The Xi Jinping Effect

Edited by Ashley Esarey
and Rongbin Han

THE
XI JINPING
EFFECT

University of Washington Press Seattle

The Xi Jinping Effect was made possible in part by a grant from The China Institute at the University of Alberta.

Additional support was provided by the Donald R. Ellegood International Publications Endowment.

Design by Mindy Basinger Hill | Composed in Garamond Premier Pro

UNIVERSITY OF WASHINGTON PRESS *uwapress.uw.edu*

LIBRARY OF CONGRESS CATALOGING-IN-PUBLICATION DATA

Names: Esarey, Ashley, editor. | Han, Rongbin, 1980– editor.

Title: The Xi Jinping effect / edited by Ashley Esarey and Rongbin Han.

Description: Seattle : University of Washington Press, [2024] | Includes bibliographical references and index.

Identifiers: LCCN 2023054096 | ISBN 9780295752808 (hardcover) | ISBN 9780295752815 (paperback) | ISBN 9780295752822 (ebook)

Subjects: LCSH: Xi, Jinping. | Political leadership—China. | China—Politics and government—2002– | China—Social policy. | China—Foreign relations—21st century.

Classification: LCC DS779.46 .X52483 2024 | DDC 320.95109/05—dc23/eng/20240319

LC record available at https://lccn.loc.gov/2023054096

∞ This paper meets the requirements of ANSI/NISO z39.48-1992 (Permanence of Paper).

Contents

Preface and Acknowledgments

Ashley Esarey

This volume is unique in its examination of the impact of Xi Jinping's leadership across a broad scope of issue areas. When Rongbin Han and I commenced planning for the project at the American Political Science Association's annual conference in 2018, no one had done anything quite like it, though scholars had written about Xi's family background, views on governance, and experiences prior to becoming the most powerful Chinese leader since Deng Xiaoping. To supplement our own skills, we needed to recruit other scholars with diverse disciplinary backgrounds. Researchers working on the project had to have sufficient expertise to consider Xi's effect—not simply on political life—but also on related topics: the anti-corruption campaign, poverty alleviation, economic inequality, religion, public service provision, state surveillance, Han-minority tensions, and China-Taiwan relations.

Consequently, we encouraged scholars worldwide to submit paper proposals and hosted the "Xi Jinping Effect" international conference at the Banff Centre in Alberta, Canada, in 2019. Six of the conference papers were published in the *Journal of Contemporary China*, volume 30, numbers 131 and 132 (2021). One of those, "Xi Jinping's Counter-Reformation: The Reassertion of Ideological Governance in Historical Perspective" by Timothy Cheek, is included here with permission of Taylor & Francis. Other papers, which complicate and even problematize the Xi effect, were reserved and developed for publication in this book. We solicited additional chapters to fill important gaps and wrote an introductory overview, and Kevin J. O'Brien drafted a concluding chapter, based on his insightful commentary at the conference. Contributors updated their analyses to account for such major developments as the COVID-19 pandemic and the 20th Party Congress in October 2022, when Xi received a green light to continue for a third term as head of the Chinese Communist Party.

As is true of all books, Rongbin Han and I incurred many debts as we labored to bring this project to fruition. Special thanks are due to the staff at the China Institute at the University of Alberta for providing the funding and administrative talent that brought the group together for the first time at the "Xi Jinping Effect" conference in Banff, including a post-conference hike to Bow Valley Falls. The project also benefited from financial support by the School of Public and International Affairs and the Department of International Affairs at the University of Georgia. Individuals who helped us mightily at various stages include Gordon Houlden, Genevieve Ongaro, Christine Park, Philippe Rheault, and Jia Wang. We are grateful to the following conference participants for enriching our conversations about Chinese politics and foreign relations: Yong Deng, Rachel Hulvey, Jue Jiang, Siqin Kan, Andy Knight, Lynette Ong, and Mark Sidel. We wish to thank Lorri Hagman, executive editor at the University of Washington Press, for early input that encouraged us to expand our group of scholars beyond political scientists and for shepherding this project along expeditiously. Several stellar participants in a July 2020 webinar, "The Xi Jinping Effect in China and Beyond," deserve our thanks: Elizabeth Economy, Joseph Fewsmith, Min Jiang, Benjamin Read, the late Ezra Vogel, and Suisheng Zhao. For advice and perceptive commentary on draft chapters (often delivered while hiking in the Cascades), we thank Stevan Harrell; we are appreciative of the excellent research assistance provided by Li Du, Solbi Kim, and Jason Zhang. Sole responsibility for any errors is ours alone.

This book is dedicated to all who seek peace, truth, and dignity for the people of China.

The Xi Jinping Effect

The Xi Jinping Effect
An Overview

Ashley Esarey and Rongbin Han

In March 2018, the Chinese National People's Congress amended the country's constitution to eliminate presidential term limits, opening the door to Xi Jinping becoming China's first "perpetual president" since the creation of term limits in the early post–Mao Zedong period. This move was symbolically groundbreaking. Though term limits have never existed for the more powerful position of head of the Chinese Communist Party (CCP), the constitutional amendment implied that Xi might not step down after ten years as paramount leader, as had his predecessors Jiang Zemin and Hu Jintao. In October 2022, the CCP extended Xi's mandate to stay on as general secretary at its 20th Congress, granting him the longest period at the helm of the party of any leader since Mao.

Without a political successor in sight, Xi carries the torch for a political agenda that has touched many aspects of Chinese political and social life. Xi's decade as China's leader has contributed to poverty alleviation, suppression of political freedom in Hong Kong, a reduction in corruption among officials, repression of non-Han peoples in Xinjiang and Tibet, the expansion of development beyond China's borders via the Belt and Road Initiative (BRI), military reform and restructuring, reemphasis on "United Front" work to win hearts and minds overseas, and the hardening of claims to sovereignty in the South China Sea and Taiwan. Meanwhile, there is growing evidence of an acceptance of Xi's political hegemony: ethnic minorities, religious groups, and even corporations are growing accustomed to playing by Xi's new formal and informal rules.[1] Unlike his predecessors Hu and Jiang, who were paramount leaders during China's boom years, Xi has rolled out bold new initiatives during a time of slowing economic growth. Yet numerous obstacles to the country's ascent loom on the horizon, including an aging population, heavily indebted local governments, persistent urban poverty, worsening income inequality, and low levels of education in rural areas.[2] Xi's policies in foreign affairs have led to pushback by foreign governments and nongovernmental organizations as well as by a small number of Chinese critics, who worry the country is headed, not toward the realization of the "Chinese dream," but toward a nightmare in which China loses comparative advantages due to rising labor costs, fights a costly war over Taiwan, commits irreparable harm to the "one country, two systems" framework in Hong Kong, and silences voices calling for improved governance.

This book considers the "Xi Jinping effect"—the impact of Xi's leadership on China's politics, economics, social life, and global governance—in the larger context of China's changing circumstances, while assessing the intended (and unintended) consequences of Xi's major initiatives. We argue that the Xi effect varies from apparent to less apparent, and even negligible depending on where one looks. While in some policy areas, the impact of Xi is highly salient, Xi's initiatives have at times fallen short as a result of China's "inherited" circumstances—domestically and internationally—or because they failed to embrace shifting trends in public opinion or to address the needs of vulnerable populations. Xi's leadership has also had "mixed effects," as his government's policies have led to change as well as new tensions and resistance. During the COVID-19 pandemic, for example, Xi sought to contain the virus through lockdowns, frequent mass testing, and made-in-China vaccines and even to benefit from the crisis through "medical diplomacy." Yet his pursuit of a "zero COVID" policy ultimately sparked protest by citizens who saw China's public health measures as unnecessarily strict, costly, or inhumane. In the chapters to follow, our contributors both assess and complicate the notion of a "Xi effect," comparing his rule to that of prior Chinese leaders, while remaining cognizant of China's changing internal and external conditions.

Early scholarship on the nature of political authority in China since Xi's 2012 rise was written before his plans for recentralizing political authority, eliminating domestic opposition, and remaking China's global status were fully apparent.[3] Some studies assumed the political positioning that enabled Xi's rise, such as support for private-sector entrepreneurship and the careful avoidance of political "mistakes," would characterize his leadership in the future.[4] Yet the scope, ambition, and rapidity of Xi's political agenda took his comrades, political opponents, and many pundits by surprise.[5] Xi utilized the power of his offices to accrue vastly greater clout as paramount leader, empower CCP institutions (as opposed to governmental ones), pursue "throwback" policies favoring once powerful state-owned enterprises, and win public support for a great restoration (*weida fuxing*) of China's power and status.

Coming to grips with the manifold changes in Chinese politics in the Xi Jinping era has made studying his leadership even more challenging. The China of Xi is not the China of Deng Xiaoping, or of his successors Jiang and Hu: Xi's CCP-led government has greater capacity to formulate and implement policies. China has become more affluent, cosmopolitan, and globally connected. The country's economic growth is also more dependent on foreign technology, capital, and markets, as well as imported energy, mineral resources, and other raw materials. Unlike the Mao period (1949–76) and the associated widespread poverty, contemporary China is plagued by disparities in wealth and education and, like other East Asian countries, has a rapidly aging population. Per capita income is roughly equivalent to that of Mexico.[6] China has the most billionaires in the world. Yet many citizens remain poor by global standards.

Intractable problems faced by Xi's predecessors have also proved difficult for him to ameliorate. Many of these problems relate to sovereignty disputes, political and social rights, and equal access to public goods, especially in education and health care; their resolution would benefit from transparency, power-sharing, and accommodation of political and cultural pluralism, to which Xi is decidedly opposed. Such challenges include movements for religious autonomy in Xinjiang and Tibet; increasing identification with Taiwan as a nation (examined by Tony Tai-Ting Liu in chapter 8); growing international support for de facto Taiwan independence; pro-democracy sentiment in Hong Kong; widespread discontent over air, soil, and water pollution within China; and the denial of full citizenship to economic migrants resulting from local government implementation of the *hukou*, or residency, system. In some areas, such as the reduction of income inequality (Martin King Whyte, chapter 4), the Xi effect has been inconsequential or even the opposite of what his government has sought.

Xi's renewed emphasis on ideological rectification for the CCP—and for the country more generally—has drawn heavily on propaganda and campaign-style strategies from the Mao period, the halcyon age of Chinese socialism.[7] As Timothy Cheek argues (chapter 2), Xi's treatment of ideology reflects both continuity and change. Even before Xi fully assumed power in January 2013, he maintained that "one cannot use the reform era to negate the pre-reform historical period, nor can one use the pre-reform historic period to negate the reform era."[8] This assertion was controversial because it implied the need to prize connections between China's largely capitalist present and intensely socialist past; one scholar suggested that Xi had embraced a "Maoist persona."[9] Indeed, Xi's throwback tendencies are reflected in the Maoist nostalgia of his speeches, his Yan'an-style "rectification" politics and ideological governance (Cheek), the personality cult associated with Xi's leadership (Musapir, chapter 7), and his antagonism to liberal democratic values.[10]

Writing about Chinese leadership at the dawn of the Xi era, the political scientist David M. Lampton observed that "leaders have become weaker, society stronger, and both leadership and society more pluralized"; he argued that it would be "difficult to maintain social and political stability without further, dramatic changes in political and governing structures and processes, as well as further evolution of China's political culture."[11] In many respects, what the East Asia expert Ezra Vogel called Xi's micromanagement of high politics, direct leadership over small groups handling salient issues, and sweeping institutional reforms can be read as an attempt to reverse the trends Lampton described.[12] Xi has attacked corruption within the ranks of the CCP and tightened control over the central government, including the People's Liberation Army. He has suppressed independent thought within China and beyond via cyber trolls, censorship, and diatribes by "wolf warrior" diplomats. Under Xi, new political institutions, such as the corruption-fighting National Supervisory Commission, the National Security Commission, and the Cyberspace Administration of China, have centralized political authority and marginalized potential adversaries. Meanwhile, the arrests of civil society activists and rights lawyers, the incarceration and reeducation of Muslims, the implementation of the National Security Law in Hong Kong, and state surveillance have narrowed the space for political participation (Deng Kai, David Demes, and Chih-Jou Jay Chen, chapter 6). To boost his popularity, Xi has provided red meat for Chinese nationalists eager to see their country's global status rise through the BRI, the construction of island bases in the South China Sea, the Chang'e-4 moon landing, and territorial conflict with Bhutan, India, Indonesia, Japan, Nepal, the Philippines, Taiwan, and Vietnam. Chinese political culture is changing, too, in ways that suggest Xi and his supporters have gambled that tighter societal control, militant foreign policy, and more power for central authorities are the best means to maintain stability.

In key respects, Xi's rule has rolled back or dismantled prominent features of political life during the reform and opening period (1978–2012). Xi's assault on Dengism includes the diminution of the status of other central leaders and the departure from "collective leadership" (*jiti lingdao*); an un-willingness to arrange an orderly (post-Xi) leadership succession; the creation of a cult of personality; a shift from a low-profile foreign policy to one that is assertive and even militant; a departure from "one country, two systems" rule for Hong Kong; the reinsertion of the CCP into citizens' lives (Musa-pir, chapter 7); and contentious relations with states in Europe and North America.[13] The 2021 CCP decision to rewrite its official history to emphasize the need for unshakable loyalty to Xi, as the transformational "founder" of the Party's ideology and the "core" of its leadership, both exemplifies and solidifies this broad movement away from Dengism.[14] The "resolution" on the Party's "historical experience" highlights Mao's accomplishments, de-emphasizes Deng's (and those of his chosen successors Jiang and Hu), and elevates momentum for Xi to guide the country in a new era, an era that we term Xi's "Restoration" (*weida fuxing*) (2013–present), not just because of what Xi has achieved but because of what he aims to achieve going forward.

Identifying and Analyzing the "Xi Effect"

Despite continuous rule by a single political party since 1949, Chinese poli-tics have nonetheless experienced repeated transformations. The Mao period saw the importation of Soviet-style government, which was disrupted by society-wide, campaign-style mobilization associated with the disastrous Great Leap Forward (1958–61) and the Cultural Revolution (1966–76). The post-Mao era broke from "continuous revolution" and ideological fer-vor, emphasizing pragmatic economic policies under Deng Xiaoping and "seeking truth from facts." By the 1980s, China transitioned away from a command economy to become market oriented and increasingly prosperous in the 1990s and early 2000s, with Jiang Zemin at the helm. The Hu Jintao administration (2002–12) sought social cohesion through the reduction of inequalities, the development of western China, and environmentalism. While tensions grew with the great powers, including the United States, on the whole democracies worldwide sought to engage China politically; China proved an attractive destination for foreign capital and international business initiatives.

Observers have identified major changes in Xi's China, though they de-bate both the nature and the extent of his leadership's effects. The political scientist Elizabeth Economy characterizes Xi's impact as "a third revolution" that "represents a reassertion of the state in Chinese political and economic life at home, and a more ambitious and expansive role for China abroad."[15]

Whereas Economy associates Xi's leadership with growing global influence and the emergence of China as a "transformative power," pundits such as Kevin Rudd see continuities in Xi's leadership, asserting that "what Xi has done is intensify and accelerate priorities and plans that have long been part of the Party's strategy."[16] Susan Shirk and other prominent scholars associate Xi's ambitious policies with overreach and strategic miscalculation that risks sowing the seeds of disaster.[17] Still others view Xi-era changes as signs of China regressing to post-totalitarian government.[18] As Minxin Pei argues, Beijing may repeat "some of the most consequential mistakes of the Soviet regime," with growing regime rigidity, even ossification.[19]

Unlike prior work on Xi's life and career before he became general secretary, this volume focuses on the impact of Xi's leadership after he came to power.[20] Our contributors take up the concept of a "Xi Jinping effect" to explore, contextualize, and problematize the influence of Xi's leadership, while drawing on their diverse disciplinary backgrounds and respective expertise. The book helps explain why the Xi effect is more salient in some areas but not others and what that tells us about the "new normal" (*xinchangtai*) of Chinese politics. The book is organized into four parts: (1) the anti-corruption campaign and ideological rectification and their impact on elite politics; (2) social policies to reduce poverty and economic inequality; (3) heightened surveillance and political control; and (4) a newly activist foreign policy.

Taking Charge and Building Faith: Anti-Corruption Campaign and Ideological Reformation

Xi Jinping's decision to launch an anti-corruption campaign of unprecedented scale was essential to establishing his political authority. The campaign targeted not just "flies," that is, officials at low bureaucratic levels, but also "tigers," including centrally appointed bureaucrats, high-ranking military officers, and former members of the Politburo Standing Committee (addressed by Andrew Wedeman in chapter 1). Utilizing an extra-legal system that governs nearly one hundred million CCP members, the campaign has sacked hundreds of officials at the provincial level or above, with many more investigated and receiving disciplinary punishment. Chinese anti-corruption campaigns in the past, though frequent since the Mao period, targeted mostly lower-level officials. Xi's anti-corruption efforts have garnered widespread public support but unsurprisingly have not played well with many officials, who, at a personal level, may have lost income and whose freedom to undertake a range of projects has been greatly curtailed. Chinese officials have become reticent to engage in the types of political experimentation that proved vital in the reform period (1978–2012).[21] Others question the economic utility of the anti-corruption campaign, seeing it as doing little to reduce economic inequality, for example, an aim more readily addressed through redistributive measures or progressive taxation (Whyte, chapter 4).

Scholarship on the anti-corruption drive has also debated the motives underlying the campaign, with some arguing that Xi's heavy emphasis on fighting corruption stems from a desire to save the CCP from domestic opposition and international subversion.[22] Other researchers such as Andrew Wedeman (chapter 1) see the campaign as an effort by Xi to reduce the influence of rival factions in the Politburo and the Politburo Standing Committee. We see the campaign as serving multiple complementary purposes—building public support for Xi's rule; reducing corrupt behavior among Party members; replacing officials with Xi loyalists tasked with remaking China's "political ecology"; increasing performance legitimacy, for example, through military restructuring and force projection; and signaling to officials high and low that they must support Xi or risk becoming a target.[23]

But is there more to the crackdown than power and control? Timothy Cheek (chapter 2) and Gerda Wielander (chapter 3) look to ideational dimensions of the Xi effect. As Cheek argues, Xi's efforts reflect a revival of ideological governance seen not only during Mao's rule but also in earlier modern Chinese regimes led by Sun Yat-sen and Chiang Kai-shek. Xi's reassertion of Party leadership is what Cheek terms a "counter-reformation" to the Deng Xiaoping–style reform of the preceding decades. Xi aims to revive the capacity of central CCP bodies and central state institutions to save China from domestic and international perils. Despite grumbling among CCP insiders, Xi appears to have unified the Party under the group élan of well-rewarded and substantive public service to recoup the CCP's faltering prestige. In doing so, Xi draws on a standard set of Party administrative practices employed since the 1940s. The rectification campaign, trumpeted by the media as a "mass line campaign," is a rewrite of the software that runs the military and security forces and the organizational muscle of the Party-state.

In part because Xi Jinping has sought to bolster public support for his government during a period of a weakening economy—a crucial source of legitimacy during the post-Mao boom—Xi has placed heavy emphasis on ideological guidance of society. For Xi, a central thrust has been the pursuit of the China Dream, or Zhongguo Meng, emphasizing China's great revival as an economic and military power.[24] The concept, first articulated in March 2013, carries both domestic and international implications. Domestically, the

China Dream indicates that the CCP hopes to draw on nationalism as a source of legitimacy, particularly a brand of nationalism that sees foreign powers as unjustly obstructing China's path to greatness. Internationally, the China Dream proposes a new positive narrative of China's rise that, when paired with Xi's BRI and with dramatic military restructuring, suggests the world must make way for China as the preeminent superpower.[25] Domestically, the China Dream thus serves as justification for greater repression of domestic dissent and more assertive or even aggressive approaches to advancing the country's interests abroad.[26] In comparison to the efforts of Xi's predecessors to pursue "peaceful rise" or "peaceful development," explications of China's place in the world that were less threatening, Xi's China Dream exemplifies the departure from Dengist "low-profile" approaches to securing global influence and the dismantling of Dengism.[27] Chasing the China Dream helps to legitimize the expansion of Chinese military action in the South China Sea, hardball tactics to suppress global recognition of Taiwanese sovereignty, "wolf warrior" diplomacy against foreign critics of Chinese human rights, and resistance to investigation of the origins of COVID-19.[28]

At the same time, Xi's China has become more conservative and more rigid ideologically. Though the purge of Bo Xilai, who was known for leftist populism and Mao-era nostalgia, prior to Xi's ascension to power seemed to indicate China's aversion to communist ideological legacies, Xi has taken a "left turn," as reflected in Xi's many paeans to Mao, his heavy emphasis on propaganda, and his Stalinist personality cult (*geren chongbai*), or what might be called "leader worship."

As Wielander argues, *faith*, or *xinyang*, has been another central term associated with Xi's political discourse. Using the Habermasian concept of a "post-secular society" as an analytical framework, she sees the reaffirmation of faith under Xi as a direct response to the challenges brought about by the pluralization of religious voices and the public sphere. Yet, instead of affording genuine validity to religion and associated values of *faith* in a post-secular world, Xi has appropriated *faith* by putting the Party and Xi at the center of political discourse, while suppressing traditional faith-based activities by Muslims, Buddhists, and Christians. The positioning of Xi as the personification of authority and the object of public adulation contributes to the state's neo-totalitarian look, most intensely in Xinjiang and Tibet, which have become epicenters for the coercive assimilation of "minoritized" peoples to Han culture and the CCP's political ideology (Musapir, chapter 7).

Socioeconomic Policies: Growth and Redistribution

Across a broadening range of economic matters, Xi Jinping has taken the position that the CCP should have greater control over decisions made by state-owned enterprises, private firms, and even foreign firms, which under Xi have been encouraged to give Party leaders greater authority. To achieve these aims, Xi has centralized economic decision-making and sidelined Peking University–trained economist Premier Li Keqiang.[29] Xi's tack thus differs from that of previous administrations in which the premier, also a member of the Politburo Standing Committee, took the lead in economic matters. Foreign pundits, in particular, point to Xi's support for the trend of "state enterprises advance, the private sector retreats" as a rollback of economic liberalization and a worrisome sign that Chinese economic growth rates will decline further and the country will risk falling into the "middle income trap."[30]

Positioning corporations to lead in next-generation technologies such as 5G and artificial intelligence has been a central component of Xi's efforts to grow the Chinese economy and solidify China's superpower status. Beijing has spent heavily on research and development in this area; it has lent diplomatic clout to firms such as Huawei that have been embroiled in disputes over corporate governance, intellectual property violations, and the security risks of products due to Chinese laws mandating data sharing by firms on national security matters. Big data approaches to state surveillance have also expanded greatly under Xi, utilizing networked video cameras, smartphones, and social media content. Led by the Cyberspace Administration of China, Xi's China has used digital forensics to suppress dissidents and human rights activists and implement broad surveillance of Chinese political, social, and economic activity (Deng, Demes, and Chen, chapter 6).

Xi's goal of leading China to greater prosperity has meant attaching more importance, at least rhetorically, to poverty reduction and redistribution of wealth. The debate over economic efficiency versus equality, that is, whether the government should prioritize economic growth irrespective of inequality or strive for fairer redistribution of wealth, has been much commented on by Chinese socialists.[31] The topic has gained prominence in China's political agenda given the country's well-known achievements in economic growth and public support for continued development, despite rising economic inequalities. At the National People's Congress meeting in 2010, then premier Wen Jiabao stressed, "We must not only develop our economy so that we can make the cake of social wealth bigger, but also set up proper institutions of income distribution to better distribute the cake."[32] Though Xi has repeatedly expressed support for fighting poverty, the Party leadership has been divided on this question, as reflected in the Dengist notion that some people could get rich first (*rang yibufen ren xian fuqilai*) and the ideological struggle between the Chongqing model and the Guangdong model, with the former emphasizing fairer redistribution and the latter attaching more importance to growth and efficiency.[33]

Unsurprisingly, considering Xi's preference for state-led poverty reduction, his government has rolled out a steady stream of measures to further poverty alleviation (*tuopin*), with considerable funding and programming in education and health care devoted to this purpose. In February 2021, in advance of the CCP's centennial celebration, Xi announced a "comprehensive victory" in the fight against poverty and the elimination of extreme poverty, declaring that nearly one hundred million people had been lifted from poverty within a decade.[34]

The evaluation of the effects of these policies by foreign observers has been less sanguine. Some economists have suggested that the metrics used in China artificially inflate the success of the country's anti-poverty campaign, though others—notably Martin Raiser of the World Bank—argue that China has actually eliminated extreme poverty in rural areas.[35] The political scientist Dorothy J. Solinger opines, however, that such narratives neglect the plight of urban poor.[36] As the scholar Jennifer Pan asserts, the safety net for low-income households (*dibao*) is insufficient to cover people's basic needs and impossible to access for millions of economic migrants living away from their hometowns.[37]

Martin King Whyte (chapter 4) considers conflicting accounts of whether Xi's China has reversed income inequality or seen increases. Whyte finds more evidence for the latter. Social programs under Xi, including the expansion of medical insurance coverage, retirement pensions, and equalizing access to education, have largely failed to lower income inequality. Whyte argues that far bolder measures are needed to create a Xi effect in this area, such as progressive income, capital gains, inheritance, and property taxes or the abolition of the *hukou* "residency" system, which discriminates against people based on their family's birthplace.

In chapter 5, Alexsia T. Chan further complicates state propaganda accounts that Xi is the champion of poor Chinese. Through her focus on access to public goods by migrants, Chan argues that inequalities in public goods provision persist because they serve the interests of resource-poor local governments. She finds that despite the newly enacted National New-Type Urbanization Plan, allegedly human-centered and oriented to the marginalized population, it is difficult to identify a clear-cut Xi effect on migrant well-being. Drawing on rich fieldwork data, Chan asserts that decentralization of migrant benefit provision has resulted in "pliable citizenship." Migrant workers' social rights are dependent on place, time, and even characteristics of the specific individual, which in turn helps the state to achieve the goals of political individualization and disempowerment. Chan argues that Xi's government has shown surprisingly little interest in centralized coordination or policy changes combating discrimination against migrants and reducing barriers to upward mobility for this large demographic.

State-Society Relations: Change and Continuity

Scholars of Chinese politics have documented shifts in state-society relations in the Xi era, with citizens and social groups responding to the state's imposition of tighter control over the society in general.[38] Journalists, lawyers, and activists face much harsher repression, with hundreds of them having been arrested. Citizens face more constraints and potentially harsher repression when engaging in popular protest, which used to be tolerated by the Party-state, as protest provides valuable policy feedback; this information in turn helps central authorities discipline local cadres for failing to maintain political stability and enables the projection of a benevolent image of the regime as a whole.[39]

Under Xi, we have also witnessed growing state control over the media and the Internet. In the realm of cyber politics, for instance, real-name registration, though introduced earlier, has been more uniformly enforced in the Xi era, and state-corporate collaboration has gained traction for a nationwide "social credit" system associated with a crackdown on corporate fraud as well as on political dissent (Deng, Demes, and Chen, chapter 6). Online critics of the regime and activists have been suppressed or silenced; state trolls, referred to as the "fifty-cent army," have been more active in manipulating public opinion and constructing Xi's public image.[40]

Deng Kai, David Demes, and Chih-Jou Jay Chen discuss the role of mass surveillance in social control, a realm where observers have identified major changes in the Xi era. Deng, Demes, and Chen argue that China under Xi features a surveillance state that results from a specific process of institutionalization and is based on an organizational and administrative infrastructure that draws heavily on digital technology. Their chapter illustrates how the government utilized new technological capabilities and street-level bureaucracies and communities to implement population control throughout the country during the COVID-19 pandemic.

In chapter 7, Musapir complements the work of Deng, Demes, and Chen by addressing the political and cultural effects of state surveillance in Xinjiang. Drawing on rare fieldwork data, interviews with Uyghurs in the diaspora, media reports, and archival sources, this contribution sheds light on the lives of Uyghurs living in fear of state surveillance and repression as well as the experiences of exiles who have lost touch with loved ones. As widely reported by the international media, and confirmed by Chinese internal documents, China has constructed "reeducation" camps in Xinjiang where millions of Uyghurs and other minorities have been forced to go through skills training courses and ideological study sessions. Musapir notes that Uyghur homes feature portraits of Xi Jinping, ostensibly a gesture of loyalty, but also a strategy to avoid mistreatment for presumed harmful thoughts, including belief in Islam. While Xi builds on his predecessors' efforts to engineer Uyghurs to become "proper" Chinese citizens, depictions of Xi's image, thoughts, and leadership in state propaganda reflect deep changes in the Uyghur heartland.

Though Xinjiang is the site of the most noticeable increase in social control during the Xi era, his leadership is also associated with the suppression of political rights and civil liberty in Hong Kong, a special administrative region that, due to its history as a British colony, has felt politically and culturally distant from Beijing. Since 2014, frustrated residents of Hong Kong have participated in waves of protests demanding direct elections for their chief executive and greater political accountability concerning the government's use of force against protesters. The Chinese central government responded to these challenges with the passage of the 2020 National Security Law, using it to justify curtailing academic and media freedom and arresting numerous activists and pro-democracy politicians. Lawyers seeking to defend the Hong Kong dissidents have been disbarred, a fate "rights lawyers" suffered previously in the People's Republic of China. Growing political tensions even led to a spike in emigration—with growing numbers of Hong Kong residents bound for Taiwan—and has cast a pall over China's relations with democracies around the world.[41]

Foreign Policy and Cross-Strait Relations: An Assertive Turn

For years, there has been running debate in Chinese media and in foreign policy circles about China's foreign policy strategy, centering on whether China should continue "keeping a low profile" or become more ambitious, to "strive for achievements" (*fenfa youwei*).[42] Observers in academic and policy circles generally agree that a strategy shift toward the latter has taken place and that it is largely attributable to Xi Jinping, despite disagreement about the effectiveness of the new approach.[43] The Chinese foreign relations scholar Yan Xuetong has argued against those critical of Chinese assertiveness, claiming that the "striving for achievement" strategy shows promise for "shaping a favorable environment for China's national rejuvenation" and "has achieved progress beyond people's expectation."[44] The assertive turn by Xi's government is unsurprising. Even before assuming power, Xi was critical of perceptions of China abroad, famously complaining of "well fed foreigners who have nothing better to do than point fingers at our affairs."[45] It is worth noting that the debate over Chinese assertiveness commenced before Xi took power; most pundits maintain that Xi's efforts have sped up China's rise, rather than proved a game changer, with some arguing that Chinese power is peaking and therefore more dangerous.[46]

In chapter 9, Brantly Womack explains how, in the new "Xi normal" of China's foreign relations, shifts in Chinese influence have played out in the context of Southeast Asia, a region where polling data suggests the People's Republic of China has become the most influential state. For Womack, both the achievements and the challenges of Xi's diplomacy toward Southeast Asia have roots in the policy trajectories of Xi's predecessors. Southeast Asians' perception of China, while certainly affected by Xi's political style, interacts with two other major factors, namely, China's economic primacy in the region and concerns about the uncertain future of American engagement.

To explain both continuity and change, Womack finds that China's regional economic clout, Xi's political style and assertiveness, and American leadership under former president Donald Trump have together contributed to patterns in Chinese relations with Southeast Asia in which all parties prioritize stability despite continuing tensions. Womack argues that while Xi has been an important contributor to development, the region worries about his arrogance and potential fallout from China's rivalry with the United States.

While China under Xi has sought to improve ties with developing countries, it has struggled to maintain good relations with the United States.

Through the BRI, China has expanded its influence across the globe, including large-scale transportation and energy projects in Southeast Asia, Africa, Central Asia, and the Middle East. Yet, since 2018, the United States and China have become embroiled in a "trade war," with both sides levying hundreds of billions of US dollars in punitive tariffs on imports.

Xi's opposition to US political influence in China and elsewhere began early in his tenure. In 2014, Xi voiced support for what in popular discourse is referred to as "de-Americanization" (*qu Meiguo hua*), and he has favored a new Asian security concept in which the region's security problems are handled by Asians.[47] Xi has proposed the notion of "community with a shared future for humankind" (*renlei mingyun gongtongti*) as an alternative to a liberal postwar world order shaped by the United States.[48]

While China collaborated with the Barack Obama administration in efforts to slow climate change, Chinese actions since the Trump presidency suggest a weakening commitment to reduce coal use by 2030, a major goal of the 2015 Paris Agreement.[49] In response to power outages and concerns over energy insecurity, China has increased production at a growing number of coal-fired power plants, leading experts to point out that increases in Chinese coal use could negate worldwide reductions.[50] Though Xi did pledge that China would stop building coal-fired plants abroad, he did not attend the United Nations Climate Change Conference (COP26) in Glasgow, where China joined India in support of "phasing down" coal use, rather than phasing it out. As Chinese foreign minister Wang Yi remarked to US climate envoy John Kerry, cooperation on climate change between the United States and China could prove a fragile "oasis" in a broader context in which the relationship resembles a "desert."[51]

China's relationship with Taiwan in the Xi era has grown tense and distant since the victory of the nominally pro-independence Democratic Progressive Party (DPP) in both presidential and parliamentary elections in 2016. Beijing broke off exchanges and intergovernmental communication, discouraged Chinese tourists from visiting Taiwan, and whittled down the number of countries maintaining formal diplomatic ties with Taiwan. The 2020 reelection of DPP president Tsai Ing-wen and the return of her party's parliamentary majority sparked an escalation in Xi's propaganda war against Taiwan's independence. Chinese state media have featured articles in which People's Liberation Army officers warned that independence was "a road to death" (*silu yitiao*). Yet, despite the fiery rhetoric, Xi's comments on Taiwan have at times been conciliatory; his government has offered a range of inducements to Taiwanese seeking opportunities in China in fields such as academia, government, and industry, including the "Made in China 2025" project to promote high-tech manufacturing. The aim is greater leverage over segments of the population that have been supportive of the DPP and encouraging the adoption of Beijing's approved political outlook, which includes skepticism of the intentions of the United States vis-à-vis Taiwan (*yimeilun*).

In chapter 8, Tony Tai-Ting Liu historicizes and contextualizes the Xi effect on China's relations with Taiwan. Liu identifies factors that shape China's Taiwan policies under Xi, including Xi's career experience in Fujian, China's domestic challenges, Taiwan's inclination toward independence, and the influence of the international community, especially that of the United States during the Trump and the Joseph Biden administrations. Comparing "hard" and "soft" aspects of Xi-era Taiwan policy, Liu finds little evidence that Chinese inducements are winning hearts and minds in Taiwan, but he does see hard policies—in particular, military coercion—as contributing to the internationalization of the "Taiwan question." Repeated Chinese air force incursions into Taiwanese airspace have rung alarm bells in North American and European capitals, prompting closer military collaboration between the United States and Taiwan, the strongest postwar expressions of Japanese support for Taiwan's security, European efforts to improve ties with Taiwan, and greater Taiwanese commitment to resist Chinese aggression.

Making Sense of the Xi Effect: Structure vs. Agency

A concluding chapter by Kevin J. O'Brien highlights the contributions of the book by asking: Is Xi a cause or an effect? If there is a Xi effect, what is it, where is it, how apparent or strong is it, and why (and why not)? Do changes associated with Xi have deep roots in the past, or can they be traced directly to his ascent? What about the future? We acknowledge that not all chapters engage all of these questions or answer them fully. After all, as O'Brien points out, this book is grappling with "one of the knottiest problems in the social sciences: sorting out the consequences of structure and agency." This book does, however, provide numerous insights to help navigate the little-charted waters of leadership politics in the Xi Jinping era as well as its domestic and global implications.

By exploring the levels and types of Xi's influence, and the different realms it affects, we break from a dichotomous view of the Xi effect and instead conceptualize it as a continuous measure: Xi's leadership has produced apparent effects in some policy areas, mixed effects in others, and fewer effects in others. The impact of Xi's leadership is visible from the ideological realm to the policy realm, as contributors to this volume argue from manifold perspectives. Many changes reverse the course of China's central government prior to his rise, dismantle post-Mao norms concerning collective leadership and leadership succession, and are unpopular even among the Chinese, especially the imposition of enhanced ideological constraints, political repression, and social control.[52] Still other policy directions are popular and somewhat progressive, including the anti-corruption campaign, poverty alleviation, promotion of social welfare, the "community with a shared future for humankind," and reductions in China's carbon footprint through renewable energy use and the electrification of transportation.

This volume seeks to contribute to the understanding of China, as a country with changing political norms and values and as a superpower facing both challenges and opportunities. To a large extent, Xi has steered his country's political life in a rigid and ruthless direction, while also moving toward an effective and popular system of authoritarian governance. The features of such a political system were exemplified by the Chinese response to COVID-19 during the pandemic. Pervasive fear and the rigidity of government policies help to explain the initial failure to contain the virus and the subsequent campaign-style measures to enforce lockdowns and mass testing, leading to a wave of public resistance in late 2022, when the "zero COVID" policy was deemed intolerable. Though aspects of China's pandemic response received widespread criticism within and beyond China, including the early suppression of whistleblowers such as Li Wenliang, the overall effectiveness of the Chinese system to prevent the spread of the virus as long as it did, especially in contrast to the United States, has helped to justify the regime's approach. Through propaganda and policy adjustments, Xi sought to leverage his government's performance during the pandemic to garner domestic support and a measure of international respect. While facing pressure and growing military constraints abroad, Xi's China has shored up authoritarian resilience through an approach to governance featuring tighter control and considerable popular support.

Notes

1. See Sarah Lee and Kevin J. O'Brien, "Adapting in Difficult Circumstances: Protestant Pastors and the Xi Jinping Effect," *Journal of Contemporary China* 30, no. 132 (2021): 902–14.

2. Dorothy J. Solinger, ed., *Polarized Cities: Portraits of Rich and Poor in Urban*

China (Lanham, MD: Rowman and Littlefield, 2019); Martin King Whyte, "China's Economic Development History and Xi Jinping's 'China Dream': An Overview with Personal Reflections," *Chinese Sociological Review* 53, no. 2 (2020): 155–34.

3. Kerry Brown, *CEO, China: The Rise of Xi Jinping* (London: Bloomsbury Academic, 2016); Kerry Brown, *The World according to Xi: Everything You Need to Know about the New China* (London: Bloomsbury Academic, 2018); Willy Lam, *Chinese Politics in the Era of Xi Jinping: Renaissance, Reform, or Retrogression?* (New York: Routledge, 2016); Steve Tsang and Honghua Men, *China in the Xi Jinping Era* (London: Palgrave Macmillan, 2016); Robert S. Ross and Jo Inge Bekkevold, eds., *China in the Era of Xi Jinping: Domestic and Foreign Policy Challenges* (Washington, DC: Georgetown University Press, 2016).

4. See Andrew Wedeman's contribution (chapter 1) for a description of how international perspectives of Xi have changed over time.

5. Brown, *CEO, China.*

6. Thomas Fingar and Jean C. Oi, "China's Challenges: Now It Gets Much Harder," *Washington Quarterly* 43, no. 1 (Spring 2020): 70.

7. Xi Jinping, "Zai jinian Mao Zedong tongzhi danchen 120 zhounian zuotanhui shang de jianghua" (Speech commemorating the 120th anniversary of Mao Zedong's birth), Central People's Government of the People's Republic of China website, December 26, 2013, http://www.gov.cn/ldhd/2013-12/26/content _2554937.htm.

8. Guo Junkui, "Xi Jinping 'Two Cannot Negates' shi shixian 'Zhongguo Meng' de kexue lunduan" (Xi Jinping's "Two Cannot Negates" is a scientific thesis to realize the "Chinese Dream"), *CPC News*, May 10, 2013, http://cpc.people .com.cn/n/2013/0510/c241220-1441140.html.

9. Willy Lam, "Xi Jinping's Ideology and Statecraft," *Chinese Law and Government* 48, no. 6 (November 2016): 412.

10. Chris Buckley and Andrew Jacobs, "Maoists in China, Given New Life, Attack Dissent," *New York Times*, January 4, 2015; Alfred L. Chan, *Xi Jinping: Political Career, Governance, and Leadership, 1953–2018* (New York: Oxford University Press, 2022), 269–70.

11. David M. Lampton, *Following the Leader: Ruling China, from Deng Xiaoping to Xi Jinping* (Berkeley: University of California Press, 2014), 8.

12. Ezra Vogel, "The Leadership of Xi Jinping: A Dengist Perspective," *Journal of Contemporary China* 30, no. 131 (2021): 693–96.

13. On Xi's utilization of state propaganda, see Ashley Esarey, "Propaganda as a Lens for Assessing Xi Jinping's Leadership," *Journal of Contemporary China* 30, no. 132 (2021): 888–901. Some of Deng's greatest achievements included the improvement of relations with the United States, Japan, South Korea, and the Soviet Union. Ezra Vogel, *Deng Xiaoping and the Transformation of China* (Cambridge,

MA: Belknap Press of Harvard University Press, 2011), 713–14. Additionally, Deng successfully negotiated with Britain for the retrocession of Hong Kong to Chinese sovereignty. See Vogel, *Deng Xiaoping and the Transformation of China*, 487–510.

14. Tony Saich, "Xi Jinping Has Made Sure History Is Now Officially on His Side," *Guardian*, November 16, 2021, https://www.theguardian.com/commentis free/2021/nov/16/xi-jinping-china-consolodation-of-power.

15. Elizabeth Economy, *The Third Revolution: Xi Jinping and the New Chinese State* (New York: Oxford University Press, 2018), 10.

16. Economy, *The Third Revolution*, 250; Kevin Rudd, *The Avoidable War: The Dangers of a Catastrophic Conflict between the US and Xi Jinping's China* (New York: PublicAffairs, 2022), 77.

17. Susan Shirk, *Overreach: How China Derailed Its Peaceful Rise* (New York: Oxford University Press, 2023); Thomas Fingar and Jean C. Oi, eds., *Fateful Decisions: Choices That Will Shape China's Future* (Stanford, CA: Stanford University Press, 2020); Carl Minzner, *End of an Era: How China's Authoritarian Revival Is Undermining Its Rise* (New York: Oxford University Press, 2018); David Shambaugh, *China's Future* (Malden, MA: Polity Press, 2016).

18. Juan J. Linz and Alfred Stepan, *Problems of Democratic Transition and Consolidation: Southern Europe, South America, and Post-Communist Europe* (Baltimore: Johns Hopkins University Press, 1996).

19. Minxin Pei, "China's Coming Upheaval: Competition, the Coronavirus, and the Weakness of Xi Jinping," *Foreign Affairs* 99, no. 3 (May/June 2020): 82.

20. On Xi's life and career before becoming general secretary, see, for example, Chan, *Xi Jinping*.

21. Fingar and Oi, "China's Challenges"; Sebastian Heilmann, "Policy Experimentation in China's Economic Rise," *Studies in Comparative International Development* 43, no. 1 (March 2008): 1–26.

22. Zach Dorfman, "China Used Stolen Data to Expose CIA Operatives in Africa and Europe," *Foreign Policy*, December 1, 2020, https://foreignpolicy.com /2020/12/21/china-stolen-us-data-exposed-cia-operatives-spy-networks.

23. Joseph Fewsmith, *Rethinking Chinese Politics* (New York: Cambridge University Press, 2021), 172; Joel Wuthnow and Phillip C. Saunders, *Chinese Military Reforms in the Age of Xi Jinping: Drivers, Challenges, and Implications* (Washington, DC: National Defense University Press, 2017); David Shambaugh, *China's Leaders: From Mao to Now* (Medford, MA: Polity Press, 2021), 305–8.

24. Geremie R. Barmé, "Chinese Dreams (Zhongguo Meng 中国梦)," in *China Story Yearbook 2013: Civilising China*, ed. Geremie R. Barmé and Jeremy Goldkorn (Canberra: Australian National University Press, 2013), 5–13; Bates Gill, *Daring to Struggle: China's Global Ambitions under Xi Jinping* (New York: Oxford University Press, 2022), 10–12.

25. On military restructuring, see David Finklestein, "Breaking the Paradigm: Drivers behind the PLA's Current Period of Reform," in *Chairman Xi Remakes the PLA: Assessing Chinese Military Reforms*, ed. Phillip C. Saunders, Arthur S. Ding, Andrew N. D. Yang, and Joel Wuthnow (Washington, DC: National Defense University Press, 2019), 45–83; Gill, *Daring to Struggle*, 28–29.

26. Stig Stenslie and Chen Gang, "Xi Jinping's Grand Strategy: From Vision to Implementation," in *China in the Era of Xi Jinping: Domestic and Foreign Policy Challenges*, ed. Robert S. Ross and Jo Inge Bekkevold (Washington, DC: Georgetown University Press, 2016), 121–22.

27. Shambaugh, *China's Leaders*, 281.

28. Zhiqun Zhu, "Interpreting China's 'Wolf-Warrior Diplomacy': What Explains the Sharper Tone to China's Overseas Conduct Recently?," *Diplomat*, May 15, 2020, https://thediplomat.com/2020/05/interpreting-chinas-wolf-warrior-diplomacy.

29. Li Keqiang has a bachelor's degree in law and a doctorate in economics, both from Peking University.

30. Ben Hillman, "The State Advances, the Private Sector Retreats," in *China Story Yearbook 2018: Power*, ed. Jane Golley, Linda Jaivin, Paul J. Farrelly, and Sharon Strange (Canberra: Australian National University Press, 2019), 294–306; Michael Wines, "China Fortifies State Businesses to Fuel Growth," *New York Times*, August 29, 2010; Dali L. Yang and Junyan Jiang, "*Guojin Mintui*: The Global Recession and Changing State-Economy Relations in China," in *The Global Recession and China's Political Economy*, ed. Dali L. Yang (New York: Palgrave Macmillan, 2012), 33–69; George Magnus, *Red Flags: Why Xi's China Is in Jeopardy* (New Haven, CT: Yale University Press, 2019).

31. Yuezhi Zhao, "The Struggle for Socialism in China," *Monthly Review: An Independent Socialist Magazine* 64, no. 5 (October 2012): 1–17.

32. Jiabao Wen, "Tongguo heli shouru fenpei zhidu ba shehui caifu 'dangao' fenhao" (Distribute the social wealth "cake" well through a reasonable income distribution system), *CNTV News*, March 5, 2010, http://news.cntv.cn/china/20100305/102492.shtml.

33. Louisa Lim, "'Cake Theory' Has Chinese Eating Up Political Debate," NPR, November 6, 2011.

34. Joe McDonald, "China Celebrates Official End of Extreme Poverty, Lauds Xi," *AP News*, February 24, 2021, https://apnews.com/article/china-celebrates-end-extreme-poverty-1449b5dc8a48483af847f4c38f64c326.

35. Indermit Gill, "Deep-Sixing Poverty in China," *Brookings* (blog), January 25, 2021, https://www.brookings.edu/blog/future-development/2021/01/25/deep-sixing-poverty-in-china; Keith Bradsher, "Jobs, Houses, and Cows: China's Costly Drive to Erase Extreme Poverty," *New York Times*, December 31, 2020.

36. Dorothy J. Solinger, "Banish the Impoverished Past: The Predicament of

19

The Xi Jinping Effect

the Abandoned Urban Poor," in *Polarized Cities: Portraits of Rich and Poor in Urban China*, ed. Dorothy J. Solinger (Lanham, MD: Rowman and Littlefield, 2019), 59–60.

37. Jennifer Pan, *Welfare for Autocrats: How Social Assistance in China Cares for Its Rulers* (New York: Oxford University Press, 2020).

38. Lee and O'Brien, "Adapting in Difficult Circumstances"; Daniel C. Mattingly, *The Art of Political Control in China* (New York: Cambridge University Press, 2020), 181–82.

39. Peter Lorentzen, "Regularizing Rioting: Permitting Public Protest in an Authoritarian Regime," *Quarterly Journal of Political Science* 8, no. 2 (February 2013): 127–58; Kevin J. O'Brien and Lianjiang Li, *Rightful Resistance in Rural China* (New York: Cambridge University Press, 2006); Lily L. Tsai, "Constructive Noncompliance," *Comparative Politics* 47, no. 3 (April 2015): 253–79.

40. Rongbin Han, *Contesting Cyberspace in China: Online Expression and Authoritarian Resilience* (New York: Columbia University Press, 2018).

41. Helen Davidson, "Number of Hong Kong Residents Moving to Taiwan Nearly Doubles in 2020," *Guardian*, February 25, 2021, https://www.theguardian .com/world/2021/feb/25/number-of-hong-kong-residents-moving-to-taiwan -nearly-doubles-in-2020.

42. Haiyan Ma and Jianmin Wu, "Zhongguo waijiao jiang changqi jianchi 'Taoguang Yanghui' fangzhen" (China will adhere to the "Keeping a Low Profile" diplomatic guideline for a long time), *China News*, July 25, 2005, http://politics .people.com.cn/GB/1026/3565534.html; Wuping Ren, "Zhongguo waijiao xuyao yinghan" (China needs tough-man diplomacy), *Global People*, January 6, 2014, http://paper.people.com.cn/hqrw/html/2014-01/06/content_1373716.htm; Xuetong Yan, "From Keeping a Low Profile to Striving for Achievement," *Chinese Journal of International Politics* 7, no. 2 (Summer 2014): 153–84.

43. On attributing this shift in strategy to Xi, see Christopher K. Johnson, "Xi Jinping Unveils His Foreign Policy Vision: Peace through Strength," *Freeman Chair China Report* (Center for Strategic and International Studies), December 8, 2014, https://www.csis.org/analysis/thoughts-chairman-xi-jinping-unveils-his -foreign-policy-vision; Jane Perlez, "Leader Asserts China's Growing Importance on Global Stage," *New York Times*, November 30, 2014.

44. Yan, "Keeping a Low Profile," 153.

45. Josh Rogin, "WikiLeaked: China's Next President Lashed Out in Mexico against 'Well Fed Foreigners,'" *Foreign Policy*, January 12, 2011, https://foreign policy.com/2011/01/12/wikileaked-chinas-next-president-lashed-out-in-mexico -against-well-fed-foreigners.

46. On China's rise, see M. Taylor Fravel, "Revising Deng's Foreign Policy," *Diplomat*, January 17, 2012, https://thediplomat.com/2012/01/revising -dengs-foreign-policy-2; Deborah Welch Larson, "Will China Be a New Type of Great Power?," *Chinese Journal of International Politics* 8, no. 4 (Winter

2015): 323–48; Kaisheng Li, "Fandui zaiyong 'Taoguang Yanghui' zhidao duiwai zhengce" (Oppose the continued use of "Keeping a Low Profile" to guide China's foreign policy), *China Newsweek*, March 7, 2012, https://opinion.huanqiu.com /article/9CaKrnJuuGq; Suisheng Zhao, "Chinese Foreign Policy as a Rising Power to Find Its Rightful Place," *Perceptions* 18, no. 1 (Spring 2013): 101–28. On China's peaking, see Andrew S. Erickson and Gabriel B. Collins, "A Dangerous Decade of Chinese Power Is Here," *Foreign Policy*, October 18, 2021, https:// foreignpolicy.com/2021/10/18/china-danger-military-missile-taiwan; Hal Brands and Michael Beckley, "China Is a Declining Power—and That's the Problem," *Foreign Policy*, September 24, 2021, https://foreignpolicy.com/2021/09/24 /china-great-power-united-states.

47. Suisheng Zhao, "President Xi's Big Power Diplomacy: Advancing an Assertive Foreign Policy Agenda," in *Mapping China's Global Future: Playing Ball or Rocking the Boat?*, ed. Axel Berkofsky and Giulia Sciorati (Milan: ISPI and Ledizioni LediPublishing, 2020), 24–36, https://www.ispionline.it/sites/default /files/pubblicazioni/ispi_mappingchina_web_1.pdf.

48. See Jacob Mardell, "The 'Community of Common Destiny' in Xi Jinping's New Era," *Diplomat*, October 25, 2017, https://thediplomat.com/2017/10/the -community-of-common-destiny-in-xi-jinpings-new-era; Jane Perlez, "Xi Jinping of China Calls for Cooperation and Partnerships in U.N. Speech," *New York Times*, September 28, 2015.

49. Ashley Esarey, Mary Alice Haddad, Joanna I. Lewis, and Stevan Harrell, eds., *Greening East Asia: The Rise of the Eco-Developmental State* (Seattle: University of Washington Press, 2020).

50. On increased production at China's coal plants, see Saich, "Xi Jinping Has Made Sure." On the effects of China's increased coal use, see Azi Paybarah, "China Says It Won't Build New Coal Plants Abroad. What Does That Mean?," *New York Times*, September 22, 2021; Centre for Research on Energy and Clean Air, "China Dominates 2020 Coal Plant Development," *Global Energy Monitor*, February 2021, https://globalenergymonitor.org/wp-content/uploads/2021/02 /China-Dominates-2020-Coal-Development.pdf.

51. Nick O'Malley, "Xi Says China Will Not Build New Coal-Fired Power Projects Abroad," *Sydney Morning Herald*, September 22, 2021, https://www.smh .com.au/world/asia/xi-says-china-will-not-build-new-coal-fired-power-projects -abroad-20210922-p58toq.html.

52. Rongbin Han, "Cyber Nationalism and Regime Support under Xi Jinping: The Effects of the 2018 Constitutional Revision," *Journal of Contemporary China* 30, no. 131 (2021): 717–33; Lee and O'Brien, "Adapting in Difficult Circumstances."

PART ONE

Taking Charge
and Building Faith

1

Corruption, Faction, and Succession
The Xi Jinping Effect on Leadership Politics

Andrew Wedeman

In the run-up to Xi Jinping's selection as general secretary of the Chinese Communist Party (CCP) in November 2012 and selection as president of the People's Republic of China in March 2013, the Western press and pundits assessed him positively. He was a "pragmatic princeling," a man with a "common touch" who was "humble," "ebullient," "affable," and "modest." Xi was described as "business friendly," "open-minded," "genial," "charismatic," "confident," "at ease with himself," and a leader" who "shunned ostentation," had a "strong sense of humor," and enjoyed watching soccer and Hollywood movies. In fact, his wife, Peng Liyuan, a famous folk singer—and major general in the People's Liberation Army (PLA)—told reporters he often stayed up too late watching overseas soccer matches and got angry when the Chinese national team lost.[1] A year later, in December 2013, Xi seemed to double down on his populist image when he wandered into a Qingfeng restaurant in western Beijing; took a place in line; ordered six steamed buns, a dish of pork liver, and some vegetables; paid the ¥21 tab; sat down at a communal table; and ate his meal while quietly chatting with fellow diners.[2]

By the time Xi was due to start his second five-year term as general secretary in 2017, he no longer enjoyed a lovable, "man of the people" image in the West. Quite the contrary, by the time of the 19th Party Congress in November 2017, Xi was being described as the "most powerful Chinese leader since Mao Zedong"; he was rapidly moving China toward "one-man rule" in which the regime used "gangster-style thuggery" and "political repression" to displace the "benevolent autocracy" of the 1990s and 2000s with a "neo-totalitarian party-state."[3] Xi had become "the chairman of everything," who "consolidated power, purged rivals and encouraged a personality cult to a degree not seen since the death of Mao Zedong in 1976."[4] Under Xi, now designated as the "core leader," the regime had taken on "all the aspects of a classic fascist state" complete with its own ideology—"Xi Jinping Thought on Socialism with Chinese Characteristics for a New Era"—and a cult of personality for "Daddy Xi" and "Mama Peng."[5] In 2020, US secretary of state Mike Pompeo declared that Xi was a "true believer in a bankrupt, totalitarian ideology."[6] President Donald Trump's national security adviser Robert O'Brien branded Xi "Josef Stalin's successor."[7]

On the eve of the 20th Party Congress in the fall of 2022, Xi was described as "the second coming of Mao Zedong," "a stern Communist monarch" who "governs much like the old emperors," "the embodiment of tyrannical one-man rule," who had "spent the past decade cracking down on potential rivals through the pretext of mass anti-corruption purges" and whose grip was "unquestionable, and . . . unrivalled."[8]

As Xi putatively morphed from a benevolent populist into a totalitarian autocrat, the Western press reported rumors of mounting opposition. In 2015, sources told a Japanese reporter that Xi had feared that the director of the Central Committee's General Office and general secretary Hu Jintao's right-hand man, Ling Jihua, had plotted an assassination in the days before the 17th Party Congress and that even after former Politburo Standing Committee member and secretary of the powerful Central Politics and Law Committee Zhou Yongkang's arrest, his supporters in Zhou's home province of Jiangsu remained a threat to Xi's safety.[9] Two years later, the Western media picked up on a speech by Liu Shiyu, the chair of the China Securities Regulatory Commission, in which Liu appeared to accuse Zhou Yongkang, Politburo member and Chongqing Party secretary Bo Xilai, Politburo member and Chongqing Party secretary Sun Zhengcai, Politburo member and Central Military Commission vice-chair General Guo Boxiong, Politburo member and Central Military Commission vice-chair General Xu Caihou, and Ling Jihua, all of whom had been arrested and charged with corruption, of plotting to "usurp the party's leadership and seize state power."[10] In 2018, rumors circulated that gunfire had been heard in downtown Beijing and that an intra-Party coup was imminent. Even though such rumors might "lack credibility" there were signs, sources claimed, that "disharmony" was increasing within the "party elite."[11]

Although talk of coup plots and assassination attempts seem to have been nothing more than feverish speculation, the sense that Xi had been ruthlessly consolidating power undoubtedly grew out of the massive anti-corruption crackdown that he ordered in late 2012 and which continued, albeit in a less visible and dramatic fashion into late 2022. Between 2013 and September 2022, the now combined Party, state, and judicial body known as the National Supervisory Commission and its subnational bureaus investigated 4,628,000 cases involving Party members, state officials, and public functionaries and punished 4,538,000 individuals. In the process, the annual number of Party members and state officials sanctioned increased over fourfold, from 153,704 in 2012 to 621,000 in 2018. Thereafter, the number sanctioned fell to 587,000 in 2019 but then increased to 627,000 in 2021.[12] As a result, over the course of ten years some 5 percent of the Party membership was punished. More critically, between 2012 and December 2022, 316 senior-level officials—those holding bureaucratic rank equivalent to that of vice minister, vice-governor, and above—were accused, charged, or sentenced on corruption charges.[13] That compares to some 50 in the dozen years prior to the crackdown. The crackdown was not, moreover, limited to the Party and state but also extended into the military. Although less well documented due to the secrecy that surrounds Chinese military affairs, the available evidence suggests that over eighty military officers holding ranks equivalent to major general and above ran afoul of corruption-related charges.[14]

Given that the number of Party cadres, state officials, and military officers holding such high ranks is likely no more than several thousand at any one time, there is little doubt that the crackdown has hit China's power elite hard. But has the crackdown fundamentally altered the structure of elite politics, and, more directly, has it enabled Xi to eliminate rival factions within the elite ranks and, as suggested by the popular discourse on the evolution of his rule, to seize absolute power within the Party? To address these questions, I begin with an analysis of the so-called Tiger Hunt and Xi's drive against high-level corruption. I then segue to an analysis of the shifting balance of power within the Politburo, followed by an assessment of the likely political future of Xi and his allies.

The Tiger Hunt

The crackdown launched in late 2012 was not unprecedented. On the contrary, it was the latest in a series of drives against corruption dating back to the founding of the People's Republic of China and beyond to the early days of the CCP, including the "Three Antis," "Five Antis," and "Four Cleans" campaigns in which hundreds of thousands of cadres and officials were subjected to "struggle sessions," humiliated, and beaten by workers and peasants mobilized by Party work teams.[15] During the post-Mao era, the leadership ordered crackdowns in 1983, 1986, 1989, and 1993. The first three focused primarily on rank-and-file corruption, or what the contemporary China media calls "flies." The 1993 crackdown shifted the focus to mid-level officials, concentrating on those holding leadership positions at the county/department and prefecture/bureau levels, officials sometimes referred to as "rats" and "wolves" in the Chinese press. The crackdown launched in 2012 shifted the focus to the senior ranks of the Party-state, to officials known as the "tigers." Officials at this level had not been entirely spared prosecution in the past. Prior to 2012, however, most senior officials charged with corruption had been linked to specific scandals, including the Wuxi Ponzi scheme that brought down Beijing Party secretary and Politburo member Chen Xitong in 1995 and the 2006 Shanghai pension fund scandal that toppled Shanghai Party secretary and Politburo member Chen Liangyu (no relation to Chen Xitong).

The crackdown launched in late 2012 was likely precipitated by two major scandals in 2011 and 2012, one involving Liu Zhijun, the minister of railways, and a second involving Lieutenant General Gu Junshan. Liu was at the center of a web of bribery linked to the construction of China's sprawling high-speed rail system. Gu was accused of accepting massive kickbacks from real estate developers and being part of an extensive illegal market for promotions in the PLA. The crackdown was then triggered by a scandal involving Chongqing Party secretary Bo Xilai that erupted when Wang Lijun, the recently demoted director of the Chongqing Public Security Bureau, attempted to defect to the United States in early 2012 and accused Bo's wife, Gu Kailai, of murdering an English businessman named Neil Heywood who had been helping her launder bribes paid by businessmen seeking to curry Bo's favor.

In December 2012, investigators from the Central Commission for Discipline Inspection, the Party's internal watchdog, began investigating Li Chuncheng, the deputy secretary of the Sichuan Provincial Party Committee and an alternative member of the 18th CCP Central Committee.[16] A relatively junior member of the Party leadership, Li was a protégé of Zhou Yongkang. Having started his career as a technician and then a junior manager in the state-owned Liaohe oil field, Zhou climbed up the ranks, becoming director of the Liaohe Oil Exploration Bureau in 1983. Two years later, Zhou was appointed a vice minister of the Ministry of Petroleum, which was reorganized into the Chinese National Petroleum Corporation (CNPC) in 1988. After serving as the commander of the Tarim Oil Exploration Headquarters and an assistant general manager of CNPC, Zhou was named general manager of the corporation in 1996. Two years later, Zhou was named minister for state land and resources. The following year, he was transferred to Sichuan and named provincial Party secretary. In 2002, Zhou became a member of the Politburo, and the following year he returned to Beijing as minister for public security. At the 17th Party Congress in 2007, Zhou was elected a member of the Politburo Standing Committee and named secretary of the powerful Politics and Law Committee. Having reached the age of seventy in 2012, Zhou retired in the days before the 18th Party Congress.

During 2013, investigators detained an increasing number of officials who had served under Zhou. As each of these "tigers" fell, Party investigators went after their henchmen and cronies in an ever-expanding attack on Zhou's network of subordinates. Investigators also launched inquiries into Zhou's family in his hometown of Wuxi, Jiangsu. An investigation into the business dealings of Zhou's son Zhou Bin quickly grew into a series of investigations of Zhou Bin's wife and her family, as well as the managers of businesses with ties to Zhou Bin, including Liu Han, the chair of the Sichuan Hanlong Group, a conglomerate with ventures in solar energy, communications, mining, and other industries. Sichuan Hanlong was actually a front for a sprawling criminal syndicate headed by Liu Han and his brother. Zhou Yongkang was placed under investigation in July 2014. He was expelled from the Party and arrested in December 2014. In April 2015, Zhou was convicted on bribery charges and sentenced to life in prison. Because Zhou was the most senior member of the Party leadership and the first former member of the Politburo Standing Committee to be charged with corruption, many observers saw the attack on him and his cronies as politically motivated.

Zhou had been a supporter of Bo Xilai. The son of Bo Yibo, a first-generation Party leader and one of the so-called Eight Immortals who formed the core of Deng Xiaoping's reform coalition, Bo rose rapidly through the ranks before spending a decade as mayor and then Party secretary of the major port city of Dalian in Liaoning Province. In 2000, Bo was promoted to governor of Liaoning. Four years later, he moved to Beijing as minister for commerce. In 2007, Bo became Party secretary of Chongqing, a provincial-level megacity in southwest China, and was elected to the Politburo. Once in Chongqing, Bo immediately launched a massive assault on Chongqing's extensive underworld. The "Sweeping the Black" campaign not only netted hundreds of gangsters, it also brought down scores of officials who had provided the "protective umbrellas" under which numerous criminal syndicates operated. Bo also launched a "Singing the Red" neo-Maoist campaign aimed at reviving the traditions of what he and others saw as the "pure" essence of the socialist revolution and attacking the "degenerate" and amoral materialism that liberal reforms has spawned.[17] Because Bo was sixty-three in 2012, it was said that even though he was too old to become general secretary, he was likely to be promoted to the Politburo Standing Committee at the 18th Party Congress in November and that he would become a counterweight to Xi. If so, Bo's abrupt fall from power following the murder of Neil Heywood and the attempted defection of Wang Lijun "fortuitously" cleared away a potential obstacle to Xi's consolidation of power after the 18th Party Congress.

In the months after the 18th Party Congress, signs emerged that Party investigators were also going after Ling Jihua. Ling had been director of the Central Committee's General Office, the agency that oversees the Party leadership's day-to-day work, including controlling access to the Party's general secretary. Ling was said to have been Hu Jintao's "hatchet man." At the time, it was widely assumed that Ling would be elected to the Politburo at the 18th Party Congress so he could act as Hu's "eyes and ears" after Hu retired.

Ling's path into the post-Hu inner circle of power, however, had been thrown into question well before the 18th Party Congress when his son, Ling Gu, plowed a Ferrari into a Beijing bridge abutment in the early hours of March 18, 2012, killing himself and critically injuring two female passengers. At the 18th Party Congress, Ling was sidelined. Instead of being elected a member of the Politburo, he was shunted off to the Party's United Front Department, the agency that works to forge and maintain ties with China's eight noncommunist parties, powerful private business leaders, intellectuals, religious leaders, celebrities, and other non-Party figures. During the summer and fall of 2014, Party investigators detained Ling's brother Ling Zhengce, an official in Ling's native province of Shanxi, and were said to be closing in on Ling's wife, Gu Liping, a businesswoman reputed to have her hands in all sorts of questionable ventures. They also began detaining a network of Shanxi officials. In December 2014, the month in which Zhou Yongkang was formally charged with corruption, Ling Jihua and Gu Liping were detained. Ling's brother Ling Wancheng, meanwhile, disappeared and was said to have fled to the United States with a cache of secret Party documents stolen by Ling Jihua as an "insurance policy" against his arrest by Xi's operatives.

Because Bo was allegedly a rival to Xi with close ties to Zhou, the attacks on these three figures at the start of the anti-corruption crackdown naturally fueled the belief that the crackdown was politically motivated and that Xi was using it to purge his factional enemies and consolidate his grip on power.

Although widely evoked in analyses of Chinese leadership politics, the meaning of *faction* is actually ambiguous.[18] The political scientist Andrew J. Nathan defines factions as networks of clientelist relationships that can form a power base for political contestation.[19] Political actors and officials in China are, however, also embedded in networks of "personalistic ties" (*guanxi*) based on overlapping life experiences.[20] Factional ties are assumed to be derived from these shared experiences—a common hometown, county, or province; childhood friends; schoolyard chums, university classmates, army buddies, or office colleagues; common acquaintances and friends; or perhaps family connections, including marriage. Ties are often assumed to be hierarchical, transitive, and instrumental, with more senior patrons mentoring "promising" protégés while also currying favor with their bosses. Subordinates are said to "swear" their loyalty and fidelity to those to whom they owe their ascent up the career ladder. Superiors are said to be able to command and mobilize their followers in pursuit of their political and personal aims. Because factions and factional maneuvering takes place behind closed doors and sometimes in hidden smoke-filled rooms, the most tangible and visible clues to factional connections are generally assumed to be found in individuals' biographical data and hence observable in the form of shared experiences.

Life coincidences, of course, do not necessarily mean that there is a true political connection. Two individuals may have gone to school together or shared an office, but rather than bosom buddies and steadfast comrades, they might in fact be bitter enemies because one beat up the other in the second grade, stole a lover in college, or stabbed the other in the back to win a boss's favor and a desired promotion or transfer. Two individuals from the same village/county/province may find each other intolerable or view each other as coming from the "wrong side of the tracks." Individuals, finally, may have double-crossed and betrayed one another in past political struggles. Biographical analysis thus provides an imperfect mapping of the factional loyalties of China's political elites.[21]

While an imperfect guide to an individual's political loyalties, "connections" nevertheless embed individuals in "communities"—groups of individuals who are linked either professionally or personally, which may then form the basis for the construction of more tightly linked "factions." Media reports identify various sorts of connections between the 316 civilian tigers, 90 senior military officers, and over 1,300 other individuals. In some cases, the nexus is explicitly corrupt. In other cases, the connection is coincidental and professional in that two individuals worked together, but their relationship may be suspect because both were accused of corruption. In other cases, the connections may be personal or familial. As noted, a "connection" need only signify a causal link, not a political link.

Using modularity measurements to first identify clusters of those implicated in the Tiger Hunt and then using eigenvalues to identify the individual at the core of each cluster yields nineteen clusters with ten or more "members," sixteen of which had a senior Party cadre or state official at their core, two clusters centered on private business operators, and a seemingly loose cluster of individuals in the telecommunications sector (see table 1.1).[22] These were not independent clusters. On the contrary, they were intertwined, including at the very top levels. In total, members of these clusters accounted for 90 percent of those implicated in or associated with the Tiger Hunt.

This analysis thus suggests that if Xi's crackdown was politically driven, its initial targets were Zhou Yongkang, Ling Jihua, Bo Xilai, and the PLA. Zhou and Ling were theoretically positioned to act as factional leaders and hence rivals to Xi. Zhou was seen by many as having taken over the leadership of the "Jiang Zemin faction" after Jiang's closest ally, Zeng Qinghong, retired at the 17th Party Congress in 2007. Although Zhou was due to retire at the 18th Party Congress, many observers assumed that he would be replaced by Bo as the Jiang faction's front man. Ling was presumably poised to move into the lead role in Hu's "Communist Youth League faction."

Both Zhou and Ling, however, were badly weakened prior to the congress. Zhou's alleged protégé Bo was under arrest. Ling was under a cloud, having failed to paper over the death of his son. It is possible that Bo and Ling were "set up" by conspiracies hatched by Xi and his inner circle. Such conspiracy theories, however, seem tenuous, since the fall of Bo was brought on by a murder committed by his wife and his fight with onetime Chongqing police chief Wang Lijun, while Ling's fall was precipitated by his son's reckless driving. The possibility that, for instance, Ling Gu's Ferrari had been sabotaged or that Gu Kailai was framed by Wang cannot, of course, be entirely ruled out.

If both Zhou and Ling Jihua were politically wounded before the 18th Party Congress, Xi presumably did not face a pressing need to launch a swift attack on the Jiang and Hu camps. The weakening of these two powerful camps certainly created conditions in which factional attacks were presumably less risky and hence would allow Xi to consolidate power more quickly. With Bo, Zhou, and Ling weakened, however, it is not clear that Xi had an immediate or pressing need to smash would-be rival cliques within the central leadership.

Similarly, none of the regional leaders represented an obvious or serious factional contender at the national level. For example, Bai Enpei, who had been a member of the 15th, 16th, and 17th Central Committees, had stepped down as secretary of the Yunnan Provincial Party Committee and chair of the Yunnan Provincial People's Congress in 2011 having reached the "normal

TABLE 1.1. Clustering of targets in the Tiger Hunt (2012–2023)

CORE INDIVIDUAL	FUNCTIONAL/ GEOGRAPHIC FOCUS	NUMBER OF MEMBERS
Zhou Yongkang, Politburo Standing Committee	Chinese National Petroleum Corporation, Sichuan, public security	302
Ling Jihua, Central Committee General Office	Shanxi, central	152
Xu Caihou, Central Military Commission	People's Liberation Army	125
Sun Lijun, vice minister	Public security	108
Bo Xilai, Politburo	Chongqing, Liaoning	103
Su Rong, provincial secretary	Jiangxi	76
Zhao Zhengyong, provincial secretary	Shaanxi	62
Pan Yiyang, regional vice-chair	Nei Menggu	60
Sun Zhengcai, Politburo	Chongqing	59
Yang Weize, Party secretary Nanjing	Jiangsu	58
Bai Enpei, provincial secretary	Yunnan	55
Zhu Mingguo, secretary Politics and Law Committee	Guangdong	52
Hao Chunrong, vice-governor	Liaoning	40
Zhou Benshun, provincial secretary	Hebei	39
Wang Sanyun, provincial Party secretary	Gansu	38
Wang Lequan, former Politburo	Xinjiang	10
Guo Wengui, Beijing Pangu Holdings	Business	59
Xiao Jianhua, Tomorrow Holdings	Business	57
Telecommunications	Business	22

Source: Compiled by the author based on media reports from both Chinese- and English-language sources.

age" of retirement and was slated for retirement from the Central Committee at the 18th Party Congress. Su Rong had not reached age sixty-five in 2012 and hence had not reached retirement age. But he would turn sixty-five in 2013. Thus, while he remained Party secretary of Jiangxi and chair of the Jiangxi Provincial People's Congress after the 18th Party Congress, he was not reelected to the Central Committee. Zhao Zhengyong, Party secretary of Shaanxi, was sixty-one in 2012 and a newly elected member of the Central Committee. But he was still a relatively junior member of the senior leadership, having assumed the governorship of Shaanxi in 2010 and been named Party secretary in 2012. More critically, the networks centered on Bai Enpei, Su Rong, Zhao Zhengyong, Pan Yiyang, Yang Weize, Zhu Mingguo, Hao Chunrong, Zhou Benshun, and Wang Sanyun were "regional networks" that were largely confined to their current provincial bases or stretched back to provinces where they had served earlier in their careers. Only Wang Lequan had held a significant leadership position at the national level. He had retired, however, in the 18th Party Congress. Moreover, his "Xinjiang cluster" had only ten identified members. As such, a factional attack by the Xi camp would likely have been more opportunistic and less a necessary component of Xi's plan to take control over the Party leadership.

As the crackdown progressed, Xi appeared to confront two new challengers. In August 2017, Party investigators detained Sun Zhengcai, a member of the Politburo and Party secretary of Chongqing. On the surface, Sun appeared to be a potential political player. Relatively young (forty-nine in 2012) and a member of the "sixth generation" of Party leaders, Sun had been elected to the Politburo at the 18th Party Congress, having previously served as minister of agriculture (2006–9) and secretary of the Jilin Provincial Party Committee. Prior to the 19th Party Congress, Sun had been identified as Xi's possible successor.[23] According to the political scientist Cheng Li, Sun was likely a protégé of former politburo members Jia Qinglin and Zeng Qinghong.[24] As such, Sun could have been a replacement for the fallen Bo Xilai. Sun had been named the Party secretary of Chongqing, the post that Bo had held prior to his political demise. Li, however, also identifies Sun as a protégé of Xi.[25] When Xi visited Chongqing in January 2016, he seemed to praise Sun and his work in the city, which was interpreted as a "nod" to Sun.[26] In July 2017, Sun vowed his "absolute loyalty" to Xi—just five days before he was pulled down—suggesting that if Sun had been part of a Jiang-led opposition faction prior to 2012, five years later he seemed to be anxiously seeking acceptance as a political ally of Xi.[27] If we see Sun as a stalwart of the Jiang faction, then his transfer to what some might have painted as Bo's neo-Maoist "red soviet" in Chongqing would have presented Xi with a factional challenge. Sun was, however, an outsider deployed to the city as an agent of Beijing and was presumably then tasked with sweeping Bo's cronies out of the city's corridors of power, not rallying them for a new struggle with Beijing. Finally, aside from his alleged ties to retired members of the Jiang camp, Sun's network did not include other powerful figures but was made up largely of personal connections.

Less than two years later, in the spring of 2020, Party investigators went after a different "political gang" (*zhengzhi tuanhuo*) putatively led by Sun Lijun, a vice minister for public security, whose members included Luo Wenjin, a retired senior official of the Jiangsu Public Security Bureau; Wang Like, secretary of the Jiangsu Provincial Party Politics and Law Committee; Deng Huilin, deputy mayor of Chongqing and a former senior official of the Central Committee's Politics and Law Committee; and Gong Dao'an, a deputy mayor of Shanghai and director of the Shanghai Public Security Bureau. Wang Like had ties to the fallen Wang Lijun and senior members of the Liaoning public security apparatus. Fu Zhenghua, minister of justice and a former vice minister for public security, and Liu Xinyun, vice-governor of Shanxi and director of the Shanxi Public Security Bureau, were also said to be part of Sun's gang. Sun was said to have been acting at the behest of Meng Jianzhu, secretary of the Central Politics and Law Committee. Meng, in turn, was alleged to be a front man for the Jiang Zemin–Zeng Qinghong–Zhou Yongkang camp. Sun and company had allegedly plotted to assassinate Xi when he visited Nanjing for a ceremony in 2017. For reasons never explained, the alleged plot fell through. In September 2022, just a month before the 20th Party Congress, Sun, Wang, and Fu were convicted of corruption and given suspended death sentences; Gong was sentenced to life in prison; Deng was sentenced to fifteen years in prison, and Liu was sentenced to fourteen years in prison.

As noted, whether these plots were real or merely rumored, there seems little question that Xi's anti-corruption crackdown struck hard at a series of sprawling networks focused on powerful figures such as Zhou Yongkang and Ling Jihua and regional networks centered on regional bosses such as Bai Enpei, Su Rong, and Zhao Zhengyong. But it is far from certain that these were "factions" in the sense that the purpose of these networks was exclusively or even largely to fight for political power. It seems rather more likely that these were networks that sought political power as a means to other ends, including, not the least, self-enrichment and power as a "protective umbrella" under which corrupt officials could feed off the state, the economy, and society.

The Politburo

The direct impact of the anti-corruption crackdown on the Politburo has been very limited. All but one of the members of the Politburo charged with corruption during the course of Xi's crackdown either fell before Xi became general secretary (Bo) or were retired—albeit newly retired—when they were detained (Zhou Yongkang, General Xu Caihou, and General Guo Boxiong). As of 2022, Sun Zhengcai was the only sitting member of the Politburo removed for corruption while Xi was general secretary. Thus, whereas four of the twenty-five members (16 percent) of the 17th Politburo were charged with corruption, only one of the forty members (2.4 percent) of the combined 18th and 19th Politburos where charged with corruption. The factional balance within the Politburo, nevertheless, changed under Xi's leadership.

Although a long-standing feature of studies of Chinese elite politics, factional studies are often "tea leaf reading" exercises in which the conclusions are largely shaped by how analysts characterize and categorize the data. While admittedly imperfect, a factional modeling of the composition of the Communist Party elite since 2012, using typologies developed by scholars who focus on biographical analysis, provides a way to assess claims that Xi has gained either absolute domination within the Party or something more akin to political hegemony.

Data on the factional alignments of members of the Politburo show that although Xi managed to move a substantial number of individuals seen as either his protégés or political allies into key Party positions at the 19th Party Congress, as of 2017 he had not eliminated either the Jiang faction or the Hu faction (figure 1.1). In fact, the Jiang faction formed the largest bloc in both the 17th and 18th Politburos, enjoying a fourteen-to-nine edge over Hu and his allies in the 17th Politburo and a fifteen-to-ten edge on the 18th Politburo.

The balance shifted in the 19th Politburo when Xi brought ten of his allies into the Politburo. Another member, Chen Quanguo, whose background did not include obvious ties to Xi, also appeared to have thrown his lot in with the Xi faction. The number of members seen as part of the Jiang faction fell from fifteen on the 18th Politburo to eight on the 19th Politburo. The number of members aligned with the Hu faction fell from ten on the 18th Politburo to just four on the 19th Politburo. The Xi faction thus clearly displaced both the Jiang and the Hu factions in the 19th Politburo. The number of members seen as not aligned with Xi nevertheless remained far from insignificant, with a total of twelve members seen as still allied with either the Jiang or Hu faction (one member of the 19th Politburo—Yang Jiechi—does not seem to have been identified with any faction).

The membership of the 20th Politburo stripped bare any possible ambiguity that Xi was in charge. All twenty-four members either were previously identified as Xi protégés or were said to have been handpicked by Xi.[28] In what some say was a direct slap in the face for former general secretary Hu Jintao, Hu Chunhua, who had been elected to the 18th Politburo and reelected to the 19th Politburo and had served as Party secretary of Guangdong, was not only not promoted to the number two slot on the Politburo Standing Committee, a position that would signal he would be promoted from vice-premier to premier when the 14th National People's Congress met in March 2023, as had been rumored, but he was unceremoniously demoted to an ordinary member of the Central Committee. His patron Hu Jintao, meanwhile, was shown being escorted off the dais of the closing session of the congress. Officially, Hu felt ill and left to receive medical attention. Hu's "illness," however, appeared to have suddenly developed when he sought to peak at a red folder said to contain a list of the theretofore undisclosed membership of the Politburo.[29] Exactly what happened remains unknown. It seems possible that Hu believed Xi would seat Hu Chunhua on the standing committee, thus leaving Hu Jintao at least a residual stake in the Party leadership. Regardless of why Hu Chunhua was dropped from the Politburo, the lineup of the 20th Politburo left Xi and his allies in total control of the Party's top leadership and as such might be seen as an end to factional politics and, with it, any notion of a collective leadership. Xi went on to pack the Central Secretariat and the Central Military Commission with his allies, thus gaining "absolute domination" of the leadership.[30]

The shifting factional balance of the Politburo and the consolidation of a factional monopoly by Xi is, however, potentially misleading, as perhaps best illustrated by Xi himself. Although a "princeling" with a powerful father, Xi started his career at the grassroots level and moved upward through the ranks, starting out as a deputy Party secretary in a county in Hebei in 1982. In 1988, he transferred to Fujian, where he served as Party secretary of a prefecture; deputy mayor of Xiamen; Party secretary of Fuzhou, the provincial capital; and ultimately governor. In 2002, he moved to Zhejiang as provincial Party secretary. Five years later, in 2007, he replaced Chen Liangyu, putatively a member of Jiang's "Shanghai gang," as Party secretary of Shanghai after Chen fell in a corruption scandal—a development that some saw as giving Hu an opportunity to attack Jiang's cronies and put one of his protégés in charge of China's financial capital. After a brief stint in Shanghai, Xi moved on to

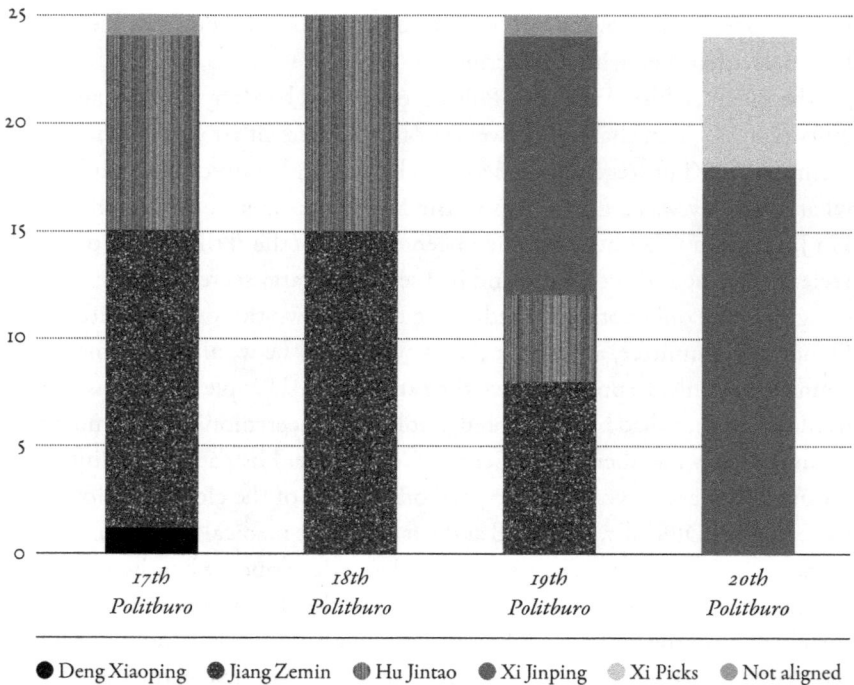

Legend: ● Deng Xiaoping ● Jiang Zemin ● Hu Jintao ● Xi Jinping ○ Xi Picks ● Not aligned

FIGURE 1.1. Factional balance of the Politburo. Sources: Barry Naughton, "The Emergence of Wen Jiabao," *China Leadership Monitor*, no. 6 (2003): 36–47; Cheng Li, "Was the Shanghai Gang Shanghaied? The Fall of Chen Liangyu and the Survival of Jiang Zemin's Faction, *China Leadership Monitor*, no. 20 (2007): 1–17, https://www.hoover.org/sites/default/files/uploads/documents/clm20cl.pdf; Cheng Li, "China's Top Future Leaders to Watch: Biographical Sketches of Possible Members of the post-2012 Politburo," *China Leadership Monitor*, pt. 1, no. 37 (2012), 1–10, https://www.hoover.org/sites/default/files/uploads/documents/CLM37CL.pdf; pt. 2, no. 38 (2012): 1–10, https://www.hoover.org/sites/default/files/uploads/documents/CLM38CL.pdf; pt. 3, no. 39 (2012): 1–9, https://www.hoover.org/sites/default/files/uploads/documents/CLM39CL.pdf; pt. 4, no. 39 (2012): 1–22, https://www.hoover.org/sites/default/files/uploads/documents/CLM39 CL2.pdf; Cheng Li, "A Biographical and Factional Analysis of the Post-2012 Politburo," *China Leadership Monitor*, no. 41 (2013): 1–17, https://www.hoover.org/sites/default/files/uploads/documents/CLM41CL.pdf; Guoguang Wu, "The King's Men and Others: Emerging Political Elites under Xi Jinping," *China Leadership Monitor*, no. 60 (2019): 1–9, https://www.prcleader.org/_files/ugd/10535f_da7effdfa8ad40979f17d561cb845a98 .pdf; Joseph Fewsmith, "China in 2007," *Asian Survey* 48, no. 1 (January/February 2008): 82–96; Willy Lam, "The Xi Jinping Faction Dominates Regional Appointments after the 19th Party Congress," *China Brief* 18, no. 2 (2018): 3–7; Zhiyue Bo, "Balance of Factional Power in China," *East Asia* 25, no. 4 (July 2008): 333–64; Zhiyue Bo, "The 16th Central Committee of the Chinese Communist Party," *Journal of Contemporary China* 13, no. 39 (2004): 223–56.

Beijing, where he became a member of the 17th Politburo and president of the Central Party School. The following year, he was elected vice president of the People's Republic of China, at which point he became seen as Hu's likely successor. The trajectory of Xi's rise to the top was thus perhaps best characterized by a gradual rise during the Jiang era (1989–2002) followed by an accelerating rise during the Hu era (2002–12). Given the acceleration of his rise under Hu and his selection to replace Chen Liangyu in Shanghai, it might appear that Xi was a member of Hu's faction, even though he had not spent time working in the Communist Youth League and hence was not an obvious member of the Hu faction. Xi was, however, generally classified as a member of the Jiang faction.

The composition of the 18th and 19th Politburo Standing Committees, meanwhile, does not appear to have shifted against Jiang's presumed allies. If we treat Xi as his own political man and Wang Qishan and Yu Zhengsheng as his close political comrades in arms, then three of the four other members—Zhang Dejiang, Liu Yunshan, and Zhang Gaoli—were from the Jiang bloc. Only Premier Li Keqiang was identified as a member of the Hu faction. Of the seven members of the 19th Politburo Standing Committee, two—Li Zhanshu and Zhao Leji—were considered members of the "Shaanxi gang," a group who had spent time in Shaanxi when Xi was living as a "sent-down youth" during the Cultural Revolution. Three—Wang Yang, Wang Huning, and Han Zheng—were identified as members of the Jiang faction, leaving Li Keqiang as the sole member of the Hu faction. Within the powerful standing committee, therefore, it did not appear that Xi made significant gains prior to 2022.

The relationship between the Jiang faction and Xi is, however, the crux of understanding the shifting factional balance within the top leadership. Some of those opposed to the regime claim that Xi is at war with the Jiang faction and that the anti-corruption crackdown is simply a smoke screen designed to disguise the political purge of the Jiang faction and, to a lesser extent, the Hu faction. As noted, specialists in factional politics, however, identify Xi as a member of the Jiang faction prior to 2012. If that is at least partially correct, then his selection as general secretary would appear to have represented a victory for the Jiang faction. If we then assume that time alone will progressively weed out the original members of the Jiang faction, one way of looking at the rise of the Xi faction at the 19th Party Congress is not as the displacement of Jiang's allies by a rival set of Xi's allies, but rather as the rejuvenation of the Jiang faction with a new generation of Xi's allies.

The assertion that Xi entered the supreme leadership as an enemy of Jiang is also difficult to sustain. Even if we assume that Xi was not a member of the Jiang faction, it would seem very unlikely that he could have become general secretary without the tacit agreement of both Jiang and Hu. Indeed, if either Jiang or Hu adamantly opposed Xi's selection, who was the "man behind the curtain" who rammed Xi down their throats? It is instead likely that Jiang and Hu reached an understanding on the leadership lineup prior to the 18th Party Congress—Xi would be named to the number one spot as general secretary and Li Keqiang, who was seen as Hu's "candidate" for general secretary, would be named to the number two spot on the Politburo and then become premier of the State Council when the National People's Congress met in March 2013. It does not appear, therefore, that Xi assumed office in the face of bitter factional opposition from Jiang or Hu, with the result that he had to fight tooth and nail from the very beginning to claim, retain, and consolidate his position as general secretary. It is, of course, possible that Jiang and Hu "naively" backed Xi's candidacy based on their belief that he would abide by the collective leadership norm and remain a "first among equals," only to have Xi double-cross them by first using the anti-corruption crackdown to attack Jiang's stalwarts and then finally disposing of Hu's allies at the 20th Party Congress.

It is also plausible that when he attacked corruption, Xi attacked protégés of Jiang and Hu because their protégés were corrupt. Data on those taken down during the Tiger Hunt suggest that high-level corruption swelled during the 1990s and 2000s because senior officials gave in to the temptation to use their public power to seek personal gains and, perhaps more crucially, because attacks on mid-level corruption launched by Jiang in the mid-1990s and sustained by Hu in the 2000s not only failed to control mid-level corruption but also failed to prevent corrupt mid-level officials from being promoted upward into the senior ranks.[31]

Given evidence that Xi faced a true surge in high-level corruption, one of the most vexing questions about Xi is whether his anti-corruption drive, as some contend, has been a venial quest to consolidate power in his own hands or was borne out of a sense, as Xi has argued, that corruption threatened to become an existential threat to the survival of the Party and hence socialism with Chinese characteristics. Put somewhat differently, was Xi's anti-corruption drive a "personal" political fight with Bo, Zhou, and Ling, or was it an "institutional" fight in which Bo, Zhou, and Ling were symptoms of a spreading cancer that Xi believed demanded immediate and radical surgery? The conundrum is, of course, that these are not mutually exclusive possibilities. Xi may well believe that he alone can cleanse the Party of the rot his two predecessors allowed to metastasize and hence sees his personal political battles as synonymous with the Party fight for survival.

Regardless of Xi's underlying motives and the factional maneuvering that has unfolded—contrary to those who have painted a picture of bitter factional infighting in which Xi and his allies have sought to politically incapacitate the elderly Jiang and his now mostly elderly lieutenants by using the anti-corruption crackdown as a disguise for a systematic political purge—the "Xi effect" on leadership politics has been more nuanced. The evidence on the shifting factional balance on the Politburo suggests that Xi and his middle-aged allies have gradually replaced the protégés of Jiang and his octogenarian allies and Hu and his septuagenarian allies.[32] If the rise of the so-called Xi faction represents an evolution of the old Jiang faction, then the 19th Politburo would seem to have been dominated by members of the older Jiang faction and the younger Xi faction, with a residual bloc of members of the Hu faction. By this evolutionary logic, the 20th Politburo represented the final exit of the last remnants of the elderly second generation of the Jiang faction and the few remaining members of the Hu faction.

The Future of the Xi Faction

At the 20th Party Congress in October 2022, Xi broke what many in the West thought was a norm laid down by Deng Xiaoping in the 1980s: members of the Politburo would not serve beyond the age of seventy and the general secretary would be limited to two five-year terms. The "two-term rule" was never codified in the Party constitution, but it was assumed to apply because the constitution of the People's Republic of China stipulated that the president was limited to two five-year terms and in the 1990s it had become the "norm" that the Party's general secretary would also be president of the People's Republic of China. As Ashley Esarey and Rongbin Han noted in their overview chapter, in March 2018 the National People's Congress amended the state constitution and eliminated the two-term limit for the presidency, a move that most saw as clearing the way for Xi to claim a third term as general secretary at the 20th Party Congress in 2022.

Many observers interpreted Xi's claiming of a third term as evidence that he planned to serve as general secretary for life and portrayed this as a play by Xi to become a second Mao Zedong. It is conceivable, however, that Xi understands that Mao's failure to arrange a proper successor capable of consolidating power led to the rise of Deng Xiaoping and the subsequent displacement of Hua Guofeng and the demise of Mao's vision of a radical

TABLE 1.2. Age of Politburo members

POLITBURO	NAME	BIRTH DATE	AGE OF 2022 RETIREES	AGE OF 2022 CARRYOVERS	AGE OF 2022 FRESHMAN	AGE OF 2022 FRESHMAN IN 2027	AGE OF 2022 FRESHMAN IN 2032
19th	Chen Quanguo	1955	67				
19th	Chen Xi	1953	69				
19th	Guo Shengkun	1954	68				
19th	Han Zheng	1954	68				
19th	Hu Chunhua	1963	59				
19th	Li Keqiang	1955	67				
19th	Li Zhanshu	1950	72				
19th	Liu He	1952	70				
19th	Sun Chunlan	1950	72				
19th	Wang Chen	1950	72				
19th	Wang Yang	1955	67				
19th	Xu Qiliang	1950	72				
19th	Yang Jiechi	1950	72				
19th	Yang Xiaodu	1953	69				
19th–20th	Cai Qi	1955		67		72	77
19th–20th	Chen Min'er	1960		62		67	72
19th–20th	Ding Xuexiang	1962		60		65	70
19th–20th	Huang Kunming	1956		66		71	
19th–20th	Li Hongzhong	1956		66		71	
19th–20th	Li Qiang	1959		63		68	73
19th–20th	Li Xi	1956		66			
19th–20th	Wang Huning	1955		67		72	
19th–20th	Xi Jinping	1953		69		74	
19th–20th	Zhang Youxia	1950		72		77	
19th–20th	Zhao Leji	1957		65		70	
20th	Chen Jining	1964			58	63	68
20th	Chen Wenqing	1960			62	67	72
20th	He Lifeng	1955			67	72	
20th	He Weidong	1957			65	70	
20th	Li Ganjie	1964			58	63	68
20th	Li Shulei	1964			58	63	68
20th	Liu Guozhong	1962			60	65	70
20th	Ma Xingrui	1959			63	68	73
20th	Shi Taifeng	1956			66	71	
20th	Wang Yi	1953			69	74	
20th	Yin Li	1962			60	65	70
20th	Yuan Jiajun	1962			60	65	70
20th	Zhang Guoqing	1964			58	63	68
	Average		69	66	62	69	70

socialist China. Xi may have further recognized that if he wants to ensure the longevity of his "China Dream," he needs to find a capable successor. It is possible, therefore, that during his first two terms as general secretary he conducted a search for a successor among the "sixth generation," but failed to identify a candidate who he felt was clean enough, capable enough, and confident enough to ensure the Party's survival. If that was the case, then Xi's decision to remove the two-term limit and claim a third term as general secretary may have been motivated by the need to search for a candidate among the "seventh generation" and hence the need to push the informal selection of a successor to the 20th Party Congress in 2022. The results of the 20th Party Congress seem to signal that Xi found the seventh generation wanting and believes that he must dig deeper and look to the "eighth generation" (senior Party members born in the early 1980s)—or beyond—for a political heir.

Data on the 20th Politburo members strongly suggest there are few apparent candidates for an heir. If we apply the supposed norm that members of the Politburo retire at or about age seventy, then the 20th Politburo includes twelve members who would not have reached age seventy by the 21st Party Congress in 2027 and only four who would not be seventy years old by the time of the 22nd Party Congress in 2032 (see table 1.2). None of the members of the 20th Politburo would meet what was said to be the pre-Xi norm for a two-term general secretary at either the 21st or 22nd Party Congress. All four of those who would not have turned seventy before the 22nd Party Congress would be sixty-eight, just two years shy of the alleged mandatory retirement age. Xi thus faces a "graying problem" and will need to choose whether to junk the seventy-year rule and allow the Party leadership to pass to a septuagenarian or even an octogenarian when he eventually retires—or passes—or to look beyond the current members of the Politburo and lower down within the ranks of the CCP for "fresh new faces" to "helicopter" up into the inner circle of power at the 21st Party Congress, by which time Xi will be seventy-four years old. Should Xi not pick an heir until the 22nd Party Congress in 2032, he would have to hang on to power—and his faculties—until he is seventy-nine years old.

Xi's removal of the remnants of the Jiang and Hu factions also does not, of course, necessarily mean an end to factionalism. On the contrary, if Xi

TABLE 1.2 *opposite page*

Sources: Wikipedia, s.v. "19th Politburo of the Chinese Communist Party," November 13, 2023, https://en.wikipedia.org/wiki/19th_Politburo_of_the_Chinese_Communist_Party, and "20th Politburo of the Chinese Communist Party," August 24 2023, https://en.wikipedia.org/wiki/20th_Politburo_of _the_Chinese_Communist_Party#All_members.

stubbornly hangs on to power, the closer he gets to a point where his aging sixth-generation lieutenants come to believe that he will elect to retire, will lose the mental and physical ability to wield power, or is likely to pass soon, factionalism is apt to increase as they vie with each other either to replace Xi or to push their protégés as potential heirs. As the political scientist Guoguang Wu points out, "Xi's men" are united mostly in their loyalty to him. Beyond that, they are split between those who are linked to Xi from days in Fujian, those who are protégés from his days in Zhejiang, and those whom he worked with in Shanghai. Others connect to Xi through his "native" province of Shaanxi. Some appear to have personal relationships with Xi's wife, Peng Liyuan, or Chen Xi, his former roommate at Tsinghua University who served as a member of the 19th Politburo, secretary of the Party Secretariat, and president of the Central Party School. Several lack long-standing ties with Xi and apparently only recently attracted his attention. Xi's men are further divided, Wu argues, into a cluster drawn from China's military industrial complex and another from the security sector. The new leadership is thus not a monolithic bloc. Wu thus predicts that as Xi reaches down into the ranks of the eighth generation, ambitious cadres will seek to form connections with members of Xi's inner circle in hopes of catching Xi's eye, while those within the inner circle will seek out protégés to build up their power bases and position themselves as kingmakers for the post-Xi era.[33] Xi's "clean sweep" of the Politburo and the exit of both the old Jiang and Hu factions may, therefore, actually lead to a new period of intensifying factional battles within the new Xi camp.

Conclusion

Assessing the "Xi Jinping Effect" on leadership politics is, admittedly, an imprecise science. Leadership politics and factional maneuvering continues to take place within a "black box" that emits only weak and fuzzy signals. Despite this persistent "fog of politics," several points seem clear. First, the "Tiger Hunt" has not targeted political factions seeking to challenge Xi's position as Party leader. It has instead struck at networks of corruption centered on a number of central and regional officials. Most of the leaders of these networks had exited the formal political game before Xi took over as Party leader and hence were no longer contenders for power at the apex of the Party apparatus, even though some likely retained a degree of informal, residual influence exercised through their protégés and connections. Second, even though Xi managed to populate the 19th Politburo and its standing committee with significant numbers of his stalwarts and reduce the number of leaders linked to the Jiang and Hu factions, Xi was himself apparently a product of the Jiang-Hu period and likely owes his selection as paramount leader to an agreement between Jiang and Hu. As such, his "packing" of the 20th Politburo with his allies constitutes less of a break with the Jiang-Hu past than a replacement of the aging leaders under Jiang and Hu with younger leaders who rose up under the aegis of members of the "Jiang-Hu generation." Third, Xi's decision to retain the role of supreme leader and not bring an obvious successor into the 20th Politburo creates a situation in which he has likely not only denied any of his sixth- and seventh-generation lieutenants the chance to lead the Party, he has shifted that chance to his current lieutenants' protégés in the eighth generation.

Xi has unquestionably established himself as a virtually unchallenged leader. If there is opposition to his domination of the Party, it appears to remain limited to the rumors and thirdhand accounts that routinely make the rounds of the Hong Kong and overseas China media. But, as argued herein, his dominance may prove transitory. If Xi is looking to the long term and seeks to perpetuate the Party's grip on power and his vision of "Socialism with Chinese Characteristics for a New Era," then he has to lay the groundwork for a post-Xi era by finding somebody to carry on his legacy, regardless of whether he retires from the front ranks and becomes a behind-the-scenes strongman like Deng or dies in office like Mao. In short, neither the anti-corruption campaign nor the putative elimination of the Jiang and Hu factions has fundamentally altered the inescapable problem of succession.

In conclusion, Xi's anti-corruption crackdown has created "gaps" in the leadership ranks by culling hundreds of corrupt senior officials—and tens of thousands of mid-level officials—which Xi has been able to fill with more junior officials who are untainted, or perhaps at least less tainted, by corruption. His decision to extend to a third term as general secretary, moreover, created time for Xi to test and groom this new generation before moving them into the front ranks of the Party. At the same time, his decision not to select an heir apparent from among the ranks of the sixth and seventh generations has likely rendered them "dead-enders"—promoted to the top but too old to serve as supreme leader. The combination of the anti-corruption crackdown and Xi's decision to remain in office thus paves the way for a generational transition from leaders like Xi, who came of age during the Cultural Revolution and the late Maoist period, to leaders who were born during the Deng era and hence came of age not in a revolutionary socialist society, but rather in a society that mixes capitalism, materialism, socialism, and Leninism. Paradoxically, Xi may have waged a life-and-death struggle with corrupted revolutionaries only to clear the way for their replacement by post-revolutionaries who have only known a system shaped by the forces that led their elders astray.

Notes

1. Sidney Leng, "China's Soccer-Mad President Xi Jinping's Passion for 'the Beautiful Game' Sparked While a Child," *South China Morning Post*, October 23, 2015, https://www.scmp.com/news/china/policies-politics/article/1871444 /chinas-soccer-mad-president-xi-jinpings-passion.

2. Matt Schiavenza, "Xi Jinping Eats Some Dumplings at a Restaurant," *Atlantic*, December 30, 2013, https://www.theatlantic.com/china/archive/2013/12 /xi-jinping-eats-some-dumplings-at-a-restaurant/282719.

3. "Xi Jinping 'Most Powerful Chinese Leader since Mao Zedong,'" *BBC News*, October 24, 2017, https://www.bbc.com/news/world-asia-china-41730948; Stein Ringen, "A Dazzling Spectacle of China's Totalitarianism," *Washington Post*, October 17, 2019.

4. Jamil Anderlini, "Under Xi Jinping, China Is Turning Back to Dictatorship," *Financial Times*, October 10, 2017, https://www.ft.com/content/cb2c8578 -adb4-11e7-aab9-abaa44b1e130.

5. Xi as "core leader": SCMP Reporter, "The Ideal Chinese Husband: Xi Dada and the Cult of Personality Growing around China's President," *South China Morning Post*, February 26, 2016, https://www.scmp.com/news/china/policies -politics/article/1918443/ideal-chinese-husband-xi-dada-and-cult-personality; "classic fascist state": Jonathan Manthorpe, "The Dawn of a Fascist China—and What It Means for Us," *iPolitics*, October 12, 2017, https://ipolitics.ca/2017/10 /12/the-dawn-of-a-fascist-china-and-what-it-means-for-us; "Xi Jinping Thought": Xiang Bo, "Backgrounder: Xi Jinping Thought on Socialism with Chinese Characteristics for a New Era," Xinhuanet, March 17, 2018, http://www.xinhuanet .com/english/2018-03/17/c_137046261.htm; cult of personality: Chris Buckley, "Xi Jinping Is China's 'Core' Leader: Here's What It Means," *New York Times*, October 30, 2016.

6. Kate O'Keeffe and William Mauldin, "Mike Pompeo Urges Chinese People to Change Communist Party; Top U.S. Diplomat Urges Allied Countries, Chinese People to Work with the U.S. to Transform the Party's Behavior," *Wall Street Journal*, July 24, 2020.

7. Daniel Lippman, "Trump National Security Adviser Compares Xi Jinping to Josef Stalin," *Politico*, June 24, 2020, https://www.politico.com/news/2020 /06/24/robert-obrien-xi-jinping-china-stalin-338338.

8. "Second coming": Peter Coy, "Xi Jinping Is the Second Coming of Mao Zedong," *New York Times*, October 7, 2022; "Communist monarch": Chris Buckley,

"As Party Meets, Xi Embodies Imperial Rule," *New York Times*, October 15, 2022; "old emperors": Michael Schuman, "Behold, Emperor Xi," *Atlantic*, October 13, 2022, https://www.theatlantic.com/international/archive/2022/10/xi-jinping -china-national-party-congress/671718; "one-man rule": Kerry Brown, "Xi Jinping Is a Captive of the Communist Party Too," *New York Times*, October 10, 2022; "anti-corruption purges": "Ishaan Tharoor, "Xi's Moment of Dominance Can't Hide His Weakness," *Washington Post*, October 17, 2022; "unrivalled": Grace Tsoi and Sylvia Chang, "How Xi Jinping Made Himself Unchallengeable," *BBC News*, October 16, 2022, https://www.bbc.com/news/world-asia-china -63210545.

9. Katsuji Nakazawa, "Power Struggle Has Xi Leery of Coup, Assassination Attempts," *Nikkei Asian Review*, May 23, 2015, https://asia.nikkei.com/Politics /Power-struggle-has-Xi-leery-of-coup-assassination-attempts.

10. "Top Chinese Officials 'Plotted to Overthrow Xi Jinping,'" *BBC News*, October 20, 2017, https://www.bbc.com/news/world-asia-china-41691917.

11. Lily Kuo, "Cracks Appear in 'Invincible' Xi Jinping's Authority over China," *Guardian*, August 4, 2018, https://www.theguardian.com/world/2018 /aug/04/cracks-appear-in-invincible-xi-jinpings-authority-over-china.

12. The numbers were compiled by the author based on the annual "The Central Commission for Discipline Inspection and the State Supervision Commission Report on the Supervision and Inspections of National Discipline Inspection and Supervision Agencies" (Zhongyang jiwei guojia jiancha tongbao quanguo jijian jiancha ji guan jiangdu jiancha, 中央纪委国家监委通报全国纪检监察机关监督检查), 2013–22, available at Central Commission for Discipline Inspection, accessed August 24, 2023, https://www.ccdi.gov.cn.

13. Andrew Wedeman, database containing information on over forty-two thousand corruption cases reported between roughly 2001 and 2022 in various Chinese- and English-language media outlets, 2022.

14. Andrew Wedeman, "Anticorruption Forever?," in *Fateful Decisions: Choices That Will Shape China's Future*, ed. Thomas Fingar and Jean C. Oi (Stanford, CA: Stanford University Press, 2020), 82–106.

15. Christopher Carothers, *Corruption Control in Authoritarian Regimes: Lessons from East Asia* (New York: Cambridge University Press, 2022).

16. All biographic data in this chapter are from China Vitae, accessed August 24, 2023, http://www.chinavitae.com/index.php.

17. Jude Blanchette, *China's New Red Guards: The Return of Radicalism and the Rebirth of Mao Zedong* (New York: Oxford University Press, 2019).

18. Alice L. Miller, "The Trouble with Factions," *China Leadership Monitor*, no. 46 (2015): 1–12, https://www.hoover.org/sites/default/files/research/docs /clm46am-2.pdf.

19. Andrew J. Nathan, "A Factionalism Model for CCP Politics," *China Quarterly*, no. 53 (1973): 34–66.

20. Lucian W. Pye, "Factions and the Politics of *Guanxi*: Paradoxes in Chinese Administrative and Political Behaviour," *China Journal*, no. 34 (1995): 35–53.

21. David Meyer, Victor C. Shih, and Jonghyuk Lee, "Factions of Different Stripes, Gauging the Recruitment Logics of Factions in the Reform Period," *Journal of East Asian Studies* 16, no. 1 (2016): 43–60; Victor C. Shih, Wei Shan, and Mingxing Liu, "Gauging the Elite Political Equilibrium in the CCP: A Quantitative Approach Using Biographical Data," *China Quarterly*, no. 201 (2010): 79–103.

22. The network analysis also identified a cluster with sixty-six members centered on Liu Tienan. Because Liu was a longtime Zhou lieutenant, I combined that cluster with the "Zhou Yongkang" cluster.

23. Chris Buckley, "Xi Jinping May Delay Picking China's Next Leader, Stoking Speculation," *New York Times*, October 4, 2017.

24. Cheng Li, "China's Midterm Jockeying: Gearing Up for 2012 (Part 1: Provincial Chiefs)," *China Leadership Monitor*, no. 31 (2010): 1–24, http://media .hoover.org/sites/default/files/documents/CLM31CL.pdf.

25. Cheng Li, "Xi Jinping's Inner Circle (Part 2: Friends from Xi's Formative Years)," *China Leadership Monitor*, no. 44 (2014): 1–22, https://www.hoover.org /sites/default/files/research/docs/clm44cl.pdf.

26. "Xi Opens Year of Political Jockeying with Nod to Chongqing Boss," *Bloomberg News*, January 5, 2016, https://www.bloomberg.com/news/articles /2016-01-05/xi-opens-year-of-political-jockeying-with-nod-to-chongqing-boss.

27. Chris Buckley, "From Political Star to 'a Sacrificial Object' in China," *New York Times*, July 23, 2017.

28. Josephine Ma, "Chinese President Xi 'Personally' Vetted Selection of Top Communist Party Team, Xinhua Says," *South China Morning Post*, October 24, 2022, https://www.scmp.com/news/china/politics/article/3196972/chinese -president-xi-personally-vetted-selection-top-communist-party-team-xinhua-says.

29. Agnes Chang, Vivian Wang, Isabelle Qian, and Ang Li, "What Happened to Hu Jintao?," *New York Times*, October 27, 2022.

30. Guoguang Wu, "New Faces of Leaders, New Factional Dynamics: CCP Leadership Politics following the 20th Party Congress," *China Leadership Monitor*, no. 74 (2022), https://www.prcleader.org/post/new-faces-new-factional -dynamics-ccp-leadership-politics-following-the-20th-party-congress.

31. Andrew Wedeman, "The Dynamics and Trajectory of Corruption in Contemporary China," *China Review* 22, no. 2 (May 2022): 21–48; Andrew Wedeman, "Flies into Tigers: The Dynamics of Corruption in China," *China Currents* 20, no. 1 (2021), https://www.chinacenter.net/2021/china-currents/20-1/flies -into-tigers-the-dynamics-of-corruption-in-china.

32. At the time of the 19th Party Congress in 2017, Jiang was ninety-one and Hu was seventy-five. Jiang died at the age of ninety-six, less than six weeks after the close of the 20th Party Congress.

33. Wu, "New Faces of Leaders."

2

Xi Jinping's Counter-Reformation

The Reassertion of Ideological Governance

Timothy Cheek

Xi Jinping is the most powerful general secretary since Deng Xiaoping, some say since Mao Zedong. Chairman Xi certainly needs all that power and a good deal of luck to achieve his stated goal of saving China by saving the Chinese Communist Party (CCP). Since Xi took top leadership in 2012 we have seen the strongest effort at inner-Party reform since the 1980s. Back then, the leadership of Hu Yaobang and Zhao Ziyang, even with the mixed support of Deng Xiaoping, set out to create a reform Leninism that would avoid the mistakes of the Cultural Revolution, but these reforms were not sufficient to enforce both political and economic reform in the teeth of sustained resistance of vested interests and political leaders committed to central planning. Ominously, it was leadership division in 1988–89 that brought a difficult situation to crisis and violent suppression of popular protests. The breakup of the Soviet Union by 1992 also reflected leadership division.[1] The lesson of Tiananmen and Mikhail Gorbachev for Xi Jinping is evident: never let the Party get that divided at the top.

Xi made this very clear at the celebration of the fortieth anniversary of reform and opening in December 2018:

> Party and government, soldiers and civilians, and schools, the East, West, North, South, and Middle—the Party leads them all. It is precisely because we always adhere to the centralized and unified leadership of the Party that we can achieve a great historical turning point, and start a new period of reform and opening up, a new journey of the great rejuvenation of the Chinese nation.... To uphold the Party's leadership, which is a major principle that determines the future and destiny of the Party and the country, the

entire Party and the whole country must without any wavering maintain a high degree of ideological consciousness, political consciousness, and consciousness of action.[2]

It is that lesson that informs Xi Jinping's reforms today. His political project is to address chronic political problems in the rule of the CCP over China as well as a host of pressing political, economic, social, and environmental issues. He aims to do this by reviving the capacity of the Central CCP and state institutions at the expense of regional and local political powers, by cauterizing the financial drain of excess state-owned enterprise profits and large-scale elite pilferage and corruption, and by unifying the Party under the firm order of public service and a group élan of well-rewarded but substantive and measurable public service, which will recoup the Party's current faltering public prestige. To do this, Xi Jinping is using a standard set of Party administrative practices employed since the 1940s to achieve these goals. The rectification campaign, trumpeted in the press today as a "mass line campaign," is one of the three legs of this political agenda. It is a rewrite of the software that runs the other two—the military and security forces and the organizational muscle of the Party-state.

Xi Jinping's efforts at a "counter-reformation" are set against previous reforms in CCP policy that he feels are not working. He believes only the Party can save China, and only ideological and organizational rectification under one supreme leader can save the Party. He insists on the prerequisites and the privileges and the power of the Party, but like a reforming pope, he requires financial celibacy, doctrinal faith, and obedient service from his cadres. As one old colleague of the general secretary puts it, Xi Jinping knows how very corrupt China is and is repulsed by the all-encompassing commercialization of Chinese society, with its attendant nouveau riche; official corruption; loss of values, dignity, and self-respect; and such "moral evils" as drugs and prostitution. It is no surprise that Xi might aggressively attempt to address these evils, perhaps at the expense of the new moneyed class.[3] This concern is not limited to Xi himself, but reflects broader concerns in the Party leadership. Before coming to power, then prime minister Wen Jiabao in 2011 acknowledged the challenges of corruption and food safety scandals, and he interpreted these as a sign of the decay of public morality and social trust. "If a country lacks citizens of high quality [*suzhi*] with moral strength," Wen pronounced, "we absolutely cannot call such a country a really strong one and a country respected by its people."[4]

Xi's campaigns have been tough on China's intellectuals and independent lawyers, but the loyalty he is demanding of them he is already demanding, much more harshly, of Party members, as addressed by Andrew Wedeman's chapter in this volume. To understand each, it is necessary to understand what links both: the Party's determination to discipline itself and society. As the political scientist Thomas Heberer concludes, the road map for modernizing China by 2049 adopted by the 19th Party Congress of the CCP in 2017 determined that achieving these goals "on the one hand, would require a 'strong' Party and strong and competent leader. On the other hand, it would need both a disciplined contingent of cadres and a disciplined, civilized and unified people."[5] Thus, it is no surprise that a key pillar of Xi's counter-reformation, cleaning up the "clergy" in the anti-corruption campaign, combines a comprehensive ideological campaign with the formidable administrative powers of a discipline campaign. Party officials from the Politburo on down are seen at study sessions. And all have seen the frightening results of the Central Commission for Discipline Inspection under Wang Qishan. However, as the scholar Ling Li notes, this commission is but the head of a system of Central Inspection Teams that "are authorized to perform mandatory inspections without cause."[6] In terms of our metaphor, these are the inquisitors for the center. Ideological governance is not only about ideas and values, it includes a robust enforcement of orthodoxy.

Analysts inside and outside of China continue to try to figure out what Xi Jinping is really up to. Is his vaunted mass line program and anti-corruption campaign a sincere effort to reform the CCP and improve the governance of China, or is it a cynical, factional effort to eliminate competitors and entrench his own power? Political scientists have struggled to interpret the "black box" of elite politics in China, with mixed results.[7] Lacking direct access to the thinking of leading Party committees, one must interpret public announcements and activities.

Almost all commentators conclude that Xi Jinping's policies first and foremost are designed to secure his personal power, as well as that of the CCP.[8] Certainly, Xi has taken into hand an impressive array of official posts—beyond his formal position as general secretary of the Party and president of the People's Republic of China: he is chairman of the Central Military Commission and Leading Group director of a dozen top committees including those on foreign affairs, Taiwan, finances and the economy, maritime rights, Internet security, and national defense and military reform, and two widely recognized as key—the Comprehensively Deepening Reforms Leadership Group and the National Security Commission. This brings considerable bureaucratic power back to Beijing and, indeed, into the hands of Xi Jinping.

Clearly, this is an effort to reverse the decentralization of Party and government decision-making that occurred under previous Party leaders.[9] However, power-hungry individuals or structural tensions between Party center and local authorities do not explain Xi's return to vigorous ideological governance in general and Party rectification doctrine in particular.

A historical perspective can add to social science studies of Chinese elite politics, grand strategy, and political economy. It can suggest patterns of governance and claims to legitimacy to look for based on the examples of prior Chinese regimes and leaders. Neither historical precedence of previous Chinese leaders nor recognizable patterns of policy practice alone can determine the actions of Xi Jinping or his colleagues, but they do shape their approach to problems and contribute to the tools and constraints with which Xi and his colleagues work.

Unsurprisingly, Mao Zedong himself identified the three legs of political power in Yan'an in 1939: Party building, military power, and the United Front.[10] The range of political and administrative activities taken by the central CCP since Xi Jinping's confirmation in November 2012 all make sense in the traditions of ideological governance in China in general and of CCP statecraft in particular. Along similar lines, the scholar David Lampton offered a trio to explain the rise of China's international power in 2008 in terms of might, money, and minds. Clearly, a comprehensive leadership program must include military security, economic productivity, and popular legitimacy or a unifying national story. China has manifestly made headway on all three fronts. Other scholars have ably addressed military-security and economic aspects of the Xi Jinping effect. More difficult for many international observers to grasp is the role of ideas, national story, of ideology in (to use Mao's terms) Party building and the United Front. Xi Jinping's administration has revived the comprehensive package of the Yan'an rectification campaign, which claimed to address military, economic, and ideological or belief issues through ideological remolding, Party discipline, and managed public mobilization. This is the Maoist form of a long-standing practice in Chinese statecraft: ideological governance. It is also not widely recognized as such in Western media and most analyses. It is for this reason that this chapter takes a well-known example from European history, the Catholic Reformation in the early modern period, as a metaphor that might help make this political constitution more legible.

It is worthwhile to define the key term in this analysis: *ideological governance* asserts a role for the government as a pedagogical state that has the responsibility to provide order and prosperity through civilizing its citizens according to the superior insights of certified transformational bureaucrats learned in a body of thought that when applied properly will bring great harmony to all under its sway, and which therefore requires and deserves freedom from competition from alternate (and presumed lesser) forms of political activity. This is something that can be called China's political constitution, in the British sense of an unwritten, working constitution.

Ideological Governance in Historical Perspective

Four phases in the history of Chinese statecraft in general and leadership in particular can help us see this "political constitution" in practice. First, there is the long-standing *habitus* of *ideological governance* in Chinese statecraft from at least the Qing emperors (1644–1911) through China's twentieth-century leaders, including Sun Yat-sen, Chiang Kai-shek, and Mao Zedong. Xi Jinping's efforts make sense within this style of politics that has characterized radically different political regimes—imperial, republican, and socialist.

Second, the proximate and specific tradition from which Xi Jinping explicitly draws is *rectification politics*, which dates most notably from the Yan'an Rectification Movement of 1942–44 and the nearly continuous set of political campaigns under the CCP since then. Generally considered a Maoist form of governance and associated with disruptive political campaigns, rectification owes as much to Liu Shaoqi and other less chiliastic Party leaders as it does to Mao, and, more importantly, it characterizes regular politics in the Party as much as it does its many disruptive mass movements. Scholars have long since documented the norms of rectification politics that characterized the Mao period, and that same pattern has held—with important changes since.[11] The core of rectification politics is the primacy of the human will when it is tempered, reformed, and regulated by a superior doctrine and implemented by a capable cadre of administrators. It does not require democracy in the electoral sense; it requires a rectified political leadership.

A third phase in this story is *reform Leninism* after the Cultural Revolution. Leaders since Mao have continued the form of rectification politics with less and less effect since the trauma of Tiananmen in 1989. This was largely because, drawing lessons from the excesses of the Cultural Revolution, leaders beginning with Hu Yaobang and Zhao Ziyang before Tiananmen but extending to Party leaders in the decades after stressed institutionalization, science, and political regulations over mobilization or ideological remolding. By the 2000s, Party campaigns from studying Jiang Zemin's "Three Represents" to a host of forgettable formulations under Hu Jintao left the ideological zeal of Party doctrine dead on arrival for most cadres. The general public largely ignored these campaigns, and the new Internet culture mocked them.

This reform Leninism generated the fourth phase, or the neo-traditional form of Chinese statecraft: *Xi Jinping's counter-reformation*. This reinterpretation of Party tradition along the lines of deeply familiar patterns of ideological governance is an institutional reaction to current events and to the decline in Party norms in recent decades. The retreat from active ideological leadership of the Party under Jiang Zemin, in the name of a Marxist fundamentalism (akin to Vladimir Lenin's New Economic Policy [NEP]) that accepted a transitional stage of capitalism in China, is now seen by Xi as the cause of China's current problems of corruption, pollution, and social unrest. In the face of the political reformation that Jiang's reliance on transforming the economic base first represented, Xi's administration constitutes a counter-reformation, a reassertion of the charismatic institution and the need for the ideological cultivation of cadres according to one orthodoxy. That orthodoxy made its official appearance in the 19th Party Congress in 2017 as "Xi Jinping Thought on Socialism with Chinese Characteristics for a New Era."[12]

Ideological Governance in Qing and Republican China

The first phase in this short history of Chinese statecraft in the modern era dates from the late imperial period (though textual echoes can be seen all the way back to the Confucian classics). Jürgen Osterhammel in his comparative study of the "civilizing mission" in Europe and the world concludes that such "civilizing" has been a continuous process in Chinese history: "The relentless urge of the Chinese elite to civilize others was directed at the peasantry, at non-Han Chinese (today called 'ethnic minorities') within the realm and at 'barbarians' along its borders."[13] Xi Jinping's "Chinese Dream," "mass line," and reimposition of a directed public sphere (that is, extensive propaganda buttressed by robust censorship and repression of dissent) are part of an institutional reaffirmation of traditions of ideological governance. In a political version of the *long durée*, cultural resources from traditional texts and a continuous chain of administrative practices from Qing emperors to Sun Yat-sen to Chiang Kai-shek to Mao can be seen. These form three traditions of Chinese ideological governance in modern China.

The Qing dynasty has bequeathed to modern China expectations and tools for ideological governance of a large and diverse territory by a relatively small ruling elite, which has been enthusiastically embraced by China's reformers and revolutionaries of varying stripes. These expectations and tools have been shaped over the twentieth century by exogenous influences (such as science and technology and the Soviet model), endogenous pressures (social disorder and elite competition), and contingent events (Japanese invasion, Cold War tensions, and the contemporary global populist moment). From traditional texts and Qing practice comes a belief in the transformative power of correct models, most notably the ancient Confucian *Classic of Rites* (Liji). Its constant repetition by Chinese governments and leading thinkers for the past two thousand years reflects a shared belief among China's cultural and political elite in the educability of humans. People can be taught how to be good, and correct ways of acting, thinking, speaking, and even sitting can directly contribute to that noble goal.[14] Thus role models, especially top leaders—like emperors—need to act well, or at least be seen to act as exemplars of morality.[15] The goal throughout, and the term that carries this long-standing orientation in Chinese statecraft today, is *jiaohua*, "to transform" the subject through moral-political education.

The significance of this tradition of ideological governance is that Chinese governments from the fourteenth century consistently insisted on giving moral lectures to local communities, when all available evidence shows that locals paid next to no attention to them.[16] These lectures proclaimed the "sacred edicts" (*shengyu*) of Ming and Qing emperors. The ritual performance of moral-political education for the people signified legitimate government regardless of whether or not anyone was paying attention. These lectures were not simply in books. Local magistrates were instructed to recite the maxims and expound upon their meaning in monthly public meetings. Handbooks, such as Li Laizhang's *Explanations of the Sacred Edict Lecture System* (Shengyu xuanjiang xiangbao tiaoyue) of 1705, literally mapped out how to hold these meetings, down to diagrams showing the placement of the tablets with the maxims and altars, and the locations of where both scholars and townsfolk should stand, as well as instruction on how to hold the meeting and fill out the registers of good and bad behavior.[17] The most painful signs of the continued salience of this approach to governance are the reeducation camps and efforts at "de-religious extremification" undertaken by the Party in Xinjiang to corral its largely non-Han Muslim population.[18]

Ideological governance continued apace in the varying regimes of twentieth-century China. The core approach shared by all governments in China down to today is political tutelage (*xunzheng*). This was Sun Yat-sen's explanation for putting democracy off for another day and the primary expression of the pedagogical state under his Nationalist Party. The founding father of China's republic, Sun came to feel by the 1920s that the Chinese people were not ready for democracy and required instead a period of political education or tutelage during which his one-party state would inculcate the masses in modern civility. This "Tutelary State," as John Fitzgerald calls it in his study of Sun's political model, was meant to awaken the Chinese people and teach them how to be modern citizens.[19] This responsibility (or presumption, depending on one's view) was enthusiastically embraced by his successors. Chiang Kai-shek, in *China's Destiny*, quotes Sun Yat-sen to say: "When there is one purpose, and it is the purpose of the entire people, and when the people all work to achieve this purpose, it is easy to succeed."[20] Chiang concludes that such unity required the complete domination of political life by the Nationalist Party to maintain order and educate the people. Chiang famously did not succeed in this unification of political wills, but, for a time, Mao did.

Rectification Politics

The next phase in this history of Chinese statecraft and the direct model of ideological governance for Xi Jinping is the one he regularly harks back to: the Yan'an Rectification. Rectification (*zhengfeng*) is the political education and reform process to train Party leaders and rank and file that Mao Zedong and his colleagues perfected in Yan'an in the 1940s. It is often employed in an orchestrated campaign, a rectification movement (such as in Yan'an in 1942–44 and in the other base areas in the years to follow, among intellectuals nationally in 1950–51, and on down every few years to Xi Jinping's campaigns today). However, rectification has characterized everyday politics under the CCP as well as Mao's famously intense campaigns.[21] When undertaken seriously, this form of political training resembles nothing so much as Bible study in small groups run by the local police department (with officers from the intelligence service and military on hand when needed). Individual study, public confession of one's sins, review of one's personnel record, and public propaganda about role models (and a few negative role models to show what is to be avoided) define a CCP rectification campaign. Such campaigns always include purges, the naming and denunciation of negative models, and the removal of offending cadres and others who cross the campaign's line. Rectification was taken to absurd and tragic extremes in the Anti-Rightist Campaign and the Cultural Revolution, but it has been a staple of political life in the CCP since the 1940s.[22] Xi Jinping's anti-corruption campaign is just such a rectification effort. So, too, is the campaign announced by the Central Political-Legal Committee that is advertised as "like the Yan'an rectification movement," which began in 2021.[23]

Rectification is the political constitution that the CCP articulated in the 1940s to address urgent political and administrative problems in the face of a lack of regular institutions or sufficient military power to force its will. How does the CCP rectification system work? It works by precisely the three components Mao outlined in 1938: Party building, control of force, and welcoming cooperative non-Party political actors. Today this means:

- articulation and consensus on the ideas and projects of *one* Party leader (the "line")
- criticism and self-criticism sessions for Party members to inculcate that line
- crackdown and prosecution of corruption via Party channels to control deviance
- repression of public criticism, irritating lawyers, and mouthy professors with the goal of managing the public message
- welcome to and use of the skills of nongovernmental organizations and "social organizations" to implement Party policy.

This adds up to one leader, one Party, and one voice—all for one project: China's rejuvenation under the Party.

One leader. This is one side of the concentration of power—from collective leadership to *primus inter pares* to an undisputed "core" leader. It is clear that the CCP leadership has agreed to let Xi Jinping serve as the single leader of this reform effort. He holds an unprecedented suite of positions, including in the newly announced National Security Council and the Leading Small Group for Comprehensive Deepening Reform. This is why the Resolution of the Third Plenum in 2013 continues to be important in conjunction with the invocation of the "mass line" tradition of public service and self- and mutual criticism.[24] Xi Jinping hopes to get the Party's self-discipline working again by controlling the message and monitoring implementation. It can be done, it has been done, but usually it is not done because diverse stakeholders blunt the effort.

One Party. This is the other side of the concentration of power—from the localities back to the center. It is done ideologically through studying the thoughts and words—the policy platform and policy approach—of the leader, usually the resolutions from each Party plenum and "important speeches." Organizationally, it is done through regular political study sessions, high and low.[25] It is backed up by the Central Commission on Discipline Inspection and through the proposed implementation of social welfare provisions to be handled directly by the central state. Financially, this is done by using the power of the state apparatus to claw back state-owned enterprise profits and take down wayward business leaders.

One voice. Rectification theory does not welcome quibbling and it will not tolerate dissent. The public voice of rectification is, indeed, the pieties of "the mass line"—which, after all, only promises to *listen* to the worries and concerns of the masses and *promises* to address them. In order to mobilize the public to do what the Party thinks is best for China—since no government would have the recourses to compel such a huge population—it needs to maintain a certain level of prestige and popularity. The central CCP has by and large succeeded in maintaining such prestige to date.[26] The widespread dissatisfaction with government in China is, as much research has reflected, directed at the *local state*. Much like African Americans in the US South in the 1960s—many Chinese look to the central government to correct the faults of the local state.

Xi Jinping believes, as can be seen in his comments from 2018 that opened this chapter, that rectification can address these challenges and achieve popular mobilization and official coordination for *one project*—bringing China to national wealth and power, the dream of Chinese reformers since the late nineteenth century—while keeping the CCP in charge.

Reform Leninism

This effort amounts to a counter-reformation in Chinese politics after the third phase in this short history: the post-Mao retreat from the excesses of rectification mobilization during the Cultural Revolution. This retreat was the "protestant reformation of the Party" started under Hu Yaobang and Zhao Ziyang in the 1980s, and continued under Jiang Zemin (and ineffectually resisted under Hu Jintao). Mao's campaigns, and particularly the Cultural Revolution, had discredited the extreme and highly emotive versions of rectification and made a mockery of mass line egalitarian claims. This led in the early post-Mao period to a search within the Party for *regularization* of political life by a return to the explicit organizational norms of Leninism—essentially a version of military hierarchy.[27] This was the work of Deng Xiaoping from 1975 and of Peng Zhen, who resuscitated "socialist legality" in the 1980s.[28] This protestant revolt against the institutional abuses of the "spiritual" side of rectification doctrine saw an emphasis on two things: socialist legality and technocratic leadership. Law and science. This served to expunge the wild excesses of emotional ideology (which had become divorced from administrative practicality) and produced a functional political package into the new century.[29]

However, this reform Leninism—regulations + science—failed to address leadership competition or to control officialdom satisfactorily. This Leninist reformation since the 1980s was meant to return to the scientific side of Leninism, in which social engineers and material engineers would join forces to produce a rational society and guide China through its necessary capitalist stage under Party tutelage. However, the absence of a compelling ideology made itself felt in leadership drift and growing official corruption. Hence Wen Jiabao's call to action in 2011 and Xi Jinping's counter-reformation.

This reform Leninism was not democratization in the accepted sense of liberal democratic politics. The CCP reformers were loath to share power, unwilling to constrain their operation by setting any law above the Party, since this would undercut its ideological governance. Such liberal restraints on political power are nearly unthinkable in the Party's doctrinal culture. To be sure, there have been liberal Party reformers who tried to imagine a path to constitutional democracy under the Party, from Hu Yaobang himself to Yu Keping in the 2000s to Cai Xia at the Central Party School in 2013.[30] Hu Yaobang, of course, was deposed in 1986, Yu Keping withdrew from government service in 2015 to take up a post at Peking University, and, most recently, Cai Xia has broken ranks and explicitly criticized Xi Jinping, resulting in her expulsion from the Party. A democratic future for the CCP is, indeed, thinkable; it simply has not taken root up to now.

Xi Jinping's Counter-Reformation

Instead, Xi Jinping has chosen to employ 1940s techniques to address problems of governance in the 2010s and 2020s. Why revive rectification politics? A comparative perspective can supplement the historical perspective. Rectification is, essentially, the political constitution of the Chinese government—in the British sense of an unwritten, working constitution in national politics (as opposed to the formal paper constitution of the Chinese state). It is useful to think of a political constitution in the terms that the historian Peter Hennessy uses to describe the operation of Britain's unwritten constitution in *The Hidden Wiring*—that peculiar combination of administrative measures used, powers agreed upon, and procedures deemed appropriate that tradition and practice have legitimated among top political actors.[31]

In the CCP's case, the political constitution that rectification doctrine represents was built in Yan'an in the 1940s in the famous Yan'an Rectification

Movement, which saw the confirmation of Mao's supreme leadership, but, more importantly, the establishment of the measures, powers, and procedures that made the CCP the most effective political administration and military force in China. Other Party leaders, such as Liu Shaoqi and Chen Yun, fleshed out the organizational methods and norms, including "self-cultivation" of Party members and the proper handling of political competition (called "inner-Party struggle").[32] The historian Philip A. Kuhn has drawn attention to the significance of such an unwritten constitutional order for twentieth-century China, which has dominated the concerns of China's politicians and thinkers. That constitutional agenda, Kuhn shows, addressed three key problems of governance: *participation, competition*, and *control*. These issues form the three dominant challenges of modern Chinese politics: (1) how political participation and public mobilization can be reconciled with enhancing the power and legitimacy of the state; (2) how political competition can be reconciled with public interest; and (3) how fiscal demands of the state can be reconciled with the needs of society.[33]

The CCP's rectification doctrine and practice address these three challenges to the modern Chinese constitutional agenda. Political scientists, particularly Frederick C. Teiwes and Franz Schurmann, have documented the centrality of the Yan'an agenda.[34] They focus on the formal procedures of rectification, but the one manifestation of this political constitution in the CCP is the political line, and, in this case, the *mass line (qunzhong luxian)*. The Yan'an Rectification in the 1940s was an implementation of this mass line to address the problems of governance in modern China, questions of political participation, leadership competition, and control of finances, officialdom, and society.[35] The Yan'an Rectification sought to unify thought and policymaking around one leader, infuse these policies and political approach into the administration through a vigorous management-training regime (self- and mutual criticism), enforce those norms with frequent police violence against infractions, and generate a popular image for the regime in the media to mobilize public support.[36] It backed up all this political work with overwhelming military power, on the one hand, and relatively effective and productive administrative and economic reforms, on the other. It was by no means perfect, nor was it without drawbacks, not least the frequent use of terror. But it beat the competition.

In summary, the Yan'an Rectification addressed the challenges of modern China's constitutional agenda by proposing a novel package of ideology and organization (hence the title of Schurmann's classic study of CCP rule in 1966). It offered *Mao Zedong Thought* to explain what to do, how to do it, and why to do it; *democratic centralism* to implement the mobilization of cadres and citizens, the management of conflict, and the exercise of state control of economic and military resources; and *self- and mutual criticism* among leaders and officials to ensure effective implementation of those ideological and organizational norms. This model is the heart of Xi Jinping's current policies, his counter-reformation.

Rectification or the mass line political order of the CCP is almost unimaginable to political theorists and politicians and the general public in the West. It is the profound acceptance of formal ideology and ideological remolding at the heart of rectification that stumps us. At root, rectification politics depends on the power of correct thought (*zhengquede sixiang*) and on the impact of it through a mobilized, faithful cadre of leaders. When it appears to be working, it makes the CCP look like a religious organization at best, like a cult at worst.[37] The mental and emotional interventions into the minds of individuals that rectification requires in order to function effectively outrages our sensibilities about individual autonomy and privacy. Our constitutional agenda is built on behavior and its consequences and not on mental states, what in Chinese political language is discussed as *jingshen* (spirit) and *taidu* (attitude).[38] Gerda Wielander's chapter in this volume gives a rich account of the role of political *faith* in Xi's politics. However, translate those words and Chinese political thought appears as either mendacious or menacing. What role in our political agenda do such "spiritual" (*jingshen*) or "attitude" (*taidu*) factors play? Certainly, political scientists, as well as publicists, are attentive to questions of attitudes, which bleeds into "values," but our political constitution is explicitly agnostic on attitudes (hate speech and behaviors around multiculturalism being an exception), and certainly our political regimes do not (at least openly) use the measure and manipulation of fundamental attitudes—one's personal thoughts and feelings—as a public political instrument.

Chinese rectification does. And Xi Jinping is currently employing this rectification politics among a Party population of some one hundred million people in order to address challenges of political participation, leadership competition, and control of the polity in China today. As the political scientist Joseph Fewsmith has commented, Xi Jinping is putting the Lenin back in Chinese Leninism.[39]

Prospects for Rectification Politics under Xi Jinping

What can one make of Xi Jinping's counter-reformation in Chinese politics? First, this is Maoism, but it is the institutional Maoism of Liu Shaoqi and Peng Zhen and not the charismatic populism of the later Mao. Put away our *Quotations from Chairman Mao* (the Little Red Book) and dig out our dusty copy of Liu Shaoqi's *How to Be a Good Communist*.[40] There is a substantial body of governance theory and experience underwriting today's rectification. This is a serious attempt to address the problems of governance, what Kuhn has termed modern China's constitutional agenda, by reclaiming *control* over the economy and over the behavior of the leadership, by channeling political *competition* among elites, and by guiding popular *participation* to unthreatening support roles in social welfare. This is Xi Jinping making good on his promise to save China by saving the CCP. Rectification is much more than "criticism sessions" or buying steamed buns and driving a Hongqi instead of an Audi. It is a comprehensive package of ideological unification, administrative control, and police power. As scholars Kerry Brown and Una Aleksandra Bērziņa-Čerenkova conclude, "Ideology in Xi's China is important because of the ways it enforces unity, creates a common purpose, and operates as a means of guiding the country, under the direction of unified CPC [Communist Party of China] rule, towards its great objective—modernization with Chinese characteristics."[41] This is the current form of ideological governance in China under Xi Jinping. And, this software is incompatible with the norms and assumptions of liberal democracy.

Second, this is political orthodoxy. Rectification talk is a public transcript for the CCP; it is the orthodoxy of the Party of Mao. As can be seen in the historical Catholic Church, and indeed within our own liberal democratic societies, the pieties of our ideals coincide with abuse of and cynicism about them. Public declaration of communist values serves as a "public transcript" to promote identity and commitment among the ruling elite. These public transcripts, as the political scientist James C. Scott has argued, have as strong a political role to play as the "hidden transcripts" of quiet dissent and resistance under authoritarian regimes.[42] And, this orthodoxy has a robust enforcement mechanism in required Party study sessions, pressure to voice agreement with Party policies, and a fearsome Discipline Inspection Commission. It is dogma with inquisitorial support. Pointing out that Xi Jinping and his colleagues, of course, are closing their eyes to the facts of power politics does not weaken the legitimating function of a plausible political orthodoxy. Multiyear survey research by a Harvard team at the Ash Center for Democratic Governance and

Innovation continues to find broad-based support for the Party's leadership, even though local leaders are often criticized.[43]

Third, Xi's counter-reformation probably will not work, at least not in terms of rectification goals of moral-personal transformation and the pure governance of the mass line. The leadership of the Communist Party today under Xi Jinping is embracing traditional values of the communist revolution to address very new problems. And just as Mao was not successful applying the economic policies of Yan'an mass mobilization to the challenges of industrialization in 1958, I do not think this application of the ideological wing of the Yan'an model is going to work in the 2020s. Rectification—with moral solutions for administrative problems, Party-run scriptural study sessions, and the demand for orthodoxy in public expression, all enforced through an independent inquisitorial police force—is no way to handle the challenges of an information society, a middle-income trap, or rising leadership in regional and global affairs.[44] One should understand why the rectification approach makes sense to Xi Jinping, but that does not mean it will produce good or sustainable governance. The China of the 2020s is not the China of the 1940s or 1960s. Globalization may not have made Chinese politics democratic, but it has certainly made Chinese society *globalized*, with international contacts and content extending to village China. As the Shanghai scholar Liu Qing has argued, this has pluralized Chinese society, and neither Chinese socialism nor Confucianism appears well equipped to deal with diversity.[45] Rectification politics requires the rigorous control of available information. Forty years of social experience since opening and reform began and over two decades of the Internet have made such propaganda control harder and harder to achieve and maintain.

Finally, the *metaphor*: Xi Jinping's counter-reformation. This metaphor compares the Catholic Reformation over a century from the Council of Trent to the close of the Thirty Years' War in 1648 with the current efforts of the CCP since about 2010 and here associated with the rule of Xi Jinping. Like all metaphors, it does not work in all respects. But metaphors are as useful when they fail as when they succeed. The failures: the "Leninist reformation" of the post-Mao reforms, as I call it, is nothing like the challenge to the old order that Luther and the German princes were to Catholic Europe. However, this highlights the shared conclusion of medieval Catholic and contemporary CCP leaders: the rot comes from within their own ranks, and most, but not all, of their counter-reformation focuses on internal rot, corruption, and loss of sense of mission. Burning heretics and disappearing rights lawyers are a nasty, but secondary, part of the primary mission:

institutional renovation. On the other hand, the frightening "vocational" reeducation centers in Xinjiang (really concentration camps bent on turning Uyghurs into Han) suggest an even darker side to ideological governance and rectification practice.[46] The Xinjiang ideological remolding camps tragically revive the human carnage of the Great Leap Forward that happened when a political technology from an earlier time was applied to new and different circumstances. The production campaigns of Yan'an and the civil war era may have contributed to effective governance in the 1940s, but they brought nationwide famine in the late 1950s. Likewise, today the terrible extension of rectification discipline from a closed group in a political party to a general population constitutes a violation of human rights on a mind-boggling scale. More tragically, the "vocational retraining" Uyghurs and others suffer in these camps as they are compelled to "reeducate" into Party-loving Han does not appear to work. Rather, these camps are likely to generate the sustained opposition the state so much fears.

In the end, and especially in light of outrage at the increased repression in China today, the counter-reformation metaphor draws our attention to the long-standing traditions of Chinese statecraft that inform not just Xi Jinping but a sufficient group of Party leaders to sustain the project for some time. That corpus of governance techniques is rectification doctrine. If this political software is dismissed, one will be hard-pressed to make sense of Xi Jinping's administration or the helmsman's place within it.

Notes

This chapter was originally published in the *Journal of Contemporary China* 30, no. 132 (2021), and is included here, with minor modification, with permission of Taylor & Francis.

1. The origins and consequences of the reform challenges into the Jiang Zemin era of the 2000s are well presented in Joseph Fewsmith, *China since Tiananmen: From Deng Xiaoping to Hu Jintao* (New York: Cambridge University Press, 2008).

2. This is the seventeenth quotation from Chairman Xi given in Xi Jinping, "Zhongguo Gongchandang lingdao shi Zhongguo tese shehuizhuyi zuibenzhi de tezheng" (The leadership of the Chinese Communist Party is the most essential characteristic of socialism with Chinese characteristics), *Qiushi* (Seeking truth), no. 14 (July 2020), http://www.qstheory.cn/dukan/qs/2020-07/15/c_1126234524.htm.

3. See "Portrait of Vice President Xi Jinping: 'Ambitious Survivor' of the Cultural Revolution," https://wikileaks.org/plusd/cables/09BEIJING3128_a.html, a leaked November 16, 2009, US diplomatic cable reprinted by WikiLeaks, cited

in Tom Phillips, "Xi Jinping: Does China Truly Love 'Big Daddy Xi'—or Fear Him?," *Guardian*, September 19, 2015, http://www.theguardian.com/world/2015/sep/19/xi-jinping-does-china-truly-love-big-daddy-xi-or-fear-him.

4. Wen Jiabao, "Jiang zhenhua ca shiqing: Tong Guowuyuan canshi he Zhongyang wenshi yanjiuguan guanyuan zuotan shi de jianghua" (Tell the truth, examine the facts: Talk at a meeting of State Council counselors and researchers at the Central Literature and History Office), *People's Daily*, April 18, 2011, 2.

5. Thomas Herberer, "Disciplining of a Society: Social Disciplining and Civilizing Processes in Contemporary China" (Ash Center for Democratic Governance and Innovation, Harvard Kennedy School, Cambridge, MA, August 2020), 43, https://ash.harvard.edu/publications/disciplining-society-social-disciplining-and-civilizing-processes-contemporary.

6. Ling Li, "Politics of Anticorruption in China: Paradigm Change of the Party's Disciplinary Regime 2012–2017," *Journal of Contemporary China* 28, no. 115 (2019): 58.

7. Frederick C. Teiwes, "The Study of Elite Political Conflict in the PRC: Politics inside the 'Black Box,'" in *Handbook of the Politics of China*, ed. David S. G. Goodman (Northampton, MA: Edward Elgar Publishing, 2015), 21–41.

8. Bates Gill, "Xi Jinping's Grip on Power Is Absolute, but There Are New Threats to His 'Chinese Dream,'" *Conversation*, June 27, 2019, https://theconversation.com/xi-jinpings-grip-on-power-is-absolute-but-there-are-new-threats-to-his-chinese-dream-118921. This is one part of the series "How China Maintains Its Power" on the *Conversation* website.

9. Sangkuk Lee, "An Institutional Analysis of Xi Jinping's Centralization of Power," *Journal of Contemporary China* 26, no. 105 (2017): 334.

10. Mao Zedong, "Introduction to *The Communist*," October 4, 1939. What Mao said precisely was: "Therefore the united front, armed struggle and Party building are the three fundamental questions for our Party in the Chinese revolution." *Selected Works of Mao Tse-tung*, vol. 2, Marxist Internet Archive, 2004, https://www.marxists.org/reference/archive/mao/selected-works/volume-2/mswv2_20.htm.

11. Frederick C. Teiwes, *Politics and Purges in China: Rectification and the Decline of Party Norms, 1950–1965* 2nd ed. (Armonk, NY: M. E. Sharpe, 1993).

12. "Resolution of the 19th National Congress of the Communist Party of China on the Revised Constitution of the Communist Party of China," October 24, 2017, trans. Xinhua News Service, http://www.xinhuanet.com/english/2017-10/24/c_136702726.htm.

13. Jürgen Osterhammel, *Europe, the "West" and the Civilizing Mission* (London: German Historical Institute London, 2006), 10, https://www.ghil.ac.uk/fileadmin/redaktion/dokumente/annual_lectures/AL_2005_Osterhammel.pdf.

14. A standard verse from the *Liji* is from the chapter "Xueji" (Record on the subject of education): "If the *junzi* [prince] wishes to transform the people and

to perfect their manners and customs, must he not start from the lessons of the school?" See Yang Guorong, *Xiankui yu Hele: Dui shengming yiyi de niliu tansuo* (*Xiankui* and *Hele:* A contrarian investigation of the meaning of life) (Hong Kong: Sanlian Shudian, 2010), 272–73.

15. See David L. Hall and Roger T. Ames, *Thinking through Confucius* (Albany: State University of New York Press, 1987); Donald J. Munro, *The Concept of Man in Contemporary China* (Ann Arbor: University of Michigan Press, 1977).

16. Victor Mair, "Language and Ideology in the Written Popularizations of the Sacred Edicts," in *Popular Culture in Late Imperial China*, ed. David Johnson, Andrew J. Nathan, and Evelyn S. Rawski (Berkeley: University of California Press, 1985), 325–59.

17. Li Laizhang, "Shengyu xuanjiang xiangbao tiaoyue" (Regulations for "Community-Security" Sacred Edict Lectures), preface dated 1705, from his collected works, *Li Shanyuan quanshu* (Complete works of Li Shanyuan). A copy is in the Harvard-Yenching Library, Harvard University.

18. James Leibold, "Surveillance in China's Xinjiang Region: Ethnic Sorting, Coercion, and Inducement," *Journal of Contemporary China* 29, no. 121 (2020): 46–60.

19. Articulated in Sun Yat-sen's "Fundamentals of National Reconstruction" (1923); see John Fitzgerald, *Awakening China: Politics, Culture, and Class in the Nationalist Revolution* (Stanford, CA: Stanford University Press, 1996), 79.

20. Chiang Kai-shek, *China's Destiny and Chinese Economic Theory* (New York: Roy Publishers, 1947), 112.

21. Teiwes, *Politics and Purges in China*, 25–62.

22. Kirk Denton provides a fine introduction and overview in "Rectification: Party Discipline, Intellectual Remolding, and the Formation of a Political Community," in *Words and Their Stories: Essays on the Language of the Chinese Revolution*, ed. Ban Wang (Leiden: Brill, 2011), 51–63.

23. Christian Sorace, "Extracting Affect: Televised Cadre Confessions in Contemporary China," *Public Culture* 31, no. 1 (2018): 145–71; Suisheng Zhao, "The Ideological Campaign in Xi's China: Rebuilding Regime Legitimacy," *Asian Survey* 56, no. 6 (2016): 1168–93. The impending political-legal rectification was announced on the WeChat group Jinri Faxue Pinglun (Today's Legal Commentary) on July 13, 2020: https://mp.weixin.qq.com/s/eVPZ85CG8A_-agJjqnDw8A.

24. "CCP Central Committee Resolution concerning Some Major Issues in Comprehensively Deepening Reform (Passed at the 3rd Plenum of the 18th Central Committee of the Chinese Communist Party on November 12, 2013)," *China Copyright and Media* (blog), November 15, 2013, https://chinacopyrightandmedia .wordpress.com/2013/11/15/ccp-central-committee-resolution-concerning-some -major-issues-in-comprehensively-deepening-reform.

25. John Dotson, "The CCP Politburo Holds Its First Collective Study Session

for 2020," *China Brief* 20, no. 11 (June 24, 2020), https://jamestown.org
/program/the-ccp-politburo-holds-its-first-collective-study-session-for-2020.

26. Edward Cunningham, Tony Saich, and Jessie Turiel, "Understanding CCP
Resilience: Surveying Chinese Public Opinion through Time" (Ash Center for
Democratic Governance and Innovation, Harvard Kennedy School, Cambridge,
MA, July 2020), https://ash.harvard.edu/publications/understanding-ccp
-resilience-surveying-chinese-public-opinion-through-time.

27. Klaus Mühlhahn, "Reform and Opening: 1977–1989," in *The Making of
Modern China: From the Great Qing to Xi Jinping* (Cambridge, MA: Belknap
Press of Harvard University Press, 2019), 491–526.

28. Pitman Potter, *From Leninist Discipline to Socialist Legalism: Peng Zhen on
Law and Political Authority in the PRC* (Stanford, CA: Stanford University Press,
2003).

29. The protestant Party ideology came at the 12th Party Congress with Hu
Yaobang; see Hu Yaobang, "Quanmian kaichuang shehuizhuyi xiandaihua jianshe de xin jumian" (Comprehensively inaugurate the new situation of socialist
modernization construction), in *Zhongguo gaige quanshu: Jingshen wenming
jianshe juan* (The encyclopedia of China's reform: The volume of constructing
spiritual civilization), ed. Zhao Yao, Hu Zhensheng, and Xu Kejun (Dalian: Dalian Chubanshe, 1992), 160–70. For an excellent analysis, see Wenjie Weng, "The
Disciplinary Reform: Sanming and the Post-Mao Civilizing Project, 1978–1984"
(master's thesis, University of British Columbia, 2021), https://open.library.ubc
.ca/soa/cIRcle/collections/ubctheses/24/items/1.0413691?o=0.

30. Cai Xia, "Advancing Constitutional Democracy Should Be the Mission of
the Chinese Communist Party (2013)," trans. Timothy Cheek, Joshua A. Fogel,
and David Ownby, *Reading the China Dream* (blog), last updated October 2022,
https://www.readingthechinadream.com/cai-xia-advancing-constitutional
-democracy.html; Fewsmith, *China since Tiananmen*; Yu Keping, *Democracy
Is a Good Thing: Essays on Politics, Society, and Culture in Contemporary China*
(Washington, DC: Brookings Institution Press, 2008).

31. Peter Hennessy, *The Hidden Wiring: Unearthing the British Constitution*
(London: Gollancz, 1995).

32. Most famously in Liu Shaoqi's essay on cadres' self-cultivation, translated
into English as "How to Be a Good Communist," from July 1939, Marxists Internet Archive, accessed December 23, 2023, https://www.marxists.org/reference
/archive/liu-shaoqi/1939/how-to-be/ch01.htm, and Chen Yun, under the same
title, and translated by Boyd Compton in *Mao's China: Party Reform Documents,
1942–44* (Seattle: University of Washington Press, 1952), 88–107.

33. Philip A. Kuhn, *Origins of the Modern Chinese State* (Stanford, CA: Stanford University Press, 2002), 1–2.

34. Teiwes, *Politics and Purges in China*; Franz Schurmann, *Ideology and*

Organization in Communist China, 2nd ed. (Berkeley: University of California Press, 1968).

35. A detailed and sympathetic account of the Yan'an Rectification and associated campaigns for production, simplifying bureaucracy, and so forth is given by Mark Selden, *The Yenan Way in Revolutionary China* (Cambridge, MA: Harvard University Press, 1971); a more critical, but sound, analysis of the politics is offered in Raymond Wylie, *The Emergence of Maoism* (Stanford, CA: Stanford University Press, 1980). Finally, a dense but powerfully detailed study of *why* rectification generated so much belief and solidarity among cadres and compliance among the general public is given in David Apter and Tony Saich, *Revolutionary Discourse in Mao's Republic* (Cambridge, MA: Harvard University Press, 1994).

36. Timothy Cheek, "Making Maoism: Ideology and Organization in the Yan'an Rectification Movement, 1942–1944," in *Knowledge Acts in Modern China: Ideas, Institutions, and Identities*, ed. Robert Culp, Eddy U, and Wen-hsin Yeh (Berkeley: Institute of East Asian Studies, University of California, 2016), 304–27.

37. Elizabeth J. Perry, "Moving the Masses: Emotion Work in the Chinese Revolution," *Mobilization: An International Journal* 7, no. 2 (2002): 111–28.

38. Timothy Cheek, "Attitudes of Action: Maoism as Emotional Political Theory," in *Chinese Thought as Global Theory*, ed. Leigh Jenco (Albany: State University of New York Press, 2016), 75–100.

39. Joseph Fewsmith, personal communication with author, August 2020.

40. Liu Shaoqi, "Lun gongchandangyuan de xiuyang" (On the self-cultivation of the Party member) (July 1939), translated in *Selected Works of Liu Shaoqi*, vol. 1, Liu Shaoqi Reference Archive, February 2004, https://www.marxists.org/reference/archive/liu-shaoqi/1939/how-to-be.

41. Kerry Brown and Una Aleksandra Bērziņa-Čerenkova, "Ideology in the Era of Xi Jinping," *Journal of Chinese Political Science* 23, no. 3 (September 2018): 323–39.

42. James C. Scott, "The Public Transcript as Respectable Performance," in *Domination and the Arts of Resistance: Hidden Transcripts* (New Haven, CT: Yale University Press, 1990), 45–69.

43. Cunningham, Saich, and Turiel, "Understanding CCP Resilience."

44. Indeed, an experienced former diplomat foresees an early end to Xi's rule. Roger Garside, *China Coup: The Great Leap to Freedom* (Berkeley: University of California Press, 2021).

45. Liu Qing, "Liberalism in the Chinese Context: Potential and Predicaments," trans. Matthew Galway and Lu Hua, in *Voices from the Chinese Century: Public Intellectual Debate from Contemporary China*, ed. Timothy Cheek, David Ownby, and Joshua A. Fogel (New York: Columbia University Press, 2020), 45–71.

46. See, for example, Sean R. Roberts, *The War on Uyghurs: China's Internal Campaign against a Muslim Minority* (Princeton, NJ: Princeton University Press, 2020); and related materials collected by the Xinjiang Documentation Project (Institute of Asian Research, University of British Columbia), accessed December 23, 2023, https://xinjiang.sppga.ubc.ca.

3

Fundamentalism
with Chinese
Characteristics
Xi Jinping and Faith

Gerda Wielander

A key aspect of Xi Jinping's leadership is the centrality of the term *faith* (*xinyang*) in his political ideology and his concomitant control of religion. *Faith* and the China Dream (Zhongguo Meng) are the two terms most closely associated with Xi Jinping's ideology. Faith—in itself not new in Party discourse—received renewed emphasis under Xi Jinping and set the ideological foundation in the first term of his leadership for the systematic control of religion, which came to define his second term. While much has been written about the China Dream, the Party's return to faith in political discourse has received less attention.

It is important to situate the reaffirmation of the concept of faith under Xi Jinping within the context of preexisting popular and intellectual discourses on faith that originated outside the Party. I argue that the reaffirmation of faith under Xi happened as a direct response to the significant rise and influence of religious voices and concepts in the public sphere, such as it exists in China. I employ Jürgen Habermas's concept of the "post-secular society" as an analytical tool to examine Xi's specific take on meeting the twin challenge of surging religious faith in China and the Party's concurrent loss of ideological control under his predecessors. The chapter should be read in conjunction with Timothy Cheek's in this volume, extending the concept of "counter-reformation" beyond the confines of the Party itself. Theories of discourse formation and the Gramscian concept of "common sense" provide further conceptual underpinnings.[1]

There is a clear link between Xi's focus on *xinyang* as a key ingredient of his political "counter-reformation" and the management of religious practice under his leadership; if centering faith within official Party discourse established the orthodoxy, closely managing religious practice was the corresponding robust enforcement. Specifically, while Xi's response to the emerging challenges of a multifaith and multicultural society recognized the continued importance of religion in people's lives and the associated value of faith in society, his strategy was to tighten control of all faith-based activity and to position the Party itself as an object of faith. As a result, China under Xi Jinping—where the importance of faith was reaffirmed yet its practice extremely tightly controlled—emerged as a fundamentalist power with serious implications for societal and ethnic relations domestically and a significant further challenge to an international order built on commonly shared values.

An in-depth reading of key texts on *xinyang*, including Xi Jinping's own writings and commentaries thereon, supplemented by academic writings, reports, and news coverage on China's religious policies and measures to manage religion, form the basis of my analysis. I use the English word *faith* to render the Chinese term *xinyang*, unless I quote an English-language source that chooses a different term in its translation.

Reaffirming Faith under Xi Jinping

At the 18th Party Congress in 2012, Xi's predecessor, Hu Jintao, stressed the importance of faith. "First of all, we must strengthen ideals and beliefs and hold fast to the spiritual aspirations of a communist. The faith in Marxism and belief in socialism and communism are the political soul of a communist; they are the spiritual mainstay that a communist relies on through every ordeal."[2] By choosing these words, Hu clearly signaled his deference to the new leader. Xi Jinping had written extensively about faith as early as 2011. His book *The Power of Faith* (Xinyang de liliang), summarized in an award-winning student essay, identified faith as the secret of earlier generations of revolutionaries, as the essence of all previous leaders' ideological contributions, and as distinctly wavering or lacking in many contemporary cadres, some of whom had started to believe in spirits and gods instead of Marxism.[3] Xi called for an unavoidable focus on faith, as nothing would be achieved without it. Starting at the individual level, the future of the country and its people depended on steadfast faith.[4]

Xi's first major policy declaration in 2013 reiterated this emphasis "Faith, belief, confidence, and real action are the guarantee for the success of our undertakings" (Xinyang, xinnian, xinxin he shigan shi women shiye chenggong de baozheng).[5] Hence, from the very start of Xi's rule, *xinyang* was a key term in his rhetoric and defined as a necessary core quality of the Chinese people, and in particular the Party's cadres. The phrase "If people have faith, the nation has hope, and the country is strong" (Renmin you xinyang, minzu you xiwang, guojia you liliang)—while associated with the spirit of the Long March but now always linked to Xi himself—became a key slogan, plastered across billboards in China's major cities.

The importance of faith is one of six main ideological points associated with Xi Jinping, but the one that is considered fundamental to all other endeavors. Xi calls faith the "calcium of the CCP [Chinese Communist Party] spirit," a source of strength to combat the "spiritual rickets," which he diagnosed in one of his early speeches when he assumed China's leadership.[6] In addition to strengthening the spiritual backbone, faith also builds a people's and a country's immunity and resistance to negative influences, according to Xi. Conversely, the danger of lacking faith lies in having nothing to rely on to resist the onslaught of capitalism or to ward off "evil winds and noxious influences."[7] Lack of faith apparently leads to two-facedness by individuals—a charge routinely leveled at Uyghurs (see Musapir's chapter in this volume)—who may make all the right noises in public but in private believe in "spirits and gods."[8] Crucially, faith cannot just be a slogan but must translate into actions people can see and experience through exemplary leadership by Party cadres (see Cheek, this volume).[9]

Generally speaking, Xi's speeches around faith, which were steeped in uncompromising, steely language—"We must cast steadfast faith like walls of bronze and iron"—stood in contrast to the mood of the multimedia campaign to promote faith among the wider population.[10] "The Chinese People Have Faith" (Zhongguo renmin you xinyang) is a popular song, released in November 2017, with lyrics that praise Chinese socialist core values:

> Core values are our faith,
> core values are our new practice,
> core values we commit to our heart,
> core values we sing out loud!
> If people have faith,
> the country has strength;
> extraordinary among the ordinary,
> our common ancestors are Yan and Huang;
> if people have faith,
> the China Dream has hope,
> with shared prosperity we speed toward a "moderately prosperous society
>   [xiaokang]"![11]

In this song (which features a rap segment), as in the associated visual campaigns, faith is closely linked to socialist core values (*shehui zhuyi hexin jiazhiguan*).[12]

The steadfast faith of early revolutionary heroes as expounded in Xi's book was also incorporated into a three-part documentary film titled *Xinyang* and broadcast in 2012 by CCTV1, the Party's main propaganda channel. The film was a three-hour lesson in CCP history and its heroes, with part 1 dedicated to the years 1921–49, part 2 to the 1950s, and part 3 to the contemporary period (leaving out a rather large chunk of time in between). The film established the orthodoxy of the CCP's version of historical events and enshrined CCP history with its holy places, and its saints, evoking a history and spirit of sacrifice and dedication. The word *xinyang* was repeated frequently throughout the three parts, which culminated in an emotional finale around the historic significance of faith to ensure the success of future endeavors.[13]

Why this sudden emphasis on faith? The use of spiritual language in Party discourse in itself is not new. However, the ascendance of the term *faith* and Xi's personal emphasis of it need to be understood in a wider discursive context. In understanding Chinese political discourse and key terms within it, I subscribe to Ernesto Laclau and Chantal Mouffe's notion that discourse is an attempt to fix a web of meaning within a particular domain and that the constitution of discourse never happens in isolation and is always contested.[14] Despite regular hegemonic interventions, the domination of a particular discourse is never complete. In the case of faith, I argue that Xi's conscious intervention, which simultaneously identified a lack of faith and firmly defined faith within the parameters of Marxism and the Party, constituted an attempt to stabilize its meaning within a web of diverse uses of the term, but also constituted an acknowledgment of its importance and significance in counter-hegemonic and popular discourses and practices.

The significance of *xinyang* as a spiritual and motivational force to ensure the success of China's endeavors was already debated in republican times owing to multicultural influences ranging from Chinese morality books to Christian writings.[15] But we can also clearly trace a recurrence of the term in the writings of dissidents and religious scholars since the 1990s, with a more pronounced resurgence in the 2000s. It is this latter context that is more relevant for Xi's reiteration of faith in Party discourse.[16]

The growth of religion and the ambivalent view the Party held of some religions, notably Christianity, in the early parts of the millennium have been well documented, and the nexus between popular civil rights activists and lawyers and the Christian faith has also attracted considerable academic attention.[17] While the relationship between activism and religious faith is complex, some of the most influential individuals have openly stated their admiration for certain religions while not necessarily being believers. Liu Xiaobo, for example, who read and wrote about Christianity during his prison sentence in the 1990s, spoke of the importance of faith even earlier: "Among people's rights and liberties, spiritual liberties [*xinling de ziyou*] are the most important—freedom of thought, expression, and faith. . . . It is a freedom that transcends utility. This is what Chinese intellectuals are missing. The result of this is not just material poverty of the nation, but an even starker national spiritual withering."[18] Liu's acerbic criticism of his fellow intellectuals finds echoes in Xi's lamentation of his fellow cadres' "spiritual rickets" twenty years later, at the end of a decade of rights activism led by a new type of intellectual whose approach to making a difference had been based on a very simple concept: to take one's rights and duties as citizens seriously. One of the most prominent individuals involved in these activities was Xu Zhiyong, who was detained in August 2013 and sentenced to four years in prison in January 2014.[19] In his closing statement to the court following his trial, Xu made repeated reference to faith.

> I believe in the power of faith, and in the power of the truth, compassion, and beauty that exists in the depths of the human soul, just as I believe human civilization is advancing mightily like a tide.[20] . . . I urge everyone to maintain their faith in freedom, justice, and love. . . . Remain steadfast in your faith in justice, always stay true to your heart, and never compromise your principles in pursuit of your goal. . . . Adhere to faith in love, because this nation has too many dark, bitter, and poisoned souls in need of redemption. . . . Our faith in the idea of building a better China, one of democracy, rule of law, freedom, justice and love, is unwavering.[21]

Zhou Guoping, a philosopher at the Chinese Academy of Social Sciences and scholar of Friedrich Nietzsche, also considered faith vital; it is one of the core messages of his book *What Are the Chinese People Missing?* (Zhongguoren queshao shenme?). The title of the book took inspiration from a chapter in Nietzsche's *Götzen-Däemmerung* titled "Was den Deutschen abgeht" (1888).[22] While Nietzsche bemoaned the German people's lack of thinking as reason for its malaise, according to Zhou the lack of both faith and the rule of law were at the heart of China's problems. In Zhou's view, the main weakness of Chinese cultural tradition lies in its emphasis on practical values and its neglect of spiritual values. To Zhou, the lack of engagement with questions of a transcendental nature was a great shortcoming in Chinese culture, as those who lacked a belief in the holy would be apathetic to their own meaning of life and unable to feel real empathy toward others and hence true social responsibility.[23] Ideologically at a far distance from Xi Jinping, both Liu Xiaobo and Xu Zhiyong were seen by many as models of the moral strength Xi wished to re-instill in his Party cadres and had found inspiration (and inspired others) through their spiritual (if not outright religious) approach.

But the importance of faith has also been expounded by mainstream scholars. In 2013, Zhuo Xinping, director of the Institute for the Study of World Religions within the Chinese Academy of Social Sciences, a scholar of Christianity, and a member of the Standing Committee of the National People's Congress, argued that the members of the Communist Party and the Chinese nation needed faith; without faith, there was no future for the country or the Party; without faith, social morality became "like a river without a source, a tree without roots."[24] Zhuo maintained that the realization of the China Dream required unity via a culture of faith. One year earlier, the chairman of the Association for the Promotion of Chinese Culture, Gao Zhanxiang, had argued: "Belief is the soul of a nation. A firm belief is . . . a spur for a state, a political party, or an individual to proceed on his or its way forward. It is a determining factor . . . as regards the flourishing or the decline, the success or the failure . . . of states, parties, and individuals."[25]

In a more eclectic take on the subject, Yuan Youjun, a professor at the Guangdong Party School and Guangdong's College of Administration, advocated the establishment of a Chinese national faith fit for the age of globalization. In his book *Seeking a Faith for Our Times* (Xunzhao shidai de xinyang), he envisaged a Chinese national faith not solely around the Party, but one that emerged from a mix of various faiths, with the following ingredients: Confucian ethics; ancestor worship, including the worship of the Yellow Emperor and Count Gong; Sinicized Christianity; socialized Taoism; globalized Buddhism; and Mao Zedong worship. Among these, Confucian ethics were supposed to take the leading role. In Yuan's view, China's history of multiple faiths provided the perfect starting point for such an amalgamated faith, a model he potentially did not see confined to China, but a suitable form of cultural globalization in times of economic globalization.[26]

The aforementioned individuals were associated with the "religious ecology" school of thought, which argued that due to foreign religious influences (notably Christianity), China's religious ecological system had been disturbed and needed to be rebalanced. Yuan Youjun's ingredients for his proposed national faith illustrate clearly how this balance should be achieved. According to one critic, Zhuo Xinping's personal views about the dangers posed by Christianity ended up as national strategy and laid the foundation for the requirement of the "Sinicization" (Zhongguohua) of religion, that is, the need for all religions to recognize Chinese politics, to adapt to Chinese society, and to express Chinese culture.[27] Whatever Zhuo's personal role, the term Sinicization was officially introduced at the Central United Front Conference held in 2015, the United Front Department being one of three separate administrative units concerned with the management of religion (the other two units being the State Administration of Religious Affairs and the patriotic organizations governing China's five officially recognized religions).

Clearly, debates around the meaning and significance of faith predated Xi Jinping's use and emphasis of the term and have continued in rather diverse ways even within the Party. All of these discourses saw faith as fundamentally positive but profoundly absent in contemporary China, yet essential for the success of one's endeavors. There was also agreement that faith was built on shared values and constituted an important motivational force that could lead to social and political transformation, that faith could be a moral and spiritual unifier, whether for smaller groups or the nation at large. There was also agreement that ritual and action were requisite to fulfilling these transformative functions. All discourses related to faith, including those of the Communist Party, placed emphasis on the salience of spiritual matters; science and faith were not contradictory pursuits.[28]

We can therefore argue that *xinyang* had become part of "common sense" in a Gramscian understanding. As Michael Gow in his analysis of socialist core values puts it, "Common sense is a canon of knowledge that frames our understanding of society, is shared intersubjectively across disparate communities, social groups and the general population, and exists at such depth that questioning it does not occur."[29] And further, "Rhetoric is a key strategic weapon in the reproduction and transformation of common sense over time and is crucial to the mobilization of common sense in the service of state interests."[30] Success in shaping common sense on the part of the hegemon is therefore crucial for the maintenance of consensus. At the point of Xi's intervention into the faith discourse, the commonsense understanding of faith was controlled not by the hegemon, that is, the Party, but by rhetoric emanating from a range of counter-hegemonic, including religious, voices. These voices had public influence and relevance, potentially undermining the secularistic certainty—also held by Marxism—that religion would disappear as a consequence of modernization.[31]

The link between modernization and secularization was built on three assumptions, according to Habermas: that a belief in the progress of science and technology promoted an anthropocentric understanding of the "disenchanted" world, which includes a belief in empiricism; that religious congregations would restrict their function to the administering of salvation, hence that religion was a private matter and had no control over law, politics, public welfare, education, and science; and that an increase in existential security would lead to a drop in personal need for religion to cope with uncontrolled contingencies through faith in a higher or cosmic power.[32] Habermas further argues that post 9/11 this link between modernization and secularization no longer held and that the world had moved into a post-secular phase, where religious voices were "translated" in a process through which contributions "pass from the confused din of voices in the public sphere into the formal agendas of state institutions."[33]

The centrality of *xinyang* in the political discourse employed by Xi came at a very particular moment in time and showed a clear awareness of the centrality of the term in counter-hegemonic discourses. Xi's emphasis on *xinyang* constituted an effort to shape common sense through rhetoric that recognized the significance of *xinyang* but imbued it with values at whose heart lay the Party and all it stands for. The adoption of *xinyang* as a concept whose commonsense understanding thus had come to be shaped by religious voices (rather than the hegemon) constituted a "translation" of said voices into the formal agenda of China's state institutions and became part of the new orthodoxy concerning the meaning and function of faith under Xi Jinping.

With doctrinal orthodoxy thus reaffirmed, reviewing the management of faith practice on the ground was the logical next step, for, as Cheek (this volume) reminds us, "a reforming pope requires . . . obedient service."

Xi's Management of Religion in a Post-Secular Context

Describing modern societies as post-secular signals a change in consciousness, which Habermas predominantly attributes to three phenomena.[34] First, in post-secular societies religion is gaining influence within public spheres through "communities of interpretation" who voice a collective view on a range of social and political issues and often emanate from communities belonging to "rival faiths" to the one considered indigenous. Second, global conflicts have undermined the secularistic belief in the foreseeable disappearance of religion; living in a secular society is no longer bound up with the certainty that cultural and social modernization can only advance at the expense of religion. Third, post-secular societies may contain "semantically

sealed off units" with "traditional cultural backgrounds" often around immigrant guest workers (as in Germany, for example).[35] These points provide
a good starting point for an analysis of Xi Jinping's policies on religious
management.

When Xi Jinping took power in 2012, "rival faiths" had not only voiced
repeated commentary on China's social and political issues but had also
gained a moral credibility sorely lacking in the Party's own leadership. As
I outlined earlier, some of the new "communities of interpretation" had
gained influence in China's equivalent of a public sphere. The politically
most influential, through public political statements, actions, and personal
conduct, were Christians or individuals and groups influenced (by their
own acknowledgment) by Christian writings. For many, they had become
the voice of morality in the face of widespread corruption, vice, and abuses
around the one-child policy, to mention just the most obvious issues. This
view became embodied in human rights lawyers' actions, a disproportionate
number of whom were Christians. Christianity was certainly a rival faith
to Communism, which, however, had strong appeal even for nonbelievers
and displayed a degree of familiarity in regard to certain practices (such as
doctrinal study groups); in fact, many house church leaders used to be Party
members. While the CCP used to tarnish Christianity as something foreign,
Yuan Youjun's book *Seeking a Faith for Our Times* is a sign that views on this
were changing and that those arguing for Christianity to be recognized as
part of Chinese cultural tradition had had an impact, not to speak of the in-
spirational "spiritual backbone" so forcefully promoted by Xi Jinping today.[36]

There is a traditional affinity between Christianity and socialism, and
Christianity has had powerful advocates in China's research and state institutions.[37] One additional aspect that had worked in Christianity's favor,
which is rarely discussed, is the fact that most of China's Christians belong
to the Han ethnic group and that the demographic profile of Christians has
changed from being predominantly female, uneducated, and rural (the "typical" Christian profile in the 1980s) to being urban, educated, professional
and with male leadership (while retaining a majority female congregation).
Contemporary Chinese Christianity arguably presents a profile of, to the
CCP, largely reasonable and compatible values argued from a shared cultural
and—this is crucial—a common ethnic base. The political challenges that
emanate from a very small number of house churches notwithstanding,
where Christianity is presented as a "rational" faith (not steeped in mysti-
cism), values and "religious utterances" were able to travel and be accommo-
dated into the state's political discourse.[38]

By the time Xi Jinping came to power, the Marxist assumption of the foreseeable disappearance for the need of religion no longer carried much weight. There were openly Christian Party members (for example, Zhao Xiao), and both Buddhism and Taoism grew in appeal across the whole population, including cadres.[39] The inclusion of a wide range of faiths into a potential national faith as suggested by Yuan Youjun and the discussion over China's religious ecology—even one that may need rebalancing—were clear evidence of the acceptance of a limited pluralistic religious landscape at the time of Xi's ascension to power. Under Xi, the Party swiftly returned to its stance—somewhat eroded under the previous leadership—that all Party members must be atheists, an expectation that has since also been extended to family members of Party members.[40]

In Xi Jinping's early days, commentators were uncertain whether Xi was good or bad news for religion in China. The passing of new regulations on religion in 2015 was greeted with the usual concern by Christian groups overseas, but more sympathetic or objective commentators interpreted the new regulations as an adaptation to new realities rather than a significant stepping up of control.[41] China had updated its religious regulations several times since Document 19 was published in 1982. Since then, these regulations had constituted a balancing act of acknowledging the importance of religions, on the one hand, while trying to control their activities within a realm acceptable to the Party, on the other, reflecting the uneasy relationship between the Party and China's religious believers. In 1982, when the country emerged from fierce religious repression under the Cultural Revolution, the aspect of acknowledgment was a welcome surprise. In the social and political realities of Xi Jinping's China, it is the controlling aspect of the relationship that is dominant.

In April 2016, Xi Jinping attended the National Religious Work Conference—in itself unusual for the highest leader to attend such a meeting—emphasizing the need to "build a socialist theory of religion with Chinese characteristics" and insisting that "religions must adhere to the direction of Sinicization, interpreting values and dogmas in a way that corresponds to the needs of China."[42] This need for "Sinicization" is not confined to belief systems that have historically been considered foreign, such as Christianity and Islam, or indeed Marxism. Even Chinese religions need to "Sinicize" in order to follow up the developments of China in the New Era and to dig into religious elements in line with core socialist values. The Central Institute of Socialism, headed by Ye Xiaowen, who from 1995 to 2009 led China's State Administration of Religious Affairs (in itself a telling career trajectory), provides lectures on religious "Sinicization" and has issued five-year plans—associated with a centrally planned economy, but here indicative of China's religious central planning—for all major religions, setting out planned developments from 2018 to 2022. For Islam, for example, this included the so-called four entries: entry into mosques of the national flag, the Chinese Constitution, love of socialist values, and the teaching of traditional classical literature. For Christianity, this meant promoting a "Chinese Christianity" and plans for a retranslation and annotation of the Bible to find commonalities with socialism and a "correct understanding" of the text.[43]

One of the early violent manifestations of this new direction was the destruction of churches and the taking down of conspicuous religious symbols (for example, large neon crosses on churches) in southeast China.[44] From 2017 onward, thus in Xi Jinping's second term in office, one could start to observe a strategic and systematic attack on religion through the invocation of "laws."[45] For all religions, this meant, among other things, the removal and destruction of places of worship or at least externally visible religious symbols; the destruction of religious statues; surveillance of even legal religious activity by a Party member, sometimes involving taking over the part of the officiator or clergy (see Musapir, this volume); the banning of under-eighteens from all religious activities, including events such as summer camps; the erasure of any "gray" areas for unregistered religious groups; the replacement of religious songs such as hymns with communist songs; the vetting of sermons; the cancellation of Tibetan language classes (vital for the practice of Tibetan Buddhism) in monasteries, and the list goes on.[46] These developments took place in parallel with the propagation of ideas of a national faith and the promotion of faith as a core ingredient to ensure the success of all endeavors, be they at the individual or national level.

These strict controls of all religion were taken even further where both an ethnic and geopolitical dimension come into play. The government's systematic campaign to control and "reeducate" Muslim Uyghurs in large-scale detention camps is the most extreme example of this control (see Musapir's chapter). While there are no sizable immigrant communities in China (as in Habermas's Germany), the Party's declared aim to reinforce ethnic unity has, in reality, heightened awareness of ethnic differences, especially where these are underpinned by significant linguistic and religious differences to Han culture.

In China under Xi Jinping, Christians are not perceived to be "semantically sealed off units," as their ethnic identity and daily practices, including religious practices, are compatible with a Han identity and some of the core values now promoted by the Chinese state. However, the state feels very differently about Islam and Muslim identities, which it considers traditional, backward, to an extent incompatible with modernized sensibilities of the Han Party-state, and even dangerous, in particular where minority ethnic groups are concerned.[47] Observing one's religion and displaying visible signs of one's belief (for example, a beard) are considered proof of backwardness and resistance to modernization; breaking such habits and assimilating to the Han majority through invasive and both physically and psychologically violent means are the most extreme manifestation of the Party's implementation of national "unity."

The Party's Answer to a Multicultural, Post-Secular Society: Forced Ethnic and Cultural Unification

With fifty-six officially recognized ethnic groups and five recognized religions, China is officially a multicultural and multifaith society. Integration into the international world order through globalization and open borders has meant that members of China's ethnic and religious minorities have once again become part of cross-border family connections and diaspora, interest groups, and networks.[48] The fact that many of China's ethnic minorities with languages, religions, and cultures distinctly different from the Han majority live in geopolitically strategic areas of China has heightened the Party-state's anxieties over national integrity and unity. China has thus experienced the key challenges posed by multicultural societies, which, to return to Habermas, is the tension between the need to protect cultural identities, on the one hand, and the need to enforce a shared sense of citizenship, on the other.[49]

In the context of faith and religion, Xi Jinping chose to respond to the challenge of multiculturalism and a plurality of values (something the Party prefers to present as a lack of values) in both the ideological and the policy realm through a process of "counter-reformation," in which United Front work played a key role. A key ingredient of the Party's ideological work and early rectification campaigns, United Front work was stepped up again under Xi Jinping, who held one of the most significant United Front conferences in three decades in 2015.[50] Religion is, of course, a central aspect of United Front work; having been introduced at the United Front conference in 2015, the requirement for the Sinicization of religion was declared national policy in the following year.

Reestablishing a strict orthodoxy in relation to the role and function of faith was an important aspect of Xi's renewed emphasis on ideological governance, as outlined by Cheek (this volume). Expected adherence to this new orthodoxy extended well beyond the confines of the Party and into the wider population, reaching levels of an inquisition in parts of the country. In this process, rather than combating the potential ill effects of renewed religious influence through dialogue, the state has instead entered the religious arena by forcing itself onto believers and demanding spiritual allegiance through a strictly regulated set of rituals and practice. Thus, China under Xi Jinping has become a quasi-religious fundamentalist power, displaying all the signs that characterize the resurgence rather than the disappearance of religion, including fundamental radicalism, and the political instrumentalization of violence.[51]

The political instrumentalization of the potential for violence innate to religious zeal was evident in China's Cultural Revolution (a period notably missing in the CCP's orthodox version of its own history) and can still be observed today. Although rhetorical emphasis is put on process and harmony—despite the metallurgic references in Xi's own pronouncements on faith—the potential and actual violence of the state is visible and present on a daily basis. It forms a vital ingredient in what the political scientist Stein Ringen refers to as China's "controlocracy" and is vividly described in Xu Zhiyong's memoir.[52] In relation to the CCP's attempts to build a faith, one can at the very least see evidence of the political instrumentalization of the people's continued need for faith. Rather than affording religious voices validity—the only way to resolve the challenges of a multicultural society, according to Habermas—the Party's strategy is to break up and forcibly assimilate.[53] The systematic detention and attempted destruction of Chinese Muslim, in particular Uyghur and Kazakh, identity together with systematic physical and psychological violence against people and cultural artifacts is a technologically sophisticated act of violence based on a zealous belief in the state project led by the Party-state along ethnic lines.[54]

In the face of the continuing need for religion/faith in the post-secular context, the Party now presents itself and all that it stands for as the only appropriate and permissible object of faith. This is evident in the way it forces people to direct religious feelings toward the Party, but also in an increasing personality cult around Xi Jinping himself. In southeast China, Christians were told to get rid of pictures of Jesus and replace them with portraits of Xi Jinping; there were accounts of reverent gatherings around a tree Xi planted in 2009 in Henan Province; and in Shenyang the Party installed red "confession boxes" in the streets (somewhat reminiscent of red telephone boxes in Britain), where people are encouraged to speak their innermost thoughts to the Party.[55] In Xinjiang, as Musapir recounts in this volume, Xi Jinping is now venerated and his image enshrined in place of anything with religious symbolism or ancestral presence in Uyghur homes. Public prayers are no longer permitted, and detainees in Xinjiang's "reeducation camps" were required to worship Xi by reciting his thought, chanting, and singing political songs.

Conclusion

According to the scholar Benoît Vermander, the Party had acted as regulator rather than purveyor of sacredness between 1980 and 2012, but in the Xi era a new regime of sacredness was put into place to redirect the flow of social and symbolic resources toward the state-sponsored channels of sacrality.[56] In Vermander's view, the "Party inspires both love and fear, functions as a church, and unites under the same ideology."[57] Under the five-year plans for the Sinicization of religion, the Party entered places of worship with the effect not of the secularization of the religious faiths whose places of worship it penetrates, but of a sacralization of the Party itself, which dresses up in religious garb, officiates at rituals, and presents itself as purveyor of a super faith at the core of which stands a spiritual Han ethnic identity based on Chinese socialist core values. These values are presented as universally shared by all Chinese; in fact, sharing and propagating these values has become a definition—and a condition—of being Chinese.

The Party responded to the continued need for religion in modern society by using spiritual language and by creating corresponding spiritual practices centered around the Party. It accepts that religious traditions and the need for interiority continues and signals this by adopting a spiritual discourse and practice of faith built around the figure of Xi Jinping and his ideology. The fierce crackdown on religions during Xi's second term in office was built on the foundations of a renewed orthodoxy on faith established during his first term that positioned the Party and its ideology as a super faith under which all religious activity needed to be subsumed. In the process, some religious utterances and values found their way from religious discourses (or discourses informed by religious values) into state discourse. This happened where the Party considered these utterances to be made from a shared ethnic and cultural base. At the same time, the recognition of the continued need for religion also led to a sacralization of the Party itself together with its increasing penetration of all parts of society, from religious places of worship to universities and privately owned companies, all the way into people's homes, as is the case in Xinjiang. Rather than leading to a secularization and decreased influence of faith, all these developments have resulted in a lack of clear distinction between religion and the state in China today, as was the case in imperial China. At the same time, the long-term consequences of these developments—in addition to the devastating effects for individuals and their families—may be similar to those of the Cultural Revolution: the long-term trauma of the separation of children from their families; the indoctrination of the young generation about the alleged ill effects of religion; the permanent destruction of cultural artifacts; and the loss of languages and cultural knowledge.

China under Xi Jinping responded to the challenges of a post-secular, multicultural, and multifaith society by attempting to create and enforce its own centralized, orthodox faith. As a result, China under Xi Jinping bears the characteristics of a political-religious fundamentalist state power built on ethnic supremacy. This "fundamentalism with Chinese characteristics" is a significant "Xi Jinping effect" with long-term domestic and international implications and an important aspect of his leadership to watch for new developments during his third and possibly subsequent terms in office.

Notes

1. On discourse formation, see Ernesto Laclau and Chantal Mouffe, *Hegemony and Socialist Strategy: Towards a Radical Democratic Politics*, 2nd ed. (London: Verso, 2001).

2. Hu Jintao, "Jianchi bu yi yanzhe zhongguo tese shehui zhuyi daolu qianjin" (Progress by steadily following the road of socialism with Chinese characteristics), China.com, November 8, 2012, http://news.china.com.cn/politics/2012-11/20/content_27165856.htm, quoted in Giorgio Strafella, "'Marxism' as Tradition in CCP Discourse," *Asiatische Studien / Études Asiatiques* 69, no. 1 (2015): 246.

3. The essay was by Hu Bao, "Xinyang shi shenme? Xi Jinping 'liuzhong yishi' zhong Xinyang" (What is faith? Xi Jinping's "six types of consciousness" stress faith), People.com, November 29, 2011, http://book.people.com.cn/GB/69839/217128/217129/15534097.html.

4. Bao, "Xinyang shi shenme?"

5. "'Eight Musts' Coalesce into Consensus," *China Copyright and Media* (blog), January 17, 2013, http://chinacopyrightandmedia.wordpress.com/2013/01/17/eight-musts-coalesce-into-consensus.

6. "Xi Jinping tan xinyang xinnian" (Xi Jinping on faith), *People's Daily*, June 7, 2017, http://cpc.people.com.cn/n1/2017/0607/c64094-29322419.html.

7. Speech made in 2015 in commemoration of Chen Yun, as quoted in "Xi Jinping tan xinyang xinnian."

8. Speech made on January 12, 2016, as quoted in "Xi Jinping tan xinyang xinnian."

9. There is a wealth of articles available on Xi Jinping's pronunciations on faith. They all make the same points, and the source "Xi Jinping tan xinyang xinnian" (cited above) constitutes a collection of the main quotations on faith in various speeches over the years while also bringing out the main points. Additional useful expositions on the subject can be found in Cary Huang, "Xi Calls for 'Staunch' Belief in Communism to Ensure National Rejuvenation as China Marks 80th Anniversary of Long March," *South China Morning Post*, October 21, 2016, http://www.scmp.com/news/china/policies-politics/article/2039017/xi-calls-staunch-belief-communism-ensure-national; and "Xi Jinping: Renmin you xinyang, minzu you xiwang, guojia you liliang" (Xi Jinping: When the people have faith, the nation has hope, and the state is powerful), Xinhua Net, February 28, 2015, http://news.xinhuanet.com/politics/2015-02/28/c_1114474084.htm.

10. Speech made in 2015 in commemoration of Chen Yun, as quoted in "Xi Jinping tan xinyang xinnian."

11. The tune is available from "Shehui zhuyi hexin jiazhiguan gequ zhanbo: 'Zhongguo renmin you xinyang'" (A musical broadcast of the Chinese socialist core values song: "The Chinese People Have Faith"), YouTube, accessed January 5, 2024, https://www.youtube.com/watch?v=c7esCE7w13g. The lyrics are available from "Changxiang zhuxuanlü xiying shijiuda. Shehui zhuyi hexin jiazhiguan gequ 'Renmin you xinyang'" (Singing the main tunes, happily greeting the 19th Party Congress. The socialist core values song "The Chinese People Have Faith"), accessed January 5, 2024, http://ent.cnr.cn/ylzt/gqzj/gqsp/20171001/t20171001_523973654.shtml.

12. Jiang Chang and Cai Mengxue, "'Dangdai zhongguo jiazhiguan' gainiande tichu, neihan yu yiyi" (The proposal, content, and meaning of the concept "contemporary Chinese values"), *Journal of Hubei University (Philosophy and Social Science)*, no. 4 (2016): 1–7 and 160.

13. *Xinyang. Women de gushi* (Faith. Our story), three-part miniseries, CCTV1, 2012, http://tv.cntv.cn/video/C38054/4ef120914f8f48b2ba89845c27ff86e1.

14. Laclau and Mouffe, *Hegemony and Socialist Strategy*.

15. Thoralf Klein, "'Our Believing in the Three People's Principles Requires a Religious Spirit': *Xin(yang)* 信仰 and the Political Religion of the Guomindang, 1925–1949," 461–96, and Chloë Starr, "From Missionary Doctrine to Chinese Theology: Developing *xin* 信 in the Protestant Church and Creeds of Zhao Zichen," 340–59, both in *From Trustworthiness to Secular Beliefs: Changing Concepts of xin* 信 *from Traditional to Modern Chinese*, ed. Christian Meyer and Philip Clart (Leiden: Brill, 2023).

16. For an in-depth Sinological engagement with the meaning and significance of *xin* or *xinyang* from ancient to contemporary times, see Christian Meyer and Philip Clart, eds., *From Trustworthiness to Secular Beliefs: Changing Concepts of xin 信 from Traditional to Modern Chinese* (Leiden: Brill, 2023).

17. On religion and the Party, see Vincent Goossaert and David Palmer, eds., *The Religious Question in Modern China* (Chicago: University of Chicago Press, 2010); Gerda Wielander, *Christian Values in Communist China* (London: Routledge, 2013). On political activism and the Christian faith, see Wielander, *Christian Values in Communist China*; Terence C. Halliday, "Under Siege: China's Christian Human Rights Lawyers," 2014, YouTube, https://www.youtube.com /watch?v=5-fXAjByWUI; Sida Liu and Terence C. Halliday, *Criminal Defense in China: The Politics of Lawyers at Work*, Cambridge Studies in Law and Society (Cambridge: Cambridge University Press, 2017).

18. Liu Xiaobo, *Zhongguo dangdai zhengzhi yu zhongguo zhishifenzi* (Chinese contemporary politics and Chinese intellectuals) (1990; repr., Taipei: Tonsan Publications, 2010), 107, translation in Gerda Wielander, "What China Is Missing—Faith in Political Discourse," in *From Trustworthiness to Secular Beliefs: Changing Concepts of xin 信 from Traditional to Modern Chinese*, ed. Christian Meyer and Philip Clart (Leiden: Brill, 2023), 602.

19. Xu's arrest was followed, in June 2015, by the start of a systematic crackdown on human rights (*weiquan*) lawyers, which has affected more than three hundred individuals and includes criminal detention, house arrest, and residential surveillance. He was detained again in February 2020. For a chronology on the crackdown on human rights lawyers, see Human Rights in China, "Mass Crackdown on Chinese Lawyers, Defenders and International Reactions: A Brief Chronology," 2017, https://www.hrichina.org/en/mass-crackdown-chinese -lawyers-defenders-and-international-reactions-brief-chronology.

20. The Chinese expression "truth, compassion, and beauty" (*zhen, shan, mei* 真善美) was originally employed by Mao, then reinterpreted in counter-discourse and featuring prominently in Xi's policies. See Michel Hockx, "Truth, Goodness, and Beauty: Literary Policy in Xi Jinping's China," *Law & Literature* 35, no. 3 (2023): 515–31, https://doi.org/10.1080/1535685X.2022.2026039.

21. Xu Zhiyong, *To Build a Free China: A Citizen's Journey* (Boulder, CO: Lynne Rienner, 2017), 281–82, quoted in Wielander, "What China Is Missing," 601.

22. A German version is available at Projekt Gutenberg–DE, accessed February 1, 2018, http://gutenberg.spiegel.de/buch/-6185/10.

23. Zhou Guoping, *Zhongguoren queshao shenme? Xifang zhexue jieshou shishang liangge anlie zhi yanjiu* (What are the Chinese people missing? Research into two historical cases of acceptance of Western philosophy) (Shanghai: Shanghai Renmin Chubanshe, 2017), 344.

24. Zhuo Xinping, *Zhongguo zongjiao yu wenhua zhanlue* (The religions in China and the strategy of culture) (Beijing: Shehui Kexue Wenxian Chubanshe,

2013), quoted in Monika Gaensbauer, *Popular Belief in Contemporary China: A Discourse Analysis* (Freiburg: Projekt Verlag, 2015), 49, cited in Wielander, "What China Is Missing," 589.

25. Gao Zhanxiang, *Xinyangli* (The power of faith) (Beijing: Beijing Daxue Chubanshe, 2012), quoted in Gaensbauer, *Popular Belief*, 49; cited in Wielander, "What China Is Missing," 589.

26. Yuan Youjun, *Xunzhao shidai de xinyang: Dangdai zhongguo guomin xinyang yanjiu* (Searching for a faith of our times: Research into contemporary Chinese citizens' faith) (Guangzhou: Guangdong Renmin Chubanshe, 2014), 4–5.

27. Statement by the former director of the religious division of the Guizhou Provincial Civil Religious Affairs Bureau as broadcast at a panel discussion on the Sinicization of religion. Christian Solidarity Worldwide, United Kingdom (CSW UK), "Sinicizing Religion in China: A Panel Discussion," organized by the CSW and the International Campaign for Tibet as a side event to the forty-seventh session of the Human Rights Council, chaired by Sophie Richardson, with Timothy Grose, Kiri Kankhwende, and Tenzin Palmo, July 15, 2021, educational video, You-Tube, 1:15:19, https://www.youtube.com/watch?v=FgGmb8i2Syo.

28. Wielander, "What China Is Missing," 603.

29. Michael Gow, "The Core Socialist Values of the Chinese Dream: Towards a Chinese Integral State," *Critical Asian Studies* 49, no. 1 (2017): 95.

30. Gow, "The Core Socialist Values," 95.

31. Habermas distinguishes between the terms *secular* and *secularistic*; he uses *secular* as a neutral term to describe the separation of church/religion and state and uses *secularistic* to describe a strong belief and political position that is characterized by denying religion a place in public life and state agendas.

32. Jürgen Habermas, "Notes on a Post-Secular Society," *Signandsight*, June 18, 2008, http://www.signandsight.com/features/1714.html.

33. Habermas, "Notes on a Post-Secular Society."

34. Habermas, "Notes on a Post-Secular Society."

35. Habermas presents the three points in a different order. See Habermas, "Notes on a Post-Secular Society."

36. For an in-depth analysis of Christianity and China's moral reconstruction, see Wielander, *Christian Values in Communist China*, chap. 2.

37. On Christianity and socialism, see Wielander, *Christian Values in Communist China*; Gerda Wielander, "Translating Protestant Christianity into China—Questions of Indigenization and Sinification in a Globalised World," in *Translating Values: Evaluative Concepts in Translation*, ed. Piotr Blumczynski and John Gillespie (London: Palgrave Macmillan, 2016), 213–36.

38. On religious utterances, see Habermas, "Notes on a Post-Secular Society."

39. Ian Johnson, *The Souls of China: The Return of Religion after Mao* (New York: Pantheon Books, 2017).

40. Grose, in CSW UK, "Sinicizing Religion in China."

41. Ian Johnson, "China Seeks Tighter Grip in Wake of a Religious Revival," *New York Times*, October 7, 2016; Gerda Wielander, "China's New Religions Regulations: An Ever-Tighter Embrace," Asia & the Pacific Policy Society, Policy Forum, November 1, 2016, https://www.policyforum.net/chinas-new-religious-regulations.

42. For a close analysis of United Front work and Sinicization of religion under Xi, see Kuei-Min Chang, "New Wine in Old Bottles. Sinicisation and State Regulation of Religion in China," *China Perspectives*, no. 1–2 (2018): 37-44. For an English translation of the full report on the plan, see Union of Catholic Asian News, "Protestant Five-Year Plan for Christianity," April 20, 2018, https://www.ucanews.com/news/protestant-five-year-plan-for-chinese-christianity/82107.

43. Lily Kuo, "In China, They Are Closing Churches, Jailing Pastors—and Even Rewriting the Scriptures," *Guardian*, January 13, 2019, https://www.theguardian.com/world/2019/jan/13/china-christians-religious-persecution-translation-bible.

44. See, for example, Union of Catholic Asia News, "Cross Burns as Chinese Officials Remove It from Church," September 27, 2017, https://www.ucanews.com/news/cross-burns-as-chinese-officials-remove-it-from-church/80327.

45. "China Passes Law to Make Islam 'Compatible with Socialism,'" *Al Jazeera*, January 5, 2019, https://www.aljazeera.com/news/2019/1/5/china-passes-law-to-make-islam-compatible-with-socialism.

46. See, for example, Anyang Wang, "Buddhist Statues Disappearing throughout China," *Bitter Winter*, February 20, 2019, https://bitterwinter.org/buddhist-statues-disappearing-throughout-china; CSW UK, "Sinicizing Religion in China."

47. There is some evidence that the treatment of Hui Muslims is nowhere near as severe as that of Uyghur and Kazakh minorities and that Hui Muslim communities have seen a revival. See, for example, Alexander Stewart, "Faith in the Future/Practices of the Past: A Sinicized Islamic Revival among the Hui of Xining," in *The Sinicization of Religion: From Above and Below*, ed. Richard Madsen (Leiden: Brill, 2021), 130–47.

48. For the historical roots of these networks, see Peter Frankopan, *The Silk Roads: A New History of the World* (London: Bloomsbury, 2015).

49. Habermas, "Notes on a Post-Secular Society."

50. Kuei-Min Chang, "New Wine in Old Bottles: Sinicisation and State Regulation of Religion in China," *China Perspectives*, no. 1–2 (2018): 37.

51. Habermas, "Notes on a Post-Secular Society."

52. Stein Ringen, *The Perfect Dictatorship: China in the 21st Century* (Hong Kong: Hong Kong University Press, 2016); Xu, *To Build a Free China*.

53. On the Party's assimilationist policies, see James Leibold, "Xinjiang Work Forum Marks New Policy of 'Ethnic Mingling,'" *China Brief* 14, no. 12 (2014): 1–12; Gerald Roche and James Leibold, "China's Second-Generation Ethnic Policies Are Already Here," *Made in China Journal* 5, no. 2 (2020): 31–35, https://

madeinchinajournal.com/2020/09/07/chinas-second-generation-ethnic-policies
-are-already-here.

54. There is now a substantial body of evidence and scholarship on the Party's actions in Xinjiang. It builds on the work of Adrian Zenz and James Leibold, which has now been supplemented by significant firsthand reporting from a range of credible international media outlets. The following piece includes links to some of the most important sources that brought awareness to this issue. See James Leibold, "Time to Denounce China's Muslim Gulag," Lowy Institute, June 19, 2018, https://www.lowyinstitute.org/the-interpreter/time-denounce-china-s-muslim -gulag. For a theorization of the contemporary Chinese colonization of Uyghur Muslims, see Darren Byler, *Terror Capitalism: Uyghur Dispossession and Masculinity in a Chinese City* (Durham, NC: Duke University Press, 2022).

55. On hanging Xi's portrait, see Tom Phillips, "Believe in Socialism Not Sorcery, China Tells Party Members," *Guardian*, November 16, 2017, https://www .theguardian.com/world/2017/nov/16/chinese-officials-believe-in-sorcery-not -socialism-says-senior-minister. On the Xi tree, see Tom Phillips, "'Enormous and Leafy': Chinese Officials Flock to Tree Planted by Xi Jinping," *Guardian*, November 13, 2017, https://www.theguardian.com/world/2017/nov/13/officials-tree -planted-xi-jinping-chinese-paulownia-henan. On confession boxes, see, for example, "Shenyang jingxian hongse liushengting xiang dang jiaoxin" (A red phonographic booth suddenly appeared in Shenyang for confession to the Party), New Tang Dynasty Television, September 26, 2017, http://www.ntdtv.com/xtr/gb /2017/09/26/a1343878.html; see also Wielander, "What China Is Missing," 594.

56. Benoît Vermander, "Sinicizing Religion, Sinicizing Religious Studies," *Religions* 10, no. 2 (2019): 4, https://doi.org/10.3390/rel10020137.

57. Vermander, "Sinicizing Religion," 18.

PART 2

Socioeconomic Policies
to Reduce Poverty

4

Xi Jinping Confronts Inequality
Bold Leadership or Modest Steps?

Martin King Whyte

Despite China's extraordinary success over the past four decades in launching an economic development boom, today that country faces daunting challenges. High on most lists is the need to combat income inequality. China's economic boom has been a primary contributor to that society's transformation from having relatively modest income gaps to becoming one of the most unequal countries on the planet.[1] The fairly uniform poverty of the late Mao Zedong era has given way to China early in the Xi Jinping era having more dollar billionaires than the United States, many of them living in lavish, gated mansions and jetting off on overseas investment forays and vacations even as tens of millions of their fellow citizens continued to live in abject poverty.[2]

Is rising income inequality a danger and, if so, why? The existing literature contends that large income gaps are problematic in any society for a variety of reasons—for example, economic demand will be weak because rich people spend less of their incomes than the poor, economic productivity will be low if most laborers are poorly compensated, and the low human capital of the poor will make them a burden on society. However, the major danger worried about in China is that rising income inequality will increase popular perceptions that the social order is unfair, provoking feelings of injustice and anger that will fuel social protest movements that threaten Chinese Communist Party (CCP) rule. As Xi Jinping took over leadership of the CCP in 2012, BBC journalist Damian Grammaticas summarized the challenge he faced: "So the job of making China a fairer place will now fall to the Communist Party's next generation of leaders, who will rule the country for the next 10 years. The fear is that China's growing inequities could undermine the legitimacy of their one-party rule, and the more unequal China becomes, the more unstable it may be."[3]

Upon examination, the potential threat of political instability arises from growing feelings of *inequity*, not from any particular level of income *inequality* per se.[4] If Chinese citizens feel that current levels of income inequality are mostly fair, with the gap between high and low incomes deserved, then they are unlikely to develop strong feelings of distributive injustice. National China surveys I directed indicate that the continuing strong income gains most families have enjoyed during the reform era have kept ordinary Chinese from getting very angry about distributive injustice, at least as of the opening years of Xi Jinping's leadership.[5] Nonetheless, for at least two decades China's leaders and many analysts have argued that if income inequality continues to rise, feelings of inequity will inevitably multiply, eventually leading to a "social volcano." In the first decade of the new millennium, it was common to see claims that surpassing a national income inequality Gini index of 0.40 (which had already occurred by about 1990) indicated that China had entered a "danger zone" for political instability, and a poll of senior officials conducted by the Central Party School in 2004 ranked China's rising income gaps as that society's most serious social problem, ahead of corruption and crime.[6]

At least since the tenure of CCP leader Jiang Zemin (1989–2002), the post-1978 sharp rise in income inequality has been considered a serious problem that needs to be addressed and reversed through new programs and public policies. Jiang's 2000 campaign to "develop the West" and the "harmonious society" programs of his successor, Hu Jintao (2002–12), were intended to shift China onto a more equitable development path.[7] However, as Hu was succeeded by Xi Jinping, there was considerable skepticism that any progress had been made in reversing rising income inequality, and many saw Xi Jinping as a more dynamic leader who might finally be able to make progress toward that goal. His years in the countryside as a sent-down youth in Shaanxi (1969–75) and later as a county CCP official in Hebei (1982–85) were seen as giving Xi special awareness of the plight of China's rural poor. These expectations seemed borne out in February 2013, soon after Xi took over, when China's State Council announced a comprehensive thirty-five-point blueprint for combating rising income inequality.[8]

What have been Xi's specific efforts aimed at combating rising inequality, and how bold versus modest have they been? What evidence do we have about trends in income inequality in China in recent years, and has the trend toward rising gaps been reversed? What do we know about how satisfied or angry ordinary Chinese citizens are about current patterns of inequality, and how much desire do they have for their government to do more to combat rising income gaps? After attempting to answer these questions, this chapter concludes with a response to the query posed in the chapter title and with thoughts on the challenges facing Xi Jinping and his eventual successors.

Before launching into this overview, a caveat is necessary. When I began to research Xi Jinping's role in combating inequality, it was generally assumed that Xi Jinping would abide by the newly established precedent of China's top leader serving two terms of five years each and then stepping aside. If that had been the case, it should have been possible to arrive at a final assessment of Xi Jinping's role in addressing income inequality (and in realms addressed in other chapters in this volume) by late 2022. However, Xi Jinping broke precedent by starting a third five-year term as CCP leader in October 2022, with some analysts predicting he will continue as leader even beyond 2027. In addition, toward the end of Xi Jinping's second term, important changes occurred that make reaching definitive conclusions about Xi's record even during his first two terms problematic. In particular, the onset of the COVID-19 pandemic early in 2020 and the zero tolerance lockdowns that had China in turmoil at the start of Xi's third term have had complex effects not only on China's economic development but also on patterns of inequality and popular attitudes toward distributive injustice issues. These same years have seen further tightening of controls over communications and freedom of expression and the spread of high-technology surveillance systems, making access to information more difficult. The full impact of these developments will not be clear for some time. Therefore, the bulk of this chapter will focus on policies and trends in regard to income inequality primarily in the years between 2012 and 2019, with tentative and somewhat speculative concluding comments about the period since then.

Xi Jinping Confronts Inequality: Specific Initiatives

Although the government's 2013 blueprint for reducing income inequality seemed to indicate that this was a high priority for Xi Jinping, in reality this plan received very little publicity subsequently and soon disappeared from view. It is apparent that Xi Jinping did not wish to be associated with concrete plans for combating inequality developed by his predecessors, Hu Jintao and Wen Jiabao. However, if one examines specific initiatives undertaken under Xi, they might be seen as constituting a substantial, multipronged effort to attack income inequality. To simplify this review, these initiatives will be grouped into three categories: efforts to lower the top and raise the bottom of China's income ladder, efforts to spread social safety net programs more broadly, and efforts to make it easier for rural Chinese to gain full citizenship rights in cities. In the pages that follow, details regarding initiatives in each category are reviewed.

Lowering the Top and Raising the Bottom of China's Income Ladder

Xi Jinping is noted for two major programs related to inequality: his campaign against official corruption and the pledge to wipe out extreme rural poverty in China by 2020. If fewer Chinese are joining the ranks of the ultrarich by corrupt means (or having their ill-gotten gains confiscated) and more Chinese are being lifted out of poverty, the result should be some reduction in overall income inequality. However, it is doubtful that these campaigns represent an effective response to rising income gaps.

THE CAMPAIGN AGAINST CORRUPTION

Obviously, the primary goal of the anti-corruption campaign is not to reduce inequality. Some skeptics claim that the main goal is not even to attack official corruption, but rather to eliminate Xi's political rivals. Even if one takes the campaign at face value, it is next to impossible to estimate what the resulting consequences for China's income distribution have been or will be. In addition to the direct effects in terms of confiscating the wealth of corrupt "tigers" targeted by the campaign, there are doubtless many hard-to-measure indirect effects as well—new investments not made and businesses not started or shut down, wealth invested abroad, restaurant banquet trade made less profitable, luxury goods attracting fewer customers, and so on. Still, it is hard to see much visible impact on China's "conspicuous consumption" culture, the boom in overseas tourism (prior to the pandemic), the rise in the costs of urban housing, increases in the number of Chinese millionaires, and so forth.

If Xi Jinping and his colleagues were serious about limiting the role of the growing wealth of China's ultrarich in aggravating income inequality, they would implement more direct and systematic redistributive measures, and currently these remain weak in the Chinese system. Progressive income taxes are paid by a relatively small number of Chinese citizens, and such taxes play a limited role in financing the Chinese government and its programs. And property taxes on family assets such as housing have been under consideration for years but appear to remain stuck at the pilot stage in only a few cities and facing considerable resistance.[9] Assets have become an increasingly important source of family incomes in recent years, and ownership of housing has been the most rapidly growing source and is by far the most important component of family wealth, so not having a comprehensive system of property taxes, not to mention capital gains and inheritance taxes, obviously means that the contribution of family wealth disparities to overall income gaps can continue to grow relatively unchecked.[10]

THE CAMPAIGN TO ELIMINATE EXTREME RURAL POVERTY

The implications for income distribution of Xi's campaign to eliminate rural poverty by 2020 are more direct. And it is true that Xi regularly stressed the importance of this goal, telling Chinese officials they must "finish the journey" and travel the "last mile" to finally eliminate extreme rural poverty.[11] It is also clear that the campaign to eliminate poverty became increasingly focused over the years (shifting from policies aimed at poverty-stricken counties to poor villages, and then to individual poor households) and employed a widening array of tactics in this effort (shifting from trying to stimulate development projects and tourism to increased funding for rural schooling, health care, livelihood payments, and rural pensions; requiring rich cities and enterprises along the coast to aid development in specific poverty-stricken locales; as well as increasingly employing mandatory resettlement to move poor villagers into housing on the outskirts of cities).[12] Late in 2020 it was announced that the campaign goal had been achieved, followed by official propaganda touting this as a personal triumph for Xi.[13] But how much credit Xi deserves in the battle against poverty is open to question on a number of grounds.

First, efforts to reduce poverty have had a high priority throughout the reform era. When Deng Xiaoping was in charge, his post-1978 market reforms were justified as a way to lift citizens out of the abject poverty in which Mao Zedong had left them. Deng and his colleagues were convinced that continuing to follow Soviet-style state socialist economic development might produce growing national strength at the expense of popular living standards, while switching to a Japanese-style export-promoting development model could dramatically improve living standards as well as raise China's gross domestic product (GDP). In urging some Chinese to get rich first, Deng indicated his conviction that Mao's mandated limits on material incentives and consumption had hindered China from developing, while market reforms would produce benefits for much of the population even if they also resulted in wider income gaps.

So the goal of reducing the proportion of the population living in poverty is hardly new, but dates back to the 1980s. The sharpest reductions in the incidence of poverty occurred during the very earliest years of the reforms, with continuing reductions in subsequent decades so that the number of Chinese living in poverty declined from about seven hundred million in 1978 to around seventy million in 2014, according to one analysis.[14] So most of the reduction in extreme poverty, from seven hundred million down to perhaps one hundred million, occurred prior to Xi Jinping assuming the leadership.[15] Furthermore, analysts agree that the primary driver of this dramatic reduction in the incidence of poverty was booming economic growth, rather than the government's anti-poverty programs.[16] Even though the latter programs provided some income relief and comfort to the poor Chinese affected by them, they didn't make it possible to reverse the national trend toward growing income inequality prior to 2010, as indicated earlier.[17]

Xi Jinping could reasonably argue that because the numbers of poor people in China had already been reduced so dramatically, lifting the remaining millions out of that state would be more difficult because these would primarily be residents of remote locales and people with very low levels of human capital, backgrounds that would make it difficult for them to become prosperous.[18] But just as reasonably, since the pace of economic development has slowed on Xi's watch, the anti-poverty engine that growth represents has become weaker.[19]

In sum, Xi Jinping can be credited with continuing to focus on the problems of rural poverty in China and making further headway in an already impressive record of accomplishment under his predecessors, mainly resulting from China's booming economy. But despite the attention his pledge has received, there is little that is particularly new or different on this front since Xi Jinping took charge beyond increased funding and administrative effort.

Xi Jinping's campaigns to attack corruption and eliminate severe rural poverty do not, on balance, reflect a bold or effective effort to reduce China's high levels of income inequality. Near the close of his second term, in August 2021, Xi Jinping announced to much fanfare a third campaign, a drive for China to pursue "common prosperity," with publicity suggesting the launching of a more comprehensive and effective set of policies to reduce income inequality. A preliminary assessment of the "Common Prosperity" campaign will be deferred to later in this chapter.

Spreading Social Safety Net Programs
and Public Goods Access to Disadvantaged Chinese

The second category of efforts to attack inequality involves initiatives that can be characterized as an attempt to transform China into more of a fully developed welfare state. These initiatives involve extensions of social safety net programs and public goods access to the majority of Chinese who did not previously have access to them. To set these programs in context, it is necessary to review the historical record.

While Mao Zedong is often regarded as a great egalitarian, the social order he and his colleagues constructed during the 1950s and maintained even through the Cultural Revolution was in fact highly unequal. Income and social class ceased to play important roles in determining the living standards and opportunities of citizens, to be sure, but where they were born and the communities and employing organizations where they lived and worked played crucial roles. Before 1949, China's Nationalist government introduced the beginning elements of a welfare state, with access to health insurance, maternity leave, pensions, and much else depending on where and for what organization a person worked within privileged sectors of society. After 1949, Mao and his colleagues built upon this foundation, leading to highly varying opportunities and entitlements for socialist citizens.[20] Even for the minority in the Mao era who were urbanites, there were clear differences in incomes, housing, benefit coverage, and much else between those who worked in high-priority state organizations and enterprises in major cities and those employed in local firms and collective enterprises in smaller cities and towns.[21] The majority of Chinese, the more than 80 percent who then lived in the countryside, were not eligible for any of the welfare state entitlements and public goods their urban counterparts enjoyed, relying instead on the meager resources of their communes, brigades, production teams, and families while bound to the soil in a system that can be characterized as "socialist serfdom."[22]

China's market reforms after 1978 and the dismantling of the commune system in the countryside by 1982 made China's system of benefits tied to employing organizations less viable. In the closing years of the twentieth century, and then increasingly in the new millennium and progressing further under Xi Jinping, China launched multiple efforts to extend welfare benefits and social safety net programs to more of the population and to move toward making eligibility for, and coverage by, those benefits less dependent on the employer and sectoral differences that had been emphasized in the socialist era.[23]

China enacted a system of minimum livelihood payments (commonly known as the *dibao* system) in 1999 to provide minimal government payments to families whose incomes fall below officially designated poverty thresholds. The program had been piloted in Shanghai starting in 1993 and was initially limited to poor families with urban *hukou* (household registrations). A few years later, experiments began at extending *dibao* payments to rural families as well, and these evolved into a nationwide rural *dibao* program starting in 2007. From that year forward, the number of rural *dibao* recipients exceeded the urban total, reaching peaks of 23.5 million urban recipients in 2009 and 53.9 million rural recipients in 2013, after which the numbers of recipients on both sides of the rural-urban divide declined.[24] Initially, the average urban *dibao* recipient received more than three times the amount of the average rural recipient, but increased state funding on the rural side reduced the ratio to close to 2:1 by 2016 (although rural *dibao* levels remained too low to live on).

The Xi era coincides with increased funding for the rural side of the program, even as *dibao* funding for urban recipients stabilized and then declined.[25] Other changes in the *dibao* program include requiring able-bodied but unemployed recipients to seek work and leave the program as well as combating unfairness in the system—both families who should be receiving *dibao* funds but are not and those who are receiving *dibao* payments even though they are not eligible.[26] In sum, Xi Jinping should be credited with some increase in *dibao* funding for rural residents and with improvements in administration, although with some retrenchment in the *dibao* coverage rate.[27] But the main credit for developing and extending the program belongs to his predecessors.

EXPANDING AND CONSOLIDATING
MEDICAL INSURANCE COVERAGE

Early in the reform era the medical insurance systems of the Mao era were dramatically cut back, with most Chinese having to pay medical bills out of pocket and facing ruin if they needed expensive medical care. According to the national China surveys I directed, in 2004 only 29 percent of Chinese adults had public medical insurance coverage, with 50.8 percent of urban *hukou* respondents covered, but only 15.4 percent of rural respondents and 9.2 percent of rural-urban migrants. In response to a sense of crisis regarding China's medical care system, a major national campaign was already underway starting in 2002 to construct a new system of village cooperative medical

TABLE 4.1. Public health insurance coverage (%)

	2004	2009	2014
Rural	15.4	89.6	94.0
Urban	50.8	75.2	94.2
Rural migrants	9.2	56.1	86.7
Total	29.0	82.4	93.4
Number of responses	3,250	2,878	2,384

Source: China Inequality and Distributive Justice Project surveys.

insurance programs, funded by a combination of individual premiums and government subsidies, as well as to increase coverage for other segments of the population. The impressive results of this high-priority effort can be seen in the figures from all three China Inequality and Distributive Justice Project (CIDJP) surveys, spanning the years from 2004 through 2014, displayed in table 4.1. Only five years later, in 2009, overall coverage by public medical insurance had risen dramatically to 82.4 percent, with rural respondents then surpassing the coverage rates of urban *hukou* respondents (temporarily). Five years after that, in 2014, public medical insurance coverage had become almost universal, at over 93 percent coverage, with only migrants trailing behind, at 86.7 percent.

However, because this expansion was constructed based on China's long-standing administrative system, there were until recently three primary medical insurance systems: one for those employed in urban enterprises and organizations (Urban Employee Basic Health Insurance, or UEBHI), one for other urban *hukou* citizens (Urban Resident Basic Health Insurance, or URBHI), and one for villagers and rural-urban migrants (New Cooperative Medical Scheme, or NCMS). Major differences in coverage and benefits and also reimbursement rates existed across plan types, as well as across localities within plan types, and many Chinese had to continue to live with fairly minimal coverage even though they were no longer uninsured. One study reported that in 2014, more than 30 percent of the health expenditures of Chinese families remained out of pocket, rather than being covered or reimbursed by insurance.[28] One further complexity of this hybrid system is that most rural-urban migrants who had health insurance (72.1 percent in the 2014 survey) remained covered by the NCMS plans in their villages of origin, rather than by the plans of their current urban employers. The spread of medical insurance coverage did not reduce the urban-rural disparities in medical care availability and quality, which research indicates remain very substantial.[29]

Although the expansion of public medical insurance coverage to most of the population was launched and primarily achieved under his predecessors, Xi Jinping can be credited with efforts to improve the levels of coverage and reimbursement rates as well as to begin to administratively consolidate the different systems. Specifically, after 2014 the two less generous legs of China's health insurance tripod, the URBHI and NCMS, were merged, a development that should simplify the lives of migrants in seeking medical treatment and reimbursement.[30] Xi Jinping, even though he is only building on the progress in health-care coverage accomplished by his predecessors, deserves some credit for pushing the process along.

EXPANDING PENSION COVERAGE

The story of efforts to expand pension coverage mirrors what happened regarding medical insurance. During the Mao era, urbanites employed by state-owned enterprises and governmental organizations received fairly generous pensions after they retired without having to make contributions during their working lives. Employees of urban collective enterprises (roughly 20 percent of the urban labor force then) received more modest pensions or more often onetime retirement payments. But the vast majority of Chinese—not only villagers but urbanites without regular jobs in state or collective firms—had no pension coverage.

In the reform era a number of changes of the existing system were enacted, particularly by pooling pension funds by sector and city, thus removing the direct financial connection between retirees and the organizations that had employed them. In 1997, a major reform of the urban pension system was enacted that required employees of state-owned enterprises (but not government agencies) to make regular financial contributions into their individual pension funds and also created similar contributory pension programs for urban private firms to cover their regular employees with urban *hukou*. In all of these plans (collectively referred to as the Urban Employee Pension System, or UEPS), participation was essentially mandatory, making eventual pension payments to those covered universal.

During the 1990s, pilot experiments began with extending pensions to rural residents. However, it took almost two decades before a national program of rural pension coverage was enacted in 2009, with pensions funded by a combination of individual and family contributions and government subsidies. Two years later, in 2011, a similar system of pensions was introduced for urbanites not employed in urban units covered via the UEPS. Both the New Rural Social Pension Scheme (NRSPS) and the Urban Social Pension

Scheme (USPS) involve voluntary participation and regular contributions from participants or their families, and in the NRSPS the basic pension at one point was said to be only ¥55 per month, which is far below any reasonable local poverty line. Nonetheless, coverage in the new plans has grown rapidly, and by 2011 there were more people covered by the NRSPS than by the UEPS, with more than three hundred million covered by each.[31] Despite this expansion, the voluntary nature of rural pension plan participation and the requirement of regular contributions over the years (at least fifteen) mean that pension coverage has not become as close to universal as coverage by medical insurance. In the CIDJP surveys, only 20 percent of respondents were covered by pensions in 2004. In 2009, this had increased slightly, to 25.9 percent, and by 2014 it was up to 48.5 percent, so still more than half of Chinese adults were not covered then, although probably pension coverage has increased since.[32]

From the dates listed it is clear that the major steps to spread pension coverage occurred prior to Xi Jinping coming to power. As with medical insurance, Xi can be credited with a decision to merge the NRSPS and USPS into a single plan after 2014, and perhaps with increasing government subsidies for this merged weaker variant of the Chinese pension system, thus raising the overall participation and coverage rates. However, the development and spread of pension coverage to rural residents as well as urbanites without formal employment has done little to counteract the way pension incomes aggravate income inequality in China today. As one recent report notes, "China's largest single transfer program—pensions—are very unequally distributed. Pensions, which on average account for more than 10 per cent of household income in China, go overwhelmingly to a minority of the population—urban retirees."[33] So Xi Jinping has continued to build upon the efforts of his predecessors, but to date these efforts have done relatively little to counteract a major contributor to overall inequality—pension incomes.

EASING AND EQUALIZING ACCESS TO ADVANCED EDUCATION

A final front of efforts to reduce inequality in the distribution of public goods concerns access to schooling, particularly advanced schooling. Again some historical context is needed. China made impressive progress during the Mao era toward eliminating illiteracy and extending basic schooling to all youths. Toward the end of that period there was even movement toward reducing the rural-urban gap in upper middle school attendance, with 18 million enrolled in upper middle schools in 1977 (although one may question the quality of schooling in the wake of the Cultural Revolution). But as the reforms were launched, there were sharp drops in upper middle school enrollments, to only 9.7 million in 1980 and 6.3 million in 1983, overwhelmingly due to a surge of dropouts and school closures affecting rural high schools.[34]

Subsequently, there was a gradual rebound in upper middle school enrollments, but until fairly recently, schooling opportunities for rural *hukou* and urban *hukou* youths increasingly diverged. In 1986, a national goal of universalizing attendance through lower middle school was mandated, with nine years of schooling considered compulsory. However, it remained difficult for rural *hukou* youths to progress on to upper middle school, much less college, while it became increasingly easy for urban *hukou* youths to do so.[35]

For many years children of rural-urban migrants were barred from attending urban public schools at all levels unless the family paid high fees. Even after 2006 when urban public schools were told they should allow migrant children to enroll without paying special fees, in large cities migrant families have generally still faced stiff barriers when trying to enroll their children in public schools. Local *hukou* youths have priority, and many cities use points systems (based on parent education, employment tenure, homeownership, and so forth) that make it difficult for most migrant families to qualify.[36] Even if migrant children are able to enroll in urban public schools, they are generally able to continue only until lower middle school graduation, the endpoint of compulsory schooling. If they want to proceed further, they have to return to the place of origin of their parents and apply for admission to rural upper middle schools, which generally require them to attend as boarders, and to pay tuition as well as room and board fees.[37] And in many of China's large cities the pendulum has swung backward since 2014, with major drives to close private migrant schools and raise the entry bars for access to public schools as a way to induce migrants to depart and thus reduce the overall urban population.[38]

The sixty million or more "left behind children" of migrants as well as rural children whose parents didn't migrate have had to cope with the limited and often distant availability and extra expenses of upper middle schooling, obstacles not faced by urban *hukou* youths. Due to the bottleneck in rural upper middle schooling, when Chinese university enrollments were rapidly expanded after 1998, with perhaps nine to ten times as many enrolled today as in 1997, the beneficiaries were overwhelmingly urban *hukou* youths.[39]

The results of these discriminatory policies are clearly visible in the relatively low levels of high school educational attainment in China compared with other middle-income developing countries. One study based on comparative census data reports that in 2015 only 30 percent of the Chinese labor force had any high schooling (that is, upper middle schooling), compared with 35 percent in Mexico, 37 percent in Turkey, 42 percent in Argentina and South Africa, and 47 percent in Brazil, not to mention the 78 percent average in member countries of the Organization for Economic Cooperation and Development.[40] The role of the *hukou* system in this poor performance is seen in a related analysis based on China's 2015 micro-census, which revealed that in 2005 90 percent of fifteen- to seventeen-year-old urban *hukou* youths had at least some high schooling, but only 43 percent of comparable rural youths did.[41]

China's leaders now recognize that to rise into the ranks of rich countries, they cannot rely on the human capital of urban youths alone. For more than a decade China has been embarked on a campaign to expand upper middle school enrollments in rural areas and to provide funds to make it easier for rural youths to complete at least that level of schooling, and perhaps college as well. The results of that campaign are striking. By 2015, the urban-rural high schooling gap had closed significantly, with 97 percent of urban youths having had some high schooling in comparison with 77 percent of rural youths.[42] However, much of the increase in upper middle school enrollments, particularly in rural areas, is in rapidly expanding and subsidized vocational and educational training (VET) schools, rather than academic high schools. In addition to the fact that VET schools are terminal, rather than preparing students for college, available research indicates that these schools provide poor-quality learning, have higher dropout rates than rural academic high schools, and generally do not lead to jobs after graduation any better than could have been obtained without a VET diploma.[43] So there has been dramatic improvement, but rural-origin youths are still shortchanged educationally.[44] And the most reasonable and cost-effective way of increasing the educational opportunities of rural-origin youths, by making enrollment in urban public schools available to all resident youths, has continued to be rejected in China's larger cities in the Xi era.

On the schooling front it is uncertain how much credit Xi Jinping deserves for the improvements in access to the higher levels of schooling that have occurred. The dramatic expansion of university education in China was launched under Jiang Zemin, and the drive to relieve the bottleneck in high schooling in rural areas began under Hu Jintao. Both initiatives have been continued by Xi Jinping, but it is not clear that he has added much that is new or has increased the pace of closing the urban-rural gap, and in the largest cities inequalities in access to advanced education have increased on Xi's watch.[45]

China has made impressive progress both before and under Xi Jinping's leadership in extending social safety net coverage to more of the population and in starting to overcome the legacy of decades of severe discrimination against Chinese of rural origins. But Xi has not boldly broken new ground regarding any of these programs. How much further progress toward inclusion and equal benefits will occur remains to be seen, and on this question China faces serious challenges. Spreading social safety net coverage to previously disadvantaged groups is one thing, but extending coverage does not mean providing equal benefits, which is very far from being the case currently. To eventually move toward equalizing benefits for all Chinese would be a very expensive proposition.[46]

Some research indicates that China may recently be moving backward, away from universal inclusion and equal social welfare benefits, rather than continuing forward. Since roughly 2010, China has experienced slowed growth in formal employment and rapid growth in the numbers of Chinese in informal employment, leading to growing wage polarization.[47] This polarization may mean that workers who lose or leave formal employment and end up in low-level, informal sector jobs will have their coverage and benefits in medical insurance plans, pensions, and so forth reduced or lost.

China's Urbanization Plan and the Effort to Phase Out Hukou-Based Discrimination

Compared with other societies, rural versus urban origin is a much larger source of overall income and other inequalities in China.[48] Because inequality rooted in *hukou*-based discrimination has been central since the Mao era, one final program launched by Xi Jinping that seemed as if it might have the potential to reduce inequality merits discussion: the major national urbanization plan launched in 2014. This plan was touted as a major step toward eventually phasing out the *hukou* system as a determinant of benefits and opportunities. (For more detailed discussion of this plan, see the chapter by Alexsia T. Chan in this volume.) Specifically, as at least a first step, a pledge was made to convert 100 million rural-urban migrants (out of the 270 million estimated in 2014) from rural/nonlocal to local urban *hukou* by 2020. Since 2014, official sources have even made the claim that China has now abolished the *hukou* system.[49]

However, even this urbanization campaign does not indicate bold new leadership in combating inequality. Chinese authorities have recognized for decades that the *hukou* system, involving discrimination based on where you (or your parents) were born, is unjust, and critics have long demanded that it be phased out. Starting in 2001 or even earlier, China made it relatively easy for migrants to obtain urban *hukou* in small cities and towns, and efforts began to develop points systems (involving such things as possessing advanced education, investing in urban housing and businesses, and having stable employment while making social insurance payments for at least five years) that would enable rural migrants who accumulate enough points to qualify for urban *hukou* conversion even in larger cities.[50] So on balance there is not that much new here, except for the specific pledge of 100 million conversions by 2020. Late in 2020, that goal was declared achieved, although by that point China had even more rural-urban migrants (more than 290 million) than in 2014 (270 million), most of them still unable to earn enough points or to otherwise qualify for full urban citizenship.[51]

Furthermore, if one looks deeper at Xi Jinping's 2014 urbanization plan, it becomes apparent that it has not produced much progress toward making it easier for migrants to enjoy equal urban citizenship and benefits, and in the largest cities ground has been lost. It may have become somewhat easier for migrants to obtain equal rights in small and medium-size cities (although one study indicates that as much as one-third of the recent rural to urban *hukou* conversions involved not migrants but rural communities reclassified as urban, without their residents' lives changing in any way).[52] Meanwhile, in Beijing and other very large cities drives were launched to reduce the overall population by making it harder for migrants to qualify for local urban registrations or send their children to public schools, in order to drive out the "low-end population" (*diduan renkou*).[53]

Chinese social policy is still based on an underlying premise that Chinese citizens can be sorted into those of high quality (*suzhi*) versus low quality, and only those in the former category are qualified to enjoy full citizenship rights in large cities. As a consequence, the millions of migrants attracted by the opportunities available in China's metropolises continue to experience severe discrimination.[54] If anything the "great wall" of *hukou* exclusion from large cities has strengthened.[55] If Xi Jinping wants to go down in history as a bold leader, he needs to find a way to eliminate institutionalized *hukou*-based discrimination.

Has China's Trend toward Widening Income
Gaps Now Been Reversed?

As noted at the outset, from early in the reform period into the new millennium, income inequality in China rose consistently and fairly sharply. Both the official National Bureau of Statistics (NBS) and the China Household Income Project (CHIP) surveys, as noted, indicated a rise in China's national Gini from around 0.30 circa 1980 to the comparatively high level of 0.49 in 2007–9, during the middle of Hu Jintao's leadership, and despite multiple efforts to reverse the trend.[56] What has happened to income inequality since?

More recent NBS and CHIP surveys report modest declines in income inequality nationally after the peak reached in 2007–9 (see table 4.2), with NBS's Gini estimates declining from 0.49 then to 0.46 in 2015, while CHIP estimates declined even more, to 0.43 in 2013.[57] Researchers at Peking University conducting the China Family Panel Study (CFPS) produced an estimate of income inequality in 2010 that was higher than either NBS or CHIP, Gini = 0.52, but they also reported a modest decline after that, to 0.48 in 2012.[58] So although there are some disagreements about the overall level of income inequality in China in recent years, several studies agree that a slight decline in income inequality occurred after 2006–9.[59] One review of available survey evidence published in 2017 welcomed this modest trend enthusiastically, referring to it as "the great Chinese inequality turnaround."[60]

However, if we examine even more recent survey data, it appears that this improvement in income distribution has stalled or even been reversed (again, see table 4.2). The 2018 CHIP survey estimate of the national Gini index remained essentially unchanged from 2013 at 0.43; the NBS Gini estimate increased slightly from 0.46 in 2015 to 0.47 in 2016 and was still at 0.47 in 2020; and the CFPS Gini estimate increased from 0.48 in 2012 to 0.50 in 2014, and then up to 0.53 in both 2016 and 2018.[61] Looking at the trend since 2007, and based on the parallel results from three separate survey-based estimates of household income inequality in China, it appears that there was a slight decline in income inequality after 2007–9, but only temporarily, with income inequality levels stabilizing or even increasing slightly after around 2013–15 and remaining at a high level compared with other countries. In other words, there has not been a "great inequality turnaround," and there is no sign of reduced national income inequality in the years since Xi Jinping became China's leader (at least up until 2018–20).[62]

Since we lack good survey data on China's income distribution after 2018, we can only speculate about whether the overall distribution of incomes has

TABLE 4.2. Post-2007 trends in China household
income inequality, Gini estimates

YEAR	NATIONAL BUREAU OF STATISTICS (NBS)	CHINA HOUSEHOLD INCOME PROJECT (CHIP)	CHINA FAMILY PANEL STUDY (CFPS)
2007	0.48	0.49	
2008	0.49		
2009	0.49		
2010	0.48		0.52
2011	0.48		
2012	0.47		0.48
2013	0.47	0.43	
2014	0.47		0.50
2015	0.46		
2016	0.47		0.53
2017	0.47		
2018	0.47	0.43	0.53
2019	0.47		
2020	0.47		

Note: All Gini coefficients rounded off to two decimal places.
Sources: NBS: Statista, "Inequality of Income Distribution in China Based on the Gini Index," December 8, 2022, https://www.statista.com/statistics/250400/inequality-of-income-distribution-in-china-based-on-the-gini-index; CHIP: Chuliang Luo, Terry Sicular, and Shi Li, "Overview: Incomes and Inequality in China, 2007–2013," in *Changing Trends in China's Inequality: Evidence, Analysis, and Prospects,* ed. Terry Sicular, Shi Li, Ximing Yue, and Hiroshi Sato (New York: Oxford University Press, 2020), 35–74; Chuliang Luo, Xu Zhang, and Shouwei Li, "Zhongguo jumin shouru chaju biandong fenxi (2013–2018)" (An analysis of changes in the extent of income disparity in China [2013–2018]), *Social Sciences in China,* no. 1 (2021): 33–54; CFPS: Yu Xie, Xiaobo Zhang, Qi Xu, and Chunni Zhang, "Short-Term Trends in China's Income Inequality and Poverty: Evidence from a Longitudinal Household Survey," *China Economic Journal* 8, no. 3 (2015): 235–51; Xiaohang Zhao, Yichun Yang, and Yu Xie, "Income Distribution," in *Zhongguo minsheng fazhan baogao, 2020–2021* (Well-being development report of China, 2020–2021), ed. Yu Xie et al. (Beijing: Peking University Press, forthcoming).

become more or less equal since then. However, there are several reasons for concern that the "leveling off of Gini at a high level" reported for 2013–18 may have been followed by a resumed increase in income inequality. First, the relative declines in formal employment in manufacturing and construction and the rapid growth of low-skilled informal employment in the service sector, and the resulting increased wage polarization reported by Scott Rozelle and his colleagues, is likely continuing, which would aggravate income inequality.

Second, over the past fifteen years or so, as noted, assets such as privately owned housing and stocks and other financial investments have gone from negligible to increasingly important sources of family incomes, with this trend likely to continue. The household income surveys used to construct the Gini estimates reported here are not good at including the very rich or measuring family wealth accurately. But tentative efforts to supplement household income surveys with other data on the wealth and incomes of Chinese ultrarich citizens yield conclusions that indicate that the battle to combat income inequality will be increasingly difficult. When the CHIP researchers employed such estimating methods, they concluded that instead of China's national Gini declining from 0.49 in 2007 to 0.43 in 2013, that index actually increased to over 0.60 that year.[63]

Third, our discussion up to this point has concerned the years before the outbreak of the COVID-19 pandemic in early 2020. It is quite clear that the massive disruptions caused by the pandemic in China fell disproportionately on the poor and disadvantaged, and particularly on migrant workers, millions of whom were thrown into unemployment and also faced disease contagion without adequate health and social service protection.[64] These trends indicate not only that there has been no clear progress in reducing income inequality in Xi Jinping's first two terms, but that he and his colleagues will face strong headwinds in any efforts to combat inequality in his third term as CCP leader.

Toward the end of his second term in office, in August 2021, Xi Jinping launched a highly publicized new campaign to promote "common prosperity." From the publicity and debates after that launch, some assume that Xi has finally decided to tackle China's very high levels of income inequality in a more comprehensive and forceful manner. It is obviously premature to judge the results of the "Common Prosperity" campaign as Xi Jinping starts his third term. However, as of the end of 2022 that campaign remained notably vague and ad hoc. Although the objectives of the campaign, to reduce income inequality and promote more broad sharing of benefits and opportunities with China's disadvantaged citizens, sound laudable (as well as fairly familiar, given the earlier pledges of CCP leaders Jiang Zemin and Hu Jintao), the actual measures adopted, such as cracking down on high-tech firms (and the private sector generally), pressuring ultrarich entrepreneurs to make large charitable donations, and eliminating the after-school academic tutoring industry, seem very unlikely to have much impact on China's large income gaps.[65] As the campaign was launched, there was active discussion of spreading the long-stalled pilot experiments with property taxes on urban housing to a wider range of cities, in preparation for implementing a national property tax system. However, the serious financial troubles in China's property firms and the weakening market for urban housing in 2022 seem to have put such plans for implementing property taxes on hold, perhaps permanently.[66] If one goes back and digs out the 2013 State Council thirty-five-point plan for combating inequality, what is striking is how much more concrete and specific that plan was compared to the vague promises of Xi Jinping's "Common Prosperity" campaign.[67]

As indicated in earlier sections of this chapter, the sort of measures that would be needed in order to reduce China's large income gaps, particularly implementing and enforcing redistributive taxation systems (for example, income, property, capital gains, inheritance) and finally and fundamentally eliminating the subordinate-caste treatment of the majority of China's population with rural *hukou* status (particularly moving dramatically to equalize the educational opportunities for rural-*hukou* youths), do not seem to be in the cards in discussions of "Common Prosperity" as of the end of 2022.[68] So although it is hard to predict China's future, and it would be nice to be proved wrong, it seems likely that "Common Prosperity" will be yet another instance of Xi Jinping failing to provide bold leadership to combat inequality.

Chinese Popular Opinions about Inequality Trends and Extending the Social Safety Net

Given multiple efforts underway to combat income inequality, how do Chinese citizens view the issues involved? In this final section, results from the CIDJP surveys are used to summarize the attitudes and preferences of Chinese citizens.[69] First, how fair or unfair do respondents think it is to base access to benefits and opportunities on one's *hukou* status, the central axis of discrimination that has dominated Chinese social life since the 1950s? Table 4.3 displays how respondents answered a range of questions about the fairness or unfairness of *hukou*-based discrimination.

In 2004, only a small minority of respondents thought it was fair to discriminate on the basis of *hukou* status, and, if anything, opposition has increased over time. In the last two rounds, for example, only 11–12 percent of respondents said it was fair to make it difficult for migrants to convert to urban *hukou* status, and 79–81 percent said country people and city people should have equal employment opportunities. Most respondents agreed that urbanites have received more benefit from China's reforms than they deserve, and most disagreed with a statement that the advantages of city folks are explained by their greater contributions to China's development.

TABLE 4.3. *Hukou* discrimination attitudes across three national China surveys (weighted % responding strongly agree + agree)

	2004 (N = 3,267)	2009 (N = 2,967)	2014 (N = 2,507)
Fair for those with urban hukou to have more opportunities than rural hukou	25.3	20.6	18.0
Fair that rural migrants cannot easily obtain urban hukou	14.9	11.5	10.8
Fair that migrant children cannot attend urban public schools	7.5	n.a.	n.a.
Fair that migrants cannot be hired in certain occupations	9.1	n.a.	n.a.
Fair that migrants are not able to obtain urban welfare benefits	9.3	8.6	8.3
Urbanites have benefited more from reforms than is fair, rural residents less	47.9	54.1	48.8
Higher living standard of urbanites is due to greater contributions to development	22.1	22.5	20.4
Country people and city people should have equal employment rights	72.8	81.4	78.9

Note: n.a. = not asked (due to policy changes by the time of the 2009 survey, migrants were supposed to be able to send children to public schools and take any job, and therefore our PRC survey partners did not want to ask these questions again).

These results indicate that there was relatively little, and declining, popular support for China's long-standing system of discrimination based on *hukou* status, at least in principle.[70]

The CIDJP surveys also contain multiple questions about opportunities to get ahead, how fair or unfair current inequalities are, and whether the government should be pursuing specific steps to achieve greater equality. In a previous publication, I summarized Chinese attitudes on such questions across the CIDJP national surveys in 2004, 2009, and 2014 and how they compared with the views of citizens in a range of other countries.[71] Briefly, despite the slowing of China's economic growth recently, Chinese citizens remained much more optimistic than their counterparts in other countries about their chances of getting ahead and improving their family's standard of living, and they were also distinctive in seeing the difference in whether people are rich versus poor as based mainly on merit factors (for example, hard work, talent, education), rather than on societal unfairness.[72]

Given this emphasis on merit, Chinese citizens also tended to feel individuals should be able to keep what they have earned even if inequality increases, and they were not particularly in favor of income redistribution schemes or limits on individual incomes. However, they were not very likely to feel that large income differences are desirable or necessary to stimulate hard work and economic growth, and they increasingly felt that the government should be doing more to guarantee jobs and minimum incomes for the disadvantaged.[73] As noted at the outset of this chapter, there is nothing in these results that suggests (as of 2014 at least) that China faced a looming "social volcano" of anger about rising income inequality, but there was growing popular support for the kinds of expanded social safety net programs discussed earlier.

These heightened expectations are even more clearly demonstrated in responses to CIDJP questions about the government's responsibility to provide public goods and benefits—in other words, to act more like a welfare state. In table 4.4a, the responses in all three surveys to questions about the relative responsibility of the government versus individuals and families are displayed.

TABLE 4.4A. Who should be responsible, the government or individuals and families?

Hukou category	Survey year	State fully	State mainly	About equally	Individual mainly	Individual fully	(Row %) total
Health care	2004	11.5	19.4	50.3	12.7	6.1	100.0
Health care	2009	10.6	42.9	42.3	3.9	0.3	100.0
Health care	2014	21.5	43.7	32.6	2.0	0.2	100.0
Primary/ secondary school	2004	17.3	26.5	33.6	15.2	7.4	100.0
Primary/ secondary school	2009	28.2	44.5	23.3	3.5	0.4	99.9
Primary/ secondary school	2014	30.5	45.6	20.6	3.1	0.2	100.0
Housing	2004	4.6	10.1	32.8	34.8	17.8	100.1
Housing	2009	3.6	15.7	46.4	27.1	7.2	100.0
Housing	2014	5.3	22.7	48.0	20.4	3.6	100.0
Eldercare	2004	13.1	20.3	38.0	17.5	11.1	100.0
Eldercare	2009	10.4	33.2	45.3	8.6	2.5	100.0
Eldercare	2014	15.5	37.6	40.9	5.0	1.0	100.0

Source: China Inequality and Distributive Justice Project surveys.

TABLE 4.4B. Who should be responsible for medical care?
(By survey and *hukou* category)

Hukou category	Survey year	State fully	State mainly	About equally	Individual mainly	Individual fully	(Row %) total
Rural residents	2004	8.0	14.2	53.2	15.5	9.0	99.9
Rural residents	2009	9.9	37.8	46.8	5.0	0.6	100.1
Rural residents	2014	22.2	43.3	32.1	2.1	0.3	100.0
Urban migrants	2004	8.7	20.9	49.0	13.8	7.7	100.1
Urban migrants	2009	11.3	48.0	36.3	3.9	0.5	100.0
Urban migrants	2014	16.6	50.6	27.2	4.7	0.9	100.0
Urban citizens	2004	14.3	32.4	42.6	8.9	1.9	100.1
Urban citizens	2009	12.3	46.7	38.5	2.5	0.0	100.0
Urban citizens	2014	17.9	46.3	33.8	1.8	0.2	100.0

Source: China Inequality and Distributive Justice Project surveys.

TABLE 4.4C. Who should be responsible for eldercare? (By survey and *hukou* category)

Hukou category	Survey year	State fully	State mainly	About equally	Individual mainly	Individual fully	(Row %) total
Rural residents	2004	10.3	12.6	44.2	18.6	14.3	100.0
Rural residents	2009	10.2	32.6	43.0	10.2	4.0	100.0
Rural residents	2014	17.3	38.5	37.4	5.6	1.2	100.0
Urban migrants	2004	7.7	27.0	37.2	15.8	12.2	99.9
Urban migrants	2009	10.8	40.2	40.7	6.9	1.5	100.1
Urban migrants	2014	17.0	32.3	40.9	8.1	1.7	100.0
Urban citizens	2004	19.8	32.9	32.9	9.6	4.8	100.0
Urban citizens	2009	11.2	38.3	43.3	6.5	0.7	100.0
Urban citizens	2014	13.4	38.8	43.8	3.6	0.4	100.0

Source: China Inequality and Distributive Justice Project surveys.

In table 4.4a, we see a very clear pattern. For each of the public goods inquired about—health care, primary and secondary schooling, housing, and care for the elderly—from the first to the third survey large increases were registered in the sentiment that provision of these goods and services should be mainly or fully the government's responsibility, rather than the responsibility of individuals and families. The proportion seeing health care as mainly or fully the government's responsibility more than doubled, from 30.9 percent to 65.2 percent, and similarly there was a more than 30 percent increase regarding the government's duty to provide primary and secondary schooling (from 43.8 percent to 76.1 percent). The proportion of respondents who saw housing as mainly or fully the government's responsibility almost doubled, from 14.7 percent to 28 percent, and in the realm that in China's Confucian culture has been seen as quintessentially the family's responsibility, eldercare, respondents went from only about one-third in 2004 seeing this as primarily a government responsibility (33.4 percent) to in 2014 a majority viewing it that way (53.1 percent). These are dramatic shifts toward the view that the government should have the primary responsibility to meet the basic welfare needs of its citizens. Since this shift was clearly already underway between the first and second surveys, perhaps the role of Hu Jintao in trying to turn China into a "harmonious society" encouraged this attitude change.[74]

The shift toward higher expectations regarding government responsibility for popular welfare involves particularly large changes for those who were deprived until recently. The contrasting patterns are visible in tables 4.4b and 4.4c. For simplicity, the focus is on only two of the four public goods covered in table 4.4a, health care and eldercare, and on the views of rural residents, rural-to-urban migrants, and urban *hukou* respondents. In 2004, urbanites, presumably still influenced by their decades of being "supplicants to a socialist state," were much more likely than villagers or migrants to say that the government should be primarily responsible for health care and eldercare.[75] By 2014, urban attitudes regarding eldercare had not changed much, but urbanites had increased their support for government responsibility for health care. However, the shifts over time in the attitudes of rural respondents and migrants were much larger, so that by 2014 all three population groups expressed very similar attitudes on these questions (with villagers actually slightly more likely than urbanites to say that the government has the primary responsibility). These data indicate that a major shift has occurred in Chinese popular attitudes toward emphasizing the government's primary responsibility to provide public goods and welfare services, and by 2014 higher expectations in this regard were very widely shared.

To sum up, Chinese citizens even in 2014 remained quite optimistic about the ability of ordinary Chinese to get ahead, and they were not all that angry about the higher income and other gaps that characterized China early in the Xi Jinping era. However, these results should not lead to complacency among China's leaders, because, at the same time, citizens wanted and expected the government to do more to help the poor and disadvantaged and to provide more robust social welfare programs benefiting everyone. Both Xi Jinping and his predecessors have encouraged rising popular expectations on the popular welfare front.

Unfortunately, no comparable national survey data on inequality attitudes are available after 2014, which is of course early in Xi Jinping's first term as

CCP leader. A number of more recent developments, including the further slowing of the Chinese growth engine, the onset of the COVID-19 pandemic in 2020 (and particularly the zero-COVID policy that was harshly enforced subsequently), the high levels of youth unemployment at the end of Xi's second term, increasingly repressive restrictions on freedom of speech and association, and the crises affecting the property market and housing values all suggest to many analysts that popular acceptance of the status quo, optimism about getting ahead, and satisfaction with Xi Jinping as China's leader may have declined since 2020, perhaps sharply.[76] However, without the ability to collect new and reliable survey data on Chinese popular attitudes, we cannot judge whether these speculations are accurate or not.[77]

Conclusion

One of the challenges China has faced, both before and since Xi Jinping became the CCP leader, is how to combat rising income inequality. I have reviewed here a wide range of policies and initiatives underway in China to examine whether they are succeeding in reining in income inequality and, if so, whether Xi Jinping should be given credit for any progress. On both counts, I end up more negative than positive. Although there is some evidence that income inequality among ordinary Chinese households declined slightly just prior to Xi Jinping becoming leader, that trend has not continued on his watch, and income inequality either leveled off or is increasing once again. In any case, China's inequality levels remain very high in comparative terms. If we take into account the growing importance of wealth inequality, the incomes of China's ultrarich, and the relative weakness to date of progressive taxation, then income inequality may well increase in the years ahead, rather than decline. Xi Jinping's recently launched "Common Prosperity" campaign seems unlikely to provide an effective route to a more equal society.

China has made substantial progress in developing programs characteristic of a modern welfare state, and particularly in beginning to spread social safety nets to its previously disadvantaged rural-origin citizens. But in reviewing these programs, and even in regard to his pledge to eliminate poverty by 2020, Xi Jinping has been building upon and extending progress already underway. Xi deserves some credit for increases in the funding of these programs as well as for reducing the administrative barriers separating the programs for rural residents (and migrants) from some urbanites. But this is still very much a work in progress, and several issues remain in doubt: whether the inequalities that derive from building these safety nets on China's very unequal administrative system can be overcome, whether the distribution of benefits from these programs is contributing much to the effort to combat rising income inequality, and whether China will be able to afford a more fully developed welfare state. And on some fronts, particularly regarding educational opportunities for rural-origin youths in large cities, China has moved backward since Xi took charge, rather than forward. Measures that could promote greater progress, such as instituting and enforcing systematic and progressive income, capital gains, inheritance, and property taxes, as well as finally abolishing *hukou*-based discrimination in determining access to opportunities and public goods, were not implemented during Xi Jinping's first two terms. However bold Xi Jinping's leadership has been in foreign affairs and in some other domestic political realms, his efforts to rein in rising income gaps have been modest and incremental rather than bold. China today remains a highly unequal society, and it will take much more bold leadership than Xi Jinping has demonstrated thus far to make China a more equal, and more equitable, society.

Notes

I received advice and assistance in preparing drafts from Kam Wing Chan, Eli Friedman, Qin Gao, Sarah Rogers, Scott Rozelle, Terry Sicular, Dorothy J. Solinger, Andrew Walder, and Yu Xie, who bear no responsibility for the use I have made of their ideas and materials.

1. As measured by the Gini statistic, in which 0 means total equality and 1 means total inequality, China went from having a modest Gini in 1980 of around 0.30 to a comparatively high level of 0.49 in 2007. See Shi Li, Hiroshi Sato, and Terry Sicular, eds., *Rising Inequality in China: Challenges to a Harmonious Society* (New York: Cambridge University Press, 2010). The trend since 2007 is discussed in a later section.

2. John Knight, Shi Li, and Haiyuan Wan, "The Increasing Inequality of Wealth in China," in *Changing Trends in China's Inequality: Evidence, Analysis, and Prospects*, ed. Terry Sicular, Shi Li, Ximing Yue, and Hiroshi Sato (New York: Oxford University Press, 2020), 109–44.

3. Damian Grammaticas, "China's Ever-Widening Wealth Gap," *BBC News*, November 1, 2012, https://www.bbc.com/news/world-asia-china-20165283.

4. Although the terms are often used interchangeably (as in the Grammaticas quotation), they are quite different. Inequality refers to the objective shape of the distribution of resources and opportunities, whereas inequity refers to a subjective assessment that a pattern of distribution differs from what is fair.

5. Martin King Whyte, *Myth of the Social Volcano: Perceptions of Inequality and Distributive Injustice in Contemporary China* (Stanford, CA: Stanford University

Press, 2010); Martin King Whyte, "China's Dormant and Active Social Volcanoes," *China Journal*, no. 75 (2016): 9–37. Popular reactions to current levels of inequalities, as revealed by the China Inequality and Distributive Justice Project (CIDJP) national surveys in 2004, 2009, and 2014, will be discussed in a later section.

6. Xinhua, "Survey of Chinese Officials' Opinions on Reform: Beijing Daily," *Xinhua News Bulletin*, November 29, 2004.

7. David S. G. Goodman, "The Campaign to 'Open Up the West': National, Provincial-Level, and Local Perspectives," *China Quarterly*, no. 178 (2004): 317–34. The "harmonious society" programs included abolishing the grain tax, eliminating tuition charges for elementary and lower middle schools, and creating village cooperative medical insurance plans. For a fuller discussion, see Li, Sato, and Sicular, *Rising Inequality in China*, chap. 1.

8. Nargiza Salidjanova, "China's New Income Inequality Reform Plan and Implications for Rebalancing" (US-China Economic and Security Review Commission, Washington, DC, March 2013).

9. See Yawen Chen and Ryan Woo, "China's Property Tax Will Be Implemented according to the City-Lawmaker," Reuters, March 14, 2019. (Thanks to Terry Sicular for alerting me to this press report.) The need to implement systematic property taxes was one of the elements of the thirty-five-point Income Distribution Plan of 2013, so the fact that little progress had been made in the six years after, and even by the end of Xi's second term as CCP leader, is notable.

10. According to the analyses in Knight, Li, and Wan, "The Increasing Inequality of Wealth in China," net wealth per capita in China increased much faster between 2002 and 2013, by 16.7 percent annually, than household incomes (which generally had been increasing by between 7 and 8 percent annually); among types of wealth, housing was the most rapidly increasing over this span (by 20.1 percent per annum); and housing wealth increased from 53 percent to 73 percent of family wealth. Wealth attributable to housing also became more unequally distributed between 2002 and 2013, with the Gini of net housing assets increasing from 0.64 in 2002 to 0.70 in 2013 (while inequality in the other relatively important source of family wealth, financial assets, actually declined modestly, from Gini = 0.69 in 2002 to 0.65 in 2013). The near total exclusion of China's millions of rural-urban migrants from the wealth creation bonanza of urban real estate is a major source of this growing wealth inequality. The lack of property taxes on housing also contributes to China's high rate of vacant urban housing units, 21.4 percent in 2017 according to a recent report, much higher than the vacancy rates in eight comparison countries. See Li Gan, Qing He, Ruichao Si, and Daichun Yi, "Relocating or Redefined: A New Perspective on Urbanization in China," NBER Working Paper No. 26585 (National Bureau of Economic Research, Cambridge, MA, December 2019), table 1, http://www.nber.org/papers/w26585. On the weakness of income redistribution in China, compared with advanced capitalist countries and Russia,

see Andrew Walder, "China's Extreme Inequality: The Structural Legacies of State Socialism," *China Journal*, no. 90 (2023): 1–26.

11. See, for example, Cissy Zhou, Frank Tang, and Zhou Xin, "Xi Jinping Tells Chinese Officials They Must 'Finish the Journey' and Shifts Focus Back to Fight against Poverty as Economy Stabilizes," *South China Morning Post*, April 22, 2019; Javier Hernandez, "Xi Jinping Vows No Poverty in China by 2020. That Could Be Hard," *New York Times*, October 31, 2017.

12. See the discussion in Lucy Hornby, "Beijing's Relentless March to Eliminate Poverty," *Financial Times*, May 29, 2019; Sarah Rogers, "The End of Poverty in China?," Research Brief No. 4 (University of Melbourne Centre for Contemporary Chinese Studies, Melbourne, August, 2016); Sarah Rogers, Jie Li, Hua Guo, and Cong Li, "Moving Millions to Eliminate Poverty: China's Rapidly Evolving Practice of Poverty Resettlement," *Development Policy Review* 38, no. 5 (2019): 541–54; Youqin Huang, "Farewell to Villages: Forced Urbanization in Rural China," in *China's Urbanization and Socioeconomic Impact*, ed. Zongli Tang (Singapore: Springer, 2017), 207–27.

13. See Tom Hancock, "Xi Declares End to Extreme Poverty in China, Meeting Party Goal," *Bloomberg News*, December 4, 2020, https://www.bloomberg .com/news/articles/2020-12-04/xi-declares-end-to-extreme-poverty-in-china -meeting-party-goal; and, for example, David Bandurski, "Propaganda Soars into Orbit," China Media Project, January 29, 2021, https://chinamediaproject .org/2021/01/29/propaganda-soars-into-orbit.

14. Chuliang Luo, Shi Li, and Terry Sicular, "The Long-Term Evolution of Income Inequality and Poverty in China," WIDER Working Paper No. 2018/153 (United Nations University World Institute for Development Economics Research [UNU-WIDER], Helsinki, December 2018), https://doi.org/10.35188 /UNU-WIDER/2018/595-4.

15. However, one recent report based on four independent national surveys claims that the poverty rates in official figures are substantially underestimated in all periods. See Chunni Zhang, Qi Xu, Xiang Zhou, Xiaobo Zhang, and Yu Xie, "Are Poverty Rates Underestimated in China? New Evidence from Four Recent Surveys," *China Economic Review* 31 (2014): 410–25.

16. See Terry Sicular, "Will China Eliminate Poverty in 2020?," *China Leadership Monitor*, no. 66 (2020), https://www.prcleader.org/post/will-china -eliminate-poverty-in-2020.

17. Li, Sato, and Sicular, *Rising Inequality in China*.

18. However, Xi's campaign was based on the erroneous assumption that there is a stable category of the persistently poor. In reality in China and elsewhere, over time many families rise above, and descend into, severe poverty as their efforts and family circumstances change. For evidence on this flux in China, see Yu Xie, Xiaobo Zhang, Qi Xu, and Chunni Zhang, "Short-Term Trends in China's

Income Inequality and Poverty: Evidence from a Longitudinal Household Survey," *China Economic Journal* 8, no. 3 (2015): 235–51.

19. As noted, the 2020 coronavirus pandemic shook China, with the economy registering negative growth of almost 7 percent in the first quarter of the year before recovering, with recovery likely to be prolonged and difficult, and with the number of COVID-19 cases in China rising sharply as Xi began his third term as CCP leader.

20. Nara Dillon, *Radical Inequalities: China's Revolutionary Welfare State in Comparative Perspective* (Cambridge, MA: Harvard University Asia Center, 2015).

21. See Andrew Walder, "The Remaking of the Chinese Working Class, 1949–1981," *Modern China* 10, no. 1 (1984): 3–48; Wang Feng, *Boundaries and Categories: Rising Inequality in Post-Socialist China* (Stanford, CA: Stanford University Press, 2008); Yanjie Bian, *Work and Inequality in Urban China* (Albany: State University of New York Press, 1994).

22. Whyte, *Myth of the Social Volcano*; Martin King Whyte, "China's Hukou System: How an Engine of Development Has Become a Major Obstacle," China-US Focus, April 24, 2019, https://www.chinausfocus.com/society-culture/chinas-hukou-system-how-an-engine-of-development-has-become-a-major-obstacle.

23. Although the focus here is on the leadership of Xi Jinping, China's premier, Li Keqiang, took major responsibility for the extension of social welfare benefits after 2014, even though Xi tended to monopolize the credit.

24. Lixiong Yang, "The Social Assistance Reform in China: Toward a Fair and Inclusive Social Safety Net" (paper presented at the United Nations conference "Addressing Inequalities and Challenges to Social Inclusion through Fiscal, Wage, and Social Protection Policies," New York, NY, June 25–27, 2018); Qin Gao, *Welfare, Work, and Poverty: Social Assistance in China* (New York: Oxford University Press, 2017). Yang notes that China's more than two hundred million urban migrants are ineligible for *dibao* support from local city governments no matter how poor they are (nor are they eligible for rural *dibao* support).

25. See Dorothy J. Solinger, "Banish the Impoverished Past: The Predicament of the Abandoned Urban Poor," in *Polarized Cities: Portraits of Rich and Poor in Urban China*, ed. Dorothy J. Solinger (Lanham, MD: Rowman and Littlefield, 2019), 59–84; Yang, "The Social Assistance Reform in China."

26. See the discussion in Dorothy J. Solinger, "Manipulating China's 'Minimum Livelihood Guarantee': Political Shifts in a Program for the Poor in the Period of Xi Jinping," *China Perspectives*, no. 2 (2017): 47–57. The 2014 CIDJP survey revealed that many Chinese were critical of how fairly the *dibao* system was operating. When asked how easy it would be for them to apply for and receive *dibao* payments if they qualified, 50.4 percent of those surveyed responded that it would be difficult or impossible. Furthermore, when presented with a statement that some people who qualify for *dibao* payments are not receiving them, 67.1

percent of respondents agreed, and when presented with the statement that some people are receiving *dibao* payments who don't deserve them, 66.7 percent agreed.

27. According to official statistics, from 2013 to 2018 the proportion of individuals receiving *dibao* payments declined from 5.47 percent to 3.24 percent. Qin Gao, personal communication with author.

28. Sonali Jain-Chandra, Niny Khor, Rui Mano, Johanna Schauer, Philippe Wingender, and Juzhong Zhuang, "Inequality in China—Trends, Drivers, and Policy Remedies," IMF Working Paper No. 2018/127 (International Monetary Fund, Washington, DC, June 2018).

29. Sean Sylvia, Yaojiang Shi, Hao Xue, Xin Tian, Huan Wang, Qingmei Liu, Alexis Medina, and Scott Rozelle, "Survey Using Incognito Standardized Patients Shows Poor Quality Care in China's Rural Clinics," *Health Policy and Planning* 30, no. 3 (2015): 322–33.

30. However, recent research indicates that this administrative merger (and the comparable pension merger to be discussed shortly) was still a work in progress as of 2017, with migrants sometimes finding that urban hospitals refuse to accept their rural medical insurance verification as well as often providing less reimbursement for medical care than could be obtained from a hospital in their rural place of origin, serving as an inducement for migrants to return to the village they came from to seek medical care. See Alexsia T. Chan and Kevin J. O'Brien, "Phantom Services: Deflecting Migrant Workers in China," *China Journal*, no. 81 (2019): 103–22.

31. See Andrea Vilela, "Pension Coverage in China and the Expansion of the New Rural Social Pension," Pension Watch Briefing No. 11 (HelpAge International, London, 2013); Robert C. Pozen, "Tackling the Chinese Pension System" (Paulson Institute, University of Chicago, July 2013), https://www.brookings.edu/articles/reforming-the-chinese-pension-system.

32. These are weighted totals. In 2004, 52.4 percent of urban respondents were covered by pensions, but only 8.1 percent of rural respondents and 6.2 percent of urban migrants. By 2014, the coverage of all three categories had increased, to 65.2, 48.7, and 32.4 percent, respectively. As with health insurance, migrants mostly began to receive coverage by enrolling in the pension plans of their rural places of origin, not of their urban employers. It should also be noted that important regional differences exist between coastal locales, which mostly provide pensions only to formal employees and not to informal workers and migrants, and inland locales, where pension plans are more inclusive but less generous. See Yujeong Yang, "The Politics of Inclusion and Exclusion: Chinese Dual-Pension Regimes in the Era of Labor Migration and Labor Informalization," *Politics and Society* 49, no. 2 (2021): 147–80.

33. Shi Li, Terry Sicular, and Finn Tarp, "Inequality in China: Development, Transition, and Policy," WIDER Working Paper No. 2018/174 (United Nations University World Institute for Development Economics Research

[UNU-WIDER], Helsinki, December 2018), 6, https://doi.org/10.35188/UNU-WIDER/2018/616-6. Another report states that according to Chinese official figures, in 2017 the average payout from the basic urban employee pension fund was ¥34,498 for the year, while the average payout from the merged rural-urban resident pension fund was ¥1,520, a ratio of more than 22:1. See China Labour Bulletin, "China's Social Security System," *China Labour Bulletin*, March 2019; also see "The Migrant Workers Who Made China an Industrial Giant Face a Bleak Retirement," *Economist*, November 30, 2019.

34. Figures as reported in Nirmal Kumar Chandra, "Education in China: From the Cultural Revolution to Four Modernisations," *Economic and Political Weekly* 22, no. 19–21 (May 1987): 121–36.

35. Qianhan Lin and Wei-Jun Yeung, "Beyond the Middle-School Gates: The Urban-Rural Divergence of School-Work Paths of China's Youth," in *Social Inequality in China*, ed. Yaojun Li and Yanjie Bian (London: World Scientific Publishing, 2023), 185–208.

36. Yi Wan and Edward Vickers, "Toward Meritocratic Apartheid? Points Systems and Migrant Access to China's Urban Public Schools," *China Quarterly*, no. 249 (2022): 210–38. Eli Friedman describes these discriminatory policies as creating an "inverted welfare state," reinforcing the advantages of the already advantaged. See Eli Friedman, *The Urbanization of People: Development, Labor Markets, and Schooling in a Chinese City* (New York: Columbia University Press, 2022).

37. See Minhua Ling, *The Inconvenient Generation: Migrant Youth Coming of Age on Shanghai's Edge* (Stanford, CA: Stanford University Press, 2019); Pei-chia Lan, "Segmented Incorporation: The Second Generation of Rural Migrants in Shanghai," *China Quarterly*, no. 217 (2014): 243–65. In many places, rural youths attending lower middle schools and even primary schools also have to board, and with the emptying out of villages and relocation of families, increasing numbers of village primary schools have closed, raising the proportion of boarding students even at entry level. One report claims that between 2000 and 2015 nearly three-quarters of all rural primary schools, more than three hundred thousand, were closed down. See "China's Grim Rural Boarding Schools," *Economist*, April 12, 2017.

38. Eli Friedman, "Just-in-Time Urbanization? Managing Migration, Citizenship, and Schooling in the Chinese City," *Critical Sociology* 44, no. 3 (2018): 503–18; Friedman, *The Urbanization of People*; Yiming Dong and Charlotte Goodburn, "Residence Permits and Points Systems: New Forms of Educational and Social Stratification in Urban China," *Journal of Contemporary China* 29, no. 125 (2020): 647–66.

39. Maocan Guo and Xiaogang Wu, "School Expansion and Educational Stratification in China, 1981–2006" (paper presented at the Annual Meeting of the American Sociological Association, Boston, June 2008); Tony Tam and Jin Jiang, "Divergent Urban-Rural Trends in College Attendance: State Policy Bias and Structural Exclusion in China," *Sociology of Education* 88, no. 2 (2015): 160–80.

40. Scott Rozelle and Natalie Hell, *Invisible China: How the Urban-Rural Divide Threatens China's Rise* (Chicago: University of Chicago Press, 2020), table 1.

41. Lei Wang, Mengjie Li, Cody Abbey, and Scott Rozelle, "Human Capital and the Middle Income Trap: How Many of China's Youth Are Going to High School?," *Developing Economies* 56, no. 2 (2018): 82–103.

42. Wang et al., "Human Capital and the Middle Income Trap."

43. Anita Koo, "Expansion of Vocational Education in Neoliberal China: Hope and Despair among Rural Youth," *Journal of Education Policy* 31, no. 1 (2016): 46–59; Guirong Li, Jiajia Xu, Liying Li, Zhaolei Shi, Hongmei Yi, James Chu, Elena Kardanova, Yanyan Li, Prashant Loyalka, and Scott Rozelle, "The Impacts of Highly Resourced Vocational Schools on Student Outcomes in China," *China and World Economics* 28, no. 6 (2020): 125–50; Ling, *The Inconvenient Generation*; Prashant Loyalka, Xiaoting Huang, Linxin Zhang, Jianguo Wei, Hongmei Yi, Yingqua Song, Yaojiang Shi, and James Chu, "The Impact of Vocational Schooling on Human Capital in Developing Countries: Evidence from China," *World Bank Economic Review* 30, no. 1 (2015): 143–70. On the quality problems of urban vocational schools, see T. E. Woronov, *Class Work: Vocational Schools and China's Urban Youth* (Stanford, CA: Stanford University Press, 2015).

44. Although China reported that about 60 percent of the total population lived in urban areas in 2019, this includes urban migrants, so perhaps only 40 percent of Chinese had urban *hukou* that year. Given higher birth rates in rural China, it is estimated that more than 70 percent of all Chinese youths have rural *hukou*. See Rozelle and Hell, *Invisible China*, 9. In other words, the large majority of Chinese youths are still being discriminated against in terms of educational opportunities.

45. For what it is worth, in the four years prior to 2012, the proportion of rural youths with some high schooling increased from 51 percent to 66 percent, and in the subsequent four years the proportion increased further to 77 percent, according to Wang et al., "Human Capital and the Middle Income Trap." On increased inequalities in access to advanced education in large cities, see Dong and Goodburn, "Residence Permits and Points Systems."

46. A recent analysis projects that if current (very unequal) benefit levels are maintained, by 2050 China will have to spend 23 percent of its GDP (compared to 11.6 percent in 2016) on education, health care, and pensions, due largely to rapid population aging. If benefit levels are equalized and raised to the levels enjoyed by citizens in rich countries today, which China says it aims to achieve, public spending in these realms could rise to 32 percent of GDP, a figure even more unsustainable. See Yong Cai, Wang Feng, and Ke Shen, "Fiscal Implications of Population Aging and Social Sector Expenditure in China," *Population and Development Review* 44, no. 4 (2018): 811–31.

47. See Scott Rozelle, Yiran Xia, Dimitris Friesen, Bronson Vanderjack, and Nourya Cohen, "Moving beyond Lewis: Employment and Wage Trends in

China's High- and Low-Skilled Industries and the Emergence of an Era of Polarization," *Comparative Economic Studies* 62 (2020): 555–89; Scott Rozelle and Matthew Boswell, "Complicating China's Rise: Rural Underemployment," *Washington Quarterly* 44, no. 2 (2021): 61–74.

48. Martin King Whyte, ed., *One Country, Two Societies: Rural-Urban Inequality in Contemporary China* (Cambridge, MA: Harvard University Press, 2010); Wang, *Boundaries and Categories*; Yu Xie and Xiang Zhou, "Income Inequality in Today's China," *Proceedings of the National Academy of Sciences* 111, no. 19 (2014): 6928–33.

49. See CGTN, "100 Million Have Settled in Urban Areas as Part of China's *Hukou* System Reform," *CGTN News*, October 8, 2020, https://news.cgtn.com /news/2020-10-08/100-million-affected-as-part-of-China-s-hukou-system -reform-UpT5zFzzHO/index.html. CGTN states, "The dual 'hukou' system, which has lasted for over half a century and divided the people into rural and non-rural population was abolished [after 2014]." However, the new urbanization plan simply stated that people should be categorized no longer as having either agricultural or nonagricultural *hukou*, but instead as having local urban *hukou* or outsider *hukou*. The great majority of migrants to China's cities, the "floating population" of voluntary labor migrants who have powered China's economic boom, are accordingly now to be termed holders of outsider *hukou*, with no change or reduction in the systematic discrimination they experience. The claim that the *hukou* system has been eliminated is patently absurd.

50. See the discussion of these earlier efforts in Fei-Ling Wang, "Renovating the Great Floodgate: The Reform of China's Hukou System," in *One Country, Two Societies: Rural-Urban Inequality in Contemporary China*, ed. Martin King Whyte (Cambridge, MA: Harvard University Press, 2010), 335–64. (Note: the city points systems used to judge qualification for conversion from outsider/rural to local urban *hukou* are not the same as the points systems discussed earlier to judge eligibility of migrant children for enrolling in urban public schools, which may vary from district to district within a city. See the discussion in Friedman, *The Urbanization of People*; Dong and Goodburn, "Residence Permits and Points Systems.")

51. CGTN, "100 Million Have Settled in Urban Areas." Obviously, rural migrants have continued to flow into Chinese cities since 2014, more than offsetting the rate of *hukou* conversions. The totals of 270 million and 290 million rural-urban migrants are based on press reports at the time, and it is not certain how they were calculated and if they are fully comparable. It is clear, at least, that the proportion of the total urban population that lacks local *hukou* increased between 2014 and 2020. See Kam Wing Chan, "What the 2020 Chinese Census Tells Us about Progress in Hukou Reform," *China Brief* 21, no. 15 (2021): 11–17.

52. See Gan et al., "Relocating or Redefined."

53. See Dexter Roberts, *The Myth of Chinese Capitalism: The Worker, the*

Factory, and the Future of the World (New York: St. Martin's Press, 2020), 32–33; Friedman, "Just-in-Time Urbanization?"; Friedman, *The Urbanization of People.*

54. One recent study found that in Shanghai, where about 40 percent of the residents are migrants, even those who had obtained Shanghai local *hukou* had a 68 percent lower chance of homeownership (controlling for education, age, gender, and other background traits) than lifelong Shanghai urban citizens, while migrants who had not converted to local Shanghai *hukou* status had a 90 percent lower likelihood of homeownership if they came from another city, and 92 percent lower if they came from a rural area. See Zhenchao Qian, Yuan Cheng, and Yue Qian, "*Hukou*, Marriage, and Access to Wealth in Shanghai," *Journal of Ethnic and Migration Studies* 46, no. 18 (2019): 3920–36.

55. Ren-Jie Hong, Yu-Chi Tseng, and Thong-Hong Lin, "Guarding the New Great Wall: The Politics of Household Registration Reforms and Public Provision in China," *China Quarterly*, no. 251 (2022): 776–97.

56. Li, Sato, and Sicular, *Rising Inequality in China.*

57. Chuliang Luo, Terry Sicular, and Shi Li, "Overview: Incomes and Inequality in China, 2007–2013," in *Changing Trends in China's Inequality: Evidence, Analysis, and Prospects*, ed. Terry Sicular, Shi Li, Ximing Yue, and Hiroshi Sato (New York: Oxford University Press, 2020), 35–74.

58. Xie and Zhou, "Income Inequality in Today's China"; Xie et al., "Short-Term Trends in China's Income Inequality and Poverty." Using a different approach that compares the top 10 percent of household incomes with the bottom 50 percent, some other scholars claim that income inequality in China has been consistently higher than official estimates indicate, but they also show some reversal and slight decline in income inequality after about 2006. See Thomas Piketty, Li Yang, and Gabriel Zucman, "Capital Accumulation, Private Property, and Rising Inequality in China, 1978–2015," *American Economic Review* 109, no. 7 (2019): 2469–96.

59. Regarding disagreements, surveys of the wealth of Chinese households conducted by the Southwestern University of Finance and Economics, termed the China Household Finance Surveys (CHFS), produced a much higher income inequality estimate of Gini = 0.61 in 2010, but other researchers have criticized this outlier estimate as due to biases in the sampling design used in the CHFS. For details, see Southwestern University of Finance and Economics, *Zhongguo jiating shouru bu pingdeng baogao* (Report on China's household income inequality) (Chengdu: Southwestern University of Finance and Economics, 2012); Terry Sicular, Shi Li, Ximing Yue, and Hiroshi Sato, eds., *Changing Trends in China's Inequality: Evidence, Analysis, and Prospects* (New York: Oxford University Press, 2020), chap. 1.

60. Ravi Kanbur, Yue Wang, and Xiaobo Zhang, "The Great Chinese Inequality Turnaround," IZA Discussion Paper No. 10635433 (Institute of Labor Economics [IZA], Bonn, 2017).

61. The NBS has released annual Gini estimates up until 2020, although the quality of the 2020 survey in the midst of the pandemic may be questioned. The CHIP surveys were carried out in 2007, 2013, and 2018, and the CFPS surveys have been carried out every two years since 2010, with the most recent survey from which Gini can be estimated being 2018.

62. The slight improvement in overall income inequality that directly preceded Xi's becoming CCP head is most likely due to growing shortages of labor from the countryside finally producing increases in the wages of migrant laborers, leading to some reduction in the urban-rural income gap. The CHIP survey estimate of the ratio of urban to rural household incomes in 2007 was an extraordinarily high 4.01, but in the 2013 survey this had been reduced to 2.56. See Luo, Sicular, and Shi, "Overview: Incomes and Inequality," table 1. However, as noted, recent research suggests that this improvement was brief, with the shift away from formal to informal employment after about 2010 leading to increasing wage polarization and poorly educated migrant laborers losing ground. See Rozelle et al., "Moving beyond Lewis"; Rozelle and Boswell, "Complicating China's Rise."

63. See Luo, Sicular, and Shi, "Overview: Incomes and Inequality."

64. See Lei Che, Haifeng Du, and Kam Wing Chan, "Unequal Pain: A Sketch of the Impact of the Covid-19 Pandemic on Migrants' Employment in China," *Eurasian Geography and Economics* 61, no. 4–5 (2020): 448–63; Meihua Luo, "China's Lockdowns Are Fueling Record Growth—in Inequality," *Sixth Tone*, July 13, 2022, https://www.sixthtone.com/news/1010753. Huan Wang, Sarah-Eve Dill, Huan Zhou, Yue Ma, Hao Xue, Prashant Loyalka, Sean Sylvia, Matthew Boswell, Jason Lin, and Scott Rozelle, "Off the COVID-19 Epicentre: The Impact of Quarantine Controls on Employment, Education and Health in China's Rural Communities," *China Quarterly*, no. 249 (2022): 183–209.

65. On the campaign's objectives, see Xi Jinping, "Making Solid Progress toward Common Prosperity," *Qiushi Journal*, English ed., updated January 18, 2022 (excerpt from speech on August 17, 2021), http://en.qstheory.cn/2022-01/18/c_699346.htm.

66. "Conditions Not Right for China to Expand Property Tax Trial This Year—Xinhua," Reuters, March 16, 2022.

67. Salidjanova, "China's New Income Inequality Reform Plan."

68. Liu Shangxi, president of the Chinese Academy of Fiscal Sciences, published a recent article in which he argued that inequality in incomes is based on inequality in capabilities, and the best way to combat income inequality would be to remove the obstacles preventing the majority of Chinese (those with rural *hukou*) from fully developing their capabilities, particularly by equalizing rural and urban educational opportunities, which is far from happening currently. See Liu Shangxi, "Zouxiang gongtong fuyu yao tupo lilun yu shixian de shuangzhong tiaozhan" (To achieve common prosperity, we must break through dual theoretical and practical challenges), Aisixiang, October 20, 2022, https://www.aisixiamg

.com/data/137271.html. (Thanks to David Kelly for providing his translation of this article.)

69. The CIDJP carried out surveys with nationally representative samples of Chinese adults between the ages of eighteen and seventy in 2004, 2009, and 2014. The surveys were based on spatial probability sampling methods and yielded sample sizes of 3,267, 2,967, and 2,507. The project involved an international team of collaborators, with the survey fieldwork carried out by the Research Center for Contemporary China at Peking University. For further information, see Whyte, *Myth of the Social Volcano*; Whyte, "China's Dormant and Active Social Volcanoes."

70. Further analysis of these responses reveals that even urban respondents are not in favor of specific *hukou*-based discriminatory practices that benefit them, although this does not mean that in their daily lives they treat migrants as social equals.

71. For my summary of Chinese attitudes across the three surveys, see Whyte, "China's Dormant and Active Social Volcanoes." The comparative data are from the International Social Justice Project (ISJP) surveys in other post-socialist and advanced capitalist countries. For details, see Whyte, *Myth of the Social Volcano*; Whyte, "China's Dormant and Active Social Volcanoes."

72. The percentage of respondents who expected their family incomes to increase during the next five years actually rose from 62 percent in 2004 to 76 percent in 2014, while the percentage who agreed with the dubious statement that "hard work is always rewarded" remained steady at about 60 percent in all three China surveys. In none of the ISJP countries surveyed was there anything close to these levels of optimism (for details, see Whyte, "China's Dormant and Active Social Volcanoes").

73. For example, the percentage of China respondents who agreed that the government should provide a minimum income guarantee to all rose from 81 percent in 2004 to 89 percent in 2014, with the latter figure among the highest compared to ISJP country surveys, much higher than the 56 percent of Americans who expressed this view.

74. See Martin King Whyte and Dong-Kyun Im, "Is the Social Volcano Still Dormant? Trends in Chinese Attitudes toward Inequality," *Social Science Research* 48 (November 2014): 62–76.

75. Deborah Davis, "Urban Households: Supplicants to a Socialist State," in *Chinese Families in the Post-Mao Era*, ed. Deborah Davis and Stevan Harrell (Berkeley: University of California Press, 1993), 50–76.

76. With regard to youth unemployment, one popular theme in the Chinese media since 2020 is the claim that many young Chinese feel they face "involution" (*neijuanhua*), having to work ever harder just in order not to fall behind, with some becoming so discouraged that they decide instead to "lie flat" (*tangping*) and stop trying, a syndrome that Xi Jinping has denounced. See Barclay

Bram, "Involution: The Generation Turning Inward and Away from Xi's Chinese Dream," Asia Society Policy Institute, November 9, 2022, https://asiasociety.org/policy-institute/involution-generation-turning-inward-and-away-xis-chinese-dream.

77. In the summer of 2023, Scott Rozelle began collaborating with colleagues in China to insert selected inequality attitude questions from the CIDJP surveys into new online surveys those colleagues have been conducting. Preliminary results reported by Rozelle suggest that there has indeed been a major shift toward more negative views among Chinese citizens regarding opportunities to get ahead and whether becoming rich depends on individual merit versus societal unfairness. However, until these new surveys are completed and the responses weighted to approximate the nationally representative samples used in the CIDJP face-to-face surveys, a process that will not be finished until after this volume goes to press, it will not be possible to judge definitively how much Chinese popular attitudes on distributive justice issues may have soured.

5

Pliable Citizenship
Migrant Inequality in the Xi Jinping Era

Alexsia T. Chan

The municipal government in Shanghai rolled out reforms in the late 2000s and early 2010s that allowed migrant children to attend primary school in the city regardless of their household registration status. However, staff at a community organization that supported migrant education told me in 2012 that migrant workers faced systematic obstacles when they tried to enroll their children in public school. Officials explained that meaningful progress would take time and that any issues they had been encountering were temporary hiccups. Five years later, workers at the same organization reported in follow-up interviews that many migrants were mired between supposedly having rights and actually obtaining access. The case was much the same in other cities.[1]

Important political changes had happened in the intervening years. Xi Jinping ascended to the top position in government and consolidated power, prompting questions about the degree of his influence. In 2014, the State Council unveiled the innovative National New-Type Urbanization Plan (2014–20).[2] The multipronged plan promised "human-centered" urbanization, marking a contrast with previous rapid economic development and committing to help those who were most marginalized. One major aim of the plan was economic. Urbanization, as it has elsewhere in the world, would lead to more economic development, higher wages for workers, and a growing middle class who could drive domestic consumption. The State Council announced, "An increasing urbanization ratio will help raise the income of rural residents through employment in cities and unleash the consumption potential, according to the plan."[3] Another key dimension was building the infrastructural and human capital support necessary to back this economic goal: "It will also bring about large demands for investment in urban infrastructure, public service facilities, and housing construction, thus providing continuous impetus for economic development."[4] The plan seemed to usher in a period of concern for the well-being of migrant workers as part of larger state goals. But the contrast between the lived experience on the ground and high-level directives suggests that less has changed than the plan promised. Municipalities still have to translate the plan's ambitious goals into social insurance plans, hospital agreements, accessible schools, classroom spots, affordable housing, transferrable pensions, and more.

Why has urban public service provision for migrant workers remained uneven and devolved to local governments? This situation is especially puzzling given that it has continued at the same time that Xi Jinping has centralized authority in many other policy areas, both domestic and foreign. His administration has ushered in an anti-corruption campaign, Belt and Road Initiative projects, and a greater commitment to improving the quality of life of Chinese citizens. But while he has poured resources into the first two, the last remains left to local governments to address through formulating and implementing policies for outsiders living and working in their cities.

Public service provision for migrants remains patchy and devolved to local government control because inequality serves the state. There has been more continuity than change between administrations in this particular governance issue. Local authorities enact social control through the contingent delivery of social services, and these practices have continued apace under Xi because they work well enough to support other state goals, namely, economic development and social stability. It allows the central government to claim commitments to increasing equality, while municipal governments can maintain a labor force for whom they do not have to provide the full set of services. However, decentralized benefits are not designed to improve the overall welfare of a group of people defined by their movement and mobility.

Municipal and district authorities use what I call "pliable citizenship," a term that reflects an outsider's social rights to the city that are dependent on place, time, and the individual migrant.[5] That is, a migrant's ability to access and use services in the city can change based on the policies and practices implemented in the city or district where the migrant happens to be working and living that year.[6] The moldability of eligibility requirements, obstacles to access, and hoop-jumping give local bureaucrats and frontline service providers some flexibility in choosing to whom they provide health care, education, housing, and other entitlements. Pliable citizenship is a component of a larger process of the "political atomization" of Chinese migrants.[7]

Despite the central government's renewed attention to the consequences of urbanization, less has changed for the people on the ground than anticipated. This finding that continuity trumps change runs counter to the notion of a universal and sweeping "Xi Jinping effect." In problematizing evaluations of Xi's influence, this chapter highlights what has largely *not* changed and why. Marginal shifts have occurred, but many of these were set in motion during the prior administration. The provision of social entitlements continues to be the responsibility of local authorities; however, people who move around the country would benefit more from a centralized system that allows transfers between cities and counties. The Xi Jinping effect on migrant inequality has been limited so far.

The Long-Standing Urbanization Challenge

The need to manage economic development, the flow of workers, and the attendant growth of cities has been a policy issue since the early 1980s. Four decades ago, rural surplus labor moved to urban centers to fuel production for the export market. Urban bias has helped induce internal migration in China, and workers continue to move today.[8] After migrants arrive and settle down, they require access to public services such as health care, housing, and education for their children. The core challenge for local governments is to maintain a steady and healthy labor force, but they are reluctant to bear the burden of fully incorporating migrant workers into the urban public welfare system. Demographic trends, structural shifts in the economy, and other changes in the past decade have reshaped the practical demands facing municipal and district officials. One aspect that has stayed consistent is statist attempts to control, manage, and channel internal migrants in order to maintain steady economic growth and social stability. It is a thorny problem that cannot be shoved aside because, ultimately, cities need workers.

Previous literature on Chinese migrant workers focuses heavily on the household registration (*hukou*) system and their second-class citizenship. The *hukou* system has long relegated internal migrants to a social underclass.[9] It dictated registered rural residents' rights to benefits in their urban destinations for several decades and tied them to their hometown or (for the second generation of migrants) their parents' hometowns. Many in the "floating population" (*liudong renkou*) at that point did not settle long-term into cities. The expectation that they would return to their village in the countryside for medical care or their children's schooling was problematic and inconvenient but was the norm. The demographics and the lifetime plans of migrants have changed. More are older, are married, have children, and would prefer to settle down permanently in their chosen destinations.[10] These trends have made it more difficult, costly, and unrealistic over time to expect migrants to live and work in one place and obtain social services elsewhere in the country.

The *hukou* system has evolved over the years and undergone changes. Recent reforms have led to "localization" of the system and related policies and procedures rather than abolishment.[11] Although it continues to exist as a national system, the entitlements that come with registration vary by place. Cities are developing their own schemes for determining who can register and through what procedures. For example, the country's capital has established its own eligibility criteria for acquiring a Beijing *hukou*.[12] At the same time, with the devolution of authority the household registration system is not necessarily the main or only determinant of migrants' social rights on the ground.

In contrast to the bright-line distinction between rural migrants and urban residents that once existed because of the *hukou* system, gradations in second-class citizenship among migrant workers have emerged.[13] Differentiation among migrant workers themselves has become politically salient. Highly educated migrants from other cities are typically more desirable than low-skilled workers who have moved from the countryside. A lawyer who has relocated to Shanghai from another city has an easier time accessing health care and education opportunities for his or her children than a nanny does who is originally from a village in Henan Province. Employment status, industry, residency period, and other factors further differentiate one migrant worker from the next in terms of urban citizenship. New gradations in second-class status are more complex, varied, and contingent.

These degrees of second-class citizenship emerged before Xi came to power. Policies, procedures, and practices are cementing them into institutions in cities, and they continue to evolve as municipal authorities' needs and preferences change. They are a direct consequence of the localization of migrant social rights in lieu of the abolishment of the *hukou* system or a national overhaul of it. In other words, they do not fit into the broader pattern of centralization of power and consolidation of authoritarianism that has characterized the Xi era so far.[14] They largely originated under Hu Jintao and have continued under Xi. Why they have persisted is part of the Xi legacy, but for reasons other than his consolidation of power.

Structural features of policy implementation affect public goods provision for migrants on the ground. Local officials are subject to the cadre evaluation system, and "street-level bureaucrats" engage in decentralized decision-making.[15] Both result in uneven public service provision for migrants. The cadre evaluation system with its mix of performance metrics and incentives shapes selective policy implementation and leaves room for discretion at the local level.[16] The decentralized implementation of services, to be clear, helps explain why there is variation in practice but not necessarily what forms that variation takes to aid social control and entrench migrant inequality. Although central leadership policies on migrant public services may change, the cadre management system and local politics and structures remain intact.

There are a number of alternative explanations for why various local governments treat migrant workers differently. The simplest reason could be wealth: richer cities can afford to spend more on public services for outsiders. But wealth does not explain why when making education accessible to migrant students, Beijing is generally exclusionary, Shanghai has had limited success, and Chengdu is doing especially well. Nor does it explain variation over time within these cities or differences between regional cities such as Dongguan and Hangzhou. Wealthier cities should be better equipped to manage an unfunded mandate, but they have other competing policy priorities, which are similar to the constraints leading cadres face within the cadre responsibility system.[17] In addition, local officials and urban residents are sometimes reluctant to share resources with rural migrants, whom some see as outsiders and troublemakers. A few megacities are seeking to cap their populations in the coming years and thus are unlikely to do anything that would lure more people, such as by expanding benefits.

Labor shortages are another alternative explanation for why some cities and not others treat migrants better. Cities in the Pearl River delta in Guangdong Province have experienced labor shortages since about 2004, but improvement in services has been more recent and dependent on limited local *hukou* reform.[18] The mechanism seems plausible, but municipalities and companies often use other ways to draw in workers when they are needed. Low-skilled labor shortages do not usually lead to changes in social service provision. Moreover, the relationship may be the reverse: the *hukou* system (and associated restrictions on benefits for workers who have relocated) may contribute to labor shortages.[19] According to the small and medium-size factory owners in Guangdong and Sichuan Provinces whom I interviewed, only the largest factories, with tens or hundreds of thousands of workers, have enough economic and political sway to try to influence local, never mind national, policy. They explained that only when a company can offer as many new jobs as a large multinational company will the local government respond directly to a particular labor shortage.[20] In those cases, the local government may offer to bus in laborers from nearby villages or provide support such as worker training.[21] Furthermore, the 2008 global economic turndown affected firms across the country, but not all cities have improved services in response. Meanwhile, workers are flocking inland, where services had already been improving. Social policy is not the main quick fix for metropolitan areas trying to resolve labor shortages.

Recent developments indicate that migrant workers may be gaining more leverage and therefore should be better positioned to demand more social protection. To be sure, some aspects of migrants' quality of life are improving and they are enjoying higher wages. Labor shortages also tip the power imbalance more toward workers, but they continue to face high institutional barriers. Meanwhile, labor unrest is on the rise. According to the China Labour Bulletin, data show that reported strikes (likely only a small fraction of total strikes in a given year) increased from 184 in 2011 to 1,257 in 2017.[22] In the first eight months of 2018 alone, 1,134 strikes had been logged on the organization's strike map.[23] In 2014, as many as forty thousand workers at the Yue Yuen shoe factory complex in Dongguan, Guangdong, in "the world's factory" in southeastern China, went on strike for two weeks. They protested what they claim had been years of inadequate social insurance and housing fund contributions the company should have paid. Yue Yuen facilities produced shoes for global brands, including Adidas, Nike, and Saucony. Although social benefits are not the most common reason workers strike, this strike was one of the largest in recent memory, according to labor activists. A Guangzhou labor dispute litigation white paper stated that unpaid social insurance accounted for more than 40 percent of arbitration cases from 2014 to 2016.[24] Some workers are beginning to seek redress for benefits owed, but the scope of their requests is often limited to the companies not paying, rather than placing the onus on the state. Labor unrest has also become more offensive, suggesting there are at least perceived openings in political opportunity.[25] Workers have demanded repayment of wage arears, better working conditions, and more. For migrants, increased leverage and assertiveness have not yet directly resulted in systematic reform of urban social services.

Many observers have assumed that the second generation of migrant workers could and would push for a stronger social safety net. Second-generation migrants are the children of the migrant workers who participated in the initial massive wave of rural-to-urban migration in the 1980s. Many were born and raised in the city, but their household registration record is still tied to their parents' and they retain their rural registration status. Some experience more anger and dissatisfaction than the first generation, and most are more highly educated than their parents.[26] That second-generation migrants are younger than first-generation migrants also means that they are healthier and less likely to have children.[27] From construction workers to factory line workers, they are more concerned about quality of life (for example, working fewer hours or in less potentially toxic job environments) than public education or health care.[28] Though individual companies may face different demands depending on the type of worker most suitable for their business, the overall cohort breakdown by first- and second-generation migrants in a city does not affect broader government policies. Where migrants have banded together to access social services in the city, it was to circumvent rules of exclusion from government-sponsored schemes or to form informal institutions to serve as private alternatives. Differences between cities in the proportion of first- and second-generation migrants do not appear to influence how the state treats migrants overall. The benefits of keeping citizenship pliable and other overriding state goals better explain public service provision for migrant workers.

Problematizing the Xi Effect

National directives toward supporting urbanization as economic development notwithstanding, there has been more continuity than change under Xi Jinping, as local authorities' use of pliable citizenship continues to shape migrant workers' benefits. The policies and practices set in motion during the Hu Jintao administration serve the central government's broader goals of economic development and social stability, and this form of inequality has been maintained under the current administration.

Top-Down View: Urbanization as Development

Urbanization is state led and state supported in China. The process of urbanizing people (and land) is seen as a means to further economic development and modernization. Central pronouncements declare a more balanced approach to urbanization that would alleviate some of the past problems and address inequity. The attention has matched other campaigns to reduce socioeconomic disparity, but concrete measures have lagged behind the words. Discussions of inequality in China often converge on two points: remarkable progress in poverty alleviation and the ever stubborn rural-urban divide.[29] Migrants, however, have not yet become fully integrated into their urban destinations. Verbal overtures about incorporating outsiders are a start, but they are not enough to improve migrant welfare without a national overhaul.

The focus on urbanization as development came from among the topmost powers in Beijing. Li Keqiang fixated on urbanization during his post as premier under Xi Jinping and made urbanization a central component of economic reform. According to Li, urbanization was the key to unlocking China's domestic consumption and subsequently improving people's welfare. His focus on urbanization and economic development was visible and widely touted when Xi first rose to power. In a 2012 article expounding his views on the urbanization drive, Li said, "Stepping up efforts to abolish the 'two-tier class system' will help rebalance urban-rural development, resolve social conflicts and unleash the untapped potential for domestic demand which will result from urbanization."[30] He drew a clear line from reducing inequality between registered urban residents and migrants to untapping rural labor and unleashing latent domestic demand. The process of urbanization itself would boost the economy as well as create the basis of future market growth by making more people city residents, who would then become urban consumers.

Li also made the link between public service provision for migrants and the urbanization process. In the same article, he pointed to the need for government responsibility in helping to provide migrant workers with health care, education, and more: "The government should formulate and ensure the seamless implementation of policies and measures which encourage migrant workers to integrate into cities, while also ensuring that they are covered by, and have equal access to basic public services, including urban social security, health care, education and culture. The government should help them solve problems concerning employment, housing, health care and children's education."[31] The article, however, did not specify the role of the central and local governments in formulating and implementing policies that would actually make migrant workers full-fledged citizens. Nor, for example, did it lay out a financial restructuring plan to increase transfers to municipal governments so they could pay for expanding their public goods systems. And it did not provide details on where new schools and hospitals for migrants and their children would be built, how these organizations would hire appropriate teachers and doctors to staff them, how migrants would be able to navigate any new eligibility and access requirements set by bureaucracies, and other logistics behind any meaningful incorporation.

The notion of urbanization as development seems to have fallen out of the national spotlight. While it is difficult to discern whether what publicly appeared to be a slow fade was the product of a completed policy goal or explicit reprioritization, it has diminished in relative rhetorical importance to other policy initiatives. At a speech seven years later, at the 2019 Summer Davos meeting, Li still emphasized the idea of putting people at the center of development priorities. But there was less weight placed on urbanization and incorporating migrants. He made broad mentions of improving people's well-being overall, saying, "The Chinese government will continue to put people first in pursuing development, explore innovative means to enhance people's well-being, and provide more quality public goods and services to better share the fruits of reform and development among our people."[32] Other economic priorities have taken center stage as the Chinese government fears a substantial slowdown in growth. That has left migrants empty-handed in terms of the significant integration that had been promoted at the start of the Xi era.

Li Keqiang was not the only vocal supporter of urbanization and improving migrant workers' welfare. A number of central proclamations and directives have shown rhetorical support for improving migrants' and their dependents' access to primary education, use of social insurance in the city, affordable housing, and pensions. The National New-Type Urbanization Plan (2014–20) suggests a longer commitment to ensuring that people moving from the countryside to the city would enjoy more services. The plan included the goal of converting one hundred million more rural residents' *hukou* into urban registrations and improving access to hospitals and schools for those already living in urban areas.[33] China's drive for urbanization is synonymous with modernization because advanced, industrialized countries are urbanized. According to the plan, different forms of migrant inequality, from public services to land rights, would be addressed as part of this process.

The Chinese Dream is another example of central concern and signaling. The amorphous and wide-reaching slogan carries grand notions of national rejuvenation but offers little in the way of specifics. Part of it seeks to address the effects of uneven development during the economic reform period. In a report to the 19th National Congress of the Communist Party of China in the Great Hall of the People in Beijing in 2017, Xi said, "What we now face is the contradiction between unbalanced and inadequate development and the people's ever-growing needs for a better life."[34] An optimistic interpretation would include in this group of people China's hundreds of millions of internal migrants. Projects focused on specific aspects of quality of life, such as the "Common Prosperity" campaign and Healthy China 2030, add more hope.[35] (See Martin King Whyte's chapter in this volume for more on inequality under Xi.) Taken together, such directives show that the Xi government appears invested in devoting attention to this large group of marginalized people in China, at least according to these announcements and plans.

Other national projects seek to direct the pace and location of urbanization. While urbanization would continue even without state intervention because China is a developing country, the Xi government is intent on speeding it up. The aim is to control the geographic concentration of movement, mostly to small and medium-size cities and to a lesser extent to urban mega-regions outside metropolises' existing central business districts. The state is devoted to leading and supporting the urbanization process insofar that it takes a certain form. A government publication called the "Key Tasks of New-Type Urbanization Construction in 2019" recommends that cities with a permanent population between one and three million people should lift residency requirements that prevent migrant workers from accessing urban social services.[36] These small and medium cities usually cannot offer the economic opportunity and co-migrant networks that are available in coastal cities, which have long been popular destinations for the "floating population." A mismatch between central state goals, local authorities' priorities and constraints, and migrant preferences ends up undermining the overarching idealistic project of deepening urbanization in a less than organic way. Li Keqiang, too, described his own plan for migrant incorporation: "Qualification requirements should be relaxed for those rural migrant workers with stable jobs and housing to become permanent urban residents of mid-sized and small cities."[37] These qualifications concerning employment stability, housing permanence, and residency status are subtle and build on a number of policies and practices that had been in place before a Xi effect could have begun.

More Continuity than Change: Pliable Citizenship in Practice

One way to evaluate the Xi Jinping effect is to assess the degree of continuity and change between administrations. It can help establish whether there is a distinct shift from changing paramount leaders and, if so, its extent. To be clear, continuity or little change does not necessarily mean that the later leader is ineffectual or that this leader is not minding the issue. If policies are sufficient or functioning, then the leader may choose to maintain them as they are. That too is a decision, though one that is less discernibly the effect of an individual. Intent, as is often the case, is difficult to measure but need not be considered to observe the outcomes of migrant inequality. This chapter focuses on the perspective on the ground of migrant workers engaged in navigating municipal and district rules on social services and the local officials and street-level service providers responsible for these public goods. Both the Hu and Xi administrations' central directives included inclusive and expansionary rhetoric. A closer look at how they are translated into municipal policies shows that city newcomers' access to public goods is actually highly differentiated and becoming more so.

The devolution of authority and responsibility for migrants' integration into cities is a major source of inequality. The central directives mentioned notwithstanding, the formulation and the implementation of specific policies to bring outsiders into the local urban public health, education, housing, and pension systems fall to municipalities. Local officials are responsible for designing schemes that dictate who does and does not qualify for benefits. For those who do qualify, they must then ensure that they have adequate access and can actually use the entitlements given to them. Officials therefore exercise discretion and devise systems such as points schemes to determine eligibility for permanent residency status. These complicated systems award points to applicants for qualifications such as having a university degree. They make it appear as if inclusion is possible and procedures do exist, but they continue to exclude most migrants. Beijing, for example, granted *hukou* only to 6,019 people who had the most points out of 124,000 applicants.[38] Few gain full citizenship.

Many city officials feel hamstrung because of crosscutting pressures. The combination of central concern and local responsibility often leads to an unfunded mandate, referred to by Chinese as "The center treats, local governments pay" (*Zhongyang qingke, dangdi maidan*).[39] Because migrants are managed locally and support from above is minimal, cities get to choose whom to incorporate and on what terms. Fully incorporating migrants would require significant resources. The Chinese Academy of Social Sciences estimated it would cost approximately ¥650 billion (or US$106 billion) a year to ensure that rural migrants have the same health care, education, and housing benefits that their urban resident counterparts have.[40] But cities cannot forego the labor of migrants. They also need them to support the local economy by ferrying takeout lunch orders to the business crowd, cleaning major city streets, building new residential construction, and more. And principals and hospital administrators must respond when migrants show up in their schools and health-care facilities looking to enroll their children or use their social insurance to receive medical treatment.

Decentralization leaves room for local governments to enact pliable citizenship. Pliable citizenship involves migrant workers' social rights being dependent on place, time, and characteristics of the individual. Their ability to qualify for, access, and use urban social services can vary based on where they live and work and their hometown or province. Being qualified does not guarantee access or use either. One year they may have a harder time enrolling their children in the local public school than the next year. They may also have more entitlements if they moved from another city instead of a village, have a formal job with a signed labor contract, work at a state-owned enterprise, or can prove long-term residency with a lease or by buying a house. One migrant's actualized citizenship may differ from another outsider's, which is a different contrast than that between a native urban resident and a registered rural counterpart. While urban authorities do have some leeway and could potentially open up their cities more, they face other pragmatic constraints.

Urban authorities, therefore, sometimes provide "phantom services" in lieu of full incorporation.[41] Many municipalities deflect demands for benefits instead of meeting them or denying them outright. City leaders often establish near-impossible eligibility requirements and require paperwork that outsiders struggle to obtain. Municipal authorities also nudge migrants to seek health care or education elsewhere by enforcing dormant rules, shutting down schools and clinics, and encouraging migrants to seek out cheaper options in another city or in the countryside. Urban officials deflect migrants for practical and political reasons. Limiting access is both cost-effective and done in a way that isolates and disempowers migrants and makes it harder for them to protest collectively. Phantom services change the locus of contention, aid "social management" (*shehui guanli*), and expose new axes of inequality.

Pliable citizenship predates the Xi era. Several years before he came to power, for example, Shanghai announced it would provide free education to all school-age migrant children. The outcome has been mixed, but the action of making the formal statement itself is noteworthy. Other cities are developing their own sets of policies and rules around public education and other types of benefits. More systematic national overhauls seem to be far off. Claims that incremental changes will eventually amount to full integration into cities are unsubstantiated so far. Xi has not recentralized fiscal responsibility and policymaking in this realm, and he has not done much to advance the incorporation of rural migrants in cities. Any changes since 2012 have happened at the edges. It would be difficult to describe this as incremental progress because the steps taken do not appear to build on each other toward a larger goal of dismantling the institutions behind migrant inequity.

The patchwork of local policies works because of the lack of centralized coordination, not in spite of it. Decentralization in migrant benefits persists beyond the Hu administration because it continues to be in Beijing's interest.

The state benefits whether it was intentionally designed this way from the top or not and regardless of whether China has the state capacity to completely overhaul the public goods system. Given the consolidation of power that follows other central policy goals, the combination of verbal commitments from the top but without resources and details to support them suggests that the current system works as is.

Devolved responsibility started before Xi, but his government has done little to advance the full incorporation of migrants. Xi's authority and efficacy are not necessarily less relevant or potent. Rather, officials have allowed an effective system (or, more accurately, a set of multiple subnational systems) to continue functioning while it is good enough. That a leader would allow a system to keep plodding along does not necessarily imply that decisions were not made about the processes in place. Insofar as this system of labor pool management suiting broader policy goals, this is unsurprising. It becomes more relevant as the Chinese economy undergoes structural adjustments, which should lead to necessary industrial upgrading but which will nonetheless involve some growing pains as the growth rate slows from the height of approximately 10 percent. But that system does not work toward primarily improving migrant welfare.

Retrenchment and reversal are underway in some places. A few of the largest cities are attempting to cap the number of people living in those metropolitan areas and are seeking to disincentivize further population growth. The Beijing Municipal Master Plan (2016–35), officially approved by the Party Central Committee and the State Council, set a goal of capping the city's population at twenty-three million by 2020.[42] Shanghai followed, with a cap of twenty-five million people by 2035. These goals seem incompatible to many given the existing population in both cities, with vulnerable migrants likely to bear the brunt of any population management policies to come. Migrant integration therefore remains uneven, especially as these cities and others in similar positions appear to inch away from full incorporation.

Whether *hukou* and public service provision reforms are gradual (as most officials say) or stalled, the effect is the same. The drawn-out process framed as incremental changes benefits the state. Pliable citizenship is a by-product of gradual reform, regardless of whether the abolishment of the household registration system or the complete integration of migrants is on the horizon. A government report compiled in 2019 by the National Health Commission's Migrant Population Service Center, the Chinese Academy of Social Sciences, the China Population and Development Research Center, and Renmin University's Population and Research Center found that less than 4 percent of migrants in fifty cities (including Qingdao and Chengdu) were able to obtain permanent residence status in their adopted city.[43] Xiao Zihua, director of the National Health Commission's Migrant Population Service Center, said, "The larger the city, the more difficult it is for migrants to integrate. . . . Migrants most want to integrate into big cities and mega-cities, but our urbanization strategy is at odds with that as we encourage them to move to small and medium cities."[44] Both the numbers and this official's statement confirm that migrants face obstacles similar to those encountered during Xi's early administration. Most outsiders continue to run up against high institutional barriers, while a select few enjoy a slim possibility of integration. Furthermore, the mismatch between the state's urbanization strategy and migrant workers' preferences lingers.

Bottom-Up View: Migrant Workers' Lived Experience

Migrants' own point of view shows how pliable citizenship works on the ground. Their lived experience reveals the ways in which a general Xi effect is overstated on the specific issue of migrant inequality. Migrants' responses in interviews conducted in the years before and after Xi Jinping came to power are remarkably similar. Qualitative descriptions of their attempts to qualify for, access, and use public services in coastal and inland cities indicate that pliable citizenship has been in practice since the period spanning the 2010s. They, too, heard about the urbanization drive and the central directives encouraging integration and better access to urban public goods. But they learned through their own experiences and those of their family, friends, and co-migrants as they encountered new bureaucratic roadblocks that only a selective group of migrants reaped newfound benefits. Disenchantment and a sense of powerlessness quickly followed their initial feeling of hope.

Almost all migrants describe a messy hodgepodge of various municipal and district systems. Every city has its own set of standards, so understanding the rules in one place is of little use once migrants move to another destination when following a new construction or manufacturing job lead. Or a school official tells them the school is full and instructs them to get in line for the following year.[45] Within a city, each district may make its own determinations about who is worthy of which benefits. Migrant children whose parents try to enroll them in public schools in the central business district often face higher barriers than if they were in a "migrant village" on the outskirts of the city, where competition for spots in high-quality schools is less fierce.[46]

Many migrants report wasted time and feelings of frustration. After they figure out what "five documents" (*wuzheng*) they need to prove eligibility, then they go about collecting them. Typically, these include a household registration booklet, proof of hometown permanent residency, a temporary residence permit, proof of local address, and proof of employment. Not all of these certifications are easily accessible, and some might be in their hometown or do not exist at all. Those who manage to gather everything must then bring their paperwork to be certified. Here, too, migrants get stuck between supposedly being eligible and being able to prove it officially. A small shop owner working in Guangzhou said, "They ask for this certificate and that certificate: proof of housing, social insurance cards, and labor contracts. It's almost impossible."[47] The few who are successful once may need to start all over the next year when their child graduates from primary school to middle school or if the family moves to another city or district. After trying, many give up and opt to send their children to live with their grandparents in their home village or to stay in boarding schools on the periphery just outside the city.[48] Part of what makes pliable citizenship work is that it is hard for outsiders to get a bird's-eye view of migrant inequality. Migrant workers know their own experiences and the shared stories of people in their networks. However, they are often in similar circumstances and are running into the same phantom services that never appear. Over time they learn to expect less and less from the promised incorporation they hear is coming.

Pliable citizenship also works by shifting responsibility to migrants themselves for obtaining their own services. While cities are the providers, the onus is on outsiders to prove their worthiness and follow the proper timeline to file paperwork. In addition to the formal rules, they must navigate and adhere to informal norms. Schools may require "voluntary" donations or other extra fees in order for children to secure a spot on the roster, as was the experience of a woman who left two children at home in Anhui Province while she worked as a street sweeper in Shanghai.[49] Specialists in hospitals may treat some people ahead of others because these patients can afford to give them red envelopes of cash, bottles of duty-free alcohol from the airport, and other gifts, as observed during transactions at hospitals in Beijing and elsewhere. If their paperwork is insufficient, as was the case of a roadside fruit and vegetable seller who did not have a storefront lease to show proof of employment, then they are told they should have secured a more formal, permanent position. A woman from Henan Province who sold vegetables in Beijing explained that she sold one head of bok choy for five *mao* (US$0.07) and earned a couple of thousand *kuai* per month, hardly enough to buy a house in her Beijing neighborhood, which she estimated to cost 10,000 *kuai* (US$1,370.00) per square meter.[50] The responsibility, and therefore the blame, is on individuals who have the least leverage.

The barriers are more than bureaucratic red tape. The practical consequences of pliable citizenship in forms such as phantom services and political atomization are not only annoyances. Excessive complexity may delay outcomes and result in inaction, but the key difference here is that the official procedures effectively keep out most migrants altogether. Few experience success or reward because most cannot accumulate enough points in points systems or provide the correct paperwork (for example, signed labor contracts or housing leases) to prove their periods of employment and residences. For city officials reluctant to welcome all newcomers and for frontline service providers strapped for resources, it is convenient to use procedural reasons for limiting access to public hospitals, public schools, low-income housing, and city pensions. Many migrants work six days per week for twelve hours or more per day. They do not have the luxury of time to constantly learn new rules and run around chasing paper trails, so many resign themselves to being empty-handed despite central calls for "human-centered" urbanization.

There are stories of success that circulate. Some cities that experienced influxes of migrants later than coastal areas seem more open. Chengdu, for example, certifies private migrant schools instead of shutting them down, as Beijing has done in the past.[51] This serves migrants better since their children are already attending them, and the buildings tend to be located in more convenient neighborhoods. Urban public hospitals may arrange agreements that allow migrants to seek a percentage of reimbursement from their rural insurance.[52] There are some stories of successfully enrolling migrant children in public schools in megacities. But when pressed, it becomes evident that it is usually a certain kind of migrant who can achieve this. Doctors, lawyers, and similarly highly educated people who have relocated from another city typically have multiple avenues of assistance. The vast majority of so-called unskilled migrant workers do not have a law school or company that can support their *hukou* change or their efforts to buy into urban social services. The gap between their aspirations and reality can be demoralizing. One report found that even 7.5 years after migrating to urban areas, rural Chinese migrants are on average less happy than they might have been had they not moved.[53] Whispers and rumors of hope have not yet materialized into widespread, deep integration across the "floating population."

Decentralization and pliable citizenship create uncertainty for migrant workers. Being perennially deflected and excluded makes it hard to plan work and life. Certain jobs, especially informal ones such as nannying, are precarious, and workers are reluctant to bring their children along when they move if they cannot be assured they can go to school during the day while they are at work.[54] The second generation of migrant workers desire to settle down long-term in cities, and not knowing whether they can use their insurance or if they will have a pension in the city when they retire makes it hard to calculate the risks and rewards of planting roots. Difficulty accessing housing is another dimension of insecurity, as tens of thousands of migrants in Beijing experienced when they were suddenly evicted from their homes after a deadly fire in an apartment building in Daxing District in 2017. The dehumanizing bureaucratic term *low-end population* lays bare how the government perceives them in terms of their supposed low value-added manual labor. From this perspective, not much has changed since Xi assumed power.

Conclusion

Urbanization presents a long-standing governance challenge for the Chinese state. Higher-paying jobs and the prospect of making life better for their children entice migrants to move from rural to urban areas, and cities need these workers to sustain local economies. These outsiders eventually require access to health care, education, and other benefits in their destinations. In the Xi Jinping era of increased power consolidation, public services for migrant workers have remained devolved to municipal governments and contingent. The state's urbanization drive is rooted in the central government's vision of development that relies less and less on export-led growth. Pressures facing municipalities and districts and the policies they have devised in response existed before Xi came to power, and the procedures and practices behind pliable citizenship are a thread of continuity between administrations. From the perspective of city newcomers, their day-to-day experience in qualifying for, accessing, and using public hospitals, schools, housing, and pensions has not changed much. The Xi Jinping effect on migrant inequality is relatively limited because pliable citizenship and decentralization work well enough to support economic growth and social stability.

Problematizing the Xi effect shows that efficaciousness must be considered in terms of the state's larger goals. The persistence of pliable citizenship suggests that the Xi administration's rhetoric about migrant incorporation fits into a narrow and particular vision of urbanization. It prefers to channel this through the growth of small and medium cities, which is not necessarily in the interest of rural-to-urban migrants themselves. Decentralization of entitlements for migrants is in service of other state goals and priorities around economic development, modernization, and increasing domestic consumer demand. The system, or more accurately various local subsystems, of urban benefits is not primarily about improving migrant welfare. The persistence of these institutions across administrations indicates that flexibility in whether and how to integrate migrant workers has endured for pragmatic reasons. Decentralization does not necessarily improve migrant welfare, but it is consistent with other state goals.

Some advantages of pliable citizenship make it practicable in the short term but may contain the seeds of their own demise. One major long-term downside is that it does not produce or maintain a healthy, stable labor force. Migrants who forego medical care or wait until they are severely ill to go to the emergency room or return home for treatment may suffer health consequences and be unable to continue working. Those families who are forced to enroll their children in makeshift private migrant schools will have a hard time attaining upward socioeconomic mobility. Another hazard is that migrant workers, who are relatively powerless as individuals vis-à-vis the state, can engage in collective action that disrupts a locality's economy or social stability because of their sheer numbers. And pliable citizenship is costly to the state itself. Policies and practices that increase bureaucracy and shift over time require resources to create and sustain. Authorities have to design procedures such as residency points systems and eligibility rules for enrolling children in school, and their frontline counterparts then have to count and keep track of these methods and accompanying documentation. In the long run, pliable citizenship will not improve overall migrant welfare and poses risks for the state. In short, there has been more continuity than change.

Institutions of population management in China have been updated and repurposed, and these structures are deeply entrenched in social policy. Factors beyond the *hukou* system affect migrant rights, giving way to the emergence of new gradations of second-class citizenship. The state nudges migrants to do what the government prefers them to do while avoiding being held accountable. Cities keep a steady pool of labor to boost local economic development without having to provide the full set of rights, and officials delay deep, systemic reform that would improve migrant welfare. Migrant citizenship is malleable relative to that of other citizens, and this inequality benefits the state.

Notes

1. Alexsia T. Chan, *Beyond Coercion: The Politics of Inequality in China* (New York: Cambridge University Press, forthcoming).

2. See State Council, "Guojia xinxing chengzhen hua guihua (2014–2020)" (The National New-Type Urbanization Plan [2014–2020]), March 16, 2014, http://www.gov.cn/zhengce/2014-03/16/content_2640075.htm.

3. State Council, "China Unveils Landmark Urbanization Plan," August 23, 2014, http://english.www.gov.cn/policies/policy_watch/2014/08/23/content_281474983027472.htm.

4. State Council, "China Unveils Landmark Urbanization Plan."

5. This chapter examines migrants' pliable citizenship across six cities in four regions, three sectors, and two types of services. The findings are based on field-work in Beijing, Chengdu, Shanghai, Guangzhou, Hangzhou, and Dongguan between 2010 and 2019. The focus is on large, top-tier municipalities rather than smaller cities, because many workers prefer more developed cities, where there are more job opportunities and higher wages. Social services are usually most contested in these desirable destinations, and this is consistent with the finding that more developed cities tend to impose higher barriers to entry for household registration. Interview with public policy scholar in Beijing, July 2017; Li Zhang and Li Tao, "Barriers to the Acquisition of Urban Hukou in Chinese Cities," *Environment and Planning A: Economy and Space* 44, no. 12 (2012): 2883–900. In one survey, 70 percent of respondents willing to settle in cities hoped to put down roots in big cities. National Health and Family Planning Commission of China, "Summary of China's Migrant Population Report for 2013," May 16, 2014, http://en.nhfpc.gov.cn/2014-05/16/c_46667.htm. Of the many public services, the chapter looks at health care and education, both crucial to human development and China's long-term growth prospects and of key importance to migrant worker families.

6. This chapter focuses on the social rights of migrants, adopting a widely used framework for understanding and categorizing citizenship. See Thomas H. Marshall, "Citizenship and Social Class," in *The Welfare State Reader*, ed. Christopher Pierson and Francis G. Castles (Malden, MA: Polity Press, 2006), 30–39.

7. Chan, *Beyond Coercion*.

8. Jeremy Wallace, *Cities and Stability: Urbanization, Redistribution, and Regime Survival* (New York: Oxford University Press, 2014).

9. C. Cindy Fan, "The Elite, the Natives, and the Outsiders: Migration and Labor Market Segmentation in Urban China," *Annals of the Association of American Geographers* 92, no. 1 (2002): 103–24; Dorothy J. Solinger, *Contesting Citizenship in Urban China: Peasant Migrants, the State, and the Logic of the Market* (Berkeley: University of California Press, 1999); Fei-Ling Wang, *Organizing through Division and Exclusion: China's Hukou System* (Stanford, CA: Stanford University Press, 2005); Martin King Whyte, ed., *One Country, Two Societies: Rural-Urban Inequality in Contemporary China* (Cambridge, MA: Harvard University Press, 2010); Jieh-Min Wu, "Rural Migrants Workers and China's Differential Citizenship: A Comparative Institutional Analysis," in *One Country, Two*

Societies: Rural-Urban Inequality in Contemporary China, ed. Martin King Whyte (Cambridge, MA: Harvard University Press, 2010), 55–81; Kam Wing Chan, "The Chinese *Hukou* System at 50," *Eurasian Geography and Economics* 50, no. 2 (2009): 197–221; Kam Wing Chan, Fang Cai, Guanghua Wan, and Man Wang, eds., *Urbanization with Chinese Characteristics: The Hukou System and Migration* (New York: Routledge, 2018); Kam Wing Chan and Li Zhang, "The *Hukou* System and Rural-Urban Migration in China: Processes and Changes," *China Quarterly*, no. 160 (1999): 818–55; Kam Wing Chan and Will Buckingham, "Is China Abolishing the *Hukou* System?," *China Quarterly*, no. 195 (2008): 582–606; Tiejun Cheng and Mark Selden, "The Origins and Social Consequences of China's *Hukou* System," *China Quarterly*, no. 139 (1994): 644–68.

10. Jonathan Unger and Kaxton Siu, "Chinese Migrant Factory Workers across Four Decades: Shifts in Work Conditions, Urbanization, and Family Strategies," *Labor History* 60, no. 6 (2019): 765–78.

11. Chan and Buckingham, "Is China Abolishing the *Hukou* System?"; Zhonghua Guo and Tuo Liang, "Differentiating Citizenship in Urban China: A Case Study of Dongguan City," *Citizenship Studies* 21, no. 7 (2017): 773–91.

12. Tao Liu and Qiujie Shi, "Acquiring a Beijing *Hukou*: Who Is Eligible and Who Is Successful?," *China Quarterly*, no. 243 (2020): 855–68.

13. On the *hukou* system, see Kam Wing Chan, *Cities with Invisible Walls: Reinterpreting Urbanization in Post-1949 China* (New York: Oxford University Press, 1994); Chan, "The Chinese *Hukou* System at 50"; Chan and Buckingham, "Is China Abolishing the *Hukou* System?"; Chan and Zhang "The *Hukou* System and Rural-Urban Migration"; Fan, "The Elite, the Natives, and the Outsiders"; Solinger, *Contesting Citizenship in Urban China*.

14. For more on Xi's power centralization and authoritarian consolidation, see Elizabeth Economy, *The Third Revolution: Xi Jinping and the New Chinese State* (New York: Oxford University Press, 2018); Carl Minzner, *End of an Era: How China's Authoritarian Revival Is Undermining Its Rise* (New York: Oxford University Press, 2018).

15. Michael Lipsky, *Street-Level Bureaucracy: Dilemmas of the Individual in Public Services* (New York: Russell Sage Foundation, 1980).

16. Susan H. Whiting, "The Cadre Evaluation System at the Grass Roots: The Paradox of Party Rule," in *Holding China Together: Diversity and National Integration in the Post-Deng Era*, ed. Barry Naughton and Dali Yang (New York: Cambridge University Press, 2004), 101–19; Kevin J. O'Brien and Lianjiang Li, "Selective Policy Implementation in Rural China," *Comparative Politics* 31, no. 2 (1999): 167–86.

17. Maria Edin, "State Capacity and Local Agent Control in China: CCP Cadre Management from a Township Perspective," *China Quarterly*, no. 173 (2003): 35–52.

18. Dali L. Yang, "China's Looming Labor Shortage," *Far Eastern Economic Review* 168, no. 2 (2005): 19–24.

19. Yuming Cui, Jingjing Meng, and Changrong Lu, "Recent Developments in China's Labor Market: Labor Shortage, Rising Wages and Their Implications," *Review of Development Economics* 22, no. 3 (2018): 1217–38.

20. Interview with factory-government liaison, Dongguan, December 2010.

21. Interviews with factory-government liaison, Dongguan, December 2010, and economics scholar, Guangzhou, January 2011.

22. The number is calculated from China Labour Bulletin, "Strike Map," 2018, http://maps.clb.org.hk/strikes/en.

23. China Labour Bulletin, "Strike Map."

24. See "Guangzhou laodong zhengyi susong qingkuang baipishu (2014–2016)" (White paper on labor dispute litigation in Guangzhou [2014–2016]),Guangzhou Shenpan Wang, May 12, 2017, http://www.gzcourt .gov.cn/upfile/File/201705/12/101657100.pdf.

25. Manfred Elfstrom and Sarosh Kuruvilla, "The Changing Nature of Labor Unrest in China," *ILR Review* 67, no. 2 (2014): 453–80.

26. Ngai Pun and Huilin Lu, "Unfinished Proletarianization: Self, Anger, and Class Action among the Second Generation of Peasant-Workers in Present-Day China," *Modern China* 36, no. 5 (2010): 493–519.

27. Interviews with migrant workers, Beijing, December 2010, and nongovernmental organization (NGO) staff member, Chengdu, July 2012.

28. Interviews with migrant workers, Beijing, December 2010, and Chengdu, July 2012.

29. See, for example, Whyte, *One Country, Two Societies*; Yuen Yuen Ang, *How China Escaped the Poverty Trap* (Ithaca, NY: Cornell University Press, 2016).

30. Li Keqiang, "Li Keqiang Expounds on Urbanization," China.org.cn, May 26, 2013, http://www.china.org.cn/china/2013-05/26/content_28934485.htm.

31. Li, "Li Keqiang Expounds on Urbanization."

32. Li Keqiang, "Full Text of Premier Li Keqiang's Speech at the Opening Ceremony of the Annual Meeting of the New Champions 2019," State Council, July 4, 2019, http://english.www.gov.cn/premier/speeches/2019/07/04/content _281476747574784.htm.

33. State Council, "Guojia xinxing chengzhen hua guihua."

34. State Council, "Xi: Principal Contradiction Facing Chinese Society Has Evolved in New Era," October 18, 2017, http://english.www.gov.cn/news/top _news/2017/10/18/content_281475912458156.htm.

35. The State Council Information Office released a white paper titled "Development of China's Public Health as an Essential Element of Human Rights" in 2017. For the text, see State Council Information Office, accessed 2019, https:// www.scio.gov.cn/32618/Document/1565200/1565200.htm.

36. National Development and Reform Commission, "2019 nian xinxing chengzhen hua jianshe zhongdian renwu" (Key tasks of new-type urbanization construction in 2019), April 2019, http://www.ndrc.gov.cn/zcfb/zcfbtz/201904/W020190408339953053184.pdf.

37. Li, "Li Keqiang Expounds on Urbanization."

38. "Beijing's Point-Based Hukou System to Open for Annual Application," Xinhua, May 17, 2019, http://www.xinhuanet.com/english/2019-05/17/c_138067093.htm.

39. Interviews with social welfare scholar, Beijing, March 2012; former education official, Chengdu, May 2012; and NGO staff member, Shanghai, July 2017.

40. "China Urbanization Cost Could Top $106 Billion a Year: Think-Tank," Reuters, July 30, 2013, https://www.reuters.com/article/us-china-economy-urbanisation/china-urbanization-cost-could-top-106-billion-a-year-think-tank-idUSBRE96T0JS20130730.

41. Alexsia T. Chan and Kevin J. O'Brien, "Phantom Services: Deflecting Migrant Workers in China," *China Journal*, no. 81 (2019): 103–22.

42. People's Republic of China Central People's Government, "Beijing chengshi zongti guihua (2016 nian–2035 nian) fubu" (Beijing Municipal Master Plan [2016–2035] released), September 30, 2017, http://www.gov.cn/xinwen/2017-09/30/content_5228705.htm; People's Government of Beijing, "Report on the Work of the Government 2018 (Part 1)," March 27, 2018, http://www.ebeijing.gov.cn/Government/reports/t1513295.htm.

43. Cited in Huizhao Huang, Shulun Huang, and Qiuyu Ren, "Government Report Calls for Serious Reform of Residency System for Migrants," *Caixin*, February 1, 2019, https://www.caixinglobal.com/2019-02-01/government-report-calls-for-serious-reform-of-residency-system-for-migrants-101377233.html.

44. Huang, Huang, and Ren, "Government Report Calls for Serious Reform."

45. Interviews with migrant workers, Beijing, December 2011.

46. Interview with school principal, Beijing, March 2012.

47. Interview with migrant worker, Guangzhou, July 2017.

48. Interview with NGO staff member, Shanghai, July 2017.

49. Interview with migrant worker, Shanghai, July 2017.

50. Interview with migrant worker, Beijing, December 2011.

51. Interviews with scholar-activist, Chengdu, May 2012, and school principal, Chengdu, May 2012.

52. Interviews with doctor, Guangzhou, July 2017, and scholar-activist, Chengdu, July 2017.

53. John Knight and Ramani Gunatilaka, "Rural-Urban Migration and Happiness in China," in *World Happiness Report 2018*, ed. John F. Helliwell, Richard Layard, and Jeffrey D. Sachs (New York: Sustainable Development Solutions Network, 2018), 67–88.

54. Interview with migrant worker, Guangzhou, July 2017.

PART THREE

Surveillance
and Political Control

6

Xi Jinping's Surveillance State
Merging Digital Technology and Grassroots Organizations

Deng Kai, David Demes, and Chih-Jou Jay Chen

From Xi Jinping's rise to power in late 2012 until the eruption of the COVID-19 pandemic in China and the rest of the world in 2020, the most significant change in Chinese politics and society was the authoritarian regime's increasing suppression of civil rights and intensifying mass surveillance. Compared with the Jiang Zemin and Hu Jintao eras, the Party-state under the strongman rule of Xi Jinping strengthened its control of civil society and tightened its censorship of both media and the Internet. In response to ongoing challenges by rights defense lawyers, nongovernmental organization activists, and various forms of collective protests, the regime implemented a severe and comprehensive crackdown.[1]

Xi Jinping's regime has achieved comprehensive mass surveillance. The country's current state of social surveillance is the product of a continuous process of institutionalization and infrastructure construction since the mid-2000s. Policy under previous leaders Hu Jintao and Wen Jiabao (2002–12) prioritized "stability maintenance," or social management to deal with collective resistance. In contrast, in response to increasing resistance and dissent, the Xi era elevates social protest management to total surveillance by mobilizing both traditional state apparatus and digital technologies.[2]

After 2015, the role of digital technology in social surveillance expanded rapidly. The COVID-19 pandemic serves as a case study to reveal the government's strategy: mobilizing grassroots governments and communities and using digital technologies for effective population monitoring and control. This approach demonstrates both the continuity and discontinuity of the Chinese surveillance state under Xi Jinping's leadership.

The Institutional Evolution of Mass Surveillance:
From Hu to Xi

As the end of the Hu administration approached in 2011, the central government enacted the 12th Five-Year Plan (2011–15), which for the first time expressed the need to build a national population database to enhance the state's intelligence gathering, social control, and emergency response capabilities.[3] In November 2013, a decision of the Third Plenary Session of the 18th Chinese Communist Party (CCP) Central Committee pointed out that the particular characteristic of social governance was that it must "address both symptoms and root causes while emphasizing the root causes, using grid management to enhance the integrated system of service and management at the grassroots level." This was the first time the term *grid management* (*wanggehua guanli*) had been mentioned in a policy document of the Central Committee.[4]

The 13th Five-Year Plan (2016–20) announced that the government would "establish a national database with basic information on the population" and "strengthen the construction of institutions such as population management, real-name registration, credit systems, and crisis early warning and intervention."[5] The document also proposed to "improve assessment and accountability mechanisms" of the government's performance in the realm of social governance.[6] In terms of grassroots governance, it prescribed to organically link "community, social organizations, and social workers" to achieve digitalized one-stop services and to increase the number of registered volunteers to 13 percent of the resident population.[7]

During the later years of Hu Jintao's administration, the Chinese state utilized its capacity to penetrate society through the existing Party-state system. However, under the leadership of Xi Jinping, the state has expanded its reach by developing social organizations and mobilizing volunteers through Party branches while closely monitoring and suppressing groups such as religious groups, ethnic minorities, dissidents, and petitioners. The Cyber Security Law was passed in June 2017, legalizing the Public Security Bureau's access to user data collected by private companies. This law strengthened and expanded data collection and surveillance under Xi Jinping's leadership at the national level. Additionally, at a work conference in the same year, Xi Jinping called for building a cybersecurity defense line, raising the level of network security protection, and strengthening the defense of key information infrastructure. He also emphasized the need to achieve all-weather and all-round awareness, as well as effective protection.[8]

Methods employed by the Chinese surveillance state to achieve its goals include grassroots grid management, extensive digital surveillance, censorship by the Cyberspace Administration of China (CAC), mandatory real-name registration, labor-intensive online monitoring, and social credit systems that evaluate individuals' daily behavior. All of these components have become integral to the Chinese surveillance state during the Xi era.

Grid Management

For decades, the smallest units of the CCP's top-to-bottom system of urban control were the "work units," or *danwei*, in government agencies, factories, schools, and neighborhood or residents' committees. However, China's economic reform process broke up this "cellular society" centered around the work unit, leading to the emergence of large numbers of employees outside of it. Urbanization further fostered the emergence of a significant "floating" population.[9] To address this shift, the grid management model was introduced as a novel approach to community governance in contemporary China. First implemented as experimental work in Beijing's Dongcheng District in 2004, this social management model involves expanding the personnel of grassroots Party organizations, extending their coverage to residential buildings, and equipping them with advanced information technology tools to monitor and address the behavior of community residents.[10] "Gridding" in China refers to the practice of subdividing a community into individual grid cells, which are then used as a unit for government management. At the grassroots level, all permanent fixtures within each grid cell are identified and coded. If any public security or criminal cases, group protests, or activities by persons considered sensitive occur within a particular grid cell, they are classified and coded.[11] Each grid cell is assigned a supervisor, a police officer, and assistants. Each staff member is equipped with an intelligent terminal or smartphone that uses a particular grid management software system to record and instantly transfer information on the situation of all people inside the cell to the grid command center at the township level. If an incident occurs somewhere, the command center will send reinforcements to deal with it.

By the end of 2016, 93 percent of communities (villages) across China had adopted grid management.[12] Grid assistants use a mobile app to upload information and report problems.[13] They also recruit volunteers from various social groups to join the grid team. For example, in the Changping District of Beijing, hundreds of couriers were recruited as grid management volunteers, and their delivery schedule in the community was fully incorporated into the state's daily grassroots governance.[14]

Grid management at the community level has become a significant source of infrastructural power for the surveillance state. Neighborhood committees gather information about social or physical disorder through real-time monitoring and grid worker patrols to identify incidents that require reporting. In this context, minor risks such as restaurant hygiene and waste management may be exaggerated or even fabricated to allow officials to "solve" them and improve their performance evaluations. Meanwhile, serious incidents such as mass protests may not be reported, as grassroots cadres may want to downplay such cases to create the illusion of good governance and avoid punishment.[15] Moreover, while grid management can identify local protests at an early stage, it can hardly stop citizens, especially the urban middle class, from rallying to express common demands, as demonstrated by the "white paper" protests against the zero-COVID policy in late 2022.

Synthesizing Surveillance

Mass surveillance in China today includes Internet surveillance, video surveillance in public areas, and other tactics making use of digital technologies. Under Xi's leadership, a significant step toward mass surveillance was the establishment of "synthetic operations centers" (*hecheng zuozhan zhongxin*) by public security departments across the country. First established in Hangzhou with the technology company Alibaba's assistance in 2013, the centers were soon promoted nationwide.[16] The synthetic operations centers integrate information from different departments within the Public Security Bureau, including cybersecurity, criminal investigation, and economic crime investigation units, together with information from the Skynet Project (*Tianwang Gongcheng*), composed of citywide surveillance cameras, as well as Internet user data collected by cybersecurity and other agencies. For example, Jiayuguan City in Gansu Province used big data provided by its synthetic operations center to integrate and analyze criminal cases. Reportedly, in 2017–19, the city assembled twenty-seven major categories, or about three hundred million pieces of data, and, through research and analysis, cracked more than 460 cases of fraud and theft, with more than thirty criminal suspects arrested.[17]

The synthetic operations centers primarily rely on intelligence collected by the surveillance infrastructure that has been established through the projects Safe City (Ping'an Chengshi), Skynet, and Bright-as-Snow (Xueliang).

Safe City is a cyber prevention and control system based on government personnel and video surveillance. During the second term of the Hu Jintao administration (2008–12), each prefecture-level city in China set up a pilot site to test the Safe City project. After 2015, the project was expanded to a nationwide network. The Skynet project was built on the foundations of Safe City, but it increased the number of surveillance cameras and also added facial recognition to improve data analysis capabilities. In 2015, it was reported that the government's blanket network of surveillance cameras in Beijing had achieved 100 percent coverage of all major streets.[18] Although authorities have tried to present the system as a crime-solving tool, the extensive coverage of Skynet has obvious applications when it comes to tracking dissidents, petitioners, and protesters.

In 2016, following Skynet, the central government approved the Bright-as-Snow Project, which enables police, grassroots cadres, and security volunteers to view public surveillance videos and face recognition results in urban communities and villages via regular TV sets and smartphones. As with the twenty million Skynet cameras already in place throughout China's urban areas, the Bright-as-Snow Project is pegged as a public safety measure to help detect all kinds of illegal behaviors more effectively. By 2020, the Chinese government was scheduled to have integrated public cameras into the online-sharing system, applying facial recognition technology to build a nationwide surveillance network to ensure public security.[19]

Through the synthetic operations centers and infrastructure projects such as Skynet and Bright-as-Snow, public security organs and grid management personnel, relying on video surveillance, as well as user data of Internet services, are able to achieve effective social surveillance.

Mass Surveillance under Xi

The implementation of mass surveillance in the Xi Jinping era began with the reformation of the State Internet Information Office into the Cyberspace Administration of China, or CAC, which places increasing emphasis on censorship and control of online activities. Under the auspices of Xi and the CAC, the state has largely successfully established the Internet real-name registration system and delegated the labor-intensive task of monitoring and censoring online activities to Internet companies. The state has also gradually established a social credit system to strengthen surveillance and control by rewarding "good" citizen behavior and punishing "bad" behavior.

The CAC as a "Super-Internet Party Branch"

On May 4, 2011, the State Internet Information Office was founded as the top state agency in charge of the supervision of online content.[20] The institution was reorganized in 2014 and became the CAC. The CAC's specific functions include the approval of news websites and content, the investigation and punishment of illegal content, censorship, and the control of video games and online publishing, videos, and other content. In addition to its in-house employees, the CAC has organized a huge team of volunteers. While these volunteers initially reported mostly fraudulent online behavior, the scope of their reporting responsibilities has been expanded to include politically sensitive content. Although the CAC does not have the authority to arrest people, it has the power to interview persons in charge, delete accounts, and shut down Internet service companies.

By 2014, various provinces and cities had established their own Internet Information Offices. Among them, the Beijing Internet Information Office has been instructed by the CAC to monitor the news content produced by China's major news portals and social media sites such as Tencent, Sina, Sohu, Netease, and Phoenix.[21] In addition, the Internet Information Offices of Shanghai, Guangzhou, and Shenzhen are responsible for the news content websites in their jurisdictions.

In 2015, the CAC implemented the "Work Regulations on Interviews of Entities Providing Internet News Information Services." These regulations specify that "the term 'interview' refers to the administrative act of a local Internet information office meeting the relevant person in charge, conducting a conversation that involves a warning, pointing out the problem, and instructing the person to rectify or correct their behavior when a serious violation of the law or regulation is committed by an entity providing Internet news information services."[22] Companies not only need to censor user-produced content but also are required to investigate content reported by netizens. They also are subject to annual inspections and daily assessments by the Internet Information Offices. Yet, it is not just the information companies themselves that are important as network monitoring forces. The Voluntary 50 Cent Party (Ziganwu), whose nationalist Internet users have been active on social media platforms since the 2000s, have been more successful in reaching Internet users with their patriotic rhetoric than state agencies have. Followers attack liberal Internet users' arguments that challenge the regime.[23] With the intervention of the Internet Information Office in the day-to-day operations of social media platforms, the Voluntary 50 Cent Party has likewise become an important force in reporting, censorship, and information gathering.

For example, on July 1, 2016, an editor at Tencent News made a typographical error that insinuated Xi had "flipped out" (*fabiao*) during an important speech (Xi Jinping fabiao zhongyao tanhua). This incident resulted in the transfer of supervisory power over Tencent from the Shenzhen Internet Information Office to the Beijing Internet Information Office. Authorities then used this incident to shut down many comment sections on social media and user-generated content channels on portals such as Sina, Netease, Sohu, and iFeng (Phoenix). This crackdown reduced the space for free speech and caused online portals that had become mainstream during the Hu administration to gradually become propaganda tools of the Party-state.[24] Meanwhile, interviews with corporate personnel increased as the state tightened its ideological control. In 2015 and 2016, the Internet Information Offices conducted 820 and 678 interviews, respectively, with relevant companies across the country. The frequency of interviews increased dramatically, reaching 2,003 in 2017 due to the implementation of the Cybersecurity Law, which went into effect on June 1, 2017.[25]

In 2017, the government promulgated regulations on data management in Internet groups, making group founders of an online forum or chat group responsible for user comments circulating in those groups. For this purpose, companies are required to equip themselves with professional staff and technical capabilities to establish real-name registration of users, censorship of online discussions, and data security protection.[26] After the implementation of these management regulations, many WeChat groups were repeatedly shut down and reopened, causing a digital limbo that became a common phenomenon. At the end of 2018, the CAC introduced twelve additional regulations to further govern postings on Weibo, WeChat group discussions, WeChat public platforms, followers' comments, chat groups, forum communities, and more. These regulations increased state control over the Chinese Internet, extending from the public sphere to the confines of private chat groups.[27] For example, in 2018, *Q Daily* (Haoqixin ribao), which was known as China's last liberal online media outlet, received a rectification notice from the CAC requesting that the site shut down and reflect on its errors for one month.[28] In November 2020, *Q Daily*'s app and official accounts on WeChat and Sina Weibo stopped receiving updates and appeared to be inactive.[29] In another example, in April 2019, the CAC alleged that Sina "continued to spread illegal and harmful information such as sensationalizing misdirection, vulgar pornography, and fake news" and punished Sina by suspending its blog and news service for a month.[30]

As the CAC has become the key actor in China's Internet governance, online public spaces are not only monitored and blocked by the state but also subject to surveillance by broad social forces. The CAC has proactively mobilized the masses by forming a large number of volunteer teams that far exceed the size of its in-house workforce. However, volunteers may report false and illegal information online, and swarms of netizens hurl insults at users who articulate liberal views or challenge official narratives. Under such conditions, the Internet police of the various Public Security Bureaus have additional time and energy to focus on monitoring the speech and activities of political dissidents.

In short, the CAC has effectively become the "Super-Internet Party Branch." The institution represents the state's significantly enhanced control over the Internet in the Xi era. Real-name registration, integration of platforms, and labor-intensive online surveillance, as well as the social credit system, are key developments under the CAC.

Real-Name Registration

Real-name registration is the most critical feature of social surveillance. It has been mandatory on China's social media networks since 2012. After the widespread adoption of smartphones, SMS (Short Message Service) verification codes have become the standard method for real-name verification. Real-name registration was not only a clearly stated policy in the 13th Five-Year Plan's chapters on social governance but was also further codified in China's Cybersecurity Law that went into effect on June 1, 2017. As of 2015, there were still 130 million mobile phone users in China who had not yet completed real-name registration.[31] In 2016, the authorities ordered their accounts blocked, requiring users to provide real-name authentication; failure to do so would result in permanent suspension of their accounts.[32] A clear goal of achieving a 100 percent real-name registration rate was set for June 30, 2017.[33]

In February 2018, the state-funded and state-controlled Cloud Big Data Industrial Development Company in Guizhou obtained the rights to operate data storage facilities for Apple's iCloud service in China.[34] Since then, almost all mainstream Internet service applications in China have completed instituting real-name registration mechanisms. To comply with the Cybersecurity

Law, in addition to Apple, companies such as Evernote, Microsoft, and Steam have all created separate Chinese versions and databases of their services. They are required to provide user data to the police upon request.[35]

The Labor-Intensive Digital Surveillance

In the Xi Jinping era, the number of mobile Internet users has increased from 420 million in 2012 to 1.051 billion in 2022, and their share of all Internet users in the country has also increased from 74.5 percent in 2012 to 99.6 percent in 2022.[36] When smartphones connect to the Internet, they can disclose a lot of private information, including personal location, movement trajectories, daily routines, web surfing habits, key logging habits, speech, address books (analog social networks), and more. With the 2017 Cybersecurity Law, the state can harvest citizens' personal information with the help of Internet companies.

In March 2019, the hacker and cyber activist Victor Gevers broke into the backbone network of China Telecom and discovered that it had been archiving chat records of large groups of users since 2018 from platforms such as Tencent QQ, WeChat, and Apple's iMessage. The database included names, ID numbers, profile pictures, GPS locations, and network information, among other details. It was synchronized with the Public Security Bureaus of various provinces and cities for purposes of censorship and surveillance.[37] This system shows that communication software companies, such as WeChat, provide data, while state-owned telecommunications companies, such as China Telecom, are responsible for integrating the data, and public security agencies conduct screening and manual reviews. The multiparty collaboration can be used to identify dissident networks and then suppress them further. It can also be used to directly silence online expression, meaning that users who engage in dissenting speech on WeChat may face banning, detention, and even criminal conviction. For instance, in 2017, Wang Jiangfeng, a petitioner from Zhaoyuan, Shandong, was arrested and sentenced to two years in prison for "picking quarrels and stirring up trouble" after he criticized Xi Jinping and Mao Zedong in a WeChat group.[38] Furthermore, his defense attorney Zhu Shengwu had his law license revoked by the Department of Justice of Shandong Province after he released to the public information relevant to the case.[39]

Monitoring online content has become a labor-intensive industry for Internet companies. In 2013, a Reuters reporter visited Sina Weibo's censorship office in Tianjin and found that the censors numbered as many as

150 people. The office operated on a rotating shift basis, with employees working twenty-four hours a day. Each censor was expected to review three thousand social media posts per hour.[40] As of 2020, social media platforms have become more diversified and, as a result, content censorship efforts have increased in scale, becoming an obligatory burden for content media. The main focus of content censorship is on netizens' responses to news posts. Often, a popular news item will attract hundreds of thousands, or even millions, of responses in a very short time. Jinan in Shandong has become known as the "content censorship capital," as companies, including People. cn (affiliated with the *People's Daily*), ByteDance, and iFeng.com (Phoenix), have all established their content censorship teams there. An investigative report by *Southern Weekly* in April 2019 later ordered to be deleted by the propaganda department, disclosed that ByteDance, which operates social media products such as Toutiao.com and TikTok, had an army of more than three thousand censors in Jinan alone.[41] The job of a "content censor" requires young people who have a college degree, stamina, and good eyesight and can work late hours. Applicants should be able to identify sensitive information. However, such work can be extremely draining, even for young people, and Internet companies have seen a significant increase in personnel costs. In other words, both the state and the private sector have to bear heavy personnel and financial burdens to ensure the smooth operation of the surveillance state.

The Social Credit System

China's social credit system can be divided into three categories. The first is "good citizen behavior," which is spearheaded by the central government. The second is the traditional personal financial credit reporting system composed of banks, which provide critical information to assess a customer's credit rating. The third category comprises unofficial private versions of social credit systems that are operated by companies such as Ant Financial's Sesame Credit. Ant Financial is the payment firm that was spun out of Alibaba. These systems use shopping habits and other user data to inform credit-style scores on an opt-in basis.[42] The private systems, such as Sesame Credit, are sometimes mistaken for government plans, but they are not officially part of the government's system.

In 2016, China's central government proposed a "unified social credit identifier system" in its policy outline. Specific policy ideas include giving priority in administrative procedures and public services to those with good credit records. In contrast, those who jeopardize public safety, disrupt public order, refuse to perform legal or military service obligations, and so forth should be considered as having poor credit records. Their access to public services or certain rights should be restricted.[43] At a government meeting in June 2016, Xi Jinping talked about "establishing a pattern of credit punishment where 'one dishonesty must lead to restriction everywhere,' so that the dishonest people cannot do anything at all."[44] The punishments include restrictions on leaving the country, buying real estate, taking airplanes or high-speed trains, going on vacations, staying in star-rated hotels, and other high-spending consumer behaviors. Moreover, the state encourages relevant mass organizations, institutions, companies, associations, and so on to provide information generated by their "red lists" (with individuals worth praising) and "blacklists" (punished persons) to government departments for reference.[45]

There are many cases where social credit was used to "blacklist" certain people, such as the famous investigative reporter Liu Hu, who was subjected to judicial persecution for exposing corruption in 2013.[46] Being placed on a blacklist can have serious consequences. In March 2018, the government announced that individuals such as Liu Hu, who were under investigation for administrative or criminal liabilities by the Public Security Bureau, would be prohibited from traveling by plane or high-speed train. Those who committed significant tax or financial violations would face similar penalties for a period ranging from several months to one year.[47] At the end of 2018, there were a total of 14.21 million blacklist records in Public Credit Information Centers across China. The courts had issued 12.77 million entries on dishonest persons and prevented 17.46 million and 5.47 million attempts to purchase air and high-speed tickets, respectively. At the same time, in that year a total of 2.17 million creditors were removed from the blacklist after paying arrears and performing penance as ordered by the court. The courts recovered a total of ¥4.44 trillion.[48]

The social credit system is extensively used, mainly for regulating the behavior of individual citizens. In economic court cases, it provides judges with a basis for rulings and guarantees the enforcement of established regulations, ensuring the implementation of restrictions and penalties. Additionally, it can reward citizens with good credit.[49] The promotion and implementation of the social credit system demonstrates the Chinese government's ability and willingness to apply technology to state governance. However, while some polls and media interviews suggest that Chinese citizens generally support the government's implementation of the social credit system and expect it to improve social trust, other sources report mixed views on this matter.[50] Regulations and implementation of the social credit system still vary greatly from city to city across China. While government propaganda emphasizes the system's potential to combat scams, fraud, and other issues, public opinion on the matter is divided. Some believe that the social credit system will improve public order and have a greater governance effect than moral persuasion alone, while others express concerns about the system's potential misuse and infringement on privacy rights.[51] However, even though citizens express high trust in the social credit system, their participation rates remain low due to concerns about the system's algorithmic and information security risks and capabilities.[52] The current literature remains cautious about the future of social credit systems, as excessive intervention may increase distrust between the state and society.

Changes in the Surveillance and Repression of Disadvantaged Groups

One of the key features of Xi Jinping's rule has been the use of digital and mass surveillance to monitor and suppress disadvantaged groups, including petitioners, ethnic minorities, religious groups, and peasants. When the rights of disadvantaged social groups are violated by local governments, they often have no recourse but to protest against the higher-level governments. However, the local governments see them as troublemakers and subject them to surveillance and repression.

Petitioners

The top priority of local governments regarding petitions has been to reduce the number of petitioners, especially those involved in collective petitions or requesting intervention from higher-level governments (known as *yueji shangfang*, or "leapfrog petitions"). Local authorities have been instructed to coordinate with governmental agencies at all levels to identify potential petitioners and intercept them before they can file a formal complaint.

According to Chinese state media, the number of petitions lodged against the government dropped by about a quarter across China between 2013 and 2016. This figure was released during a major propaganda campaign to highlight the country's achievements during Xi's first five-year term.[53] One reason for the decrease in the number of petitions received by relevant authorities was the announcement, in 2014, of new petitioning procedures by the National Public Complaints and Proposals Administration (NPCPA, or Guojia

Xinfangju). Starting May 1 of that year, petition authorities would no longer accept in-person visits from petitioners who "skipped levels" (leapfrogged), while written petitions sent via the Internet or traditional mail would not be subject to such restrictions.[54] The ban on leapfrog petitions and the new transparency regarding petition information have increased local governments' willingness to address petitioner complaints. As a result, the number of petitions and visitors to the NPCPA in Beijing has significantly decreased.[55]

Furthermore, the promotion of "online petitions" has reduced the need for in-person petitions. Petitioners can now track their petitions online and check which departments are handling their cases, as well as learn about processing results. In the first half of 2018, the number of online petitions processed by the NPCPA accounted for more than 50 percent of all petitions, demonstrating that the Internet has become the primary channel for petitioning in China.[56]

Although changes to the petition system have reduced the number of petitioners, especially those who go to Beijing, they have shifted most of the pressure to local governments. As a result, petitioners often face violent interception and detention, on the one hand, and increased government control and mediation efforts, on the other. For example, the government uses digital monitoring to intercept petitioners. Not only are their WeChat conversations monitored, but they are also frequently harassed or detained by the police.[57] In 2017, a facial recognition system was installed in the waiting area of Shanghai's main railway station, and efforts to investigate and detect suspicious persons during key periods were strengthened.[58]

However, despite these measures, people still engage in leapfrog petitions. For instance, in November 2017, over two thousand private teachers from more than twenty provinces across the country went to petition at the Ministry of Education in Beijing. According to one petitioner, the authorities had intercepted many fellow petitioners through surveillance on WeChat. While digital surveillance and local grassroots stability control measures may have reduced the number of participants in the petition, they did not succeed in preventing it from happening.[59] Another example concerns the petition of peer-to-peer (P2P) financial victims. In August 2018, many individuals who had suffered significant financial losses due to the collapse of P2P online lending platforms went to Beijing to petition the government. However, Shanghai police reportedly used special devices to search the contents of mobile phones in subways and railway stations, possibly in an attempt to intercept petitioners.[60] Nevertheless, these preemptive measures failed to prevent all petitioners from traveling to Beijing.

The Chinese government has been particularly severe in suppressing collective mobilization of religious groups. This is evident not only in the strengthening of social suppression in both Xinjiang (see Musapir's chapter in this volume) and Tibet but also in the targeting of religious organizations and activities in Han-majority areas. For example, in 2013, Zhejiang launched an urban renewal campaign that specifically targeted the houses of Christians, which were deemed illegal structures. In just one year, 100 churches and 426 crosses were razed in Zhejiang alone.[61] During the demolition process, dozens of protests by the affected communities and conflicts with the police occurred.

In 2018, observers noted the most severe religious repression in China in recent years. One of the earliest indications of this crackdown was the removal of Christian and Islamic books from online bookstores on March 30. The situation was particularly challenging in Henan, which has a sizable Christian population. Even the Three-Self Patriotic Movement, China's state-controlled church, faced suppression there. In August of that year, the city of Yongcheng in Henan Province forced the temporary closure of 100 out of 180 Three-Self churches.[62] Official justifications for the closures and demolitions of churches have varied, ranging from a supposed lack of parishioners to allegations that the churches were built illegally or located too close to government buildings and schools.[63] In December 2018, China's largest Protestant house church, the Early Rain Covenant Church in Chengdu, was forcibly disbanded, affecting hundreds of parishioners. Its founder, Wang Yi, his wife, and several priests were either criminally detained or forcibly disappeared.[64]

In addition to heavy-handed clampdowns, new social surveillance methods have emerged in China. The state has intensified its investigation of the religious population and gained comprehensive access to their data, enabling the creation of big data platforms for surveillance purposes.[65] For instance, in Henan Province, the government has launched the Religious Affairs Management and Service Platform to register and classify Protestants.[66] Jiangxi Province has not only collected and documented basic information on religious sites but has also established Bright-as-Snow Project systems at these sites, which have instilled fear in many believers.[67]

Mass Surveillance in Times of COVID-19

During the COVID-19 pandemic from 2019 to 2022, surveillance facilities that were initially intended to target specific groups of people expanded their monitoring scope to include the general public. As a result, grassroots communities were able to monitor the entire local population in order to meet the requirements for pandemic control. For example, in Pinghu, a county-level city in Jiaxing, Zhejiang, China mobilized grassroots-level governments and communities to monitor and control its population during the COVID-19 pandemic.[68]

Grassroots Control: The Case of Pinghu

In 2019, Pinghu became the first city in Zhejiang Province to implement the so-called Red Property (Hongse Wuye) project, which aims to integrate government, residents, and construction companies under state leadership in small commercial housing communities. The implementation of Red Property has given grassroots community Party committees more power and organizational resources, extending control from the "grid manager" (*wanggezhang*) to the "hallway manager" (*loudaozhang*) of residential housing, resulting in even more finely tuned community control.[69]

On January 23, 2020, Wuhan, the epicenter of the pandemic, announced a citywide lockdown. However, one day before that, the Pinghu County Party Committee had already convened a meeting to convey instructions from their superiors and establish a leading group for pandemic prevention and containment work. Working groups were established in all subdistricts (*jiedao*) at the township level and in relevant departments, with their main tasks including improving hospital fever clinics and infection control, centrally regulating farmers' markets and various business sites, strengthening disinfection and ventilation on public transport, and supervising large-scale public gatherings during the Spring Festival.[70] On January 27, the Pinghu government established three checkpoints to carry out meticulous inspections based on the community grid. They took the temperature of drivers at road checkpoints and isolated people who had come into contact with infected persons. In addition to the cadres currently on the job, the government also mobilized veterans, retired cadres, and young volunteers to participate in this work.[71] On January 31, the city of Pinghu established 162 temporary Party organizations and frontline posts (*chongfenggang*). Communist Party members were mobilized to assist at medical work posts and centralized isolation work posts, as well as to provide one-on-one care for home isolation and carry out inspection work at checkpoints.[72] Despite all of these efforts, the number of newly infected people in Zhejiang continued to rise from the end of January to February in all cities, including Pinghu.

On February 3, the Pinghu government announced a lockdown of the city, refusing entry to individuals without local household registration and controlling the movement of people and vehicles entering or leaving the city.[73] On February 6, the municipal government issued a public notice on closed community management, which relied on grassroots community and village Party committees for implementation. Specific measures included closing residential communities, isolating residents who had traveled through pandemic areas within the previous fourteen days, and escalating propaganda efforts.[74]

Besides controlling social activities and population mobility through community gridding, local governments were also under pressure to resume industrial production. To facilitate this resumption, the Pinghu government established an online platform for companies to declare their readiness to resume work and stationed Party and government officials in these companies. In early February, over two hundred officials were deployed to guide and supervise pandemic prevention measures, report difficulties to the municipal government, and assist companies in resuming production.[75] The number of stationed cadres had increased to 709 by the end of the month.[76] To address the labor shortage, the Pinghu government reached out to local governments in inland provinces to recruit workers, arranged transportation for returning workers through chartered buses and flights, and established mutual recognition of their respective health codes.

The Health Code: Data-Based Governance during a Pandemic

While many communities across the country remained under strict control in February 2020, business activities gradually resumed. At this time, the health code—a quick response (QR) code on a mobile phone rating the user's risk of exposure to the coronavirus—began to play an essential role in the government's containment efforts. The apps that facilitated the health code were hosted by China's top technology companies: Alibaba, Tencent, and Baidu. At checkpoints throughout the city, police and security guards demanded that anyone seeking to enter or leave must present the health QR code. A green code granted unrestricted movement, while a yellow code required seven days of quarantine, and red meant fourteen days of quarantine.

To receive a rating, users must download an app embedded in one of the tech giants' ubiquitous payment, messaging, or search engine platforms, which require users to register their basic personal information and health condition. By March, the codes were widely adopted by local governments, public facilities, businesses, and farms across the country. When the code is scanned, a limited amount of personal data is accessed through the phone. Some codes pull mobile phone data from telephone companies to see where the user has been, while others confirm personal health information, such as whether the user has completed a mandatory quarantine. The data used to generate the health code comes from three main sources: self-reported information, including personal details provided by users when applying for or updating their health code; travel information obtained through location-based services; and information provided by various institutions, such as the local government's e-government system, the community e-pass, the city's resumption of work application database, and the city's fever clinic patient database. The system links and integrates this data and assesses the health status of residents according to rules and algorithms set by the local government. As such, it has become a digital tool for population control in various scenarios during the pandemic.[77]

The reason why China was able to build the health code system so quickly lies in the "national big data strategy" proposed by the Chinese government's 13th Five-Year Plan in 2016. The strategic plan included an investment in resources to establish an information-sharing platform for government departments, aimed at promoting "industrial transformation and upgrade, as well as innovation in social governance."[78] The public data and e-government management measures of Zhejiang Province stipulate that public management and service agencies in Zhejiang should share public data with each other free of charge. Unless there is a legal, regulatory, or rule basis, these agencies are not allowed to refuse data-sharing requests from other agencies.[79] Policies and regulations such as these help to break down information barriers between various government departments. Population databases, including those maintained by the police, medical services, and household registration departments, form the basis of government-owned data. When the government expresses a demand to enterprises with strong research and development capabilities, such as Alibaba and Tencent, these companies swiftly connect various databases and invest in their use. In other words, the extensive health code program was made possible because of the close cooperation and information sharing between these tech giants and the government.

The case of health codes is emblematic of the "data-based national governance" approach in contemporary China. The development of digital tools, their test runs, and their widespread promotion generally take only a few days to complete. With the help of these digital tools, the state has been able to greatly reduce costs while building a more comprehensive, accurate, and effective system of population control.

Conclusion

Under the leadership of Xi Jinping, the Chinese government has exhibited a greater obsession with control and repression than its predecessors. Protesters and dissidents are increasingly likely to be labeled as gangsters, prosecuted, and imprisoned under charges of picking quarrels and provoking trouble (*xunxin zishi zui*) and are subjected to surveillance and censorship under the guise of national security. The state has invested heavily in developing the infrastructure and technologies required for intrusive mass surveillance. New laws and regulations, such as the National Security Law and the Cybersecurity Law, have been introduced, and new government agencies, such as the CAC, have been established to monitor, control, and even arrest dissidents and protesters. The collusion between the state and businesses, as reflected in measures such as real-name registration, labor-intensive censorship, and social credit systems, has enabled the government to infiltrate society deeply. In particular, disadvantaged groups protesting rights violations are now subject to more comprehensive and effective surveillance and suppression than ever before.[80]

Xi Jinping's regime has established a system of mass surveillance. The outbreak of the COVID-19 pandemic in 2020 provided the Chinese government with an opportunity to further enhance its extensive surveillance of the population, using invasive methods in the name of public health and safety. Officials quickly utilized the population's smartphones to identify and isolate individuals who might have been spreading the virus. Few would dispute that such measures may infringe on the privacy and human rights of individual citizens. However, it is doubtful that the government's monitoring apps will be fully disabled post-pandemic and fade into oblivion. Instead, they are likely to become a permanent fixture in everyday life, allowing the government to track down criminals and monitor potential protesters, as well as to collect and analyze instances of social discontent and specific demands.

Chinese politics can be characterized by a tendency toward responsiveness without accountability.[81] While this is true in some cases, the white paper protests held in November 2022 against the government's strict zero-COVID policy exhibited features of China's "surveillance state." Protesters who held up white sheets of paper during the demonstrations were later arrested based on facial recognition, the physical location of their cell phones, or their activities in private chat groups on social media. Some individuals even reported that photos of the protests were remotely deleted from their devices. The state's response to the white paper protests has shown that when protesters express political demands, the state will use the power of its surveillance apparatus, such as closed-circuit television footage and individuals' digital footprints, to identify and arrest them. This differs from the state's response to protests with nonpolitical demands. While the authorities will still monitor and collect information on these protests, local and central governments will actively work to demobilize the protesters, and arrests are less common. In the era of mass surveillance under Xi Jinping, the surveillance apparatus has supplanted the information collection process. However, the state's strategy of adopting different responses for different social groups to maintain stability and reduce social discontent remains unchanged, with surveillance technologies and grassroots organizations used to consolidate Communist Party rule. This trend has led some scholars to label China's approach as "digital authoritarianism," "digital totalitarianism," or "digital Leninism."[82]

Notes

This work is supported by the Grand Challenge Project of Academia Sinica, titled "Constructing Social Surveys under the Totalitarian Regime in Contemporary China" (grant no. AS-GC-111-H01).

1. Chih-Jou Jay Chen, "Peasant Protests over Land Seizures in Rural China," *Journal of Peasant Studies* 47, no. 6 (2020): 1327–47; Chih-Jou Jay Chen, "A Protest Society Evaluated: Popular Protests in China, 2000–2019," *Mobilization: An International Quarterly* 25, no. 5 (2020): 641–60; Chih-Jou Jay Chen and Yongshun Cai, "Upward Targeting and Social Protests in China," *Journal of Contemporary China* 30, no. 130 (2021): 511–25.

2. In 2014, Chinese Communist Party general secretary Xi Jinping first introduced his "holistic view of national security" (*zongti guojia anquan guan*), which rhetorically put social stability on par with national defense. Xi's theory was later codified in the 2015 National Security Law.

3. Zhongguo Zhengfuwang, "Zhonghua Renmin Gongheguo guomin jingji he shehui fazhan di shier ge wunian guihua gangyao" (Outline of the Twelfth Five-Year Plan for National Economic and Social Development of the People's Republic of China), chap. 41, "Di sishiyi zhang: Jiaqiang gonggong anquan tixi

jianshe" (Strengthening the construction of the public security system), March 16, 2011, http://www.gov.cn/2011h/content_1825838.htm.

4. Zhongguo Zhengfuwang, "Shiba jie san zhong quanhui 'jueding,' gongbao, shuoming (quanwen)" ("Decision," communiqué, and notes of the Third Plenary Session of the Eighteenth Central Committee [full text]), November 12, 2013, http://www.ce.cn/xwzx/gnsz/szyw/201311/18/t20131118_1767104.shtml.

5. Zhongguo Zhengfuwang, "Zhonghua Renmin Gongheguo guomin jingji he shehui fazhan di shisan ge wunian guihua gangyao" (Outline of the Thirteenth Five-Year Plan for National Economic and Social Development of the People's Republic of China), March 17, 2016, http://www.gov.cn/xinwen/2016-03/17/content_5054992.htm.

6. Zhongguo Zhengfuwang, "Zhonghua Renmin Gongheguo guomin jingji he shehui fazhan di shisan ge wunian guihua gangyao."

7. Zhongguo Zhengfuwang, "Zhonghua Renmin Gongheguo guomin jingji he shehui fazhan di shisan ge wunian guihua gangyao."

8. Xi Jinping, "Jianchi zongti guojia anquan guan" (Upholding the overall outlook on national security), Renminwang, August 14, 2018, https://web.archive.org/web/20181004052957/http://theory.people.com.cn/n1/2018/0814/c419481-30227228.html.

9. See also Alexsia T. Chan's chapter in this volume.

10. Jingning Kang, "Guonei shequ wanggehua guanli yanjiu zongshu" (A review of domestic research on community grid management), Chinese Social Science Net, October 28, 2013, https://web.archive.org/web/20210921165523/http://www.cssn.cn/sf/bwsf_gl/201312/t20131205_895684.shtml.

11. Huirong Chen and Sheena Chestnut Greitens, "Information Capacity and Social Order: The Local Politics of Information Integration in China," *Governance* 35, no. 2 (2022): 497–523.

12. Feng Xiong, "Shehui zonghe zhili zouchu wanggehua guanli jingzhun fuwu zhi lu" (Comprehensive social governance is advancing grid-based management precision service), Xinhuanet, September 19, 2017, https://web.archive.org/web/20180918052713/http://www.xinhuanet.com/legal/2017-09/19/c_1121689554.htm.

13. "Beijing chengshi guanli wanggehua shixian 16 ge qu quan fugai" (Beijing urban management grid to achieve full coverage of 16 districts), Xinhuanet, December 12, 2018, https://web.archive.org/web/20181213125534/http://www.xinhuanet.com/local/2018-12/12/c_1123843069.htm.

14. "Kuaidi xiaoge dang wanggeyuan, zan!" (The courier boy as a grid officer: Like!), Xinhuanet, March 14, 2019, https://web.archive.org/web/20200809201732/http://www.xinhuanet.com/2019-03/14/c_1124233496.htm.

15. Jianhua Xu and Siying He, "Can Grid Governance Fix the Party-State's Broken Windows? A Study of Stability Maintenance in Grassroots China," *China Quarterly*, no. 251 (2022): 843–65.

16. Shujun Yu, "Hangzhou Gongan tuijin 'hecheng zuozhan' jianshe dazao poan 'jiandao'" (Hangzhou Public Security Bureau promotes the construction of "composite operations" to create "sharp knives" for solving cases), Zhongguowang, December 11, 2015, https://web.archive.org/web/20151211144157/http://www.china.com.cn/txt/2015-12/11/content_37293609.htm.

17. "Jiayuguan 'zhihui xin jingwu' zhimi chengshi anquan wangluo" (Jiayuguan "intelligent new police work" weaving city security network), Xinhuanet, July 17, 2019, https://web.archive.org/web/20190717052551/http://www.gs.xinhuanet.com/news/2019-07/17/c_1124763845.htm.

18. Dapeng Wang and Jianing Wang, "Beijing 3 wan tantou jiankong suoyou zhongdian jiemian 'Tianwang' jiben xingcheng" (Beijing deploys 30,000 surveillance cameras to monitor all key streets, "Skynet" basically taken shape), Renminwang, May 25, 2015, http://politics.people.com.cn/n/2015/0525/c1001-27049946.html.

19. Yu Zhang, "Ba 'Xueliang Gongcheng' jiancheng shouhu renmin anning de 'qianliyan'" (Building the 'Bright-as-Snow Project' into a 'telescope' to protect the people's peace of mind), Renminwang, June 22, 2018, http://legal.people.com.cn/n1/2018/0622/c42510-30075878.html.

20. "Guojia Hulianwang Xinxi Bangongshi sheli" (State Internet Information Office established), *Guangming Daily*, December 22, 2011, http://epaper.gmw.cn/gmrb/html/2011-12/22/nw.D110000gmrb_20111222_7-04.htm?div=-1.

21. See, for example, Cyberspace Administration of China, "Tengxun Weixin, Xinlang Weibo, Baidu Tieba shexian weifan 'Wangluo Anquan Fa' bei li'an diaocha" (Tencent WeChat, Sina Weibo, Baidu Post under investigation for violating the "Cybersecurity Law"), August 11, 2017, http://www.cac.gov.cn/2017-08/11/c_1121467425.htm; Cyberspace Administration of China, "Guojia Wangxinban zhidao Beijingshi Wangxinban yuetan Fenghuangwang fuzeren" (Cyberspace Administration of China directed the Beijing Internet Information Office to interview the person in charge of Phoenix), February 15, 2020, http://www.cac.gov.cn/2020-02/15/c_1583303419227448.htm; "Beijingshi Wangxinban zeling Tengxun, Xinlang, Souhu deng wangzhan guanting weigui zicai lanmu" (Beijing Internet Information Office ordered Tencent, Sina, Sohu, and other websites to shut down illegal self-published columns), *Paper*, March 2, 2017, https://www.thepaper.cn/newsDetail_forward_1630860.

22. Cyberspace Administration of China, "Hulianwang xinwen xinxi fuwu danwei yuetan gongzuo guiding" (Work regulations on interviews of entities providing Internet news information services), April 28, 2015, http://www.cac.gov.cn/2015-04/28/c_1115112600.htm.

23. Rongbin Han, *Contesting Cyberspace in China: Online Expression and Authoritarian Resilience* (New York: Columbia University Press, 2018).

24. Tao Wen, "Dianping Zhongguo: 'Fabiao' shijian he meiti jianguan de fansi" (Commentary on China: Rethinking the "flipping out" incident and media

regulations), *BBC News China*, August 1, 2016, https://www.bbc.com/zhongwen/simp/china/2016/08/160801_cr_tengxun_print_mistake.

25. NGOCN, "1998 ci yuetan, wanganfa de 500 tian" (1,998 interviews, 500 days of the Cybersecurity Law), *China Digital Times*, October 16, 2018, https://chinadigitaltimes.net/chinese/597730.html; "Wangxinban yuetan shilu" (Internet Information Office interview transcript), *Matters*, August 14, 2018, https://reurl.cc/ObpN4y.

26. Cyberspace Administration of China, "Hulianwang qunzu xinxi fuwu guanli guiding" (Internet group information service management regulations), September 7, 2017, http://www.cac.gov.cn/2017-09/07/c_1121623889.htm.

27. Jihong Chen, Jiawei Wu, and Zehan Xue, "Zhijing shuju hegui yuannian: Biaoxi 'Wangluo Anquan Fa' peitao falu fagui he guifanxing wenjian" (A tribute to the first year of data compliance—an analysis of the supporting laws, regulations, and normative documents of the Cybersecurity Law), Zhonglun Zixun, January 18, 2019, http://www.zhonglun.com/Content/2019/01-18/1220212637.html.

28. "Shanghai, Beijing Wangxinban yuetan Haoqixin ribao: Zeling quanpingtai shenru zhenggai yige yue" (Shanghai and Beijing Internet Information Offices interview Q Daily: Whole platform ordered to engage in in-depth rectification for one month), *Guanchazhe*, August 3, 2018, https://m.guancha.cn/society/2018_08_03_466779.shtml.

29. "'Haoqixin ribao' app yi zao quanwang xiajia" (Q Daily app suspected to be taken down nationwide), iFeng, April 22, 2019, http://tech.ifeng.com/a/20190422/45563204_0.shtml.

30. "Xinlang duoge yingyong bei xialing tingzhi gengxin xiajia yige yue" (Multiple apps by Sina were ordered to stop updates and be removed from the App Store for a month), Voice of America China, April 17, 2019, https://www.voachinese.com/a/china-sina-to-temporarily-suspend-some-apps-due-to-violations-20190417/4879537.html.

31. "'Shishang zuiyan' shoujika shimingzhi lai le!" (The "strictest ever" cell phone card real-name system is here!) Wenhuiwang, August 29, 2015, http://news.wenweipo.com/2015/08/29/IN1508290007.htm.

32. "Zhongguo Zhengfu shoujin shouji shimingzhi, Taobaowang jiang quanmian jinshou shouji haoma" (Chinese government tightens cell phone real-name registration system, Taobao will be completely banned from selling cell phone numbers), *Initium*, September 2, 2016, https://theinitium.com/article/20160902-dailynews-phone-real-name.

33. "Zhongguo Zhengfu shoujin shouji shimingzhi."

34. Pingguo: Zhongguo neidi de iCloud fuwu jiang zhuan you guonei gongsi fuze yunying (Apple: iCloud Service in Mainland China to be Transferred to Domestic Company for Operation), 2018/1/10, Xinhuanet, https://web.archive.org/web/20180117131853/http://www.xinhuanet.com/fortune/2018-01/10/c_129787466.htm.

35. Examples include the Chinese versions of Evernote and Steam, which separated from their holding companies in 2018 and 2021, respectively, to satisfy the Chinese government's demands for the implementation of real-name registration.

36. "Di 50 ci 'Zhongguo hulian wangluo fazhan zhuangkuang tongji baogao' fabu" (The 50th "Statistical Report on the Development of the Internet in China" is published), *Guangming Daily*, September 1, 2022, http://www.gov.cn/xinwen /2022-09/01/content_5507695.htm.

37. "Heike da jiemi zhangwo Zhongguo jianshi wangmin tiezheng" (Hackers reveal that they have hard evidence that China is spying on Internet users), Radio Free Asia, March 4, 2019, https://www.rfa.org/cantonese/news/hacker -03042019075827.html.

38. Long Qiao, "Fengci 'Mao Zei' 'Xi Baozi' Shandong wangmin Wang Jiangfeng panxing liangnian" (For satirizing "Thief Mao" and "Xi Baozi," Shandong netizen Wang Jiangfeng sentenced to two years in prison), Radio Free Asia, April 12, 2017, https://www.rfa.org/mandarin/yataibaodao/renquanfazhi/q12 -04122017101221.html.

39. "709 an wunian hou Zhongguo weiquan lushi chujing ruhe?" (Five years after the 709 case, what is the situation of Chinese human rights lawyers?), Voice of America China, July 9, 2020, https://www.voachinese.com/a/rights-lawyers -709-case-5-years-07092020/5495846.html.

40. Li Hui and Megha Rajagopalan, "At Sina Weibo's Censorship Hub, China's Little Brothers Cleanse Online Chatter," Reuters, September 11, 2013, https:// www.voanews.com/a/reu-sina-weibo-censorship-online-chatter/1748103.html.

41. Leizi, "Jinan: Jueqi de hulianwang shenhe zhidu" (Jinan: The rising capital of Internet auditing), *Southern Weekly*, April 22, 2019, https://chinadigitaltimes .net/chinese/607993.html.

42. "Cong dangandai dao xinyong pingfen Zhongguo shifou zheng zouxiang 'Aoweier shi' jiankong shehui" (From file bags to credit scores: Is China moving toward an "Orwellian" surveillance society?), *BBC News China*, October 17, 2018, https://www.bbc.com/zhongwen/trad/chinese-news-45886126.

43. State Council, "Guowuyuan guanyu jianli wanshan shouxin lianhe jili he shixin lianhe chengjie zhidu jiakuai tuijin shehui chengxin jianshe de zhidao yijian" (Guidance of the State Council on the establishment and improvement of joint incentives for trustworthiness and joint discipline systems to speed up the construction of social credit), November 18, 2016, http://www.gov.cn/zhengce /content/2016-06/12/content_5081222.htm.

44. "Xi Jinping: Tuijin shehui chengxin tixi rang shixin zhe cunbu nanxing" (Xi Jinping: Promote the social credit system so that dishonest people cannot do anything at all), Xinhuanet, June 27, 2016, https://credit.shaanxi.gov.cn/311 /32797.html.

45. "Zhonggong Zhongyang Bangongting Guowuyuan Bangongting yinfa 'guanyu jiakuai tuijin shixin bei zhixing ren xinyong jiandu, jingshi he chengjie

jizhi jianshe de yijian'" (General Office of the CPC Central Committee and General Office of the State Council issue "opinions on accelerating the construction of credit supervision, warning and punishment mechanism for defaulted executors"), Xinhuanet, September 25, 2016, https://web.archive.org /web/20190818025619/http://www.xinhuanet.com//politics/2016-09/25 /c_1119620719.htm.

46. Megan Palin, "Big Brother: China's Chilling Dictatorship Moves to Introduce Scorecards to Control Everyone," *News AU*, September 19, 2018, https:// www.news.com.au/technology/online/big-brother-chinas-chilling-dictatorship -moves-to-introduce-scorecards-to-control-everyone/news-story/6c821cbf15378 abod3eeb3ec3dc98abf.

47. "Lu tui shehui xinyong xitong 5 yue qi shixin zhe xian da huoche feiji" (Mainland to promote social credit system, people without credit will be restricted from taking trains and flights beginning in May), Central News Agency, March 22, 2018, https://www.cna.com.tw/news/acn/201803170239.aspx; National Development Commission, "Guanyu zai yiding qixian nei shidang xianzhi teding yanzhong shixin ren chengzuo minyong hangkongqi tuidong shehui xinyong tixi jianshe de yijian" (Views on appropriate restrictions on air travel over a certain period of time for persons with serious credit issues to ride civil aircraft and on the promotion of constructing a social credit system), March 2, 2018, http://www.ndrc.gov.cn/zcfb/zcfbtz/201803/t20180316_879624.html.

48. Zhongguo Zhengfuwang, "2018 nian shixin heimingdan niandu fenxi baogao fabu" (2018 annual analysis report on the blacklist of credit losers released), February 19, 2019, http://www.gov.cn/fuwu/2019-02/19/ content_5366674.htm.

49. Xin Dai, "Enforcing Law and Norms for Good Citizens: One View of China's Social Credit System Project," *Development* 63, no. 1 (2020): 38–43.

50. Genia Kostka, "China's Social Credit Systems and Public Opinion: Explaining High Levels of Approval," *New Media & Society* 21, no. 7 (2019): 1565–93.

51. "Cong dangandai dao xinyong pingfen."

52. Li Haili and Genia Kostka, "Accepting but Not Engaging with It: Digital Participation in Local Government-Run Social Credit Systems in China," *Policy & Internet* 14, no. 4 (2022): 845–74.

53. Jun Mai, "Fewer Chinese Citizens Filing Petitions against Authorities as Beijing Tries to Curb Use," *South China Morning Post*, August 23, 2017, https:// www.scmp.com/news/china/policies-politics/article/2107944/fewer-chinese -citizens-filing-petitions-against.

54. Zhongguo Zhengfuwang, "Guojia Xinfangju yinfa guanyu jinyibu guifan xinfang shixiang shiyi banfa" (The National Public Complaints and Proposals Administration issues measures on the further standardization of petition matters), April 23, 2014, http://www.gov.cn/xinwen/2014-04/23/content_2665286.htm.

55. Shiwei Xing, "Guojia Xinfangju guanyuan: Jinjing shangfang renshu xiajiang jianshao Beijing yali" (Official from the National Public Complaints and

Proposals Administration: Number of petitioners to Beijing falls, reducing the pressure on Beijing), Renminwang, February 9, 2015, http://politics.people.com .cn/BIG5/n/2015/0209/c1001-26528977.html.

56. Zong Zhang, "Wangshang shouli xinfang zhidu 5 nian lai wangshang xin-fang liang zhanbi guoban" (After 5 years of accepting petitions online, the volume of online petitions accounts for more than fifty percent), Renminwang, July 27, 2018, http://legal.people.com.cn/n1/2018/0727/c42510-30173593.html.

57. Long Qiao, "Tianjin fangmin weixin fa jiankong shipin zao xingju" (Tianjin petitioner who sent surveillance video via WeChat detained), Radio Free Asia, October 9, 2017, https://www.rfa.org/mandarin/yataibaodao/renquanfazhi /q11-10092017103348.html.

58. "Tielu jinjing mingqi shixing erci anjian" (People taking train to Beijing will be subject to two security checks beginning tomorrow), *Shanghai Labor News*, cited in *Xinmin Evening News*, October 8, 2017, https://wap.xinmin.cn /content/31323254.html.

59. Feng Gao, "Liangqian minban jiaoshi Beijing shangfang Jiaoyubu zaixian weiquan renhai" (Two thousand private teachers petition in Beijing: Ministry of Education again faced with huge crowd of rights defenders), Radio Free Asia, November 30, 2017, https://www.rfa.org/mandarin/yataibaodao/renquanfazhi /gf1-11302017104403.html1.

60. Long Qiao, "Huochezhan yancha chengke shouji weidu P2P touziren" (Train station to strictly check passengers' cell phones to intercept P2P investors), Radio Free Asia, August 8, 2018, https://www.rfa.org/mandarin/yataibaodao /meiti/q11-08082018091713.html.

61. "2014 nian Zhongguo weiwen yu renquan zhuangkuang nianzhong zong-jie" (2014 year-end summary of the state of stability maintenance and human rights in China), Minsheng Guancha, February 16, 2015, https://www.msguancha .com/a/lanmu12/2015/0216/11888.html.

62. Tao Jiang, "San tian nei 21 zuo zhengfu guankong de sanzi jiaotang zao chafeng" (In a matter of three days, 21 government-controlled Three-Self churches were closed down), *Bitter Winter*, September 7, 2018, https://zh.bitterwinter.org /21-state-sanctioned-churches-shut-down-in-three-days-video.

63. Shuji Zeng, "Henan quansheng qingchai jiaotang shizijia qiangzhi gua guoqi gua Xi xiang" (In all of Henan churches and crosses are demolished or forced to hang national flags and pictures of Xi), Radio France International, September 6, 2018, https://www.rfi.fr/tw/中國/20180906-河南全省清拆教堂十字架強制掛國旗掛習像.

64. "2018 nian Zhongguo shehui kongzhi nianzhong zongjie" (2018 year-end summary of social control in China), Minsheng Guancha, February 19, 2019, https://www.msguancha.com/a/lanmu2/2019/0219/18358.html.

65. "2018 nian Zhongguo shehui kongzhi."

66. Tao Jiang, "Henan mimi jianli zongjiao renyuan shujuku: Chaoxi fenlei

shishi jiankong" (Henan secretly establishes database of religious personnel: Ultra-detailed classification, real-time monitoring), *Bitter Winter*, May 21, 2019, https://zh.bitterwinter.org/database-of-believers-established-in-henan.

67. Zhe Tang, "Xueliang Gongcheng shixian zongjiao changsuo neiwai quanfugai wu sijiao jiankong ling xintu kongju" (Bright-as-Snow Project to achieve full coverage inside and outside of religious venues: No-blind-spot surveillance stokes fear in believers), *Bitter Winter*, August 3, 2019, https://zh.bitterwinter.org/cameras-monitor-chinas-religious-venues-24-7.

68. Unless otherwise noted, the information in this section is based on Deng Kai's field research in Pinghu. As a Pinghu native, he was stationed in Pinghu since returning to his hometown for the Spring Festival in 2020. Although it was not possible to conduct face-to-face interviews due to the epidemic, Deng observed the situation on the ground, collecting and verifying various messages from the government and the community.

69. Wei Xiao, "Pinghu fabu quansheng shouge 'Hongse Wuye' difang biaozhun" (Pinghu releases province's first local standard for "Red Property"), Zhejiang Online, February 28, 2019, https://town.zjol.com.cn/cstts/201902/t20190228_9556182.shtml.

70. "Pinghu Shiwei Changweihui yanjiu bushu Xinxing Guanzhuang Bingdu ganran de feiyan yiqing fangkong gongzuo" (Pinghu Municipal Committee's Standing Committee to study the deployment of prevention and control measures in face of COVID-19 outbreak), Pinghu Fabu WeChat Public Account, January 22, 2020, https://mp.weixin.qq.com/s/3UH9yeCp7CQRgN77DUK8EA.

71. "Pinghu Shiwei Changwei (kuoda) huiyi zhaokai, dui yiqing fangkong gongzuo zai yanjiu zai bushu" (Pinghu Municipal Committee Standing Committee [extended] meeting held, again studying and deploying epidemic prevention and control measures), Pinghu Fabu WeChat Public Account, January 27, 2020, https://mp.weixin.qq.com/s/CrqVuXWk47HzteyB189X3A.

72. "162 ge linshi dangzuzhi, Pinghu shixian yiqing fangkong qianyan dang de zuzhi quan fugai" (162 temporary Party organizations, Pinghu to achieve full coverage of Party organizations at the forefront of epidemic prevention and control), Pinghu Fabu WeChat Public Account, February 1, 2020, https://mp.weixin.qq.com/s/frB71wolwakcVGmALGsy3g.

73. "'Zhongyao tonggao': Jiri qi, yange xianzhi fei Jiaxing shiji renyuan jinru Pinghu!" ("Important notice": Beginning today, non–Jiaxing City residents are strictly restricted from entering Pinghu!), Pinghu Fabu WeChat Public Account, February 3, 2020, https://mp.weixin.qq.com/s/QpwouE2d_J-NQLvSCr_1dA.

74. "Pinghu quanmian shishi xiaoqu fengbishi guanli!" (Pinghu to fully implement the locked-down management of communities!), Pinghu Fabu WeChat Public Account, February 6, 2020, https://mp.weixin.qq.com/s/DGGHAJ97iid982a14PNMRA.

75. "Pinghu 200 duo ming ganbu bianshen 'zhu qi zhidaoyuan,' quebao qiye

kai fu gong shengchan fangyi liangbuwu" (More than 200 cadres in Pinghu turned into "in-house instructors" to ensure that enterprises can resume production and also engage in epidemic prevention), Pinghu Fabu WeChat Public Account, February 9, 2020, https://mp.weixin.qq.com/s/mCvrNaQNIEmdv Ua6jJcozw.

76. "Pinghu 709 ming jiguan ganbu bianshen 'HR renli ziyuan zhuli'" (709 cadres in Pinghu turned into "human resource assistants"), Pinghu Fabu WeChat Public Account, March 1, 2020, https://mp.weixin.qq.com/s/eWXxPrNaitCK MQ2HmmRIZA.

77. "'Zhuli yiqing zuji zhan' Hangzhou jiankangma shi zenme shengcheng de?—Alibaba jiankangma xitong zhuli yiqing fangkong he fugong fuchan" ("Helping to stop the epidemic," how is the Hangzhou health code generated?—Alibaba health code system to help epidemic prevention and control to resume work and production), Hangzhoushi Kexue Jishu Xiehui, February 26, 2020, https://mp.weixin.qq.com/s/J1r0HMvJoKFtWG8ymhqnUg.

78. Zhongguo Zhengfuwang, "Zhonghua Renmin Gongheguo guomin jingji he shehui fazhan di shisan ge wunian guihua gangyao," 139.

79. Zhejiang Zhengwu Fuwuwang, "Zhejiangsheng gonggong shuju he dianzi zhengwu guanli banfa" (Public data and e-government management measures of Zhejiang Province), March 27, 2017, http://www.zjzwfw.gov.cn/art/2017/3/27 /art_1177809_6090045.html.

80. Chen, "A Protest Society Evaluated"; Chen, "Peasant Protests over Land Seizures."

81. Bruce J. Dickson, *The Party and the People: Chinese Politics in the 21st Century* (Princeton, NJ: Princeton University Press, 2021).

82. Sebastian Heilmann, "Leninism Upgraded: Xi Jinping's Authoritarian Innovations," *China Economic Quarterly* 20, no. 4 (2016): 15–22.

7

Love through Fear
The Personality Cult
of Xi Jinping in Xinjiang

Musapir

Since Xi Jinping conducted a four-day inspection tour in Xinjiang in April 2014, images and slogans displayed on large murals in Xinjiang's streets have depicted him as the unquestioned leader and "soulmate" (Uy.: *qelbdash*) of the Uyghur, Kazakh, and other ethnic minorities in Xinjiang. One common slogan on murals proclaims: "Xi Jinping is the soulmate of all the peoples of Xinjiang, breathing together and sharing the same fate" (Xi Jinping yu Xinjiang ge zu renmin xin lian xin, tong huxi, gong mingyun; Uy.: Xi Jinping bilen Xinjiangdiki her millet helqi qelbdash, hemnepes, teqdirdash).[1] During fieldwork in 2016, I commonly saw propaganda photographs of Xi together with Uyghurs in their homes posted in public spaces such as streets, village centers, urban squares, and restaurants and circulated via online and print-based state media. A common caption was "Xi Jinping is joining hands and laughing with happy Uyghurs." The ubiquity of slogans and images claiming solidarity between the Chinese Communist Party (CCP) leadership and ethnic minority peoples, and the happiness and gratitude of the latter, is not new. But depictions of the intimate relationship between Xi and the peoples of Xinjiang have extended beyond public representation into everyday reality as his presence has come to permeate Uyghur public spaces, homes, families, and daily life.

Xi Jinping is now venerated, and his image enshrined in place of anything with religious symbolism or ancestral presence in Uyghur homes. In 2016, his picture was displayed on the living room wall of almost every Uyghur household I visited throughout southern Xinjiang, the Uyghur homeland that locals refer to as Altishahr.[2] Members of the Uyghur diaspora have confirmed that the same is true in their families' homes in Xinjiang.[3] The picture is often a solo portrait of Xi, but it is common to find it displayed next to one of Mao Zedong; some people display a group portrait of the five paramount leaders of the CCP: Mao, Deng Xiaoping, Jiang Zemin, Hu Jintao, and Xi. Viral TikTok videos from 2019 offer a further glimpse into how pervasive Xi Jinping's presence has become, beyond the mere ubiquity of his image.[4] In one widely circulated video, a Uyghur woman tells her toddler son to kiss "grandfather Xi" (Uy.: *Xi chong dada*).[5] The child runs toward the picture of Xi on the wall and starts kissing it. Another noteworthy example shows a Uyghur man playing a traditional two-stringed *dutar* and singing a song to a Uyghur folk melody in a crowded room. The lyrics to his improvised song are

Xi Jinping atimiz,	Xi Jinping is our father,
Partiye animiz.	The Party is our mother.
Partiyening sayiside,	Under the Party's protection,
Hatijem yatimiz.	We sleep soundly.
Dini esebi unsur kelse,	If we see religious extremists,
Gum qilip atimiz.[6]	Bang! We will shoot them.

The word *father*, *atimiz*, is usually reserved for fathers or ancestors within the community and has sacred connotations. Its use with reference to Xi Jinping in this song is particularly jarring.[7]

How and why has Xi Jinping come to penetrate every aspect of domestic Uyghur life to the point that he is portrayed and apparently accepted as a father, a protector, and even a soulmate? In analyzing the cult of personality around Xi Jinping, communication studies scholars Liangen Yin and Terry Flew acknowledge that local officials and state-controlled media have played a role in its creation, but they claim that the cult has been "primarily driven" by Chinese netizens and thus by society.[8] This chapter argues against such an interpretation, at least in the case of Xinjiang. There, support and love for Xi Jinping has arisen not from a bottom-up appreciation of his actions, but rather from the internalized fear that Uyghurs have to live with every day. Constant surveillance and carefully orchestrated top-down political pressure to demonstrate loyalty and trustworthiness to the CCP and its vision of the Chinese nation have driven Uyghurs to participate in Xi Jinping's cult of personality out of fear for their lives. Gerda Wielander, in her chapter in this volume, argues that Xi has simultaneously worked to increase control over religion in China and "to position the Party itself as an object of faith." As she notes, the government's attempts to manage faith have been taken to extremes among Uyghurs (and other Turkic Muslims) in Xinjiang. As I show here, Uyghurs' "veneration" of and "love" for Xi come from a place of intimidation and extreme self-consciousness, rather than free will. Xi's ubiquitous presence is a reminder of his power. As one Uyghur said to me, "[His picture] is always there, looking at you, as if it is listening to you." Expressions of loyalty to and affection for Xi can therefore be understood as a creative form of political action that establishes a household as "safe" (*fangxin*) in the hope that this will protect family members from disappearing into one of Xinjiang's many so-called reeducation camps.

Since Xi Jinping came to power in 2012, the encroachment of his image and politics into everyday life in Xinjiang has been a gradual, insidious process, profoundly shaped by the entanglement of China's "War on Terror" with the pursuit of Xi's "Chinese Dream" (Zhongguo Meng) of rejuvenating the Chinese nation by cultivating a unified Chinese identity, culture, and civilization under the authority of the CCP.[9] Although state-society and interethnic tensions in Xinjiang have been increasing since the early 2000s, Uyghur elders told me that when Xi took office as Party general secretary and launched his high-level anti-corruption campaign in late 2012 they were hopeful and envisioned a new form of government that valued its people.[10] As Andrew Wedeman discusses in his contribution to this volume, Xi's drive against corruption, while not unprecedented, was notable for its focus on senior-ranking Party officials. However, Xi's speech at the Second Xinjiang Work Forum (May 28–29, 2014) made it abundantly clear that cracking down on terrorist activities and reinforcing ethnic unity were the key priorities in Xinjiang. The political scientist James Leibold notes that this speech marked the beginning of a major shift in China's ethnic policies framed around a "new strategic intent: the erosion of ethnic differences."[11] The shift to an assimilationist "second generation" in ethnic policies was proposed by Tsinghua scholars Hu Angang and Hu Lianhe in 2011. It has been implemented under Xi as a way to deal with anti-state resistance (or "terrorism") in Tibet, Xinjiang, and, since 2019, Hong Kong and "to ensure integration, promote nationalism, and create a homogeneous society."[12] Although the state may say that it supports different ethnic communities, Xi Jinping's Chinese Dream of a unified Chinese nation is Han-centric.[13] Its strict and inflexible definition of what it means to be "Chinese" is built on Han language, traditions, values, history, and culture, with no space for dissent or diversity. The economist Ilham Tohti, the most outspoken of Uyghur intellectuals to raise warnings about the rise of such "Han chauvinism" (*da Hanzu zhuyi*), a term coined by Mao Zedong in the 1950s to criticize Han ethnocentrism, was sentenced to life imprisonment for separatism in 2014. The shift toward this "virulent form of cultural nationalism" and its effects on the lives of ethnic minorities have been made very clear in the concrete manifestations of the Chinese Dream in Xinjiang.[14]

China watchers agree that an obvious shift toward assimilation in China's ethnic policy has heavily affected the Uyghur cultural and political land-scape.[15] Since 2017, there has also been extensive media coverage of the mass internment and treatment of Uyghurs in "reeducation" camps in Xinjiang, documented by scholars including the anthropologist Adrian Zenz, who has analyzed open source online data, satellite images, and survivors' testimonies.[16] The political scientist Anna Hayes connects this extreme repression to the CCP's anxieties over external influences on Xinjiang, which is a critical frontier region in China's expansion into Central Asia and the Middle East through the Belt and Road Initiative.[17] The primary focus has thus been on the Party-state's response to terrorism in Xinjiang and its current treatment of the Uyghur people. My aim here is to foreground what it feels like to live as a Uyghur in Xinjiang under the Xi Jinping administration, based on interviews and observations carried out during annual research visits to Xinjiang from 2012 to 2016 and in the Uyghur diaspora up to the present, as well as analysis of public content on social media, Chinese state-controlled media sources, the large archive of links and resources compiled by the anthropologist Magnus Fiskesjö (continuously updated), and the community-based Xinjiang Victims Database, which contains personal testimonies on the disappearances of friends and relatives.[18] These materials illuminate the intensive internalized fear produced by the unprecedented extension of surveillance under the Xi Jinping administration, how this fear has intersected with intense pressures to assimilate into the Chinese nation, and the resulting destruction of Uyghur family life, language, religion, and culture as Uyghurs adapt to an undifferentiated Chinese identity and life based on Han culture. Looming over all of this is the irony of Xi Jinping as an omnipresent, absent, and imaginary "father" who commands public loyalty and affection under the threat of violence. While Xi's leadership might not have had a particularly pronounced impact in some areas of Chinese politics, economics, and social life (see the chapters by Martin King Whyte and Alexsia T. Chan in this volume), in the everyday lives of Uyghurs and other minoritized people in Xinjiang "the Xi Jinping effect" has been profound.

Surveillance and Fear

Since the implementation of the "People's War on Terror" in 2014, access to Xinjiang has been increasingly restricted. The chapter by Deng Kai, David Demes, and Chih-Jou Jay Chen (this volume) outlines the intensification of mass surveillance across China under Xi Jinping's leadership. What they refer to as "the surveillance state" has been particularly intrusive in Xinjiang, where it has been used to enforce increasingly restrictive control over the everyday lives of Uyghurs. In 2016, the new Party secretary Chen Quanguo, former Party secretary of the Tibet Autonomous Region, introduced the grid management system, which subdivides communities into small units for the purposes of information gathering and monitoring.[19] This unprecedented security apparatus has brought everyday life in Xinjiang under highly policed surveillance. Fear was omnipresent among Uyghurs when I visited in 2016; people were extremely cautious about what they said and did. Journalists' reports from 2017 and 2018 showed heavily restricted areas, empty streets, and a proliferation of surveillance cameras.[20] In 2019 and 2020, they witnessed residents going through security checks robotically even without police supervision, knowing that any misbehavior would have severe consequences.[21] This increase in surveillance has created a widespread environment of distrust and pervasive fear, which has its own internalizing function. Even without being noticeably watched, Uyghurs tend to control and censor themselves out of fear of being seen or caught doing something that would raise suspicion. As one Uyghur told me, "We don't even dare to think, let alone do or say anything."[22]

Chen Quanguo tested his neighborhood grid surveillance system while in charge of the Tibet Autonomous Region, but expanded it massively in Xinjiang through the use of both technologies (for example, cameras, facial recognition) and people, with neighbors assigned to spy on each other.[23] In more densely populated urban areas of the Uyghur homeland, "convenient" police stations were established every fifty to two hundred meters. Regular inspections of homes by police or neighborhood-level cadres became possible at any time.[24] The state outlawed "suspicious" beards, veils, and Islamic baby names. Anyone who had ever studied or taught the Quran or even saved or viewed religious content on their smart devices became subject to imprisonment under charges of extremism or terrorism.[25] Uyghur residents' passports were confiscated, and those who had previously traveled abroad or had relatives abroad became targets of political indoctrination. According to local rules, people were not only to spy on their neighbors but also to make sure they behaved well. "They would take your credit card, cut your electricity or water [for the whole neighborhood] if you failed to report any suspicious person or behavior in the neighborhood," said one resident.[26] "They will catch you anyway. Cameras are everywhere," they continued, "so we had better report them while we can." Xinjiang increased its security budget by 365 percent in 2016.[27] In 2018, Lucas Niewenhuis, the newsletter editor at the China Project, reported that the state had arrested 227,000 people from Xinjiang in 2017, an increase of 731 percent from 2016.[28] Xinjiang has become a land of "criminals." Although its residents constitute only 1.5 percent of the total population of the People's Republic of China, they accounted for one in every five persons arrested in 2017. These statistics do not even begin to address the hundreds of thousands of Uyghurs who have been detained without formal charge or sentencing. Several Uyghurs told me that they slept in their clothes because they had seen their neighbors arrested in the middle of the night in their pajamas, with no time to change.

The fear of disappearing without a trace and the fear of losing loved ones without any explanation haunt Uyghurs every day. Both in person and via media, people can no longer talk to each other without the fear of being overheard and caught saying something they should not. In an effort to save themselves, they go silent. As surveillance intensified in 2017, many people buried their smartphones or threw them into the river, and those who kept them returned them to their factory settings and deleted the contact information of any friends and relatives outside of China. As the anthropologist Linda Green observes, silence when used as "a survival strategy" is simultaneously a "powerful mechanism of control" that creates more fear and divides people further.[29] If people cannot speak to each other, they cannot trust each other. Another level of terror was created by the awareness that those detained on suspicion of being a "religious extremist," "separatist," or "two-faced person" (*liangmian ren*) were being put under pressure to inform on other people who may have committed similar crimes.[30] These crimes could include any incident of criticizing the state or overtly displaying religiosity, even if it happened years ago. Detainees were told that if they provided at least three names and incidents, it would be better for both them and their family. Survivors testified at the Uyghur Tribunal (London, June 2021) that they were asked to provide this information while enduring torture. This contributed to a massive increase of detainees held without factual evidence. As a Uyghur elder stated, "During the Cultural Revolution, we were accused of being a 'two-hearted person' [*liangxin ren*]. Now we are accused of being two-faced persons. It's impossible to prove our loyalty to them."[31]

What makes surveillance in Xinjiang so powerful is the use of technology to make it a routine part of everyday life, inevitably sparking comparisons to George Orwell's *1984*. On top of the surveillance cameras on every street corner, all residents of Xinjiang are required to install surveillance smartphone apps such as Cleannet Bodyguard (Jingwang Weishi) or the Integrated Joint Operations Platform (IJOP), which gather data on whatever the user does and flag any suspicious activity, from photos to videos and even WiFi login data.[32] Facial recognition technologies have been installed at checkpoints throughout the region, following Uyghurs wherever they go and constantly cataloging their travel, making them feel as if they are never free from monitoring.[33] They have also been integrated into smartphone apps. As of April 2021, citizens are required to download the National Anti-Fraud Center (Guojia Fanzha Zhongxin) smartphone app, developed by the Ministry of Public Security in China. A user's name, phone number, ID number, address, and facial scan are all required to create an account. The app then has access to nearly everything on the phone, including the microphone, camera, contacts, SMS (Short Message Service) code, call log, and browsing history.[34] The required use and the nature of this app have created considerable discussion among netizens nationwide.

The ubiquitous surveillance enabled by technology has created an atmosphere of proactive self-censorship and changed how people think about the state, which has an increasingly omnipotent presence. In making surveillance a routine part of everyday life, the Party has also made fear routine, forcing people to live in a chronic state of anxiety while appearing normal.[35] Surveillance at the community level has created an internalized embodiment of fear and distrust that has forced people to present an inauthentic self in daily life. Party-state control of ethnic minority communities through fear is not just a top-down management approach. It is also a strategy to facilitate assimilation through internalization of rules and norms and by weaponizing neighbor against neighbor. It has deeply penetrated the bodies and minds of Uyghurs. While I have been able to communicate with some Uyghurs in Xinjiang, mostly via chat rooms or video games, they rarely speak to me in the Uyghur language and keep their messages in Chinese as short as possible. Fear has facilitated a dystopian reality, driving people to do whatever they have to do to physically survive, including the performance of inauthentic "happiness" that mediates structural violence and state terror.[36] This fear is the primary fuel behind the cult of personality surrounding Xi Jinping in Xinjiang—the reason why he is praised in songs and why parents teach children that he is their grandfather. After all, as the Uyghur expression goes, "Tamningmu quliqi bar" (Walls have ears).

Destroying Families

The "War on Terror" strategy and the "Chinese Dream" vision of Han-based national identity have had a significant impact on Uyghur families. Xi Jinping's political control in Xinjiang has dismantled family bonds by making the very notion of family and kinship precarious and fear-driven. Of the twelve million Uyghurs native to the region, it is estimated that between one and two million have been detained for longer or shorter periods in camps since 2017, and many have been sent on to jail or forced labor camps.[37] This high number of detentions means that nearly every Uyghur, including those who have been forced into exile or are otherwise living abroad, has a friend or family member who has been taken.[38] One person in Australia counted fifty-two extended family members and friends who had been taken to camps as of February 2019.[39] Those who have survived the camps and managed to leave China have testified that they experienced physical and psychological trauma in the camps and were forced to disown their Islamic beliefs while showing gratefulness to the CCP.[40] There have also been reports of deaths inside the camps, not only of the elderly but also of youths.[41]

Since the reeducation system has targeted Uyghur men between the ages of twenty and fifty, many women have struggled to support their families financially. This is particularly the case in villages, where most women do not have jobs and the majority of male breadwinners (agricultural workers, small business owners) have been incarcerated. Many children have had both parents disappeared. Effectively orphaned, these children have been placed in boarding schools and orphanages where, under state care, they are educated in Chinese language and Han culture.[42] Some members of the Uyghur diaspora who left their children with family members when they went abroad to work or study (or were forced to flee) have told me that they recognized their sons and daughters in TikTok videos made by the teachers of those schools. Even children who live with their parents are instructed to speak Chinese in public spaces, even to their parents.[43] This creates a huge disconnect between generations. A popular Uyghur saying goes, "Nowadays grandparents and grandchildren need a translator."

In most cases, communication between Uyghurs abroad and their relatives in the Xinjiang Uyghur Autonomous Region ceased entirely for between one and three years starting in 2017. Those in the diaspora could only connect to each other to share their hopelessness, represented by the typical expression "I don't know if they are alive or dead." They no longer asked each other, "How is your family?" but rather "Have you been able to get in touch with them?" The testimonies featured in the Xinjiang Victims Database are powerful and relatable. Uyghurs and Kazakhs are pictured holding their loved ones' photos and talking about their mothers, fathers, brothers, sisters, husbands, and children. While many detainees were released over the course of 2019 and 2020, and some contact was reinstated, albeit under tight control, many diaspora Uyghurs have endured tremendous anxiety, guilt, and feelings of powerlessness.[44] Among those whom I have encountered, many show symptoms of trauma, despair, and depression.[45]

As people lost loved ones to the camps and were unable to contact them, more than 1.2 million Han citizens were being placed into Uyghur houses under the "Becoming Family" (Jiedui Renqin) campaign, another measure that Chen Quanguo tested in the Tibet Autonomous Region and expanded in Xinjiang and that was ongoing at the time of writing.[46] Every two months, state cadres spend at least five days in the assigned villagers' home, to assess their loyalty and ability to speak standard Chinese (Putonghua)—now referred to as the "national language" (Guoyu)—and to report on any suspicious activities.[47] These "sent-down" state employees also study Xi Jinping's reports and thoughts with the family. According to Darren Byler's study of the campaign in 2018, Han cadres often did not fully grasp the consequences of their actions and saw it as an opportunity to work toward the goals of the state in a way that would benefit their careers.[48] Videos of Han family members "happily" joining Uyghur families who seem distressed are common on TikTok. For example, in one video, while a Han cadre performs as an intimate family member, a boy asks, "If Dad comes home, can he stay?," and the mom answers, "I don't know if he can come."[49] According to government documents, the behavior of Uyghurs in front of these Han family members, as well as in other aspects of daily life, will affect how long the loved ones will be detained.[50]

This integration of Han Chinese into Uyghur households has been promoted under the slogan "Our Chinese Dream—a family of ethnic unity" (Women de Zhongguo Meng, minzu tuanjie yi jiaqin).[51] In the place of the Uyghur family comes the "Chinese" family, instituted and inserted into Uyghur homes by the Xi Jinping regime. Uyghur pioneers of ethnic unity, "Becoming Family," and interethnic marriage are celebrated by the state as model China Dream catchers.[52] For Uyghurs in Xinjiang, however, the dream is one of survival. Living in fear and silence, they have no choice but to be family with Han "brothers" and "sisters" and assimilate into a greater Chinese "family," even if this is a process that destroys their Uyghur family.

More than simply another layer of surveillance of Uyghur political loyalties, the "Becoming Family" campaign is therefore part of efforts to reengineer Uyghur identity, culture, and values in line with Xi Jinping's vision of a Han-based national culture and identity. According to Xi: "Every ethnic group must tightly bind together like the seeds of a pomegranate."[53] The pomegranate, a symbol of beauty and fertility in Uyghur culture and literature, has become a symbol of ethnic unity, which for non-Han people means giving up or denouncing fundamental parts of their own family, religion, and cultural identity. In a 2018 government white paper on ethnic policy in Xinjiang, state authorities declared that "Chinese" culture should be considered the core of all other ethnic cultures, which "have their roots in the fertile soil of Chinese civilization. All ethnic cultures in Xinjiang have borrowed from Chinese culture from the very beginning."[54] This distinction between "ethnic cultures" and the "Chinese culture," asserting that the former have borrowed from the latter, suggests that Han culture represents a central core; it is a superior culture that emerged prior to others. In August 2018, the mayor of Ürümqi made this even more explicit, declaring that "Uyghurs are not descendants of Turks" and instead are "members of the Chinese family," effectively erasing Uyghur history.[55] In state media and broader social discourse, the differences between Han and Uyghur culture are continuously emphasized to make plain that one is desirable and the other is not. Han culture is elite, superior, and civilized and associated with patriotism and modernity, while Uyghur (and Muslim) culture is represented as backward and violent and, since the Chinese "War on Terror" campaign, has been increasingly criminalized.

Criminalizing Uyghur Distinction, Reengineering Identity

"This is worse than the Cultural Revolution" is a common phrase I heard during interviews both inside and outside Xinjiang.[56] The increasing politicization of and hostility toward any aspect of Uyghur religious life has effectively removed religiosity, from everyday greetings to weddings and funerals, while an ever-tightening cultural space has weakened the use of the Uyghur language across generations. During my fieldwork in 2016, I heard that religious books and books deemed illegal were being confiscated and burned. One villager told me that, although people were very afraid, they were unwilling to burn books that were sacred, so they threw them into local rivers. In some cases, the sluice gates of irrigation canals became blocked with discarded books. Although Uyghur-language publications had previously been subject to the approval of state censors, the effective criminalization of the Uyghur language now makes it impossible for anything Uyghur—other than propaganda and expressions of loyalty—to remain within the boundaries of state-permitted speech. For either aesthetic or historical purposes, the practical value of the Uyghur language continues to diminish due to state oppression.[57]

Many small bookshops that catered to the Uyghur language have closed down, and even the larger state-owned bookshops no longer support Uyghur publications to any significant extent. For the most part, only texts translated into Chinese remain. Online spaces have also witnessed significant decreases in Uyghur language use, with many sites being shut down or their owners disappearing. TV programs rarely have any Uyghur-language content. If they do, it must have Chinese subtitles. TikTok videos display young Uyghurs speaking Chinese. This is in strong contrast to what I observed on social media in the early 2010s, when many people were shown speaking their mother tongue. People are required to learn Chinese at home to complete assignments for each week's neighborhood political education gathering. As one Uyghur resident stated: "Every time I was finally able to contact my mother, I learned that she was doing homework, every day copying Chinese characters, each one hundred times."

The language shift is most obvious in traditional Uyghur music and popular media. For example, Uyghur Muqam, a UNESCO (United Nations Educational, Scientific, and Cultural Organization) intangible cultural heritage featuring traditional music and dance, was performed in Chinese during the seventieth anniversary of the founding of the People's Republic of China in 2019. This brought distress to many Uyghurs, according to my contacts in the diaspora. The 2020 Xinjiang New Year's gala hosted a few young Uyghur musicians, yet there was not a single trace of the Uyghur language or traditional dance. The expression of state-curated ethnic difference via song and dance performances by "happy" and exoticized Uyghurs has long been a staple of such official events. These examples show that even this is disappearing and "being swallowed up by Hanness" as Uyghur language and arts disappear from public life.[58] Expressions of devotion to Xi and the Party seem to have become the only safe way of using Uyghur language and Uyghur cultural forms such as folk songs.

The disappearance of visible and well-known members of the Uyghur cultural elite demonstrates the Party's message even more clearly to the public, further intensifying and routinizing internalized fear. The Uyghur Human Rights Project has reported that more than 380 Uyghur intellectuals have disappeared since 2017, among whom the anthropologist Rahile Dawut and the geographer Tashpolat Tiyip once made international headlines for their scholarly work. There is growing public demand for the Chinese government to be transparent and provide information regarding their fates. When we look at the many public figures who have disappeared, from human rights activists to scholars, it is evident that those whose work is related to Uyghur language and the preservation of Uyghur identity, culture, and history have been targeted.[59] Exiled Uyghur poet and filmmaker Tahir Hamut Izgil stresses that the attack on and eradication of intellectuals who had been leading research on Uyghur art, culture, and history not only serves as an example to citizens but also causes widespread despair throughout Uyghur society.[60]

The attack on Uyghur culture has extended to the removal of physical traces of Uyghur beliefs, values, and identity in the landscape under the policy of "Sinicizing" religion, which has been intensified and diversified under Xi Jinping.[61] A five-year plan to "Sinicize Islam" was adopted in 2019, justified as the regulating of "non-state-approved religious beliefs."[62] Journalists and Uyghur researchers have uncovered systematic destruction of sacred sites, mosques, and cemeteries through satellite imagery data and in-person visits. Uyghur researcher Bahram Sintash confirmed the disappearance of more than one hundred mosques and sacred shrines (*mazars*) by comparing satellite images over a span of several years.[63] In the name of the "standardization" of old graves, many cemeteries have been relocated without community approval, and some cemeteries near town centers have been transformed into parks or residential areas.[64] Praying at sacred places, a central part of Uyghur life for centuries, has been prohibited. This is ironic since camp detainees have been forced to effectively worship President Xi by learning his thoughts and chanting or singing songs in his praise in order to receive their meals.[65] As Zenz highlights, religiosity is equated to addiction and the internment camps are seen as treatment centers, as if religion is a disease or drug to be overcome.[66] The only way to be "free" from religion is through state-sponsored treatment, and with this treatment comes the erasure and replacement of one's religious beliefs and cultural values.

The criminalization and destruction of the Uyghur language, culture, and faith are tangible manifestations of the ways in which Party-state authority intensifies fear. Intense pressure on Uyghurs to demonstrate loyalty and patriotism through performing an undifferentiated Han-based Chineseness, combined with the effective criminalization of Uyghur identity and ubiquitous surveillance of their lives and actions, has left many Uyghurs with little choice but to abandon their own culture, language, and traditions. Some have even changed their names to Han names.[67] Uyghur cultural festivals have disappeared from public life. Communities now celebrate traditional Han festivals such as Chinese New Year, the Dragon Boat Festival, and even Tomb-Sweeping Day. Those who do not celebrate have been fined, according to reports from the region.[68] Uyghur friends in Xinjiang testified that in some cases when Han "family" members visited Uyghur homes during Chinese New Year, they forced Uyghurs to write couplets and eat pork dumplings together—a major violation of Uyghur halal traditions. Many small Uyghur towns have held Chinese traditional dances as a way of celebrating Chinese New Year.[69] They perform traditional Peking operas, learn classical Chinese poems, and speak and eat like they are Chinese. If state media broadcasts are to be believed, Uyghur children are studying the Chinese classics dressed up in costumes representative of the Ming era, the last Han-led dynasty.[70]

All of these examples show that the state, under the leadership of Xi Jinping, is intolerant of the existence of Uyghurs as a people with a very different language, culture, and religion. The securitization and the destruction of Uyghur families, religion, and culture are threatening the very existence of Uyghurness, a process that some commentators have referred to as "cultural genocide" or "ethnic cleansing."[71] The CCP's end goal is to reengineer the entire Uyghur population to fit a Chinese nationalistic vision and interests based on Han values and traditions. The anthropologists Amy Anderson and Darren Byler, in their analysis of Uyghur music, argue that the act of criminalizing a culture's language sends the message that the language and its associated culture have no value in mainstream society.[72] People are being taught and shown through propaganda, the "Becoming Family" program, and the internment camps that adopting Han culture is the better, pragmatic choice for Uyghur people; they are expected to be grateful that so many people, from camp personnel to Han "family" members, are willing to help them assimilate. It is no wonder that under this state of oppression, fear, and censorship we witness elderly mothers ending conversations with phrases such as "Party bless you, my child" or "Xi Jinping bless you."

"Love" Xi Jinping with Fear

The fear that Uyghurs have internalized has resulted in outward obedience to Xi Jinping and the Party. As Byler and the human geographer Sarah Tynen have demonstrated, for most, if not all, Uyghurs in China there is no room to show resistance—instead, life centers around survival and existence.[73] This reflects a significant change in the lives of Uyghurs under the Xi administration. Studies of Uyghur-state and Uyghur-Han relations in the 1990s and the first decade of the twenty-first century analyzed Uyghur ethno-nationalist sentiment and documented people's resistance to Han state nationalism through everyday language and activities, as well their everyday acts of "symbolic resistance" to assimilation.[74] Since Xi Jinping's rise as paramount leader in 2012, however, life in Xinjiang has shifted to survival through the active performance of Han-based Chinese national identity and "full-hearted" support and love for Xi in daily life.

Xi Jinping has become larger than life. His words and image have come to offer the only safe means for Uyghurs to express their "solidarity" with and loyalty to the Party. Just as Uyghurs used to greet each other using a Mao quotation during the Maoist period, it is becoming common to quote Xi Jinping in daily conversation. Although no one trusts each other, they trust that these texts can be used without fear as a way to express their loyalty. The political scientist Rongbin Han's recent study of popular nationalism and regime support in China suggests that there is a measure of freedom of expression and space for some criticism of the regime under Xi among domestic as well as overseas Chinese netizens.[75] However, this does not extend to Uyghur netizens, whose online posts and comments are full of "love" and "gratitude" to the nation, to the greatest leader, Xi Jinping, and "hope" for achieving the Chinese Dream. The overwhelming patriotic and monolithic tone of Uyghur social media results from the extreme fear that pushes people to express loyalty through love and gratitude in order to survive.

Internment camp survivors have testified that as part of their reeducation, policy documents and speeches written by Xi Jinping were used as study materials that they were required to memorize to demonstrate their knowledge and loyalty to the Party. They were forced to chant "Thanks to the Party! Thanks to the Motherland! Thanks to Chairman Xi!" (Ganxie dang! Ganxie zuguo! Xiexie Xi Zhuxi!) before each meal.[76] This reinforced the message that their thoughts had to be aligned to the Party, and more specifically to Xi Jinping. Former detainees have refuted the idea that the camps have in any way been places of learning or vocational training.[77] They have all been about learning the Chinese language, Xi Jinping Thought (Xi Jinping Sixiang), and Xi's speeches, as well as self-criticism of Uyghur traditional and religious beliefs.[78] Some have said that all they did was watch television with only one channel, which showed nothing other than footage of Xi Jinping's visits to other countries and how he is helping them to develop.

Outside the camps, Uyghurs study Xi Jinping Thought with their Han "family members" and at regular neighborhood political education gatherings, which they are required to attend. They display Xi's image in their living rooms and hold song and dance gatherings where Uyghur musicians improvise lyrics thanking "father Xi Jinping" for teaching them how to be "modern" Chinese citizens. Showing any lack of love for Xi, the Party, Chinese nationalism, or Han culture is interpreted as a sign of disloyalty and extremism. As one elder told me, "They call us extremist, yet not realizing how extreme they are." In this case, fear is not silent anymore; it is expressed through demonstrations of "love." In a video that circulated on Uyghur social media in 2018, a group of Uyghur village women sing together:

Xi dada, Xi dada	Father Xi, father Xi
Yishen zhengqi ying tianxia	Winning the world with righteousness
Renmin de Xi dada, baixing de Xi dada	Father Xi of the people, father Xi of the commonfolk
Zhongguo de Xi dada, shijie de Xi dada.	Father Xi of China, father Xi of the world.[79]

There are a growing number of songs in both Uyghur and Chinese dedicated to praising Xi Jinping. In Xinjiang, it has become a political duty to learn and perform these songs.

Based on available ethnographic data, it is unclear whether all performances of devotion to Xi, from public singing to the display of his image in the "private" space of the home, are official requirements or a response to the political climate in Xinjiang—a means of demonstrating loyalty and avoiding being sent to a reeducation camp. They are likely a combination of both. Several recent exiles from Xinjiang have confirmed that neighborhood-level cadres directly ask residents to display a photo of Xi Jinping and other core leaders of the CCP. As every family receives daily checkups from these cadres, it is dangerous to take the pictures down. This has driven people to engage in the cult of personality around Xi Jinping in fear of their lives.

The image of "father" or "soulmate" Xi has penetrated deep into Uyghur life. No matter how his cult of personality began—whether it was promoted by Xi Jinping, his supporters, or genuine grassroots admiration—in Xinjiang, Xi Jinping has become the highest symbol of state power. Party officials such as Chen Quanguo, as well as the Han family cadres sent to Xinjiang, help to reinforce and maximize the effects of Xi's cult of personality. By extension, Xi's Chinese Dream attempts to make the ideals of the past and the future (a unified China) a reality in the present. Ostensibly, Xi Jinping placates the current generation's fears and provides safety to future generations. Yet when his personality cult is intertwined with an internalized fear, resistance to Xi's "love" is not an option. The absurd horror of forced assimilation and cultural genocide is thus normalized in contemporary Uyghur society, at least on the surface. There is no space to voice any criticism of Xi or the Party in this tightly controlled region. Uyghurs in Xinjiang understand that demonstrating their knowledge of Xi Jinping Thought and venerating him publicly are the safest ways to show loyalty and thereby continue to survive.

Conclusion

When Uyghur elders advise young people to remain calm if faced with force-ful confrontation, they often use the idiom "The one who fears will throw the first punch" (Qorqqan awal mush koturer). Violence here is a sign not of strength, but of fear. Some Uyghurs have pointed out that the extreme assimilationist policies implemented under Xi Jinping are the result of state and Han fear of Uyghurs and their differences, and the possibility of sepa-ratism. This fear has been projected onto and internalized by the Uyghurs of Xinjiang by way of mass internment camps and ubiquitous surveillance, the disintegration of Uyghur families, and the replacement of Islam with the personality cult of Xi Jinping. It is clear that the Chinese state's ethnic policies have entered a new phase under Xi with an emphasis on assimilation and a growing Han-based cultural nationalism. Given extreme state pressure, it seems that the majority of Uyghurs have no choice but to accept the terms of the "Chinese Dream" and adopt an undifferentiated Chinese identity built solely on Han cultural traditions, even if that means having their culture and way of life transformed into something foreign to them. Only a complete reversal of the policies implemented in the name of the "War on Terror" and Xi's "Chinese Dream" could offer freedom from the fear of the state for Uyghurs in Xinjiang.

At present, Uyghurs are never free from fear; the difficulty of expressing the depth of their fear and terror has been a challenge in the writing of this chapter. Fear of disappearance and detention, and of family destruction, are overwhelming. These fears are exacerbated by other fears—fears of showing ethnic pride, of not being loyal enough, and of not showing enough love for Xi Jinping. As more and more Uyghurs describe themselves as a "people destroyed" and as having "broken spirits," the state defends its strategy in Xinjiang and circulates propaganda images of "happy" Uyghurs.[80] Cognitive dissonance, indeed. Since 2014, images of Xi Jinping have become unavoidable in Xinjiang, embedded into every facet of daily life. No one dares to criticize him: he is the new god; his words guarantee safety. People venerate Xi Jinping; they learn his words and thoughts, talk about them, and cite them to protect themselves and their families. The extent of Xi Jinping's direct involvement in causing this tragic effect is unclear. What is certain is that his image, views, and leadership have transformed the deepest corners of the Uyghur homeland and everyday life.

Notes

Musapir is the pen name of a Uyghur scholar. Search for other works by this author on ORCID, https://orcid.org/0000-0002-9547-1352.

1. For an example, see the image of a mural showing Xi surrounded by Uyghur children accompanying the article from the Associated Press, "With Parents Detained, Chinese State Cares for 'Uighur Orphans,'" *VOA News*, September 21, 2018, https://www.voanews.com/a/with-parents-detained-chinese-state-cares-for-uighur-orphans-/4581363.html. The first part of the Chinese slogan can be more literally translated as "Xi Jinping's heart is connected to the hearts of all the peoples of Xinjiang." I have chosen to follow the nuances of the Uyghur slogan, which uses the term *qelbdash*. *Qelbdash* means "soulmate" in the sense of a person who is your closest friend, who can deeply understand you, and who shares your thoughts.

2. Altishahr means "six cities" and is the historical name for the Tarim Basin region.

3. Interviews and conversations with members of the Uyghur diaspora.

4. The videos cited in this article have been gathered from other members of the Uyghur diaspora and are in the author's personal archive.

5. While "Xi *dada*" is sometimes translated as "Uncle Xi" from the Chinese, in Uyghur it means "father Xi"; *chong dada* means "grandfather." In this article, I follow the Uyghur meaning.

6. Although the last words of the first and sixth lines share the same phonetic spelling (*atimiz*), they have different etymological roots, with *ata* meaning "father," and *at* meaning "shooting" or "horse."

7. Personal observation, shared by several other members of the Uyghur diaspora who have expressed this to me in personal communications.

8. Liangen Yin and Terry Flew, "Xi Dada Loves Peng Mama: Digital Culture and the Return of Charismatic Authority in China," *Thesis Eleven* 144, no. 1 (2018): 80–99.

9. See Peter Ferdinand, "Westward Ho—the China Dream and 'One Belt, One Road': Chinese Foreign Policy under Xi Jinping," *International Affairs* 92,

no. 4 (2016): 941–57; Michael Gow, "The Core Socialist Values of the Chinese Dream: Towards a Chinese Integral State," *Critical Asian Studies* 49, no. 1 (2017): 92–116.

10. On the heightening of tensions in Xinjiang, see Gardner Bovingdon, *The Uyghurs: Strangers in Their Own Land* (New York: Columbia University Press, 2010); Joanne N. Smith Finley, *The Art of Symbolic Resistance: Uyghur Identities and Uyghur-Han Relations in Contemporary Xinjiang* (Leiden: Brill, 2013); Michael Clarke, "China's 'War on Terror' in Xinjiang: Human Security and the Causes of Violent Uighur Separatism," *Terrorism and Political Violence* 20, no. 2 (2008): 271–301.

11. James Leibold, "Xinjiang Work Forum Marks New Policy of 'Ethnic Mingling,'" *China Brief* 14, no. 12 (2014): 1–12.

12. Gerald Roche and James Leibold, "China's Second-Generation Ethnic Policies Are Already Here," *Made in China Journal* 5, no. 2 (2020): 32, https://madeinchinajournal.com/2020/09/07/chinas-second-generation-ethnic-policies-are-already-here; see also James Leibold, "Planting the Seed: Ethnic Policy in Xi Jinping's New Era of Cultural Nationalism," *China Brief* 19, no. 22 (2019): 1–32.

13. Ben Hillman, "Xinjiang and the 'Chinese Dream,'" *East Asia Forum*, October 24, 2018, https://www.eastasiaforum.org/2018/10/24/xinjiang-and-the-chinese-dream.

14. Leibold, "Planting the Seed."

15. This shift in policy and its affects have been discussed by scholars such as Tashi Rabgey, James Millward, and Darren Byler in the podcast *Sinica*, https://thechinaproject.com/series/sinica. See also the articles by Martin Lavička, Anonymous, Ildikó Bellér-Hann, and Rune Steenberg in "Voiced and Voiceless in Xinjiang: Minorities, Elites, and Narrative Constructions across the Centuries," special issue, *Asian Ethnicity* 22, no. 1 (2021).

16. See, for example, Adrian Zenz, "New Evidence for China's Political Re-education Campaign in Xinjiang," *China Brief* 18, no. 10 (2018): 1–45.

17. Anna Hayes, "Interwoven 'Destinies': The Significance of Xinjiang to the China Dream, the Belt and Road Initiative, and the Xi Jinping Legacy," *Journal of Contemporary China* 29, no. 121 (2020): 31–45.

18. Magnus Fiskesjö, "China's 'Re-education'/Concentration Camps in Xinjiang / East Turkestan and the Wider Campaign of Forced Assimilation Targeting Uyghurs, Kazakhs, Etc.," Uyghur Human Rights Project, last revised March 21, 2021, https://uhrp.org/bibliography. This archive not only provides extensive information and evidence about the current situation, but it also could serve as a catalyst for future truth and reconciliation in China by providing valuable resources. Xinjiang Victims Database, last accessed January 5, 2024, https://shahit.biz/eng. I also interviewed people who actively volunteer for or add content to this database.

19. On Chen Quanguo, see James Leibold and Adrian Zenz, "Chen Quanguo:

The Strongman behind Beijing's Securitization Strategy in Tibet and Xinjiang," *China Brief* 17, no. 12 (2017): 1–28. For a brief description of grid management, see Deng, Demes, and Chen, in this volume.

20. Josh Chin and Clément Bürge, "Twelve Days in Xinjiang: How China's Surveillance State Overwhelms Daily Life," *Wall Street Journal*, December 19, 2017, https://www.wsj.com/articles/twelve-days-in-xinjiang-how-chinas -surveillance-state-overwhelms-daily-life-1513700355.

21. Hanna Burdorf, "A Police State Going into Hiding," *Art of Life in Chinese Central Asia*, January 31, 2020, https://livingotherwise.com/2020/01/31/a-police -state-going-into-hiding.

22. Personal communication with author, 2016.

23. International Campaign for Tibet, "The Origin of the 'Xinjiang Model' in Tibet under Chen Quanguo: Securitizing Ethnicity and Accelerating Assimila- tion," December 19, 2018, https://savetibet.org/the-origin-of-the-xinjiang-model -in-tibet-under-chen-quanguo-securitizing-ethnicity-and-accelerating-assimilation; Leibold, "Planting the Seed," 48.

24. Each neighborhood has a residents' committee (*ahaliler komteti*) that functions as a bridge between local government and residents; in Chinese these administrative units in urban areas are called *shequ* and in villages *dadui*. In pres- ent-day Xinjiang, *ahaliler komteti* cadres are the main heads of surveillance acting on behalf of the government. See Sarah Tynen, "Uneven State Territorialization: Governance, Inequality, and Survivance in Xinjiang, China" (PhD diss., Univer- sity of Colorado, 2019).

25. Tanner Greer, "48 Ways to Get Sent to a Chinese Concentration Camp," *Foreign Policy*, September 13, 2018, https://foreignpolicy.com/2018/09/13/48 -ways-to-get-sent-to-a-chinese-concentration-camp.

26. Personal communication with author, 2016.

27. Adrian Zenz and James Leibold, "Xinjiang's Rapidly Evolving Security State," *China Brief* 17, no. 4 (2017): 21–27.

28. Lucas Niewenhuis, "A Police State of Historic Proportion: Criminal Ar- rests Up 731 Percent in Xinjiang," China Project, July 25, 2018, https://thechina project.com/2018/07/25/a-police-state-of-historic-proportion-criminal-arrests -up-731-percent-in-xinjiang.

29. Linda Green, "Living in a State of Fear," in *Fieldwork under Fire: Contem- porary Studies of Violence and Culture*, ed. Carolyn Nordstrom and Antonius Robben (Berkeley: University of California Press, 1995), 118–19.

30. "China Condemns Two Ex-Xinjiang Officials in Separatism Cases," *AP News*, April 7, 2021, https://apnews.com/article/world-news-race-and-ethnicity -beijing-china-national-security-e4d7a915a2e3ebb6c6f50778a2aec81a.

31. Interview with author, Xinjiang, 2016.

32. James Leibold, "Surveillance in China's Xinjiang Region: Ethnic Sorting, Coercion, and Inducement," *Journal of Contemporary China* 29, no. 121 (2020):

46–60. On the IJOP system and app, see also Human Rights Watch, *China's Algorithms of Repression: Reverse Engineering a Xinjiang Police Mass Surveillance App* (New York: Human Rights Watch, 2019), https://www.hrw.org/sites /default/files/report_pdf/china0519_web.pdf.

33. Nithin Coca, "China's Xinjiang Surveillance Is the Dystopian Future Nobody Wants," *Engadget*, February 22, 2018, https://www.engadget.com/2018 -02-22-china-xinjiang-surveillance-tech-spread.html.

34. Yujie Xue, "Anti-Fraud App from Chinese Police Sees Soaring Downloads amid Complaints of Forced Installs," *South China Morning Post*, April 12, 2021, https://www.scmp.com/tech/policy/article/3129222/anti-fraud-app-chinese -police-sees-soaring-downloads-amid-complaints#.

35. Here I have drawn inspiration from Linda Green's discussion on the routinization of terror and its effects in Guatemala. See Green, "Living in a State of Fear," 108.

36. Gene Bunin, "How the 'Happiest Muslims in the World' Are Coping with Their Happiness," *Art of Life in Chinese Central Asia*, July 31, 2018, https:// livingotherwise.com/2018/07/31/happiest-muslims-world-coping-happiness.

37. Stephanie Nebehay, "U.N. Says It Has Credible Reports That China Holds Million Uighurs in Secret Camps," Reuters, August 10, 2018, https://www.reuters .com/article/us-china-rights-un/u-n-says-it-has-credible-reports-that-china-holds -million-uighurs-in-secret-camps-idUSKBN1KV1SU; Zenz, "New Evidence"; Vicky Xiuzhong Xu, Danielle Cave, James Leibold, Kelsey Munro, and Nathan Ruser, *Uyghurs for Sale: "Re-education," Forced Labour and Surveillance beyond Xinjiang* (Barton, ACT: Australian Strategic Policy Institute, 2020).

38. Sarah Parvini, "'They Want to Erase Us.' California Uighurs Fear for Family Members in China," *Los Angeles Times*, August 9, 2019, https://www.latimes .com/local/lanow/la-me-california-uighur-muslims-china-20190610-story.html.

39. Fergus Hunter, "Detained and in Danger: The Tortured Australian Families Who Fear for Their Missing Loved Ones," *Sydney Morning Herald*, November 17, 2018, https://www.smh.com.au/politics/federal/detained-and-in-danger-the -tortured-australian-families-who-fear-for-their-missing-loved-ones-20181115 -p50g5q.html; Kate Lyons, "17 Australian Residents Believed Detained in China's Uighur Crackdown," *Guardian*, February 10, 2019, https://www.theguardian .com/australia-news/2019/feb/11/revealed-17-australian-residents-believed -detained-in-chinas-uighur-crackdown.

40. Gerry Shih, "'Permanent Cure': Inside the Re-education Camps China Is Using to Brainwash Muslims," *Business Insider*, May 17, 2018, https://www.business insider.com/what-is-life-like-in-xinjiang-reeducation-camps-china-2018-5.

41. Eva Dou, Jeremy Page, and Josh Chin, "China's Uighur Camps Swell as Beijing Widens the Dragnet," *Wall Street Journal*, April 17, 2018, https://www .wsj.com/articles/chinas-uighur-camps-swell-as-beijing-widens-the-dragnet -1534534894; Shohret Hoshur and Alim Seytoff, "Uyghur Muslim Scholar Dies

in Chinese Police Custody," trans. Alim Seytoff and Paul Eckert, Radio Free Asia, January 29, 2018, https://www.rfa.org/english/news/uyghur/scholar-death-01292018180427.html; Shohret Hoshur, "Uyghur Teenager Dies in Custody at Political Re-education Camp," trans. Alim Seytoff and Joshua Lipes, Radio Free Asia, March 14, 2018, https://www.rfa.org/english/news/uyghur/teenager-03142018154926.html.

42. Emily Feng, "Crackdown in Xinjiang: Where Have All the People Gone?," *Financial Times*, August 5, 2018, https://www.ft.com/content/ac0ffb2e-8b36-11e8-b18d-0181731a0340; John Sudworth, "China Muslims: Xinjiang Schools Used to Separate Children from Families," *BBC News*, July 4, 2019, https://www.bbc.com/news/world-asia-china-48825090. Reporters from CNN tracked down some of these children in Xinjiang and Istanbul and provided extensive detail of this tragedy of family separation. See David Culver, "CNN Finds Stranded Uyghur Children," CNN, March 24, 2021, https://www.cnn.com/videos/world/2021/03/24/china-xinjiang-children-culver-pkg-intl-hnk-vpx.cnn.

43. Darren Byler, "China's Government Has Ordered a Million Citizens to Occupy Uighur Homes. Here's What They Think They're Doing," *ChinaFile*, October 24, 2018, https://www.chinafile.com/reporting-opinion/postcard/million-citizens-occupy-uighur-homes-xinjiang.

44. Nathan Vanderklippe, "Exporting Persecution: Uyghur Diaspora Haunted by Anxiety, Guilt as Family Held in Chinese Camps," *Globe and Mail*, August 12, 2018, https://www.theglobeandmail.com/world/article-exporting-persecution-uyghur-diaspora-haunted-by-anxiety-guilt-as.

45. Further research needs to be done on the mental health and trauma many members of the Uyghur diaspora live with.

46. Human Rights Watch, "China: Visiting Officials Occupy Homes in Muslim Region," May 13, 2018, https://www.hrw.org/news/2018/05/14/china-visiting-officials-occupy-homes-muslim-region.

47. Zhiyun Zhao, "Zizhiqu dangwei jueding: 12 yue jizhong kaizhan minzu tuanjie 'jieqin zhou' huodong" (The Party Committee of the Autonomous Region has decided to focus on the "Unity Week" of ethnic unity in December), *Bingtuan News*, December 11, 2017, http://web.archive.org/web/20180812111510/http://www.bt.chinanews.com/bingtuan/20171211/8699.shtml (site discontinued).

48. Byler, "China's Government."

49. Darren Byler (@dtbyler), "An incredible scene of Han state workers invading a Uyghur home," Twitter, November 4, 2019, https://twitter.com/dtbyler/status/1191474404472963072.

50. "Document: What Chinese Officials Told Children Whose Families Were Put in Camps," *New York Times*, November 16, 2019, https://www.nytimes.com/interactive/2019/11/16/world/asia/china-detention-directive.html.

51. Sunzhen Song and Zhang Ziwei, "Xinjiang wulumuqi: Shequ juban 'women de zhongguo meng, minzu tuanjie yijia qin' ying xinchun lianhuan hui" (Urumqi,

Xinjiang: "Our Chinese Dream, National Unity and One Family" New Year celebration party held by the community), *Sina*, January 14, 2020, https://k.sina.cn /article_3164957712_bca56c10020014h4j.html?from=news&subch=onews.

52. See, for example, Darren Byler, "On Qurbanjan Semet's Photobook 'I Am from Xinjiang on the Silk Road,'" *Art of Life in Chinese Central Asia*, September 3, 2015, https://livingotherwise.com/2015/09/03/on-qurbanjan-semets-photobook -i-am-from-xinjiang-on-the-silk-road.

53. Austin Ramzy and Chris Buckley, "'Absolutely No Mercy': Leaked Files Expose How China Organized Mass Detentions of Muslims," *New York Times*, November 16, 2019, https://www.nytimes.com/interactive/2019/11/16/world /asia/china-xinjiang-documents.html.

54. State Council Information Office, "Cultural Protection and Development in Xinjiang," November 15, 2018, http://www.xinhuanet.com/english /2018-11/15/c_137607548.htm.

55. Shan Jie, "Uyghurs Are Not Descendants of Turks: Urumqi Mayor," *Global Times*, August 26, 2018, https://www.globaltimes.cn/content/1158545.shtml.

56. Central Asia Program, "Symposium on China's Mass Incarceration of Uyghurs: Contextualizing the Re-education Camps," November 27, 2018, YouTube, https://www.youtube.com/watch?v=IYVfnRLK9mU.

57. Byler wrote a series of columns for the China Project about this issue. See, for example, Darren Byler, "'Ethnic Extinction' in Northwest China," China Project, July 7, 2021, https://thechinaproject.com/2021/07/07/ethnic-extinction -in-northwest-china.

58. Amy Anderson and Darren Byler, "'Eating Hanness': Uyghur Musical Tradition in a Time of Re-education," *China Perspectives*, no. 3 (2019): 17–26.

59. Eziz Eysa, interview with author, 2019.

60. Tahir Hamut Izgil, interview with author, 2020.

61. See "China Passes Law to Make Islam 'Compatible with Socialism,'" *Al Jazeera*, January 5, 2019, https://www.aljazeera.com/news/2019/1/5/china-passes -law-to-make-islam-compatible-with-socialism.

62. Li Qingqing, "China Explores Effective Governance of Religion in Secular World," *Global Times*, January 6, 2019, http://www.globaltimes.cn/content /1134750.shtml [page no longer active], accessed February 15, 2020.

63. Bahram Sintash, "Demolishing Faith: The Destruction and Desecration of Uyghur Mosques and Shrines," Uyghur Human Rights Project, October 28, 2016, https://uhrp.org/report/demolishing-faith-the-destruction-and-desecration-of -uyghur-mosques-and-shrines.

64. Eva Xiao, Pak Yiu, and Andrew Beatty, "Even in Death, Uighurs Feel Long Reach of Chinese State," *Taipei Times*, October 14, 2019, https://www.taipeitimes .com/News/feat/archives/2019/10/14/2003723889.

65. Brian McGleenon, "Inside China's Secret 'Concentration Camps' Where Detainees 'Pray to President Xi Jinping,'" *Daily Express*, May 28, 2019, https://

www.express.co.uk/news/world/1132815/china-re-education-camps-muslim
-minority-crack-down-uyghur-oppression-xi-jinping-xinjiang.

66. Adrian Zenz, "'Thoroughly Reforming Them towards a Healthy Heart Attitude': China's Political Re-education Campaign in Xinjiang," *Central Asian Survey* 38, no. 1 (2019): 102–28.

67. Guo Cheng and Rizwangul, "Mandatory Name Change Campaign Reflects the Sharpening of Assimilation Policy against Uighurs," International Uyghur Human Rights and Democracy Foundation, March 10, 2018, https://www .iuhrdf.org/content/mandatory-name-change-campaign-reflects-sharpening-as-similation-policy-against-uighurs.

68. Darren Byler, "Images in Red: Han Culture, Uyghur Performers, Chinese New Year," *Art of Life in Chinese Central Asia*, February 23, 2018, https://living otherwise.com/2018/02/23/images-red-han-culture-uyghur-performers-chinese -new-year.

69. See, for example, "Wen su xian: She huo xunyan nao xinchun" (Wensu County celebrating new year), China News Service Xinjiang, December 30, 2022, https://www.xj.chinanews.com.cn/dizhou/2022-12-30/detail-ihcihaha6948914 .shtml. For an image of Uyghurs celebrating Chinese New Year in Yengeriq Village, Awat County, Aksu, in 2018, see the news website Tianshannet, February 16, 2018, http://uy.ts.cn/system/2018/02/16/035099046.shtml.

70. "Uyghurs Asked to Celebrate Chinese New Year in 2018," February 20, 2018, YouTube, 8:35–8:40, https://www.youtube.com/watch?v=dyp9XL24b wE&ab_channel=TheArtofLifeinChineseCentralAsia.

71. Azeem Ibrahim, "China Must Answer for Cultural Genocide in Court," *Foreign Policy*, December 3, 2019, https://foreignpolicy.com/2019/12/03/uighurs -xinjiang-china-cultural-genocide-international-criminal-court; "What Congress Can Do Now to Combat China's Mass Ethnic Cleansing of Uighurs," *Washington Post*, May 23, 2019, https://www.washingtonpost.com/opinions/global-opinions /what-congress-can-do-now-to-combat-chinas-mass-ethnic-cleansing-of-uighurs /2019/05/23/fe906c68-7d6a-11e9-a5b3-34f3edf1351e_story.html.

72. Anderson and Byler, "'Eating Hanness.'"

73. Darren Byler, "Spirit Breaking: Capitalism and Terror in Northwest China," *Art of Life in Chinese Central Asia*, July 22, 2019, https://livingotherwise .com/2019/07/22/adam-hunerven-capitalism-and-terror-in-northwest-china; Tynen, "Uneven State Territorialization."

74. Bovingdon, *The Uyghurs*; Smith Finley, *The Art of Symbolic Resistance*.

75. Rongbin Han, "Cyber Nationalism and Regime Support under Xi Jinping: The Effects of the 2018 Constitutional Revision," *Journal of Contemporary China* 30, no. 131 (2021): 717–33.

76. Gerry Shih, "China's Mass Indoctrination Camps Evoke Cultural Revolution," *AP News*, March 29, 2018, https://apnews.com/article/kazakhstan-ap

-top-news-international-news-china-china-clamps-down-6e151296fb194f85ba69a 8babd972e4b.

77. Gene Bunin, "There Was No Learning at All," *Art of Life in Chinese Central Asia*, December 13, 2019, https://livingotherwise.com/2019/12/13/there-was-no-learning-at-all.

78. Gene Bunin and Darren Byler have interviewed many camp survivors.

79. Mamtimin Ala (@MamtiminAla), "Uyghur women are praising Xi Jin-ping, singing 'Zhongguo de Xi dada, shijie de Xi dada' [Father Xi of China, father Xi of the world]," Twitter, April 20, 2019, https://twitter.com/MamtiminA /status/1119699224420126720.

80. On Uyghur self-descriptions as a "people destroyed" and as having "broken spirits," see, respectively, Bunin, "How the 'Happiest Muslims in the World' Are Coping," and Byler, "Spirit Breaking."

PART FOUR

Foreign and Cross-Strait Relations

8

Xi Jinping's Taiwan Policy
Soft Gets Softer, Hard Gets Harder

Tony Tai-Ting Liu

Since 2016, relations across the Taiwan Strait have greatly deteriorated. Compared with China-Taiwan relations from 2008 to 2016, when "peace," "dialogue," and "exchange" described bilateral relations, the relationship subsequently is better described by "estrangement," "antagonism," and "hostility." Despite Beijing's claim that the pro-independence position of Tsai Ing-wen and the Democratic Progressive Party (DPP) government should be blamed for setting relations back, Xi Jinping's militant attempts to compel Taiwan to have a closer relationship with China have contributed to the worsening of ties.

What are Xi's policies toward Taiwan, and what are their implications? How do his Taiwan policies differ from those of prior Chinese leaders? It is clear that the relationship between China and Taiwan has greatly deteriorated, despite Chinese efforts to win new support from certain sectors of Taiwanese society. As Xi Jinping consolidated power, Beijing's stance vis-à-vis Taiwan hardened considerably. His positions contrast sharply with those of Hu Jintao's government, which adopted a softer stance toward Taiwan, emphasizing exchange and cooperation. Through his centralization of power, Xi Jinping has the dominant voice in shaping China's approach toward Taiwan relations. A number of factors, both domestic and international, have contributed to the formation of Xi Jinping's Taiwan policies.

Cross-Strait Relations: From Cooperation to Stagnation

Since 2008, Taiwan-China relations have experienced a pendulum swing from exchange and cooperation to antagonism and stagnation. When the

Nationalist Party candidate Ma Ying-jeou won the presidential election, some observers foresaw peaceful relations.[1] Beijing and Taipei agreed to a diplomatic truce—Beijing wouldn't try to disrupt Taiwan's diplomatic relations with states that formally recognize Taipei and not Beijing—and reinitiated dialogue between the semiofficial Association for Relations Across the Taiwan Straits (ARATS) and the Strait Exchange Foundation (SEF). Restrictions on the "three links" (*santong*)—postal, transportation, and trade connections between China and Taiwan—were lifted, allowing greater people-to-people exchange. In 2010, representing Beijing and Taipei, respectively, ARATS and SEF signed the Economic Cooperation Framework Agreement (ECFA) and initiated major steps toward the integration of the Chinese and Taiwanese economies.

From 2008 to 2012—during Ma Ying-jeou's first term as president—expectations grew on the prospect of talks concerning the question of political unification. Subsequent developments, however, scuttled such hopes. In 2011, the Nationalist Party and the DPP geared up for the 2012 presidential election. Meanwhile, China was preparing for a change in political leadership, as Hu Jintao and Wen Jiabao neared their final year in office. The benefits of the ECFA were hotly debated while Taiwan rebounded from the global economic downturn, precipitated in part by the subprime mortgage crisis in the United States. Uncertainties prevented Beijing and Taipei from major political negotiations.

Xi Jinping's rise as paramount leader in late 2012 commenced a sea change in China-Taiwan relations. Xi expressed global ambitions as well as a determination to resolve disputes over Taiwan's political status, possibly during his time in office. At the 2013 Asia-Pacific Economic Cooperation (APEC) conference, Xi expressed the sentiment of "China and Taiwan being one family" and told Taiwan's representative in the talks, former vice president Vincent Siew, that "political differences across the Strait cannot pass from generation to generation and must be resolved gradually."[2] Xi's positions on such matters resonated with some in Taiwan, but not with the majority of the population, which, polls indicate, seeks the perpetuation of the status quo and has come to see Taiwan rather than China as its nation. Unsurprisingly, Xi's remarks generated debates on the future of China-Taiwan ties within Taiwan, though without arriving at a public consensus. Over time, the grim global economic outlook and concerns over the rapid pace and scope of economic integration with China led to growing disapproval of the Ma Ying-jeou government and the rise of anti-government social movements. A frustrated population—students and young people in particular—occupied

Taiwan's legislature in March 2014, signaling to the Ma government that it should do more to protect Taiwan's sovereignty and halt the pursuit of further economic integration with China.

The Sunflower occupation, named for flowers donated to protesters, proved a pivotal factor in Taiwan-China relations, contributing indirectly to more bilateral friction. In 2016, when the DPP's presidential candidate, Tsai Ing-wen, won handily and the DPP returned its first-ever parliamentary majority, relations with the Xi government rapidly worsened. China began adopting measures aimed at isolating Taiwan in international relations. The ARATS-SEF communication channel was severed. Beijing discouraged tourists and students from visiting Taiwan. Cross-strait exchanges came to an abrupt halt, with the result that Taiwan would commence decoupling from China and pursue more diversified regional and global trade relations.

On January 2, 2019, at the Great Hall of the People in Beijing, Xi Jinping made an open statement in light of the fortieth anniversary of the issuance of the "Message to Compatriots in Taiwan" (Gao Taiwan tongbao shu).[3] Xi stated that "the future of Taiwan lies in national reunification, and the well-being of the people hinges on the rejuvenation of the Chinese nation" and that "peaceful reunification and 'one country, two systems' is the best approach."[4] President Tsai Ing-wen responded by rejecting the 1992 Consensus, a notion first advanced by Nationalist politician Su Chi, that Taiwan is part of China but that Taiwan and the People's Republic of China may disagree on what that means exactly. She asserted that "Taiwan absolutely will not accept the 'one country, two systems'" plan devised by Deng Xiaoping for unifying Hong Kong and Macau with China.[5] Xi's and Tsai's divergent statements showcased what appear to have become increasingly intractable positions. Presumably, resolving such wide differences peacefully would require a long time horizon and much trust building. Yet, such an impasse was clearly unsatisfactory for Xi, who has since expressed keen interest in compelling closer economic and political relations, with military force, if necessary.[6]

The relationship between China and Taiwan deteriorated further in August 2022, when US House of Representatives Speaker Nancy Pelosi made a formal visit to Taiwan. China responded with live-fire military exercises, including missile launches that flew over Taiwan, reminding some of the 1995–96 Taiwan Strait crisis. The resulting spike in tensions attracted global attention as well as expressions of support for Taiwan from North American and European capitals. Chinese military encroachments also indicated how dangerous the Taiwan Strait had become. Despite changes in the international environment, including the outbreak of the COVID-19 pandemic in

Wuhan, China's slowing economic growth, and the Russia-Ukraine war, which have ostensibly weakened China's global influence, Xi Jinping remains insistent on "gradually resolving the Taiwan issue."

The Xi Jinping Factor

Xi Jinping's eagerness to resolve the "Taiwan question" may stem from his lengthy administrative experience in Fujian, the Chinese province that is culturally and geographically closest to Taiwan. After his first posting as the vice mayor of Xiamen in 1985, Xi Jinping spent a total of seventeen years in Fujian, serving as the municipal secretary of Fuzhou and provincial governor of Fujian. As governor, Xi met with Taiwanese businesspeople, including notable figures such as the chair of TPV Technology, Jason Hsuan, and the later chair of Yulon Motor Corporation, Kenneth Yen.[7] In addition, Xi established the Xiamen Taiwanese Business Association (Xiamen Taishang Huiguan), the first of its kind in China.[8] As a result of Xi Jinping's experiences in Fujian, he is more familiar with Taiwan and Taiwanese than his predecessors Jiang Zemin and Hu Jintao were, despite Xi never having visited Taiwan.

While Xi Jinping's desire to create a great political legacy is clear, his ambitions may be easier imagined than achieved. Mao Zedong brought New China to its feet, Deng Xiaoping set the country on the course of economic development, Jiang Zemin guided the country to prosperity, and Hu Jintao led China toward peaceful development and great power status. As Xi has considered how to make his mark, reunifying Taiwan with China has gained appeal, as a task that his predecessors were unable to achieve. Xi has thus sought to position China as militarily powerful enough to conquer and reunify Taiwan by force, possibly in a very short period of time.[9]

Xi assumed the role of paramount leader at a time of numerous obstacles to the country's ascendance, including great power rivalry with the United States. The Taiwan issue is one that Xi Jinping thought he could leverage—not only to shift popular attention away from China's domestic problems (see the chapters by Martin King Whyte and Alexsia T. Chan in this volume, for example) but also to challenge the global status of the United States.

Xi Jinping has had to contend with an identity shift in Taiwan toward seeing Taiwan (and not China) as the nation. This long-term development is certain to make unification more difficult to attain. Xi Jinping has therefore felt the need to act in order to prevent Taiwan from drifting further away. With pro-independence sentiment increasing in Taiwan, supported by the so-called *tianrandu*, or the generation born with a Taiwanese identity, trends in self-identification suggest that time is not on China's side.

Meanwhile, the Tsai administration has adopted an active approach toward cross-strait relations. The DPP has urged Beijing to undertake dialogue and negotiations without set preconditions. In an interview with CNN in 2021, Tsai Ing-wen noted that she had not abandoned the possibility of improved relations with China and would sit down with Xi Jinping for talks.[10] At the same time, Taipei, seeking to internationalize a dispute that China claims is purely a domestic political affair, compared Taiwan's democratic successes to global democratic backsliding and drew attention to the threat that autocracies pose to a rules-based international order.[11] In doing so, Taipei implies that all countries concerned about democracy should lend their support to Taiwan.

In 2018, Xi Jinping attempted to prevent new inroads by Taiwan to win greater international clout, assigning Liu Jieyi, former ambassador to the United Nations, to head the Taiwan Affairs Office (TAO). Liu's rich experience in foreign affairs set him apart from previous TAO directors. In 2022, Song Tao, a career diplomat and former head of the Chinese Communist Party's (CCP) International Liaison Department (Zhongyang Weiyuanhui Duiwai Lianluobu), replaced Liu as the TAO's director. Compared with his predecessor, Song is associated with a softer approach toward Taiwan. Song has advocated not only a return of cross-strait exchanges but also a lifting of bans on Taiwanese products. On March 16, 2023, the TAO announced the cessation of bans against fish imports from Taiwan, and some observers credited Song Tao with playing a role in the move.[12] Nonetheless, it remains to be seen whether the TAO's shift in outlook represents the beginning of a reconciliatory trend or is simply part of Xi Jinping's strategy to apply both "carrot and stick" strategies toward Taiwan.

Xi Jinping's Two-Pronged Taiwan Policy

To date, Xi Jinping's approach to Taiwan could be understood as involving soft and hard policies. Soft policies refer to "persuasive" actions that attempt to influence individual preferences in Taiwan through material and nonmaterial inducements. Hard policies, in contrast, describe coercive actions that imply or involve the use of military force. Lin Chong-pin, former deputy defense minister of Taiwan, has used the expression "Hard gets harder, soft gets softer" to describe Xi Jinping's Taiwan policies.[13] Lin has argued that hard initiatives such as military threats and diplomatic isolation have limited utility; hence Beijing has adopted an approach under Xi that employs both soft and hard policies, with a growing emphasis on the latter.[14] Moreover, as Brantly Womack points out in his chapter in this volume, there is an inverse correlation between the growth of China's hard power and the reduction of its soft power.

Charm Offensive

Beijing's soft policies are directed toward winning the hearts and minds of the Taiwanese people. In contrast with Hu Jintao's policy of "exchange and unilateral concessions" (*jiaoliu rangli*), characterized by an emphasis on people-to-people exchange and further opening of the Chinese market to Taiwanese goods and products, under Xi Jinping Beijing adopted the policies of the "Three Middles and One Young" (Sanzhong Yiqing) and "One Generation, One Line" (Yidai Yixian).[15] The new policies are aimed at courting the favor of groups within Taiwanese society that are traditionally least favorable toward China. Unlike the policies toward Taiwan in the Hu Jintao period, Xi Jinping's soft policies target specific demographics that have been disinclined toward deeper political or economic engagement with China. The "Three Middles and One Young" policy targets the three "middles": small and medium-size enterprises, middle and lower social classes, and the population in central and southern Taiwan.[16] The "One Young" arm of this policy targets Taiwan's youth, a demographic seen as playing a pivotal role in the future direction of national identity. The policy's underlying rationale is that if China can sway the most resistant Taiwanese demographics, then reunification may simply be a matter of time. As Chinese military strategist Sun Tzu puts it in *The Art of War*, "Winning a war without a fight remains the highest principle of strategy" (Buzhan er qurenzhibin, shanzhi shanzheye).[17] Toward such a goal, Chinese state-sponsored tourism, usually involving visits to "patriot education centers" (*aiguo jiaoyu jidi*), history museums, and monuments commemorating anti-Japanese movements, has been a common tactic designed to reeducate young people from Taiwan. At the same time, Beijing has also provided start-up funding for Taiwanese youths seeking to establish business in China, as a way to win favor with this typically pro-Taiwan independence-leaning demographic.

The issuance of a mainland travel permit (*taibaozheng*) to Taiwanese residents is another example of China's charm offensive at work. Issued in card form beginning in July 2015, the permit serves as the primary identification for Taiwanese in China, replacing the traditional booklet form of the permit that was stamped upon entry to the country. The travel permit is valid for five years and eliminates the hassle of a visa application. The mainland travel permit also serves as personal identification for opening a bank account, acquiring a mobile phone number, and making online hotel and high-speed rail reservations in China. In other words, the permit allows Taiwanese residents to enjoy many of the everyday privileges of Chinese citizens without having to carry a Republic of China passport. Due to the proximity of China and Taiwan and the ease of travel through direct flights, the mainland travel permit serves as an inducement for Taiwanese to live and work in China.

In March 2017, Yu Zhengsheng, chairman of the Chinese People's Political Consultative Conference, announced the "One Generation, One Line" policy to focus on "strengthening engagement and exchange with the grass roots of society (one line) and Taiwan's youth (one generation), in order to strengthen the public foundation for developing peace in cross-strait relations."[18] "One Generation, One Line" marked a new emphasis on improving relations with laborers in foundational industries, such as agriculture, forestry, fishing, and animal husbandry, and Taiwan's youth generally. The "One Generation, One Line" policy complements the "Three Middles and One Young" policy's aim of influencing the most anti-China groups in Taiwanese society. The inclusion of laborers in "One Generation, One Line" reflects their political salience and potential vulnerability: labor comprises a large group with generally lower levels of education and economic well-being. Laborers have also traditionally supported the DPP. By investing in efforts to influence laborers, Beijing seeks to undermine societal support for the DPP. An example of this policy at work is the provision of residence permits for Taiwan residents (*Taiwan jumin juzhuzheng*) in China. Individuals holding this permit are considered Chinese nationals and enjoy the same privileges as Chinese citizens.

In February 2018, the TAO introduced thirty-one policies preferential to Taiwan, as later captured and reformulated in the "Several Measures to Promote Further Cross-Strait Economic and Cultural Exchange Cooperation" (Guanyu jinyibu cujin liangan jingji wenhua jiaoliu hezuo de ruogan cuoshi), officially released in November 2019.[19] The new policies are representative of Xi Jinping's Taiwan policies. In sectors ranging from finance and medicine to education, the preferential treatments include such new privileges as the right to practice medicine, participate in the "Made in China 2025" strategic project, and apply for professional licenses in China. In addition, China opened the door to Taiwanese talent who are keen to work in academia, the Chinese civil service, or the finance industry—sectors that require skills and professional training.[20] China has also organized regular job exhibitions catering to young, skilled laborers from Taiwan in cities such as Shanghai and Xiamen. To spur westward migration, China has promised generous start-up funding and job opportunities to young "compatriots in Taiwan," as well as opportunities to visit China through low-cost, state-organized tours.[21]

Overall, China's charm offensive seeks to target a large swath of the Taiwanese society, with policies designed to cater to Taiwanese social and economic needs. It is worth noting that from "Three Middles and One Young" and "One Generation, One Line" to the thirty-one preferential policies, Xi's government has demonstrated a nuanced understanding of Taiwan that has kept up with social and economic developments on the island.

Hard Offensive

Compared to its soft policies, Beijing's hard policies are aimed at the Taiwanese government, or, more specifically, the DPP government under President Tsai Ing-wen and Vice President Lai Ching-te, who, following the DPP's defeat in local elections, has taken over as party chairman. China's hard offensive toward Taiwan comprises three categories of actions: diplomatic isolation, military intimidation, and economic sanctions. The different actions are carried out simultaneously, though military intimidation and economic sanctions appear most prominently in news headlines.

Beginning in 2016, the year Tsai was inaugurated as president, Beijing ceased all communications with Taipei. Aside from the termination of communication between ARATS and SEF, the TAO cut off communication with its counterpart, the Mainland Affairs Council in Taiwan. The hotline between Beijing and Taipei—established when relations were better—became useless. No known calls were made during the spike in military tensions associated with the "Pelosi crisis" of August 2022. In 2016, the number of inbound Chinese visitors to Taiwan fell for the first time in eight years. Reminiscent of an earlier time, the flow of people became one-way again, largely limited to Taiwanese traveling on business. The outbreak of the COVID-19 pandemic in 2020 further exacerbated cross-strait relations as both China and Taiwan shut down their respective borders. The small "three links" (*xiao santong*) for business, travel, and postal service between Taiwan's offshore islands Kinmen and Matsu and China were severed in February 2020 as a result of the pandemic and did not resume until March 2023.

In addition to cutting off communication channels, Beijing has launched a series of attacks on Taipei in the area of international representation. Taiwan took the first blow in terms of participation in international organizations. In 2017, for the first time in eight years, Taiwan was not invited to participate in the annual World Health Assembly under the status of an observer.[22] As the World Health Assembly is the central decision-making body governing the World Health Organization (WHO), a functional organization of the United Nations, membership is restricted to recognized nation-states. Beijing has argued for the "One China" principle in the assembly—an arrangement in which Taiwan is treated as a subnational polity that is represented by China—effectively barring Taiwan from any meaningful participation.[23] Based on similar reasoning, Beijing has also prevented Taiwan from taking part in the triennial International Civil Aviation Organization meeting since 2016. Taiwan's exclusion from international organizations, particularly the WHO, attracted global attention when the COVID-19 pandemic broke out. Due to its exposure from a large number of inbound travelers, Taiwan faced an immediate challenge to it public health system when the first suspected cases of coronavirus emerged in China. Resistance from China was the reason Taiwan was barred from the WHO, even during the height of the pandemic, despite global support for Taiwan's inclusion.

Taiwan suffered other diplomatic setbacks during the Xi era, when a number of states that had formally recognized Taiwan as a sovereign state and maintained official diplomatic relations with Taipei (but not Beijing) broke off ties. The nation of São Tomé and Príncipe switched its diplomatic recognition from Taiwan to China in 2016, and a number of other states followed suit: Panama (2017), the Dominican Republic (2017), Burkina Faso (2018), El Salvador (2018), Kiribati (2019), the Solomon Islands (2019), and Nicaragua (2021). Only fourteen states formally recognize Taiwan (officially known as the Republic of China), compared to twenty-two states from 2008 to 2016, when Beijing and Taipei had a "diplomatic truce" (*waijiao xiubing*). Taiwan's only "friendly nation" (*youbangguo*) in Africa, where China has considerable influence, is Eswatini, a small landlocked state. The situation has become serious enough that the United States, which itself has unofficial ties with Taiwan, has attempted to stem Taiwan's loss of diplomatic partners. For example, in response to the switch in diplomatic recognition by Panama, the Dominican Republic, and El Salvador to the People's Republic of China, the United States recalled its top representatives in the three states. Since 2021, the United States has expressed grave concern for the potential geopolitical implications of a security pact between China and the Solomon Islands.[24]

Before switching recognition to Beijing, the Solomon Islands had long shared good diplomatic relations with Taiwan.

Following Tsai Ing-wen's reelection as president in 2020, China imposed a series of economic sanctions on Taiwan, some of which were informal, through bans on agricultural products, meat, and fish. In January 2021, while the pandemic raged, China banned pork imports from Taiwan, claiming that the meat was unsafe due to Taiwan's decision to open its market to US pork, which some argued posed health risks because of the presence of ractopamine, a feed additive. The Chinese ban raised doubts from observers, who wondered whether Beijing's concerns were genuine or an act of retaliation against Taiwan.[25] In March 2021, China banned pineapples from Taiwan after the alleged discovery of pests. Six months later, China banned Taiwan's wax apples (*lianwu*) and custard apples (*shijia*). In response to the pineapple ban, Taipei sought to rebrand its fruit as "freedom pineapples" to win support from major trading partners such as Japan and the United States, framing the dispute as a clash between democracy and authoritarianism.[26] Beijing continued with another wave of sanctions in 2022. From grouper fish to traditional pastries, alcohol, and tea, Beijing broadened the targeted goods beyond agricultural products, signaling to Taipei and the world Chinese efforts to exert leverage over numerous sectors of the Taiwanese economy.

Perhaps losing patience with such incremental tactics, Xi Jinping's China topped off its diplomatic and economic maneuvers with military actions aimed at cowing Taiwan to surrender. In March 2019, two J-11 fighter jets crossed the median line of the Taiwan Strait and entered into Taiwan's air space, the first deliberate breaching in two decades. Since then, Beijing has greatly increased the number of times that its fighter jets and spy planes circle the island, cross the median line of the Taiwan Strait, or harass the Taiwanese fighter planes that confront such encroachments. According to Taiwan's Ministry of Defense, from 2020 to 2022, the number of Chinese planes that intruded into Taiwan's air defense identification zone increased from 380 to 1,727. The number of Chinese planes deployed more than doubled, from 538 in 2021 to 1,241 in 2022.[27] Besides showing off the capability of its air force, China's constant intrusions into Taiwanese air space have contributed to a looming tension and unleashed the specter of war in the Taiwan Strait. The *Economist* magazine put an image of the marine space around Taiwan on the cover of its May 2021 issue, labeling it as "the most dangerous place on Earth."[28]

Taiwan Strait: To War or Not to War?

Since 2016, Xi Jinping has issued verbal warnings and threats toward Taiwan. He has lashed out at "Taiwanese independence activists" (*taidufenzi*), threatening to defeat them in the pursuit of unification with or without the use of force. At the 19th National Congress of the CCP, Xi Jinping highlighted unification of the fatherland through the "one country, two systems" model and asserted that "China has sufficient capabilities to defeat Taiwanese independence of any form."[29] A few months later, at the 13th National People's Congress, Xi proclaimed, "Our great fatherland absolutely cannot lose even an inch of Chinese territory."[30] Perhaps the strongest statement relating to Taiwan came in the 2019 speech commemorating the "Message to Compatriots in Taiwan": "China must be and will be unified. . . . Cross-strait reunification is the trend of history. Taiwan Independence goes against the trend of history and will lead to a dead end. . . . We are willing to create broad space for peaceful reunification, but will leave no room for any form of separatist activities. . . . We make no promise to renounce the use of force and reserve the option of taking all necessary means."[31]

Many observers consider the 2019 statement as expressing Xi Jinping's determination and perhaps growing impatience vis-à-vis the Taiwan issue.[32] In light of rising tensions, pundits have speculated about when Beijing could be more or less likely to carry out its "endgame" or seek to force Taiwan's unification through military means. The "two centenaries" (*liangge yibainian*) of 2021 and 2049 were considered possible dates: 2021 marked the centenary of the founding of the CCP, while 2049 will mark the centenary of the establishment of the People's Republic of China.[33] Perhaps due to the COVID-19 pandemic, war did not break out in the Taiwan Strait in 2021. However, the fact that the antagonism between China and Taiwan grew during the pandemic has increased anxieties about the future of the Taiwan Strait. In 2023, Xi Jinping commenced his third term as the president of China, a development made possible through constitutional reforms in March 2018 that eliminated term limits for the position of PRC president (see Ashley Esarey and Rongbin Han, this volume). Attention has turned to 2027 as a potential year for conflict. Some observers claim that war is likely to break out in 2027 for two reasons: (1) it will mark the centenary of the establishment of the People's Liberation Army, and (2) Xi Jinping will be completing his final term in office, that is, if he does not seek another term.[34]

If Xi remains keen to resolve the Taiwan issue, then developments since 2020 suggest that he may need to take action rather than postponing it indefinitely. Besides Taiwan's changing national identity, new factors may diminish China's prospects for continued economic development and political stability. The COVID-19 pandemic's unpopular "zero COVID" policy slowed the rate of China's economic development and generated domestic political opposition, while disrupting global supply chains and hurting the global economy. In November 2022, the "white paper revolution"—popular protests in response to a deadly apartment fire that killed ten people and injured nine others in Ürümqi—broke out in cities across China, prompting Beijing to rapidly lift COVID-19 restrictions.

Russia's troubled invasion of Ukraine has also proved unsettling for China. The fact that Russia has struggled to conquer Ukraine after more than a year of war has emboldened people to call for caution with respect to Chinese plans to launch a tricky amphibious invasion of Taiwan. At the same time, a number of commentaries have appeared comparing Taiwan to Ukraine and proposing that Russo-Chinese collaboration might make it possible for Xi Jinping to invade Taiwan soon.[35]

During much of the pandemic, Taiwan proved to be one of the safest societies in which to live. A related reputational boost and efforts to strengthen ties to democracies worldwide have drawn attention to the need to support Taiwan diplomatically and decry acts of Chinese aggression. Taiwan's donation of face masks and medical supplies strengthened partnerships with countries in North America and Europe. Such tactics helped to win the support of at least one country, Lithuania, which subsequently opened a trade and representative office in Taiwan in November 2022, to Beijing's great displeasure. In response to China's growing military challenges, Taiwan also used support for its "freedom" discourse to attract visits by legislative representatives from Canada, France, Germany, Japan, Lithuania, South Korea, Switzerland and the United States, among others, which elevated the island nation's international status. In some instances, heightened awareness of Taiwan's situation has spilled into the security realm. For example, Japan sees "Taiwan contingency as a contingency for Japan," linking the two island nations' security.[36] In January 2023, the European Parliament's Common Security and Defense Policy and the Common Foreign and Security Policy asserted that the belligerence of China's military destabilizes global security and urged the European Commission to promote strategic cooperation with Taiwan.

At the same time, growing global awareness of the grave security situation in the Taiwan Strait has contributed to a Chinese security dilemma about how best to proceed: further offensive measures toward Taiwan increase international support and military aid for Taipei, diminishing China's sense of security. Further, should Beijing back down with respect to its sovereignty disputes with Taipei, Taiwan could gain more room to pursue even de jure independence, which could come with dire consequences for the popularity of Xi Jinping's rule in China. Hence Xi continues to "make no promise to renounce the use of force and reserve the option of taking all necessary means."[37] Yet Beijing's pressure on Taiwan risks driving it further away from unification in a negative feedback loop that has led Taiwan to look to the United States for greater military support, while strengthening its own defense capabilities.

Under Tsai Ing-wen and the DPP administration, Taiwan has sought to balance against the threat posed by China in a sharp contrast from the integrationist strategy of the Ma Ying-jeou administration (2008–16). Under Tsai's leadership, Taiwan has made efforts to improve its defense capability and to deepen security cooperation with the United States. Guided by the motto "War can be avoided only by preparing for war" (Beizhan caineng zhizhan), the Tsai Ing-wen administration has emphasized "all-out defense," a concept that stresses the participation of everyone in society, including women, in support of national defense.[38] In January 2022, the Taiwan Ministry of National Defense launched the All-Out Defense Mobilization Agency (Guofangbu Quanmin Fangwei Dongyuanshu), a new ministry tasked with the mobilization of reservists during wartime as well as disaster relief. The Tsai administration has extended the period of mandatory military service from four months to one year, as of January 2024. Currently, Taiwan's Ministry of Education is considering the possibility of mobilizing students over the age of sixteen, regardless of gender, for military training and the formation of youth protection groups. Taiwan has authorized several large military procurements from the United States, from both the Donald Trump and Joseph Biden administrations, ranging from spare parts for fighter jets to missiles, torpedoes, and anti-tank munition-laying systems.[39] In 2022, under the United States' State Partnership Program, the US National Guard began training Taiwan's military for a range of defensive actions. In January 2023, the United States announced the appropriation of funds to help Taiwan participate in the International Military Education and Training program to improve the interoperability of forces and the capability for joint military operations.[40] In addition to improving its military strength, Taiwan-US cooperation shores up perceptions of Taiwan as a sovereign state, thereby undermining Chinese claims that Taiwan is an errant subnational polity.

Conclusion

China-Taiwan relations in the Xi Jinping era have moved in a downward spiral, leaving the impression that war could be imminent. Nancy Pelosi's visit to Taiwan in August 2022, ostensibly to show her support for Taipei, triggered large-scale Chinese military maneuvers and military crisis. Unlike China's territorial disputes with India or fellow claimants to territory in the South China Sea, conflict between China and Taiwan has the potential to ignite a global war. Thus, it is fitting to consider the future of cross-strait relations, highlighting the challenges and opportunities ahead as well as factors that might affect whether or not war will break out.

A Xi Jinping effect on the bilateral relationship could be the most decisive factor in the near future. The prospect that Xi could serve indefinitely as China's top leader greatly contributes to uncertainty concerning the future of relations across the Taiwan Strait. Xi's willingness to depart from tradition, with respect to his tenure as paramount leader and in other areas of politics noted in this volume, suggests that the actions of prior Chinese leaders who pursued a "long game" with Taiwan, rather than military confrontation in the near term, are poor predictors of what Xi might do. Cross-strait relations have changed significantly since Deng Xiaoping's time. Xi Jinping may indeed wonder whether the goal of peaceful reunification is still feasible. If one assumes that Xi Jinping will remain in power for another decade and the relationship between China and Taiwan fails to improve, Xi might be tempted to hazard the use of force to compel Taiwan's unification with China. Should Xi leave office, as mentioned by Brantly Womack (this volume), in China's relationship with Taiwan such questions as "After Xi, what?" and "After Xi, when?" will undoubtedly emerge.

Developments in Taiwan are also important indicators for whether tension will continue to dominate Taiwan-China relations. Since 2016, the 1992 Consensus has lost appeal for the Taiwanese population, to the extent that the concept is little discussed in Taiwan. The discourse on independence has come to dominate discussions on Taiwan's relations with China. Whether an alternative discourse can emerge that effectively counterbalances the independence discourse could be critical to improving relations. Such a development might involve, for example, a stronger voice for proponents of the political status quo, a large segment of the population that is usually silent. Whether the pro-independence DPP or the traditionally pro-unification Nationalist Party comes out on top in presidential elections could also decide Taiwan's stance toward China in the near term. Over the long term, however, perceptions of China and its political system will heavily influence Taiwanese deliberations over the sort of relations Taipei should pursue with Beijing. Regardless of future electoral outcomes, a healthy democracy with vibrant discussion among different groups may well prove to be Taiwan's best defense against the threat of externally imposed authoritarianism.

In a context in which relations across the Taiwan Strait appear to offer little room for optimism, one should not discount the possibility that new developments may halt or slow down further acceleration of tensions. How the war in Ukraine turns out, whether it wraps up soon and with a Russian defeat, could offer some light for resolving tensions in the Taiwan Strait, particularly if China concludes that it cannot afford a similarly costly debacle during a time of sputtering economic growth. As the COVID-19 pandemic winds down, China and Taiwan may negotiate the reopening of the minor links that facilitated exchanges between Xiamen and Kinmen and Matsu. Should people-to-people exchange recommence more broadly, positive spill-overs into other policy areas may follow. Finally, in relation to Xi's pursuit of the China Dream, Taiwan presents a critical dilemma, with potentially enormous economic and political implications: Does the prospect of unification with Taiwan represent a strategic opportunity or a dangerous trap that poses risks for arguably more significant Chinese developmental objectives? In other words, is the pursuit of the unification of Taiwan essential for China's political ambitions or a great misstep with more potential downsides than benefits for China's continued rise? Xi's answer to these questions may prove critical to the future course of Taiwan-China relations.

Notes

1. See Fu-Kuo Liu, "Ma Ying-jeou's Rapprochement Policy: Cross-Strait Progress and Domestic Constraints," in *Political Changes under Ma Ying-jeou: Partisan Conflict, Policy Choices, External Constraints and Security Challenges*, ed. Jean-Pierre Cabestan and Jacques deLisle (New York: Routledge, 2014), 175–94.

2. Alan Romberg, "From Generation to Generation: Advancing Cross-Strait Relations," *China Leadership Monitor*, no. 43 (2014): 1–23, https://www.hoover.org/sites/default/files/uploads/documents/CLM43AR.pdf.

3. The "Message to Compatriots in Taiwan" was first issued by the Standing Committee of the National People's Congress in 1979. The statement called for the termination of the military standoff between China and Taiwan and the commencement of cross-strait exchange, including the opening of the three links. At

the same time, China announced an end to its regular shelling of Kinmen. The statement is a definitive description of China's position toward Taiwan and represented a shift away from a more bellicose stance.

4. Taiwan Work Office of the Chinese Communist Party Central Committee, "Xi Jinping: Working Together to Realize Rejuvenation of the Chinese Nation and Advance China's Peaceful Reunification," April 12, 2019, http://www.gwytb .gov.cn/wyly/201904/t20190412_12155687.htm.

5. Office of the President of the Republic of China, "President Tsai Issues Statement on China President Xi's 'Message to Compatriots in Taiwan,'" January 2, 2019, https://english.president.gov.tw/News/5621.

6. See Wayne Chang, Yong Xiong, and Ben Westcott, "Chinese President Xi Jinping Vows to Pursue 'Reunification' with Taiwan by Peaceful Means," *CNN World*, October 9, 2021, https://edition.cnn.com/2021/10/08/china/xi-jinping -taiwan-reunification-intl-hnk/index.html.

7. Hong-da Lin, "Yi sheng Jiansheng xiong toulu Xi Jinping de Taishangxue" ("Brother Jiansheng" exposes Xi Jinping's thinking toward Taiwanese businessmen), *Wealth Magazine*, April 19, 2018, https://www.wealth.com.tw/articles /af19f0db-c00d-4cdd-8574-5bf8e61d58d7.

8. Guo-Cheng Song, "Xi Jinping shiqi de duitai zhengce" (Taiwan policy in the Xi Jinping period), *Taipei Forum*, May 22, 2012, http://140.119.184.164 /view_pdf/04.pdf.

9. See Oriana Skylar Mastro, "The Taiwan Temptation: Why Beijing Might Resort to Force," *Foreign Affairs* 100, no. 4 (July/August 2021): 58–67.

10. William Ripley, Eric Cheung, and Ben Westcott, "Taiwan's President Says the Threat from China Is Increasing 'Every Day' and Confirms Presence of US Military Trainers on the Island," *CNN World*, October 28, 2021, https://edition .cnn.com/2021/10/27/asia/tsai-ingwen-taiwan-china-interview-intl-hnk/index .html.

11. Trevor Sutton, "The Anomaly of Taiwanese Democracy," *Washington Monthly*, March 11, 2020, https://washingtonmonthly.com/2020/03/11/the -anomaly-of-taiwanese-democracy.

12. See Jin-Hong Lai and Zheng-Lu Chen, "Lu shishanyi, tai er shuichan huifu jinkou" (China gives out good will, resuming import of two Taiwanese seafoods), *United Daily News*, March 16, 2023, https://udn.com/news/story /7333/7034501?from=udn_ch2_menu_v2_main_cate.

13. Wang Yu-ping, "Xuezhe guandian: Hu Jintao duitai yingdeyueying ruand-eyueruan" (Academic perspective: Hu Jintao toward Taiwan—hard gets harder, soft gets softer), *Liberty Times*, January 30, 2005, https://news.ltn.com.tw/news /politics/paper/11168.

14. Lin Chong-pin, "Shijiudahou Xi Jinping duitai: Ruanshouweigong, ying-shouweishou, yizai gaibian Taiwan minyi" (Xi Jinping toward Taiwan after the

19th CCP National Congress: Soft policies as offense, hard policies as defense, aimed at changing public opinion in Taiwan), *Independent Opinion@Common-Wealth Magazine*, March 30, 2018, https://opinion.cw.com.tw/blog/profile/70/article/6740?utm_source=Facebook&utm_medium=Social&utm_campaign=Daily.

15. Yu Yuan-Jie, "Liangan jiaoliu sanshi nian: Sanzhongyiqing dao yidaiyisian zhi tongzhan fenxi" (Thirty years of cross-strait exchange—an analysis of the CCP United Front from "Three Middles and One Young" to "One Generation, One Line"), *Clear Current Bimonthly*, no. 11 (September 2017): 12–17.

16. The social classes category also refers to those with lower income.

17. *The Art of War* by Chinese strategist Sun Tzu (544–496 BC) is generally believed to have been compiled between 515 and 512 BC. One of the most well-known lessons from the classic is "Winning a war without a fight remains the highest principle of strategy," or, simply, to claim victory without losing soldiers is the best strategy in war.

18. "Quanguo zhengxie huiyi kaimu Yu Zhengsheng zuo gongzuo baogao" (Yu Zhengsheng's work report at the opening of the Chinese People's Political Consultative Conference), *Wenwei News*, March 3, 2017, http://news.wenweipo.com/2017/03/03/IN1703030027.htm.

19. See Central People's Government of the People's Republic of China, "Guanyu jinyibu cujin liangan jingji wenhua jiaoliu hezuo de ruogan cuoshi" (Several measures to promote further cross-strait economic and cultural exchange cooperation), November 4, 2019, http://www.mod.gov.cn/big5/topnews/2019-11/04/content_4854414.htm.

20. Taiwan Affairs Office of the State Council of the People's Republic of China, "Guanyu fayin guanyu cujin liangan jingji wenhua jiaoliu hezuo de ruogan cuoshi de tongzhi" (On the announcement of the measures on stimulating cross-strait economic and cultural exchange and cooperation), February 28, 2018, http://www.gwytb.gov.cn/wyly/201802/t20180228_11928139.htm.

21. Huang Pei-jun, "Zhongguo tongzhantuan xuanqian dajiangjia shiwutian xinaotuan zhiyao liangqianba" (Chinese "tongzhan" tour, major discount before election—fifteen days for only 2,800 NT), *Liberty Times*, October 31, 2019, https://news.ltn.com.tw/news/politics/paper/1328670.

22. Ministry of Foreign Affairs of the Republic of China (Taiwan), "Republic of China (Taiwan) Rejects WHO Characterization of Its Participation in World Health Assembly and Expresses Its Strong Dissatisfaction to WHO Secretariat," May 12, 2017, https://www.mofa.gov.tw/en/News_Content.aspx?n=1EADDCFD4C6EC567&s=161DC7A70C4856E0.

23. See Czeslaw Tubilewicz, "Friends, Enemies or Frenemies? China-Taiwan Discord in the World Health Organization and Its Significance," *Pacific Affairs* 85, no. 4 (2012): 701–22.

24. "US Reassessing Aid to Solomon Islands after Taiwan Ties Cut," Reuters, September 19, 2019, https://www.reuters.com/article/us-taiwan-diplomacy-usa-solomons-idUSKBN1W32RL.

25. Roy Lee, "China's Agricultural Bans Don't Yet Threaten Taiwan's Economic Security," *East Asia Forum*, December, 10, 2022, https://www.eastasia forum.org/2022/12/10/chinas-agricultural-bans-dont-yet-threaten-taiwans-economic-security.

26. Nick Aspinwall, "Taiwan Promotes 'Freedom Pineapples' in Response to China's Import Ban," *Diplomat*, March 6, 2021, https://thediplomat.com/2021/03/taiwan-promotes-freedom-pineapples-in-response-to-chinese-import-ban.

27. "Chinese Incursions Nearly Doubled Last Year," *Taipei Times*, January 3, 2023, https://www.taipeitimes.com/News/front/archives/2023/01/03/2003791889.

28. See "The Most Dangerous Place on Earth," *Economist*, May 1, 2021, https://www.economist.com/leaders/2021/05/01/the-most-dangerous-place-on-earth.

29. Xi Jinping, "Secure a Decisive Victory in Building a Moderately Prosperous Society in All Respects and Strive for the Great Success of Socialism with Chinese Characteristics for a New Era," Xinhua News Agency, October 18, 2017, http://www.xinhuanet.com/english/download/Xi_Jinping's_report_at_19th_CPC_National_Congress.pdf.

30. "Speech Delivered by Xi Jinping at the First Session of the 13th NPC [National People's Congress]," *China Daily* (Hong Kong), March 21, 2018, https://www.chinadailyhk.com/articles/184/187/127/1521628772832.html.

31. "Highlights of Xi's Speech at Gathering Marking 40th Anniversary of Message to Compatriots in Taiwan," *Xinhua News*, January 2, 2019, http://www.xinhuanet.com/english/2019-01/02/c_137715300.htm.

32. See Shih-Min Chen, "Xi Jinping de zhanlue zhuanxian yu taihai jushi de bianqian: 2021–2018" (A shift in Xi Jinping's strategy and the changing cross-strait security situation: 2012–2018), *Prospect Quarterly* 20, no. 2 (2019): 56.

33. Yiu Chung Wong, "Independence or Reunification? The Evolving PRC-Taiwan Relations," *Baltic Journal of European Studies* 9, no. 2 (2019): 120.

34. See Mallory Shelbourne, "Davidson: China Could Try to Take Control of Taiwan in 'Next Six Years,'" *USNI News*, March 9, 2021, https://news.usni.org/2021/03/09/davidson-china-could-try-to-take-control-of-taiwan-in-next-six-years; Derek Grossman, "Taiwan Is Safe until at Least 2027, but with One Big Caveat," *The RAND Blog*, November 10, 2021, https://www.rand.org/blog/2021/11/taiwan-is-safe-until-at-least-2027-but-with-one-big.html.

35. See William H. Overholt, "Ukraine Offers No Easy Lessons on Taiwan," *Global Asia* 17, no. 2 (2022): 36–39; David Keegan and Kyle Churchman, "Taiwan and China Seek Lessons from Ukraine as Taiwan's International Position Strengthens," *Comparative Connections* 24, no. 1 (2022): 89–100.

36. See Kunihiko Miyake, "Shinzo Abe's No-Nonsense Message to Beijing," *Japan Times*, December 21, 2021.

37. Ministry of Foreign Affairs of the People's Republic of China, "Full Text of the Report to the 20th National Congress of the Communist Party of China," October 25, 2022, https://www.fmprc.gov.cn/eng/zxxx_662805/202210/t20221025_10791908.html.

38. Peter Wood, "Taiwan's 'All-Out Defense' in Context of Aggressive PLA [People's Liberation Army] Exercise," *OE Watch*, no. 7 (July 2022): 9–10.

39. For a complete list of US military arms sales to Taiwan, please refer to the press release section of the Defense Security Cooperation Agency website, accessed January 2, 2024, https://www.dsca.mil/press-media/major-arms-sales.

40. Li Yi-hsuan, "US Funding Taiwan Military Training," *Taipei Times*, January 25, 2023, https://www.taipeitimes.com/News/front/archives/2023/01/25/2003793116.

9

Xi Jinping's Diplomatic New Normal

The Reception in Southeast Asia

Brantly Womack

The study of international relations is often criticized for assuming that unitary national actors make foreign policy. However, a party-state like the People's Republic of China does not allow the public articulation of diverse internal points of view, and its leadership thus presents a credible persona of unity. In fact, of course, the leadership is constrained by its appreciation of the conflicting variety of domestic interests, but the character of the leadership, and especially of core leaders, is decisive.[1] Nevertheless, the choices faced by leaders are shaped by the realities of their situations, and foreign affairs are a process of interaction rather than simply action.[2] The dialectic of structure and agency, noted by Kevin O'Brien in the conclusion to his chapter in this volume, is even more complex in foreign affairs than it is in domestic politics.

Xi Jinping is certainly the face on China's current brand of foreign policy, and his assertive diplomacy, emphasizing China's big power status and centrality to Asia, is in striking contrast to the more modest note sounded by Deng Xiaoping. Moreover, as Andrew Wedeman details (this volume), Xi clearly expects to be a dominant influence on Chinese politics and policy in his third term as Party secretary. Not only is there no successor in sight after the 20th National Party Congress, but he has followed his declaration of a "new normal" in 2014 with the announcement of a new era of socialism with Chinese characteristics at the 19th National Party Congress in 2017. In foreign policy, his announcement of the Belt and Road Initiative (BRI) in 2013 attracted worldwide attention, and more recently his Global Development Initiative (2021) and Global Security Initiative (2022) attempt a more multilateral approach to global leadership, but with Xi Jinping as the initiator.[3]

But the effectiveness of a brand is best judged by the audience reaction, and different audiences react differently. In the United States, Xi's personalistic authoritarianism has put his face on general American concerns about a "Thucydides Trap," a coming confrontation with a rising power, and has encouraged its repackaging as the centerpiece of a new Cold War between democracy and authoritarianism.[4] Europe shares American concerns about China's technological challenge and the authoritarianism personified by Xi, but it is also committed to an economic world order in which China now plays an essential part. In Africa and Latin America, China presents a welcome alternative to US and European connectivities, but the honeymoon of easy loans has morphed into concerns about debt and about an uncertain global economy. Nevertheless, while China's loans can be seen as part of current problems, China also remains a key component of prospects for solutions in the developing world.

China is itself a regional power, and its success as a regional power is the foundation of its prospects as a global power.[5] China's region, Pacific Asia, comprises Northeast Asia (the Koreas, Japan), Greater China (mainland China, Taiwan, Hong Kong, Macau), and the ten countries of Southeast Asia, all members of ASEAN, the Association of Southeast Asian Nations. Pacific Asia is not merely places contiguous on a map. Although political relationships in Pacific Asia are problematic, unlike in South America and South Asia there is a thick web of economic activity. Pacific Asia, called "Factory Asia" by the World Trade Organization, has more intraregional trade than "Factory Europe" or "Factory America."[6] Moreover, the aggregate production of Pacific Asia, measured in terms of purchasing power parity, is now greater than that of the United States and the European Union combined, and it is growing faster.[7] China has been central to the Pacific Asian region since 2008, and it was central before the Opium War in 1840. While the Xi effect could be analyzed in China's interactions with Korea or Japan, as Tony Tai-Ting Liu has done (this volume) for the cross-strait relationship, the diversity of Southeast Asia, in terms of politics, economics, and specific issues, provides an opportunity to differentiate Xi Jinping's personal influence both from contextual factors and from the interactive effects of recent Sino-American relations.

In Southeast Asia, in general, the China brand looms much larger than it did under Xi's predecessors, but its attractiveness is reduced. There appears to be an inverse correlation between the growth of China's hard power and the reduction of its soft power. This is all the more remarkable given Southeast Asia's simultaneous disappointment with President Donald Trump. The Joseph Biden era began with a double honeymoon in Southeast Asia by replacing Trump and contrasting to Xi, but the divisiveness of its portrayal of a global struggle between democracy and autocracy has continued Southeast Asian uneasiness concerning the United States.

With 650 million people and a strong sense of regional community, Southeast Asia can be seen as the most significant section of China's regional neighborhood. Three vectors converge to frame current Southeast Asian attitudes toward China. The first is China's regional economic primacy, the second is Xi Jinping's political style and assertiveness, and the third is concern about American leadership. The general result is that the region already views China as its most influential external power. It lacks confidence in the quality and reliability of Xi Jinping's China as a benevolent leader but does not see an alternative. For Southeast Asia, the continuing global political crisis that began with Trump's election and the American withdrawal from the Trans Pacific Partnership (TPP) has made a stable and open relationship with China more necessary, but not more attractive.

China's general prestige and attractiveness as seen from the vantage point of Southeast Asia has been through several major phases in the past forty years. From 1978 to 1991, China's shift to reform and openness reduced regional anxieties outside Indochina. Moreover, the hostility between China and Vietnam during this period led to the formation of an anti-Indochinese entente of China, the United States, and the members of ASEAN at that time—quite a change from the days of the American war in Vietnam.[8] After Western sanctions were imposed in 1989 in the wake of Tiananmen, China began to focus on regional "good neighbor" policies, and these plus China's economic growth led to a friendlier but still distant attitude in ASEAN. Meanwhile, ASEAN became a truly regional organization in the 1990s, adding the remaining four regional countries by 1999.

The next phase of the relationship was the golden decade of China–Southeast Asian relations, from 1998 to 2008.[9] In the Asian financial crisis of 1997 everyone was concerned about a regional currency race to the bottom, but China was willing and able to maintain the value of the Hong Kong dollar and of the renminbi, earning the admiration and gratitude of the region. China moved quickly from good neighbor to major collaborator. The year 2002 was the banner year, featuring the founding of the ASEAN-China Free Trade Area (ACFTA), China becoming the first nonmember to sign ASEAN's Treaty of Amity, and the proclamation of the "Declaration on Conduct of Parties in the South China Sea." The ACFTA created the world's third-largest free trade area, and China's share in ASEAN's merchandise trade increased from 8 percent in 2004 to 21 percent in 2018.[10]

I use 2008 as the end point of the golden decade because the turbulence of the global financial crisis appeared to affect everyone except China. The region became anxious about its dependency on China. China's assertiveness in the South China Sea was the focal point of regional anxiety, though in fact China's basic claims had not changed.[11] China's relationships in Southeast Asia reached a new low in May–July 2014 when the insertion of an oil platform in waters contested by Vietnam led to a serious crisis.[12] The sobering experience of the crisis has led both China and Vietnam to consider how to reduce the likelihood of future crises. The crisis with Vietnam was followed by the regional standoff over a 2016 decision by a United Nations arbitration tribunal that rejected China's claims to island sovereignty in the South China Sea and to historical waters reaching along the coasts of Vietnam and the Philippines.

Despite continuing tensions in the South China Sea, since 2016 China's relationship with Southeast Asia has entered a "new normal" era in which all sides consider stability the bedrock of their diplomacy. Of course, the expected normalcy of 2019 was blindsided by COVID-19 in 2020, and stability then required the prerequisite of recovery. But maintaining stability—with China, with the United States, in ASEAN, and also in the domestic politics of the various Southeast Asian countries, especially Myanmar—is a fundamental concern in the region. With China, the sovereignty disputes in the South China Sea as well as Southeast Asia's asymmetric relationship require caution. However, China's economic development as well as its BRI policies have recentered Pacific Asia, including Southeast Asia. The new high-speed rail links under construction are a powerful component and symbol of the new connectivity.[13] Xi Jinping has been an important contributor to this development, but the region remains concerned about his arrogance and the possible side effects of China's confrontation with the United States. Since Xi takes personal credit for the BRI and is likely to remain in power for the foreseeable future, I think that the "Xi normal" is a suitable term. By contrast, the politics of the United States under President Trump have demonstrated that it is not necessarily a reliable ally, and the Biden presidency is friendlier to American allies in the region but even more hostile to China. The "Biden normal" in foreign affairs appears to be a Cold War framing linking China and Russia as enemies, and even though Biden and the Democrats may be upended in 2024, the general Republican attitude is no different.

The Economic Recentering of Pacific Asia

The most important vector influencing China's relationship with Southeast Asia is the size, connectivity, and prospects of its economy. Neither the regional nor the Chinese economy is shrinking, though China hit a trough in 1989 and Southeast Asia did the same in 1997 and 2008. As figure 9.1 illustrates, the Chinese economy has grown faster than that of Southeast Asia. It doubled the region in 2006 and is currently 274 percent of the region's size and steady at that level. By comparison, the economy of the United States is 271 percent of Latin America's. In terms of sheer economic mass as well as population, Southeast Asia stands in the shadow of China.

Another important finding of the chart is that China's relative rate of growth has been declining since 2011, and it is now almost at the region's average. The large annual differences of 2007–10 were due to the contrast between China's steadiness and the region's fluctuation. At present, the poorer Southeast Asian countries are growing at China's rate or better, while the richer are still slightly behind. China's continuing growth prospects are therefore less scary to its neighbors than they were ten years ago, although clearly China is not going away. Indeed, the region is more concerned about a possible Chinese slowdown than another leap forward, concerns that are heightened by China's trade war with the United States and the economic effects of the pandemic.

However, scale matters. China's economy grew at 6.1 percent in 2019, possibly slower than some Southeast Asian countries, but its added production in 2019 is more than the entire Thai economy.[14] The proportional relationship of China's economy to the region is likely to remain similar to that of the United States and Latin America at roughly triple that of the region, varying according to which country has a crisis, but generally stable or with gradual increments.[15] Of course the reason for the preponderances is different. The United States has a much higher per capita gross domestic product (GDP) than Latin America and roughly half the population, while China has twice the population of Southeast Asia.

Another important dimension of China's economy vis-à-vis Southeast Asia is its rise in developmental status. I use per capita GDP as a rough indicator of relative levels of development.[16] As figure 9.2 illustrates, there have been dramatic changes in China's relative status over the past forty years. Initially, China's per capita GDP was beneath the "poor four" of ASEAN. It did not rise above that group until 1988, but by 2000 it had doubled their per capita gross national product (GNP). China has been climbing relative to the

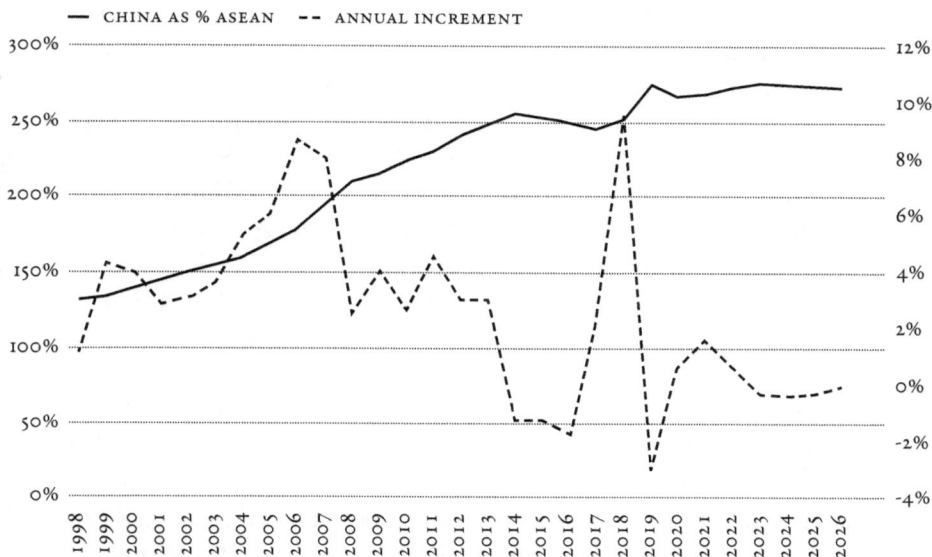

FIGURE 9.1. China's gross domestic product (GDP) (purchasing power parity) as percentage of ASEAN. Source: Calculated from International Monetary Fund (IMF), *World Economic Outlook* (Washington, DC: IMF, October 2022).

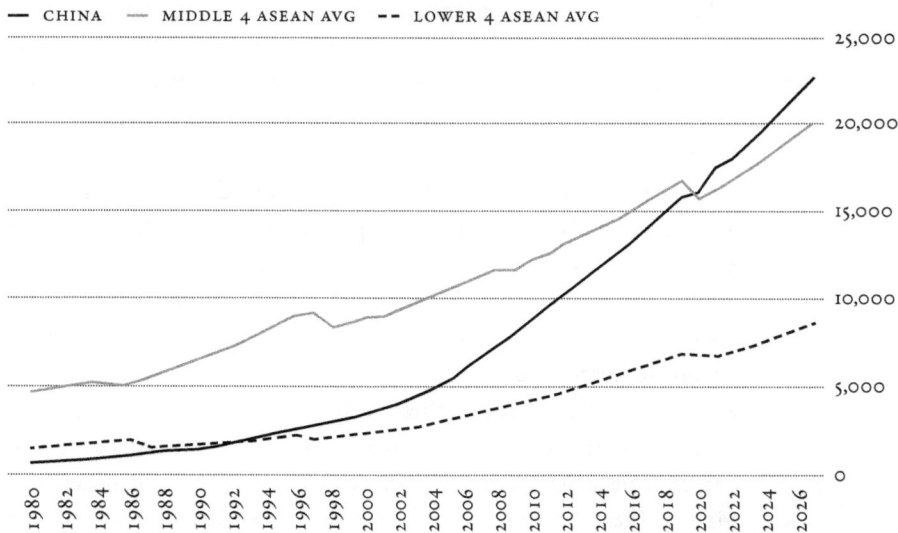

FIGURE 9.2. China's and ASEAN's GDP per capita purchasing power parity. Source: Calculated from International Monetary Fund (IMF), *World Economic Outlook* (Washington, DC: IMF, October 2022). The "ASEAN middle" are Indonesia, the Philippines, Thailand, and Malaysia. The "ASEAN lower" are Vietnam, Laos, Cambodia, and Myanmar.

middle ASEAN countries since the 1997 Asian financial crisis, and in 2020 its GDP per capita surpassed their average for the first time. When the United States looks at China it sees an economy with four times its population but one-fourth its GNP per capita, therefore a demographic power but not an equal in developmental status. China has only 18 percent of Singapore's per capita GDP, but Singapore has four-tenths of 1 percent of China's population, and Shanghai's per capita GDP is 38 percent of Singapore's. In terms of general relative development, however, Southeast Asia looks sideways if not up at China. A visit to Shanghai or Shenzhen only confirms the perception, and China's own infrastructure miracles lend credibility to the promises of the BRI.

The most direct economic linkage between China and Southeast Asia is trade. In 2004, China's merchandise trade was 8 percent of ASEAN's global trade and ASEAN's internal trade was three times higher.[17] By 2017, China's trade had climbed to 17 percent of global trade and 74 percent compared to internal trade. In 2019, China's trade with Myanmar exceeded Myanmar's trade with the rest of ASEAN.[18] Although ASEAN as a region consistently runs a slightly favorable overall balance of trade, it has run a deficit with China that ran in the single digits before 2013, reached a high of 22 percent in 2016, and in 2017 was 17 percent. Imports from China equaled 91 percent of internal ASEAN imports that year and were 20 percent of global imports. The US trade exposure to China is comparable to that of ASEAN, but the American trade imbalance is considerably more acute. A corollary of this is that China's 14 percent share of ASEAN's sales abroad is important to the regional economy.

Although the BRI has attracted global attention to Chinese investments abroad, China is still playing catch-up with the developed world in terms of investment.[19] In Southeast Asia, China's investment has almost doubled its share of global investment from the launch of the BRI in 2014–17, from 4.8 percent to 8.4 percent. Compared to intra-ASEAN investment, China's share has risen from 28 percent to 42 percent. Thus, it is not the existing level of investment that is impressive, but rather the dynamic. Besides the prospective growth of Chinese investment, the emphasis of the BRI on transformative infrastructure projects is welcome.[20] Given the already lowered expectations of emerging markets in 2019, the BRI took on added significance, and its projects remain central to prospects of post-pandemic progress.[21]

One of the five categories of connectivity promoted by Xi Jinping in the BRI is people-to-people contact, and Chinese tourism has leapt forward in the past few years before jumping back from COVID-19 in 2020. In 2013, Chinese tourists constituted 12 percent of ASEAN's total tourists and 23 percent of its tourists from outside ASEAN. In 2017, China furnished 20 percent of the total and one-third of non-ASEAN tourists, more than Europe, the United States, and Japan combined. From 2013 to 2019, visits to ASEAN by Chinese rose 155 percent, while non-Chinese visits went up by 24 percent.[22] Tourism accounts for over 10 percent of the GDP of the Philippines, Thailand, Malaysia, Laos, and Cambodia.[23] Of course, the contact provided by tourism is a mixed blessing even without the specter of epidemics. Residents not profiting from tourism are inconvenienced by crowded facilities and cultural friction. Nevertheless, tourism broadens the direct people-to-people experience, and the experience is deepened by increasing numbers of students going to China. The target that had been set for 2020 of one hundred thousand students was already doubled in 2018.[24]

Because of ASEAN, the Southeast Asian region has more economic integration and coherence in outlook than any other region on China's periphery, and it is adamantly open and global in its diplomacy. Nevertheless, with twice the population and three times the production, it is hardly surprising that China is again becoming the center of attention in Southeast Asia. If we add China's rapid increases in connectivity with the region, then integration amplifies centricity. Finally, although China's growth is slowing in the "Xi normal" era, it is still expected to exceed the growth of the United States and other developed countries. And while developing countries such as India or Ethiopia might occasionally match or exceed China's rate of growth, China has already achieved a massiveness of production that guarantees its continuing primacy in the developing world for the foreseeable future. China's prominence has become part of regional common sense. In a 2018 poll of regional opinion leaders, 73 percent thought that China had the most economic influence, compared to 11 percent for ASEAN and only 8 percent for the United States.[25] In the 2019 version of the same survey, China moved up to 79 percent.[26] Thanks to COVID-19, China moved down to 72 percent in 2020, but came back up to 77 percent in 2021.[27]

One could say, therefore, that, as far as Southeast Asia is concerned, Xi Jinping's notion of "a community of common destiny" is a reality rather than a dream. The question remains whether a shared destiny remains one of mutual benefit and respect.

Xi Jinping and Southeast Asia

The effect of Xi Jinping's leadership on regional perceptions has been mixed. On the one hand, all ASEAN states were founding members of the BRI and of the Asia Infrastructure Investment Bank (AIIB). Meanwhile, the earlier institutional relationships such as the ASEAN China Free Trade Area continue to grow, and China supports the Regional Comprehensive Economic Partnership (RCEP), an ASEAN initiative that gained new importance when the United States pulled out of the Trans Pacific Partnership (TPP). Besides the ASEAN countries, the RCEP includes Japan, South Korea, Australia, and New Zealand. It is the first trade agreement covering all of Pacific Asia, and its members represent one-third of the global population and one-third of the global GDP.

In addition, the major objections to Xi's leadership raised by the United States and other developed countries have a quite different salience in Southeast Asia. The region is not happy about the treatment of Uyghurs, but it has its own problems, including the treatment of the Rohingya in Myanmar and their refugee status elsewhere, and also Rodrigo Duterte's mass executions of drug suspects in the Philippines. At a deeper level, there is strong sentiment that Asian values are different from Western values and that official judgments should not be made concerning the internal affairs of other countries. American sanctions and interventions are often viewed as high-handed. As for intellectual property, most Southeast Asian countries share China's situation with regard to innovation transfer. They are also on the receiving end rather than on the protecting end. Finally, the region did not share American illusions that China's economic development would lead to democratization. Democratization has had its ups and downs in Southeast Asia, and tolerance of regime differences is part of the culture of ASEAN. And the concern raised by Kiron Skinner, chief of policy planning in Trump's State Department at the time, that rivalry with China is "the first time that we will have a great power competitor that is not Caucasian" sounds a bit different when heard by other non-Caucasians.[28]

On the other hand, there are three aspects of Xi's leadership that heighten the region's concerns about their increasing asymmetric integration with China: the encouragement of Chinese nationalism, Xi's aspirations of global leadership, and his personalistic authoritarianism. Chinese nationalism encouraged by Xi is the major source of worry and the one most directly tied to the South China Sea disputes. While Xi's campaigns such as "China Dream" may have the immediate objective of raising collective self-regard

234

Womack

within China, in combination with efforts to increase China's international presence, China under Xi's leadership appears more alien and intrusive to others. Moreover, there is little effort to control the overt nationalism of publications such as *Global Times* and of social media. Articles projecting Chinese nationalism or militarism produce allergic reactions among China's vulnerable neighbors. Disputed sovereignty is by its nature a hot-button issue for all sides, and Xi's abandonment of Deng Xiaoping's low-profile approach to foreign policy makes the Chinese claim more threatening.[29]

Since the oil rig incident in 2014 and the Philippines arbitration in 2016 there has been an ebb in maritime confrontations, and there has been slow progress on arriving at a code of conduct for the South China Sea. All sides declared their intention of arriving at a code by 2021, derailed by COVID-19, and China has been pushing for its completion.[30] However, the continuing militarization of maritime features and the rhetoric of Chinese netizens are disturbing, especially to Vietnam and the Philippines. Besides the tendency for Chinese nationalism to stimulate counter-Chinese nationalism in Southeast Asia, there is the special regional problem of a history of tensions and crises regarding ethnic Chinese in Southeast Asia. While ethnic Chinese have been on the defensive for much of the past seventy years, there is concern that with the new assertiveness of China, current ethnic balances could be upset.[31]

A second concern is with the global turn of Xi Jinping's ambitions. Reasonable people in the region are not worried about China expanding its land boundaries toward the south. China settled its last land border dispute with Southeast Asia in 2001, and its basic southeastern border was set in the fifteenth century with the defeat of the Ming annexation of Vietnam.[32] But coping with American rivalry has become Xi's dominant concern, and that poses several derivative risks for the region. The most basic problem is that it threatens to make the region into a passive venue of great power tensions. This was Southeast Asia's fate during the American war in Vietnam, and it was a major reason for the founding of ASEAN.[33] For the past twenty-five years, ASEAN's prestige and agency have blossomed, and arguably the rise of China has helped rather than hurt its prominence. But the region's significance and autonomy will be reduced if both China and the United States fixate on their bilateral relationship—whether a rivalrous new Cold War or a collaborative Group of Two (G2)—and deduce regional policies from their global concerns. For example, China's militarization of the South China Sea is aimed primarily at countering American capabilities, but it has the secondary effects of making regionally based demilitarization unlikely and stimulating American military activities in the region.

A second related problem with incipient US-China rivalry is that most other countries would prefer not to choose between them. While Southeast Asia welcomed the growing American interest in the region exemplified by the "pivot toward Asia," it would be a disaster to be exclusively on one side or the other in a Cold War–type confrontation. In the 2019 survey of Southeast Asian elites, 79 percent wanted to avoid taking sides and to strengthen ASEAN, though only 3 percent wanted to keep the superpowers out of the region.[34] In the 2020 survey, despite a more jaundiced view of China and high hopes for the Biden administration, the percentage wanting to avoid taking sides increased to 84 percent.[35]

Regional countries have leverage as long as both sides are trying to entice friends and partners, but to take sides would mean either to lose access to China's markets, products, and connectivity or to cut off a vital buffering relationship beyond Asia. Since the choice would be an unwelcome one, whichever side attempts to force the choice would thereby become the proximate threat. If both sides force a choice, the best policy for other countries would be to reduce exposure to both by strengthening non–great power relationships and regional institutions such as ASEAN.[36]

The third aspect of Xi Jinping's leadership that worries Southeast Asia is his increasing tendency toward personalistic authoritarianism. The region is not shocked by this tendency. It has plenty of its own experience with this genre of leadership. Cambodia's Hun Sen was in power from 1979 until succeeded by his son in 2023. But precisely because of this background, there are concerns about the long-term reliability and quality of Chinese leadership. Xi's deinstitutionalization of Party and state processes and muzzling of contrary views and criticism have not improved the quality and sensitivity of Chinese diplomacy. Yang Jiechi, Xi's former chief foreign policy adviser, is infamous in the region for reminding Singapore's foreign minister in 2010 that China is a big country but Singapore is a small one. "Wolf warriors" may be popular in China, but Southeast Asia faces the toothy end of the wolves. And while Xi's consolidation of personal power at the 20th Party Congress promises stability in the medium term, it doesn't guarantee consistency in policy, and it raises the questions of "after Xi, what?" and "after Xi, when?"

Public opinion in Southeast Asia reflects both awareness of China's arrival as a global power and reservations about its nationalism, rivalry with the United States, and leadership. The fourth wave of the Asian Barometer Survey, the most extensive and detailed political opinion survey of East Asia, was conducted in China, Japan, and South Korea and all Southeast Asian countries except Brunei in 2014–16 and contained some questions relating to international perceptions.[37] The timing is useful because it captures Xi's first years and the effect of Barack Obama's pivot toward Asia. Opinions differed widely, and varied according to current country-specific interactions, but, in general, American influence on Asia was viewed more positively (73 percent) than Chinese influence (56 percent).[38] However, as one researcher put it simply, "Prosperity attracts East Asians."[39] This trait benefits the prestige of Japan and Singapore, and it also accounts for a smaller rise in esteem for China and little change for the United States despite the efforts of Obama and Hillary Clinton. China was viewed as "the main driver of regional integration and greater economic openness."[40] The difference in political systems between China and respondents' countries had little effect, leading the researchers to conclude that "China's one-party authoritarian system is no longer an obstacle to its ascendance in the region."[41] In 2016, China was, if not the coming attraction for the region, the coming reality.

In sum, Xi Jinping's coming to power in 2012 did not define a new era in China–Southeast Asian relations, but it has reshaped them. The age of anxiety replaced the golden age already in 2008, as China appeared to leap forward while others, especially the United States, fell back. However, Xi brought anxiety to its highest point with the crises of 2014 and 2016. Since then, few would disagree that China is now the major economic and political influence. But the "Xi normal" has not created a comfort zone for China's neighbors. China's soft power and political prestige lagged behind perceptions of its economic might and dynamic.

The Trump Vector

The election of Donald Trump in 2016 created a global political crisis comparable to the global economic crisis of 2008.[42] The main effect of both crises was the creation of systemic uncertainty. The big difference between the two is that with Trump the uncertainty continued to deepen, and even after his departure uncertainty remains as a cloud over American diplomatic predictability. As in 2008, the crisis created the opportunity for China to leap forward in prominence, this time in terms of political prestige and visibility. But just as its earlier economic advances generated anxieties in Southeast Asia, China's political prominence is unsettling.

The structural uncertainties introduced by Trump were evident from the beginning of his administration and can be divided into five dimensions: policy content, implementation, continuity, adaptability, and duration. First, Trump's assertions of policy preferences were occasionally contradictory or inconsistent. Second, implementation was hampered by frequent changes of key personnel and by the demoralization of the diplomatic, intelligence, and military communities. Third, Trump took pride in disrupting continuity with previous administrations. Fourth, although his style of bargaining to a crisis point and then compromising involved a certain kind of flexibility, he did not admit mistakes, nor did he learn from them. Fifth and last, but not least, although Trump lost the 2020 election, the strength of the Republican Party and of the Trump faction within it raises the question of a possible return of right-wing politics—with or without Trump himself—in 2024. And the riot at the Capitol on January 6, 2021, raises the prospect of a new level of violence in American domestic politics.

The regional Trump shock in Asia began on the first day of his presidency when he abandoned the TPP. Organizing the TPP option was the capstone of Obama's "pivot to Asia." Trump's quick scuttling of the TPP demonstrated that his talk about "America First" was not just campaign rhetoric. His personal style and his tweets aimed at his right-wing domestic base have continued to alienate and irritate the region. After Trump's first hundred days in office in 2017, a poll of Southeast Asian foreign policy elites showed that while 70 percent supported active US involvement in the region, only 4 percent thought that Southeast Asia was an American priority.[43] A majority thought that the United States now considered Southeast Asia unimportant or irrelevant, and 72 percent thought that the US global image had deteriorated over the previous four months. The United States was considered an undependable ally by 44 percent and highly undependable by 11 percent. Two-thirds did expect the United States to continue its involvement in the South China Sea, but did not expect continuing interest in human rights or international law. While half expected ASEAN to strengthen intraregional cooperation, three-quarters considered China most influential in the region now and for the next ten years, followed by ASEAN (18 percent), Japan (5 percent), and the United States (4 percent). If the United States created a strategic vacuum, then 80 percent expected China to be the major beneficiary. These low expectations of the Trump administration stemmed not from anticipated economic losses (only 9 percent expected "huge losses" from America First), but rather from Trump's initial policies and general uncertainties.

A similar elite poll conducted in November–December 2018 confirmed the initial judgments of Trump and of Xi.[44] The United States and China were equally distrusted, at 51.5 percent for China and 50.6 percent for the United States. There were surprisingly low ratings for China from its presumptive friend Cambodia (21 percent trusted) and for the United States from its ally Thailand (14 percent trusted). The political nature of the current crisis was underlined by the contrast between 43 percent considering the regional outlook uncertain and 55 percent being optimistic about the regional economy. More expected to benefit rather than to lose in a US-China trade war, but most were uncertain about it. Only Vietnam (78 percent) and the Philippines (62 percent) considered military tensions a major problem, but many were worried about ASEAN becoming the arena of major power competition (62 percent). Most thought that US global and regional power and influence had deteriorated over the past year (59 percent), and only Vietnam thought the United States had done better (47 percent positive, 32 percent negative). There was an even split on the reliability of the American security role in the region. One-third considered it reliable (especially Vietnam and Cambodia), one-third were unsure (especially Indonesia, Laos, and Myanmar), and one-third were doubtful (especially Malaysia, Brunei, and Thailand). The general view of the BRI was positive, but there was concern about China's ultimate ambitions in the region. While China was clearly the leading economic power (73 percent), the responses regarding political and strategic influence are more diverse: 45 percent choose China, 31 percent choose the United States, and 21 percent choose ASEAN. Singapore ranks the United States and China equally; China is the leader everywhere else. Two-thirds expect the United States and China to be strategic competitors.

One year later, *The State of Southeast Asia* survey documented a continuation of China's rise in prominence in an atmosphere of increasing general concern.[45] China's status as the leading economic power in the region grew from 73 to 79 percent, and it was now seen as the leading political and strategic power by 52 percent, almost twice the American share of 27 percent and three times ASEAN's 18 percent. But people are not happy about the trend. Eighty-five percent of those who consider China the largest political influence are worried about China's influence in their own country. Seventy-nine percent do not want to choose sides in a global rivalry, but if they had to, 46 percent would choose China and 54 percent the United States.

It is important to note that only three ASEAN states preferred the United States to China in 2019, namely, Vietnam (86 percent), the Philippines (83 percent), and Singapore (61 percent); the other seven preferred China, but by smaller margins. The gap is a reminder of the diversity of attitudes within ASEAN, as well. Vietnam's relation to the United States actually improved under Trump. He visited Hanoi twice, US military actions in the South China Sea were welcome, Vietnam's trade was improved by Trump's trade war with China, and human rights criticism disappeared. Over the course of 2019, respondents became significantly more worried about domestic political instability, economic downturn, and climate change, followed distantly by military tensions and terrorism, but military tensions related to the South China Sea ranked first for Vietnam and the Philippines. Many were concerned that new initiatives regarding the Indo-Pacific might sideline ASEAN's initiatives.

The elite poll conducted immediately after the defeat of Trump in the 2020 election documented the region's vast relief and its hope for an American return to predictability.[46] Now 68 percent expected US engagement in the region to increase, as opposed to only 10 percent the previous year. Confidence that the United States "will do the right thing" under Biden rose from 30 percent to 48 percent, and confidence in the United States as a strategic partner rose from 35 percent to 55 percent. This is especially impressive considering the confusion in American politics that persisted until January 2021 (when the poll concluded) and the poor performance of the United States in the COVID-19 crisis. But positive attitudes should not be mistaken for a regional swing toward the United States. Only 6 percent had full confidence in the United States as a strategic partner, and 84 percent wanted to strengthen ASEAN and avoid a choice between the global powers. The United States is seen as one of a number of hedges against China but not as an alternative. Japan and the European Union, while not as powerful, are more popular, and there is a positive reception of the new regional trade organization, the Regional Comprehensive Economic Partnership (RCEP).

The New Normal of China's Soft Power in Southeast Asia

Given the ebbing of American hegemony, it is notable that the world's general confidence in China's leadership has decreased while perceptions of its importance have increased. According to a global poll in October 2018, 70 percent see China as moving forward over the past decade, 34 percent consider China the leading economic power, and only 19 percent think that having China as the leading power is good. Despite generally low opinions of Trump, 60 percent prefer American leadership.[47] In Europe as well as in Asia there is nostalgia for the "good old days" before Trump.[48] This promises a post-Trump rebound effect, already visible in the 2020 ASEAN poll, but a full return to earlier confidence is unlikely, and a return of American economic hegemony is far less likely.

The reasons for the lag in confidence concerning China are complex. Part of the gap is due to negative aspects of Xi's diplomacy and part to China's party-state system, though, in any case, changing asymmetric relations generate anxieties. Using the political scientist Joseph Nye's original definition of soft power as the ability to achieve cooperation without rewards or sanctions, China's soft power appears to be far behind its hard power capabilities.[49] Clearly, soft power is more complex than an automatic accompaniment of power, the "gleam on the sword." Indeed, in the case of Vietnam, it seems that the vividness of China's hard power accounts for Vietnam's extreme suspicion. Up close, a sword in a neighbor's hand is not attractive, nor are the bared teeth of a neighbor's diplomats.

Especially under Xi Jinping, China has certainly attempted to develop the persuasiveness of its soft power. Xi's slogans of "win-win" and the "community of common destiny" attempt to emphasize the mutual benefit of specific initiatives and the general situation of shared needs and goals. But "win-win" is unconvincing in asymmetric relationships.[50] The larger side is proportionally less exposed to risk in the transaction and can more freely take chances. If a BRI project fails, China loses money, but the other side loses its budget and the next election. Moreover, while the tighter bond forged by cooperation enables the smaller side to participate in accomplishing something desirable, it leaves the residue of a closer relationship with a stronger power.[51] That closer relationship can be comfortable only if the larger power is trusted. Trust requires confidence that the autonomy and core interests of the smaller side will be respected. In turn, the larger side must be confident that the smaller side is not scheming against it. The most important factor in creating mutual trust is mutual respect over time. Eventually, the stability of the relationship becomes the commonsense expectation of both sides.

The term *new normal* is therefore a bit of a contradiction. A relationship becomes normal as it ages. In the instance of China and Southeast Asia, the rise of China has been too recent and there is the even more recent problem of sharpening global rivalry. China has reasons to be confident that Southeast Asia will not balance against it, and Southeast Asia has reasons to be confident that China will respect its collective and individual autonomy. But there are doubts on both sides, and Southeast Asia is at best a collective actor rather than a unitary one. Appropriate diplomacy is necessary on both sides in order to embed normalcy.

On the Southeast Asian side, diplomatic appropriateness and stability are made more difficult by the number and variety of sovereign actors. Each has a long and idiosyncratic relationship with China. Consider the examples of Vietnam, Singapore, and the Philippines. Vietnam's party-state is most similar to China's and their party-to-party relations are considered more important than their state-to-state diplomacy. Nevertheless, no country in the region is more suspicious of China than Vietnam. Righteous resistance to China is a central part of Vietnamese national identity, underlined by hostility from 1978 to 1991.[52] Singapore's small size and affluence creates nervousness in its regional relationships as well as with China. It is like a small orphan with a fat wallet in a raucous playground, and it relies on its agility to survive. Singapore's military expenditures as a percentage of its GDP are double the average of Pacific Asia and 1.8 times that of China, and conscription at age eighteen is compulsory.[53] The Philippines continues to have a close but fraught relationship to the United States. More important than the formal alliance (often ignored by both sides) is the thick web of transnational family connections. Remittances from the United States were $11 billion in 2017, ranking behind only Mexico, China, and India and contributing 4 percent of its GDP.[54] Moreover, political swings in the Philippines have led to dramatic changes in attitudes toward China with each new president. In 2014, during Benigno Aquino's presidency only 32 percent of Filipinos had a positive view of Xi, but six months into Duterte's presidency in 2017 it had risen to 53 percent.[55] Nevertheless, China's power and influence was still considered a threat by 77 percent.

The fluctuation and diversity of China's bilateral relations with Southeast Asian countries underlines the importance of ASEAN. ASEAN is key to the China–Southeast Asia relationship because it pools (but does not compress) the divergent perspectives of its members and reduces the asymmetry of their individual relationships with China.[56] By creating a regional international profile and point of attention, ASEAN strengthens the collective autonomy of its members.[57] Just as importantly, inclusivity is the essence of its foreign policy. Thus ASEAN facilitates both sides of the asymmetric relationship. It reassures its members, but not by suggesting an alliance against outsiders. In the China–Southeast Asia relationship over the past twenty-five years, ASEAN has had the opposite function of the North Atlantic Treaty Organization (NATO) between Europe and Russia.

Even the researchers at the ASEAN Studies Centre in Singapore were surprised at their findings that ASEAN was considered second only to China as the country/organization with the most economic influence in Southeast Asia, and with substantial political influence as well.[58] ASEAN's strength is its weakness: because it operates by consensus it cannot force its membership, and because it is not an alliance it cannot threaten others. Its challenge is to preserve credible centrality as connectivity with China continues to strengthen and as great power rivalry hardens.

Conclusion

China's diplomacy toward Southeast Asia under Xi Jinping has followed the successful lines of his predecessors. He has continued to develop exchanges of official visits at all levels. In 2020, Xi's first official overseas trip was to Myanmar. The first top official whom Xi met after the confirmation of his third term as Party secretary in 2022 was General Secretary Nguyen Phu Trong of Vietnam. The BRI has provided an umbrella and label for a general commitment to expand China's domestic and international connectivity. Xi has shown respect for ASEAN itself and for ASEAN's continued leadership in its various initiatives such as the RCEP, the East Asia Summit, and the East Asia Community. Although bilateral tensions with Vietnam and the Philippines reached their high points under Xi, like his predecessors he was careful to keep the crises from crossing a threshold into hostility or from creating more lasting and generalized enmity.[59] To a great extent the region's nostalgia for American presence and concerns about China's growth are due to its decreasing exposure to the United States and increasing exposure to China rather than to bad diplomacy or aggressive actions on China's part. The United States seems less threatening because it is less capable of threatening.

The problematic features of Xi's diplomacy also have their roots in previous policy. Even before 2008 the domestic discussion of China's peaceful rise occurred in the context of a new interest in the rise of great powers.[60] In the South China Sea the number of incidents increased after 2008, whether by central direction or by a loosening of the leashes of various Chinese units operating there. The problem of maritime loose cannons continued under Xi until 2014, when the severity of the oil rig crisis with Vietnam led to some leash-tightening but not significant accommodation. But the cannons continue to multiply. Xi's physical and military building of the maritime points under Chinese control was central policy, though that also had precedents.

Perhaps the major personal failings of Xi's regional diplomacy thus far are problems of omission rather than of commission. The general contours of the China–Southeast Asia relationship are more favorable for a stable, mutually beneficial asymmetric relationship than they have ever been. Southeast Asia needs no further persuasion that a positive relationship with China is essential. China should be confident that Southeast Asia and ASEAN will not abuse its favors. The shock of China's post-2008 growth rate is over. China under Xi aspires to sustainable stability, not leaps forward, and Southeast Asia can view China as a socio-economy more similar to itself in problems and aspirations. Southeast Asians appreciated China's help during the

COVID-19 crisis.[61] Both China and Southeast Asia have to deal with the problem of American nationalism and unpredictability, though from different perspectives. Southeast Asia does not want to choose between global rivals, and even less does it want to become again the venue for global conflict.

In these circumstances China has the opportunity—thus far not grasped—to confirm a normal relationship with Southeast Asia. The basic diplomatic challenge is to provide a credible framework for the relationship that guarantees Southeast Asia's individual and collective autonomy and core interests. While China does not see itself as threatening regional autonomy, it needs to convince Southeast Asia that respect for regional interests is not a matter of changeable policy. The first step would be to sign a code of conduct for the South China Sea. What matters with the code is that it would provide a mutually agreeable and binding structure for interactions despite continuing differences over sovereignty. The fact of the signing of the code would be more important than its content. The second step would be to continue to emphasize that increased connectivity to China would enhance rather than restrict connectivity elsewhere, including connectivity with the United States. The most effective response to American containment would be not counter-containment but rather openness.[62] Joining the revised TPP would be a brilliant move that would push forward openness while preventing containment. A third step would be developing cooperative institutions to cope with regional problems shared by China such as natural disasters, effects of global warming, and fisheries.

China is no longer a rising power vis-à-vis Southeast Asia. It is a risen power, but it is not all-powerful, and it will never be. The age of hegemony is over. What has already replaced the hegemony of the United States is a multinodal web of interacting relationships in which relative power matters, but is not decisive.[63] Even if the United States disappeared, China would not be all-powerful. This is the basic context of the Xi normal in China–Southeast Asia relations. Xi Jinping's task is how to stabilize and institutionalize a mutually beneficial asymmetric relationship. He has not taken off in a contrary direction, but there are important steps not yet taken.

Notes

1. Suisheng Zhao, *The Dragon Roars Back: Transformational Leaders and Dynamics of Chinese Foreign Policy* (Stanford, CA: Stanford University Press, 2022).

2. Camilla T. N. Sørensen, "The Roots of China's Assertiveness in East Asia:

Analysing the Main Driving Forces in Chinese Foreign Policy," *Copenhagen Journal of Asian Studies* 39, no. 2 (December 2021): 10–32.

3. Yi Wang, "Jointly Advancing the Global Development Initiative and Writing a New Chapter for Common Development," Ministry of Foreign Affairs of the People's Republic of China, September 21, 2022, https://www.fmprc.gov.cn/eng/zxxx_662805/202209/t20220922_10769721.html; Yi Wang, "Acting on the Global Security Initiative to Safeguard World Peace and Tranquility," Ministry of Foreign Affairs of the People's Republic of China, April 24, 2022, http://us.china-embassy.gov.cn/eng/zgyw/202205/t20220505_10681820.htm.

4. Graham Allison, *Destined for War: Can America and China Escape Thucydides's Trap?* (Boston: Houghton Mifflin, 2017).

5. Brantly Womack, *Recentering Pacific Asia: Regional China and World Order* (Cambridge: Cambridge University Press, 2023).

6. World Trade Organization (WTO), *Global Value Chain Development Report 2019: Technological Innovation, Supply Chain Trade, and Workers in a Globalized World* (Geneva: WTO, 2019).

7. In dollar value, Pacific Asia was 73 percent of combined US and EU production in 2021. China was 62 percent of Pacific Asia's total production. Calculated from International Monetary Fund (IMF), *World Economic Outlook* (Washington, DC: IMF, October 2022).

8. Until the accession of Vietnam in 1995, the members of ASEAN were Thailand, Indonesia, Malaysia, Singapore, Brunei, and the Philippines.

9. Brantly Womack, "China and Southeast Asia: Asymmetry, Leadership and Normalcy," *Pacific Affairs* 76, no. 4 (Winter 2003/4): 529–48.

10. Jayant Menon and Anna Cassandra Melendez, "Upgrading the ASEAN-China Free Trade Agreement," *East Asia Forum*, August 14, 2019, https://www.eastasiaforum.org/2019/08/14/upgrading-the-asean-china-free-trade-agreement.

11. Alastair Iain Johnston, "How New and Assertive Is China's New Assertiveness?," *International Security* 37, no. 4 (Spring 2013): 7–48; Bjorn Jerden, "The Assertive China Narrative: Why It Is Wrong and How So Many Bought into It," *Chinese Journal of International Politics* 7, no. 1 (Spring 2014): 47–88; Brantly Womack, "China and the Future Status Quo," *Chinese Journal of International Politics* 8, no. 2 (Summer 2015): 115–37.

12. The oil rig crisis was certainly the lowest point in Vietnam's recent relationship with China, and it has had lasting effects. Alexander Vuving, "Where to Now for Vietnam after Trong?," *East Asia Forum*, February 27, 2021, https://www.eastasiaforum.org/2021/02/27/where-to-now-for-vietnam-after-trong.

13. David M. Lampton, Celina Ho, and Cheng-Chwee Kuik, *Rivers of Iron: Railroads and Chinese Power in Southeast Asia* (Berkeley: University of California Press, 2020).

14. Calculated from Central Intelligence Agency, *The World Factbook*, accessed December 23, 2023, https://www.cia.gov/the-world-factbook; estimate from the IMF, *World Economic Outlook* (Washington, DC: IMF, 2019), https://www.imf.org/en/Publications/WEO/Issues/2019/10/01/world-economic-outlook-october-2019.

15. In the past twenty years, the United States has fluctuated between 313 percent and 239 percent of the Latin American economy, according to the IMF.

16. There are numerous problems with equating per capita GNP to wealth and poverty. However, the most extreme problems of inflated gross national products (GNPs) per capita are due to resource export, which does not affect these comparisons.

17. All China-ASEAN trade, investment, and tourism figures calculated from *ASEAN Statistical Yearbook 2018* (Jakarta: ASEAN Secretariat, December 2018), https://www.aseanstats.org/wp-content/uploads/2019/01/asyb-2018.pdf.

18. John Reed, "China and Myanmar Sign off on Belt and Road Projects," *Financial Times*, January 18, 2020.

19. Evelyn Goh and Nan Liu, "Chinese Investment in Southeast Asia, 2005–19: Patterns and Significance," SEARBO Policy Briefing, *New Mandala*, August 11, 2021, https://dokumen.tips/documents/chinese-investment-in-southeast-asia.html?page=2.

20. See Dewi Fortuna Anwar, "Indonesia and the ASEAN Outlook on the Indo-Pacific," *International Affairs* 96, no. 1 (2020): 111–29, especially 121.

21. Jonathan Wheatley, "Investors Look to Emerging Markets amid IMF's Prognosis," *Financial Times*, April 12, 2019.

22. Calculated from ASEAN Stats Data Portal, "Visitor Arrival to ASEAN Member State States by Origin Countries," accessed March 2, 2021, https://data.aseanstats.org/visitors.

23. *ASEAN Tourism Strategic Plan 2016–2025* (Jakarta: ASEAN Secretariat, 2015), https://asean.org/wp-content/uploads/2012/05/ATSP-2016-2025.pdf.

24. The target was set in 2010 at the 13th ASEAN-China Summit. The current estimate is for students in both directions. Tommy Koh, "ASEAN and China: Past, Present, and Future," Tembusu College, National University of Singapore, October 22, 2018, https://tembusu.nus.edu.sg/news/2018/asean-and-china-past-present-future.

25. Tang Siew Mun, Moe Thuzar, Hoang Thi Ha, Termsak Chalermpalanupap, Pham Thi Phuong Thao, and Anuthida Saelaow Qian, *The State of Southeast Asia: 2019 Survey Report* (Singapore: ISEAS–Yusof Ishak Institute, 2019), https://www.iseas.edu.sg/images/pdf/TheStateofSEASurveyReport_2019.pdf. This is an annual online survey of "policy influencers and informers" in Southeast Asia. It tries to include a spectrum of responders from across government, academic, and other specialist areas. The 2022 survey included sixteen hundred respondents.

26. Tang Siew Mun, Hoang Thi Ha, Anuthida Saelaow Qian, Glenn Ong, and

Pham Thi Phuong Thao, *The State of Southeast Asia: 2020 Survey Report* (Singapore: ISEAS–Yusof Ishak Institute, 2020), https://www.iseas.edu.sg/images/pdf/TheStateofSEASurveyReport_2020.pdf.

27. Sharon Seah, Hoang Thi Ha, Melinda Martinus, and Pham Thi Phuong Thao, *The State of Southeast Asia: 2021 Survey Report* (Singapore: ISEAS–Yusof Ishak Institute, 2021), https://www.iseas.edu.sg/wp-content/uploads/2021/01/The-State-of-SEA-2021-v2.pdf; Sharon Seah, Joanne Lin, Sithanonxay Suvannaphakdy, Melinda Martinus, Pham Thi Phuong Thao, Farah Nadine Seth, and Hoang Thi Ha, *The State of Southeast Asia: 2022 Survey Report* (Singapore: ISEAS–Yusof Ishak Institute, 2022), https://www.iseas.edu.sg/wp-content/uploads/2022/02/The-State-of-SEA-2022_FA_Digital_FINAL.pdf.

28. Joel Gehrke, "State Department Preparing for Clash of Civilizations with China," *Washington Examiner*, April 30, 2019.

29. Womack, "China and the Future Status Quo."

30. Carlyle A. Thayer, "South China Sea: China and the Code of Conduct," *Thayer Consultancy Background Brief*, January 11, 2020, https://www.scribd.com/document/489530542/Thayer-Consultancy-Annual-Report-for-2020.

31. Bilahari Kausikan, "Two Global Trends That Will Shape Singapore's Future" (speech, Overseas Chinese Banking Corporation Forum, Singapore, July 12, 2018).

32. James Anderson and John Whitmore, eds., *China's Encounters on the South and Southwest: Reforging the Fiery Frontier over Two Millennia* (Leiden: Brill, 2014).

33. Lee Hsien Loong, "The View from Singapore and Southeast Asia" (speech, 18th Shangri-La Dialogue, Singapore, June 2019).

34. Tang et al., *The State of Southeast Asia: 2020 Survey Report*, 28.

35. Seah et al., *The State of Southeast Asia: 2021 Survey Report*, 32.

36. Brantly Womack, "Asymmetric Parity: US-China Relations in a Multinodal World," *International Affairs* 92, no. 6 (November 2016): 1463–80.

37. Asian Barometer Survey, accessed December 23, 2023, https://www.asianbarometer.org.

38. Yun-han Chu and Yu-tzung Chang, "Xi's Foreign-Policy Turn and Asian Perceptions of a Rising China," *Global Asia* 12, no. 1 (Spring 2017): 104–11.

39. Kai-Ping Huang and Bridget Welsh, "Trends in Soft Power in East Asia: Distance, Diversity and Drivers," *Global Asia* 12, no. 1 (Spring 2017): 112–17.

40. Min-Hua Huang and Mark Weatherall, "Democratic Distance and Asian Views of Chinese and American Influence," *Global Asia* 12, no. 1 (Spring 2017): 118.

41. Huang and Weatherall, "Democratic Distance," 119.

42. Brantly Womack, "International Crises and China's Rise: Comparing the 2008 Global Financial Crisis and the 2017 Global Political Crisis," *Chinese Journal of International Politics* 10, no. 4 (Winter 2017): 383–401.

43. ASEAN Studies Centre, "How Do Southeast Asians View the Trump Administration?," May 3, 2017, https://www.iseas.edu.sg/wp-content/uploads/2017/05/ASCSurvey40517.pdf.

44. Tang et al., *The State of Southeast Asia: 2019 Survey Report*.

45. Tang et al., *The State of Southeast Asia: 2020 Survey Report*.

46. Seah et al., *The State of Southeast Asia: 2021 Survey Report*.

47. Kat Devlin, "5 Charts on Global Views of China," Pew Research Center, October 2018, https://www.pewresearch.org/fact-tank/2018/10/19/5-charts-on -global-views-of-china.

48. Guy Chazan and Michael Peel, "Confidence in NATO in Sharp Decline," *Financial Times*, February 10, 2020.

49. Joseph Nye, *Bound to Lead: The Changing Nature of American Power* (New York: Basic Books, 1990).

50. Brantly Womack, "Beyond Win-Win: Rethinking China's International Relationships in an Era of Economic Uncertainty," *International Affairs* 89, no. 4 (July 2013): 911–28.

51. Evelyn Goh, ed., *Rising China's Influence in Developing Asia* (New York: Oxford University Press, 2016).

52. Brantly Womack, *China and Vietnam: The Politics of Asymmetry* (New York: Cambridge University Press, 2006).

53. World Bank, "World Development Indicators," 2019, http://datatopics .worldbank.org/world-development-indicators.

54. Pew Research Center, "Remittance Flows Worldwide in 2017," April 3, 2019, https://www.pewresearch.org/global/interactives/remittance-flows -by-country.

55. Laura Silver, "How People in Asia-Pacific View China," Pew Research Center, October 16, 2017, https://www.pewresearch.org/fact-tank/2017/10/16/how -people-in-asia-pacific-view-china.

56. Alice Ba, *(Re)Negotiating East and Southeast Asia: Region, Regionalism, and the Association of Southeast Asian Nations* (Stanford, CA: Stanford University Press, 2009); Amitav Acharya, *ASEAN and Regional Order: Revisiting Security Community in Southeast Asia* (New York: Routledge, 2021).

57. Nguyen Vu Tung, *Flying Blind: Vietnam's Decision to Join ASEAN* (Singapore: ISEAS–Yusof Ishak Institute, 2021).

58. Tang et al., *The State of Southeast Asia: 2019 Survey Report*, 22.

59. Frances Yaping Wang and Brantly Womack, "Jawing through Crises: Chinese and Vietnamese Media Strategies in the South China Sea," *Journal of Contemporary China* 28, no. 119 (2019): 712–28.

60. Gotelind Müller, *Documentary, World History, and National Power in the PRC: Global Rise in Chinese Eyes* (London: Routledge, 2013).

61. Seah et al., *The State of Southeast Asia: 2021 Survey Report*.

62. Wang Jisi, "Qualitative Change in US China Policy in 4 Perspectives," *Global Times*, June 16, 2019, http://www.globaltimes.cn/content/1154466.shtml.

63. Womack, *Recentering Pacific Asia*, chap. 5.

10

Understanding the Xi Effect

Structure versus Agency

Kevin J. O'Brien

Is there a Xi Jinping effect? And if there is, what is it? These seem like straight-forward questions, but this volume shows that they are not easily answered. This is so because even if an unmistakable change in the wake of Xi's rise to preeminence can be identified in a sphere such as great power diplomacy, a second set of questions immediately follows.[1] Is the Xi effect apparent in many policy areas or just a few? If only in some areas, why in those? Do changes associated with Xi have deep roots in the past, or can they be traced directly to his ascent and a break with the Hu Jintao era or perhaps the entire reform period ushered in by Deng Xiaoping? What about the future? Although it is difficult to make out the outlines of a post-Xi China, or even to hazard a guess when it might begin, are the changes evident since Xi's rise likely to persist, or are reversals in the offing when he leaves the scene?

The editors of this volume have slyly forced the contributors to grapple with one of the knottiest problems in the social sciences: sorting out the consequences of structure and agency. How much is Xi a vessel or manifestation of larger changes, separate from him, taking place in China or in the international political-economic system, and how much is Xi a captain of the ship taking China in directions that could not be foreseen based on the exhaustion of export-led growth, technological change, problems in the West, the Thucydides Trap, decades of economic development and military modernization, efforts to cope with a more complex society, and whatever else Leninist state capitalism entails at this juncture in world history. Is Xi, as one of the participants at the Banff conference that inspired this book (Timothy Cheek) put it, a cause or an effect?

Starting with the first question: Is there a Xi effect? The answer that emerges from this volume is a qualified "yes." To be sure, there are notable and striking continuities that should not be downplayed, on issues such as limited attempts to address inequality, as Martin King Whyte demonstrates, or how migrants remain precarious participants in the urban public goods regime, as explained by Alexsia T. Chan. And there may be aspects of the pre-Xi past that were not fully appreciated in the Hu Jintao years, including the continuing importance of ideology (Cheek; Ashley Esarey and Rong-bin Han) and the fragility of collective leadership, which have been carried through to the current era.[2] But it is difficult to make the case that Xi has just been more of the same. If Li Keqiang had won the leadership race, as many expected in the late 2000s, it is not a big stretch to argue that China would be a materially different country today. Would we see growing tensions with the United States? Probably. A larger Chinese presence in the South China Sea (Brantly Womack)? Quite likely. A vigorous anti-corruption campaign directed at "tigers" as well as "flies" (Andrew Wedeman), "total surveillance" of Uyghurs and increasingly of Han (Musapir; Deng Kai, David Demes, and Chih-Jou Jay Chen), "One Belt, One Road," the casting aside of leadership succession norms, a remarkably hard crackdown on free speech and the rights protection movement (Esarey and Han)? Probably not. Elite politics, in other words, is back. What top leaders, especially Xi, want clearly matters. How Xi vanquished his opponents and concentrated power in his own hands so that he has a degree of discretion not seen since Deng Xiaoping is a topic that China scholars must strive to understand better, even if our ways of knowing what takes place in the halls of Zhongnanhai have not improved as much as would be ideal.[3] We need to be reading leadership statements and public announcements closely and parsing them skillfully so that we can learn what Xi and others at the top seek.[4] This is true because, policy misimplementation and opposition by political rivals aside, a substantial portion of what Xi calls for is happening.

That is the case for change and agency, and against continuity and structure. In this volume, that leadership matters is most evident in Tony Tai-Ting Liu's chapter on Xi stepping up pressure on Taiwan, his confidence that he knows Taiwan better than other top leaders, and his focus on resolving the Taiwan issue in the near future. But we also see Xi's hand at work in domestic politics, concerning the mistreatment of Uyghurs (Musapir), the scope of the anti-corruption campaign (Wedeman), and Xi's presiding over a centralization of power that has benefited Xi more than anyone else.[5]

Now, allow me to tack back against this line of thinking or at least complicate it and problematize the Xi effect. First, as seen in Gerda Wielander's "fundamentalism with Chinese characteristics," there are many paradoxes and ironies in the Xi effect. Wielander shows that tighter control of faith-based activity and efforts to position the Communist Party as a sacralized object that subsumes all religions is both familiar and unfamiliar.[6] Or in Timothy Cheek's chapter on ideological governance and Xi's "counter-reformation," Xi's use of ideology echoes the governing style of Liu Shaoqi and Mao Zedong, but is not merely a return to the Yan'an rectification model, as twenty-first-century leaders continue to confront Qing dynasty problems and play their usual pedagogical role, but have also developed new lessons to teach. The main content of the Party's curriculum for Cheek lies in texts such as Liu Shaoqi's *How to Be a Good Communist* and the 1981 "Resolution on Certain Questions in the History of Our Party," the Party's "holy scripture" on the Maoist past, while a new resolution on Party history in 2021 elevated Xi's thought and stature to Deng's and Mao's level. Again, a mixture of new and old. Familiar instruments of rule repurposed to achieve sometimes unfamiliar goals. One might also note the reemergence of campaigns and work teams as routine means to carry out repression and policy implementation.[7] Is this evidence of a Xi effect? It is perhaps more precisely thought of as a governance technique that resonates or rhymes with the past, which is being deployed strategically to deal with today's challenges (Cheek).

Continuity, in other words, cannot be ignored, as lessons of history are reapplied and transformed, and also built upon and extended. For Whyte, government attention to poverty reduction dates to the 1980s and the biggest successes occurred before Xi's time in office.[8] A new blueprint for combating inequality appeared in 2013, but the plan has received little publicity since, and despite additional funding for rural "minimum livelihood payments" (*dibao*), "the main credit for developing and extending the program belongs to his predecessors." On health care, Xi built on earlier progress and deserves some credit for "pushing the process along" and improving the extent of coverage and reimbursement levels, as well as beginning to reduce administrative barriers that make it difficult for rural residents to use their medical insurance in cities. As for educational access, Whyte argues that Xi has continued Jiang Zemin's effort to increase college enrollment and Hu Jintao's to break through bottlenecks in rural schooling, "but it is not clear that he has added much that is new or has increased the pace." Likewise for Chan: efforts to improve the quality of life for urban migrants have not received the resources or attention devoted to other signature policies, such as the anti-corruption campaign or the Belt and Road Initiative. Inequality continues to serve the state as local authorities use access to the urban public goods regime as a means of social control.[9] For Chan, continuity trumps change and this "runs counter to the notion of a universal and sweeping 'Xi Jinping effect.'" (That former premier Li Keqiang was more prominent than Xi in defining and promoting China's urbanization strategy also raises questions about Xi's participation in this area.) The chapters on social policy highlight continuities and variation in the Xi effect by sector, depending on whether Xi and other top leaders believe that a policy is working well enough (Chan). Allowing a policy to persist and incremental fine-tuning to occur is a leadership decision of sorts (Chan), but it is not evidence of a significant Xi effect.

Structural factors also limit the impact of any one person, however powerful. Some recent developments are not due to Xi per se, but are instead coterminous with his time in office. Although "total surveillance" is unquestionably a leadership initiative, and is likely related to Xi's personal ambition and his preference for strongman rule, it is also the result of a long process of institutionalization and the creation of laws, regulations, and agencies that facilitate societal monitoring (Deng, Demes, and Chen). Furthermore, using smartphones for contact tracing during the coronavirus pandemic (Deng, Demes, and Chen) and placing location apps on every smartphone in Xinjiang (Musapir) depend on increases in processing speed that have little to do with Xi and much to do with technological progress. Even the chapters on foreign policy highlight structural changes that have offered Xi new options.[10] For Brantly Womack, Xi's personal preferences and "assertiveness" are secondary. The size, connectivity, and prospects of the Chinese economy are driving China's diplomatic relationship with Southeast Asian nations, and growing economic ties are causing the countries in the region to look for a positive relationship with their powerful neighbor. Xi's role is mainly to stabilize and institutionalize a mutually beneficial asymmetric relationship. The importance of causes other than Xi is also evident in the hardening of China's Taiwan policy and military force becoming a more viable option to pursue reunification (T. Liu). This is partly a result of Xi coming to power and partly a result of Taiwan's Democratic Progressive Party returning to power.

Some of the chapters are less about the Xi Jinping effect than about what has changed (or not) in the Xi era. Liu takes on this issue most directly by arguing that it is plausible to assume that because Xi has stripped many of his political opponents of their authority and concentrated power in his own hands (compare Wedeman), "Xi Jinping has the dominant voice in shaping China's approach toward Taiwan relations." Chan also worries that intentions and "the discernible effect of an individual" are difficult to measure. Other authors artfully elide the issue of Xi's influence in a given policy realm and instead explain what is new, what is old, and what resonates to a greater or less extent with the past. Given the opaqueness of Chinese leadership politics, this is an entirely reasonable analytical move, even if it steers some distance away from the Xi effect and specifying what can be attributed to structure and what to agency. This reminds us that we can seldom pinpoint what even the strongest leaders in a secretive authoritarian system are personally responsible for and that rock-solid counterfactuals are never available in the social sciences.[11] Even Xi is sometimes an object rather than a subject, acted upon rather than acting, as the world situation, Chinese history, his rivals, the bureaucracy, and the society he rules over influence his choices. In this sense, Karl Marx was right when he wrote that "men make their own history, but they do not make it as they please; they do not make it under self-selected circumstances, but under circumstances existing already, given and transmitted from the past."[12] Even though Xi has considerable leeway to act independently, there are structures and long-standing practices that shape and limit the opportunities available to him.

Understanding the Xi Effect

Notes

1. On great power diplomacy, see Suisheng Zhao, "President Xi's Big Power Diplomacy: Advancing an Assertive Foreign Policy Agenda," in *Mapping China's Global Future: Playing Ball or Rocking the Boat?*, ed. Axel Berkofsky and Giulia Sciorati (Milan: ISPI and Ledizioni LediPublishing, 2020), 24–36, https://www.ispionline.it/sites/default/files/pubblicazioni/ispi_mappingchina_web_1.pdf.

2. On ideology, see also Christian Sorace, Ivan Franceschini, and Nicholas Loubere, eds., *Afterlives of Chinese Communism: Political Concepts from Mao to Xi* (Acton: Australian National University Press, 2019); Kerry Brown and Una Aleksandra Bērziņa-Čerenkova, "Ideology in the Era of Xi Jinping," *Journal of Chinese Political Science* 23, no. 3 (September 2018): 323–39; Christian Sorace, *Shaken Authority: China's Communist Party and the 2008 Sichuan Earthquake* (Ithaca, NY: Cornell University Press, 2017). On collective leadership, see Cheng Li, *Chinese Politics in the Xi Jinping Era: Reassessing Collective Leadership* (Washington, DC: Brookings Institution Press, 2016).

3. For evidence that Xi is a stronger leader than Deng in some regards, but not in others, see Ezra Vogel, "The Leadership of Xi Jinping: A Dengist Perspective," *Journal of Contemporary China* 30, no. 131 (2021): 693–96.

4. For Xi's evaluation of the Maoist era, see Joseph Fewsmith, "Mao's Shadow," *China Leadership Monitor*, no. 43 (Spring 2014): 1–9, https://www

.hoover.org/sites/default/files/uploads/documents/CLMJF.pdf. On the al-most-lost art of reading and interpreting leadership statements and other public announcements, see Alice L. Miller, "Valedictory: Analyzing the Chinese Leadership in an Era of Sex, Money and Power," *China Leadership Monitor*, no. 57 (2018), 1–17, https://www.hoover.org/sites/default/files/research/docs/clm57-am-final.pdf; Frederick C. Teiwes, "The Study of Elite Political Conflict in the PRC: Politics Inside the 'Black Box,'" in *Handbook of the Politics of China*, ed. David S. G. Goodman (Northampton, MA: Edward Elgar Publishing, 2015), 21–41.

5. On Xi's centralizing of power, see Sangkuk Lee, "An Institutional Analysis of Xi Jinping's Centralization of Power," *Journal of Contemporary China* 26, no. 105 (2017): 325–36; Elizabeth Economy, *The Third Revolution: Xi Jinping and the New Chinese State* (New York: Oxford University Press, 2018).

6. For more on religion and "paradoxes and ironies" in a leader's influence, see Sarah Lee and Kevin J. O'Brien, "Adapting in Difficult Circumstances: Protestant Pastors and the Xi Jinping Effect," *Journal of Contemporary China* 30, no. 132 (2021): 902–14. They offer "a reminder that there is a bottom-up element to the Xi effect and that the consequences of leadership change are mutually constituted by society and the state" (903).

7. Kristen E. Looney, *Mobilizing for Development: The Modernization of Rural East Asia* (Ithaca, NY: Cornell University Press, 2020); Elizabeth J. Perry, "From Mass Campaigns to Managed Campaigns: 'Constructing a New Socialist Countryside,'" in *Mao's Invisible Hand: The Political Foundations of Adaptive Governance in China*, ed. Sebastian Heilmann and Elizabeth J. Perry (Cambridge, MA: Harvard University Press, 2011), 30–61; Kristen E. Looney, "China's Campaign to Build a New Socialist Countryside: Village Modernization, Peasant Councils, and the Ganzhou Model of Rural Development," *China Quarterly*, no. 224 (2015): 909–32; Kevin J. O'Brien and Yanhua Deng, "Preventing Protest One Person at a Time: Psychological Coercion and Relational Repression in China," *China Review* 17, no. 2 (June 2017): 179–201.

8. See also Shujie Yao, "Economic Development and Poverty Reduction in China over 20 Years of Reforms," *Economic Development and Cultural Change* 48, no. 3 (April 2000): 447–74.

9. Alexsia T. Chan and Kevin J. O'Brien, "Phantom Services: Deflecting Migrant Workers in China," *China Journal*, no. 81 (2019): 103–22.

10. For an influential treatment of structure, which also makes room for agency, see William H. Sewell Jr., "A Theory of Structure: Duality, Agency, and Transformation," *American Journal of Sociology* 98, no. 1 (July 1992): 1–29.

11. On the use (and abuse) of counterfactuals in the study of world politics, see James D. Fearon, "Counterfactuals and Hypothesis Testing in Political Science," *World Politics* 43, no. 2 (January 1991): 169–95.

12. Karl Marx, "The Eighteenth Brumaire of Louis Bonaparte," in *Karl Marx and Friedrich Engels: Selected Works* (Moscow: Progress Publishers, 1969), 1:398.

Chinese Character Glossary

aiguo jiaoyu jidi 爱国教育基地

Beizhan caineng zhizhan 备战才能止战

Buzhan er qurenzhibin, shanzhi shanzheye 不战而屈人之兵，善之善者也

chongfenggang 冲锋岗

da Hanzu zhuyi 大汉族主义
danwei 单位
dibao 低保
diduan renkou 低端人口

fabiao 发飙
fangxin 放心
fenfa youwei 奋发有为

Ganxie dang! Ganxie zuguo! Xiexie Xi Zhuxi! 感谢党！感谢祖国！谢谢习主席！
"Gao Taiwan tongbao shu" 告台湾同胞书
geren chongbai 个人崇拜
guanxi 关系
"Guanyu jinyibu cujin liangan jingji wenhua jiaoliu hezuo de ruogan cuoshi" 关于进一步促进两岸经济文化交流合作的若干措施

Guofangbu Quanmin Fangwei Dongyuanshu 国防部全民防卫动员署

Guojia Fanzha Zhongxin 国家反诈中心

Guojia Xinfangju 国家信访局
Guoyu 国语

Haoqixin ribao 好奇心日报
hecheng zuozhan zhongxin 合成作战中心

Hongse Wuye 红色物业
hukou 户口

jiaohua 教化
jiaoliu rangli 交流让利
jiedao 街道
Jiedui Renqin 结对认亲
jingshen 精神
Jingwang Weishi 净网卫士
jiti lingdao 集体领导
junzi 君子

kuai 块

liangge yibainian 两个一百年
liangmian ren 两面人
liangxin ren 两心人
lianwu 莲雾
Liji 礼记
liudong renkou 流动人口
loudaozhang 楼道长

mao 毛

neijuanhua 内卷化

Pingan Chengshi 平安城市
Putonghua 普通话

qu Meiguo hua 去美国化
qunzhong luxian 群众路线
rang yibufen ren xian fuqilai 让一部分
　人先富起来

renlei mingyun gongtongti 人类命运
　共同体
Renmin you xinyang, minzu you
　xiwang, guojia you liliang 人民有信
　仰，民族有希望，国家有力量

santong 三通
Sanzhong Yiqing 三中一青
shehui guanli 社会管理
shehui zhuyi hexin jiazhiguan 社会主
　义核心价值观
shengyu 圣谕
Shengyu xuanjiang xiangbao tiaoyue
　圣谕宣讲保条约
shijia 释迦
silu yitiao 死路一条
suzhi 素质

taibaozheng 台胞证
taidu 态度
taidufenzi 台独分子

Taiwan jumin juzhuzheng 台湾居民
　居住证
tangping 躺平
tianrandu 天然独
Tianwang Gongcheng 天网工程
tuopin 脱贫

waijiao xiubing 外交休兵
wanggehua guanli 网格化管理
wanggezhang 网格长
weida fuxing 伟大复兴
weiquan 维权
Women de Zhongguo Meng, minzu
　tuanjie yi jiaqin 我们的中国梦，民
　族团结一家亲
wuzheng 五证

Xi Jinping fabiao zhongyao tanhua
　习近平发表重要谈话
Xi Jinping Sixiang 习近平思想
Xi Jinping yu Xinjiang ge zu renmin
　xin lian xin, tong huxi, gong ming-
　yun 习近平与新疆各族人民心连
　心，同呼吸，共命运
Xiamen Taishang Huiguan 厦门台商
　会馆
xiao santong 小三通
xiaokang 小康
xinchangtai 新常态
xinling de ziyou 心灵的自由
xinyang 信仰
Xinyang, xinnian, xinxin he shigan
　shi women shiye chenggong de
　baozheng 信仰、信念、信心和实干
　是我们事业成功的保证
Xinyang de liliang 信仰的力量
Xueliang 雪亮
xunxin zishi zui 寻衅滋事罪
Xunzhao shidai de xinyang 寻找时代
　的信仰
xunzheng 训政

Yidai Yixian 一代一线
yimeilun 疑美论
youbangguo 友邦国
yueji shangfang 越级上访

zhengfeng 整风
zhengquede sixiang 正确的思想
zhengzhi tuanhuo 政治团伙
Zhongguo Meng 中国梦

"Zhongguo renmin you xinyang" 中国人民有信仰
Zhongguohua 中国化
Zhongguoren queshao shenme? 中国人缺少什么
Zhongyang qingke, dangdi maidan 中央请客，当地买单
Zhongyang Weiyuanhui Duiwai Lianluobu 中央委员会对外联络部
Ziganwu 自干五

Selected Bibliography

This bibliography contains academic sources that are most central to the study of the Xi Jinping era in China, including books, book chapters, journal articles, and reports by academic institutions, research institutes, or organizations. Citations of additional sources accompany each chapter in this volume.

Acharya, Amitav. *ASEAN and Regional Order: Revisiting Security Community in Southeast Asia*. New York: Routledge, 2021.

Allison, Graham. *Destined for War: Can America and China Escape Thucydides's Trap?* Boston: Houghton Mifflin, 2017.

Anderson, Amy, and Darren Byler. "'Eating Hanness': Uyghur Musical Tradition in a Time of Re-education." *China Perspectives*, no. 3 (2019): 17–26.

Anderson, James, and John Whitmore, eds. *China's Encounters on the South and Southwest: Reforging the Fiery Frontier over Two Millennia*. Leiden: Brill, 2014.

Ang, Yuen Yuen. *How China Escaped the Poverty Trap*. Ithaca, NY: Cornell University Press, 2016.

Anwar, Dewi Fortuna. "Indonesia and the ASEAN Outlook on the Indo-Pacific." *International Affairs* 96, no. 1 (2020): 111–29.

Apter, David, and Tony Saich. *Revolutionary Discourse in Mao's Republic*. Cambridge, MA: Harvard University Press, 1994.

Ba, Alice. *(Re)Negotiating East and Southeast Asia: Region, Regionalism, and the Association of Southeast Asian Nations*. Stanford, CA: Stanford University Press, 2009.

Bandurski, David. "Propaganda Soars into Orbit." China Media Project, January 29, 2021. https://chinamediaproject.org/2021/01/29/propaganda-soars-into-orbit.

Barmé, Geremie R. "Chinese Dreams (Zhongguo Meng 中国梦)." In *China Story*

Yearbook 2013: Civilising China, edited by Geremie R. Barmé and Jeremy Goldkorn, 5–13. Canberra: Australian National University Press, 2013.

Bian, Yanjie. *Work and Inequality in Urban China*. Albany: State University of New York Press, 1994.

Blanchette, Jude. *China's New Red Guards: The Return of Radicalism and the Rebirth of Mao Zedong*. New York: Oxford University Press, 2019.

Bo, Zhiyue. "Balance of Factional Power in China." *East Asia* 25, no. 4 (July 2008): 333–64.

———. "The 16th Central Committee of the Chinese Communist Party." *Journal of Contemporary China* 13, no. 39 (2004): 223–56.

Bourke, Joanna. "Fear and Anxiety: Writing about Emotion in Modern History." *History Workshop Journal* 55, no. 1 (2003): 111–33.

Bovingdon, Gardner. *The Uyghurs: Strangers in Their Own Land*. New York: Columbia University Press, 2010.

Bram, Barclay. "Involution: The Generation Turning Inward and Away from Xi's Chinese Dream." Asia Society Policy Institute, November 9, 2022. https://asiasociety.org/policy-institute/involution-generation-turning-inward-and-away-xis-chinese-dream.

Brown, Kerry. *CEO, China: The Rise of Xi Jinping*. London: Bloomsbury Academic, 2016.

———. *The World according to Xi: Everything You Need to Know about the New China*. London: Bloomsbury Academic, 2018.

Brown, Kerry, and Una Aleksandra Bērziņa-Čerenkova. "Ideology in the Era of Xi Jinping." *Journal of Chinese Political Science* 23, no. 3 (September 2018): 323–39.

Byler, Darren. "Spirit Breaking: Uyghur Dispossession, Cultural Work, and Terror Capitalism in a Chinese Global City." PhD diss., University of Washington, 2018.

———. *Terror Capitalism: Uyghur Dispossession and Masculinity in a Chinese City*. Durham, NC: Duke University Press, 2022.

Cai, Yong, Wang Feng, and Ke Shen. "Fiscal Implications of Population Aging and Social Sector Expenditure in China." *Population and Development Review* 44, no. 4 (2018): 811–31.

Carothers, Christopher. *Corruption Control in Authoritarian Regimes: Lessons from East Asia*. New York: Cambridge University Press, 2022.

Chan, Alexsia T. *Beyond Coercion: The Politics of Inequality in China*. New York: Cambridge University Press, forthcoming.

Chan, Alexsia T., and Kevin J. O'Brien. "Phantom Services: Deflecting Migrant Workers in China." *China Journal*, no. 81 (2019): 103–22.

Chan, Alfred L. *Xi Jinping: Political Career, Governance, and Leadership, 1953–2018*. New York: Oxford University Press, 2022.

Chan, Kam Wing. "The Chinese *Hukou* System at 50." *Eurasian Geography and Economics* 50, no. 2 (2009): 197–221.

———. *Cities with Invisible Walls: Reinterpreting Urbanization in Post-1949 China*. New York: Oxford University Press, 1994.

———. "What the 2020 Chinese Census Tells Us about Progress in Hukou Reform." *China Brief* 21, no. 15 (2021): 11–17.

Chan, Kam Wing, and Will Buckingham. "Is China Abolishing the *Hukou* System?" *China Quarterly*, no. 195 (2008): 582–606.

Chan, Kam Wing, Fang Cai, Guanghua Wan, and Man Wang, eds. *Urbanization with Chinese Characteristics: The* Hukou *System and Migration*. New York: Routledge, 2018.

Chan, Kam Wing, and Li Zhang. "The *Hukou* System and Rural-Urban Migration in China: Processes and Changes." *China Quarterly*, no. 160 (1999): 818–55.

Chandra, Nirmal Kumar. "Education in China: From the Cultural Revolution to Four Modernisations." *Economic and Political Weekly* 22, no. 19–21 (May 1987): 121–36.

Chang, Kuei-Min. "New Wine in Old Bottles: Sinicisation and State Regulation of Religion in China." *China Perspectives*, no. 1–2 (2018): 37–44.

Che, Lei, Haifeng Du, and Kam Wing Chan. "Unequal Pain: A Sketch of the Impact of the Covid-19 Pandemic on Migrants' Employment in China." *Eurasian Geography and Economics* 61, no. 4–5 (2020): 448–63.

Cheek, Timothy. "Attitudes of Action: Maoism as Emotional Political Theory." In *Chinese Thought as Global Theory*, edited by Leigh Jenco, 75–100. Albany: State University of New York Press, 2016.

———. "Making Maoism: Ideology and Organization in the Yan'an Rectification Movement, 1942–1944." In *Knowledge Acts in Modern China: Ideas, Institutions, and Identities*, edited by Robert Culp, Eddy U, and Wen-hsin Yeh, 304–27. Berkeley: Institute of East Asian Studies, University of California, 2016.

Chen, Chih-Jou Jay. "Peasant Protests over Land Seizures in Rural China." *Journal of Peasant Studies* 47, no. 6 (2020): 1327–47.

———. "A Protest Society Evaluated: Popular Protests in China, 2000–2019." *Mobilization: An International Quarterly* 25, no. 5 (2020): 641–60.

Chen, Chih-Jou Jay, and Yongshun Cai. "Upward Targeting and Social Protests in China." *Journal of Contemporary China* 30, no. 130 (2021): 511–25.

Chen, Huirong, and Sheena Chestnut Greitens. "Information Capacity and Social Order: The Local Politics of Information Integration in China." *Governance* 35, no. 2 (2022): 497–523.

Chen, Shih-Min. "Xi Jinping de zhanlue zhuanxian yu taihai jushi de bianqian: 2021–2018" (A shift in Xi Jinping's strategy and the changing cross-strait security situation: 2012–2018). *Prospect Quarterly* 20, no. 2 (2019): 49–93.

Cheng, Tiejun, and Mark Selden. "The Origins and Social Consequences of China's *Hukou* System." *China Quarterly*, no. 139 (1994): 644–68.

Chiang, Kai-shek. *China's Destiny and Chinese Economic Theory*. New York: Roy Publishers, 1947.

Chu, Yun-han, and Yu-tzung Chang. "Xi's Foreign-Policy Turn and Asian Perceptions of a Rising China." *Global Asia* 12, no. 1 (Spring 2017): 104–11.

Clarke, Michael. "China's 'War on Terror' in Xinjiang: Human Security and the Causes of Violent Uighur Separatism." *Terrorism and Political Violence* 20, no. 2 (2008): 271–301.

Cui, Yuming, Jingjing Meng, and Changrong Lu. "Recent Developments in China's Labor Market: Labor Shortage, Rising Wages and Their Implications." *Review of Development Economics* 22, no. 3 (2018): 1217–38.

Cunningham, Edward, Tony Saich, and Jessie Turiel. "Understanding CCP Resilience: Surveying Chinese Public Opinion through Time." Ash Center for Democratic Governance and Innovation, Harvard Kennedy School, Cambridge, MA, July 2020. https://ash.harvard.edu/publications/understanding-ccp-resilience-surveying-chinese-public-opinion-through-time.

Dai, Xin. "Enforcing Law and Norms for Good Citizens: One View of China's Social Credit System Project." *Development* 63, no. 1 (2020): 38–43.

Davis, Deborah. "Urban Households: Supplicants to a Socialist State." In *Chinese Families in the Post-Mao Era*, edited by Deborah Davis and Stevan Harrell, 50–76. Berkeley: University of California Press, 1993.

Denton, Kirk. "Rectification: Party Discipline, Intellectual Remolding, and the Formation of a Political Community." In *Words and Their Stories: Essays on the Language of the Chinese Revolution*, edited by Ban Wang, 51–63. Leiden: Brill, 2011.

Dickson, Bruce J. *The Party and the People: Chinese Politics in the 21st Century*. Princeton, NJ: Princeton University Press, 2021.

Dillon, Nara. *Radical Inequalities: China's Revolutionary Welfare State in Comparative Perspective*. Cambridge, MA: Harvard University Asia Center, 2015.

Dong, Yiming, and Charlotte Goodburn. "Residence Permits and Points Systems: New Forms of Educational and Social Stratification in Urban China." *Journal of Contemporary China* 29, no. 125 (2020): 647–66.

Dotson, John. "The CCP Politburo Holds Its First Collective Study Session for 2020." *China Brief* 20, no. 11 (June 24, 2020). https://jamestown.org/program/the-ccp-politburo-holds-its-first-collective-study-session-for-2020.

Economy, Elizabeth. *The Third Revolution: Xi Jinping and the New Chinese State*. New York: Oxford University Press, 2018.

Edin, Maria. "State Capacity and Local Agent Control in China: CCP Cadre Management from a Township Perspective." *China Quarterly*, no. 173 (2003): 35–52.

Elfstrom, Manfred, and Sarosh Kuruvilla. "The Changing Nature of Labor Unrest in China." *ILR Review* 67, no. 2 (2014): 453–80.

Esarey, Ashley. "Propaganda as a Lens for Assessing Xi Jinping's Leadership." *Journal of Contemporary China* 30, no. 132 (2021): 888–901.

Esarey, Ashley, Mary Alice Haddad, Joanna I. Lewis, and Stevan Harrell, eds. *Greening East Asia: The Rise of the Eco-Developmental State.* Seattle: University of Washington Press, 2020.

Fan, C. Cindy. "The Elite, the Natives, and the Outsiders: Migration and Labor Market Segmentation in Urban China." *Annals of the Association of American Geographers* 92, no. 1 (2002): 103–24.

Fearon, James D. "Counterfactuals and Hypothesis Testing in Political Science." *World Politics* 43, no. 2 (January 1991): 169–95.

Ferdinand, Peter. "Westward Ho—the China Dream and 'One Belt, One Road': Chinese Foreign Policy under Xi Jinping." *International Affairs* 92, no. 4 (2016): 941–57.

Fewsmith, Joseph. "China in 2007." *Asian Survey* 48, no. 1 (January/February 2008): 82–96.

———. *China since Tiananmen: From Deng Xiaoping to Hu Jintao.* New York: Cambridge University Press, 2008.

———. "Mao's Shadow." *China Leadership Monitor*, no. 43 (Winter 2013): 1–9. https://www.hoover.org/sites/default/files/uploads/documents/CLMJF.pdf.

———. *Rethinking Chinese Politics.* New York: Cambridge University Press, 2021.

Fingar, Thomas, and Jean C. Oi. "China's Challenges: Now It Gets Much Harder." *Washington Quarterly* 43, no. 1 (Spring 2020): 65–82.

———, eds. *Fateful Decisions: Choices That Will Shape China's Future.* Stanford, CA: Stanford University Press, 2020.

Finklestein, David. "Breaking the Paradigm: Drivers behind the PLA's Current Period of Reform." In *Chairman Xi Remakes the PLA: Assessing Chinese Military Reforms*, edited by Phillip C. Saunders, Arthur S. Ding, Andrew N. D. Yang, and Joel Wuthnow, 45–83. Washington, DC: National Defense University Press, 2019.

Fitzgerald, John. *Awakening China: Politics, Culture, and Class in the Nationalist Revolution.* Stanford, CA: Stanford University Press, 1996.

Frankopan, Peter. *The Silk Roads: A New History of the World.* London: Bloomsbury, 2015.

Friedman, Eli. "Just-in-Time Urbanization? Managing Migration, Citizenship, and Schooling in the Chinese City." *Critical Sociology* 44, no. 3 (2018): 503–18.

———. *The Urbanization of People: Development, Labor Markets, and Schooling in a Chinese City.* New York: Columbia University Press, 2022.

Gaenssbauer, Monika. *Popular Belief in Contemporary China: A Discourse Analysis.* Freiburg: Projekt Verlag, 2015.

Gan, Li, Qing He, Ruichao Si, and Daichun Yi. "Relocating or Redefined: A New Perspective on Urbanization in China." NBER Working Paper No. 26585,

National Bureau of Economic Research, Cambridge, MA, December 2019. http://www.nber.org/papers/w26585.

Gao, Qin. *Welfare, Work, and Poverty: Social Assistance in China.* New York: Oxford University Press, 2017.

Gao, Zhanxiang. *Xinyangli* (The power of faith). Beijing: Beijing Daxue Chubanshe, 2012.

Garside, Roger. *China Coup: The Great Leap to Freedom.* Berkeley: University of California Press, 2021.

Gill, Bates. *Daring to Struggle: China's Global Ambitions under Xi Jinping.* New York: Oxford University Press, 2022.

Goh, Evelyn, ed. *Rising China's Influence in Developing Asia.* New York: Oxford University Press, 2016.

Goodman, David S. G. "The Campaign to 'Open Up the West': National, Provincial-Level, and Local Perspectives." *China Quarterly,* no. 178 (2004): 317–34.

Goossaert, Vincent, and David Palmer, eds. *The Religious Question in Modern China.* Chicago: University of Chicago Press, 2010.

Gow, Michael. "The Core Socialist Values of the Chinese Dream: Towards a Chinese Integral State." *Critical Asian Studies* 49, no. 1 (2017): 92–116.

Green, Linda. "Living in a State of Fear." In *Fieldwork under Fire: Contemporary Studies of Violence and Culture,* edited by Carolyn Nordstrom and Antonius Robben, 105–28. Berkeley: University of California Press, 1995.

Guo, Maocan, and Xiaogang Wu. "School Expansion and Educational Stratification in China, 1981–2006." Paper presented at the Annual Meeting of the American Sociological Association, Boston, June 2008.

Guo, Zhonghua, and Tuo Liang. "Differentiating Citizenship in Urban China: A Case Study of Dongguan City." *Citizenship Studies* 21, no. 7 (2017): 773–91.

Habermas, Jürgen. "Notes on a Post-Secular Society." *Signandsight,* June 18, 2008. http://www.signandsight.com/features/1714.html.

Haili, Li, and Genia Kostka. "Accepting but Not Engaging with It: Digital Participation in Local Government-Run Social Credit Systems in China." *Policy & Internet* 14, no. 4 (2022): 845–74.

Hall, David L., and Roger T. Ames. *Thinking through Confucius.* Albany: State University of New York Press, 1987.

Han, Rongbin. *Contesting Cyberspace in China: Online Expression and Authoritarian Resilience.* New York: Columbia University Press, 2018.

———. "Cyber Nationalism and Regime Support under Xi Jinping: The Effects of the 2018 Constitutional Revision." *Journal of Contemporary China* 30, no. 131 (2021): 717–33.

Hayes, Anna. "Interwoven 'Destinies': The Significance of Xinjiang to the China Dream, the Belt and Road Initiative, and the Xi Jinping Legacy." *Journal of Contemporary China* 29, no. 121 (2020): 31–45.

Heilmann, Sebastian. "Leninism Upgraded: Xi Jinping's Authoritarian Innovations." *China Economic Quarterly* 20, no. 4 (2016): 15–22.

——. "Policy Experimentation in China's Economic Rise." *Studies in Comparative International Development* 43, no. 1 (March 2008): 1–26.

Hennessy, Peter. *The Hidden Wiring: Unearthing the British Constitution*. London: Gollancz, 1995.

Herberer, Thomas. "Disciplining of a Society: Social Disciplining and Civilizing Processes in Contemporary China." Ash Center for Democratic Governance and Innovation, Harvard Kennedy School, Cambridge, MA, August 2020. https://ash.harvard.edu/publications/disciplining-society-social-disciplining-and-civilizing-processes-contemporary.

Hillman, Ben. "The State Advances, the Private Sector Retreats." in *China Story Yearbook 2018: Power*, edited by Jane Golley, Linda Jaivin, Paul J. Farrelly, and Sharon Strange, 294–306. Canberra: Australian National University Press, 2019.

Hockx, Michel. "Truth, Goodness, and Beauty: Literary Policy in Xi Jinping's China." *Law & Literature* 35, no. 3 (2023): 515–31. https://doi.org/10.1080/1535685X.2022.2026039.

Hong, Ren-Jie, Yu-Chi Tseng, and Thong-Hong Lin. "Guarding the New Great Wall: The Politics of Household Registration Reforms and Public Provision in China." *China Quarterly*, no. 251 (2022): 776–97.

Huang, Kai-Ping, and Bridget Welsh. "Trends in Soft Power in East Asia: Distance, Diversity and Drivers." *Global Asia* 12, no. 1 (Spring 2017): 112–17.

Huang, Min-Hua, and Mark Weatherall. "Democratic Distance and Asian Views of Chinese and American Influence." *Global Asia* 12, no. 1 (Spring 2017): 118–22.

Huang, Youqin. "Farewell to Villages: Forced Urbanization in Rural China." In *China's Urbanization and Socioeconomic Impact*, edited by Zongli Tang, 207–27. Singapore: Springer, 2017.

Jain-Chandra, Sonali, Niny Khor, Rui Mano, Johanna Schauer, Philippe Wingender, and Juzhong Zhuang. "Inequality in China—Trends, Drivers, and Policy Remedies." IMF Working Paper No. 2018/127, International Monetary Fund, Washington, DC, June 2018.

Jerden, Bjorn. "The Assertive China Narrative: Why It Is Wrong and How So Many Bought into It." *Chinese Journal of International Politics* 7, no. 1 (Spring 2014): 47–88.

Jiang, Chang and Cai Mengxue. "'Dangdai zhongguo jiazhiguan' gainiande tichu, neihan yu yiyi" (The proposal, content, and meaning of the concept "contemporary Chinese values"). *Journal of Hubei University (Philosophy and Social Science)*, no. 4 (2016): 1–7 and 160.

Johnson, Christopher K. "Xi Jinping Unveils His Foreign Policy Vision: Peace through Strength." *Freeman Chair China Report* (Center for Strategic and International Studies), December 8, 2014. https://www.csis.org/analysis /thoughts-chairman-xi-jinping-unveils-his-foreign-policy-vision.

Johnson, Ian. *The Souls of China: The Return of Religion after Mao.* New York: Pantheon Books, 2017.

Johnston, Alastair Iain. "How New and Assertive Is China's New Assertiveness?" *International Security* 37, no. 4 (Spring 2013): 7–48.

Kanbur, Ravi, Yue Wang, and Xiaobo Zhang. "The Great Chinese Inequality Turnaround." IZA Discussion Paper No. 10635433, Institute of Labor Economics (IZA), Bonn, 2017.

Keegan, David, and Kyle Churchman. "Taiwan and China Seek Lessons from Ukraine as Taiwan's International Position Strengthens." *Comparative Connections* 24, no. 1 (2022): 89–100.

Keping, Yu. *Democracy Is a Good Thing: Essays on Politics, Society, and Culture in Contemporary China.* Washington, DC: Brookings Institution Press, 2008.

Klein, Thoralf. "'Our Believing in the Three People's Principles Requires a Religious Spirit': *Xin(yang)* 信仰 and the Political Religion of the Guomindang, 1925–1949." In *From Trustworthiness to Secular Beliefs: Changing Concepts of xin* 信 *from Traditional to Modern Chinese,* edited by Christian Meyer and Philip Clart, 461–96. Leiden: Brill, 2023.

Knight, John, and Ramani Gunatilaka. "Rural-Urban Migration and Happiness in China." In *World Happiness Report 2018,* edited by John F. Helliwell, Richard Layard, and Jeffrey D. Sachs, 67–88. New York: Sustainable Development Solutions Network, 2018.

Knight, John, Shi Li, and Haiyuan Wan. "The Increasing Inequality of Wealth in China." In *Changing Trends in China's Inequality: Evidence, Analysis, and Prospects,* edited by Terry Sicular, Shi Li, Ximing Yue, and Hiroshi Sato, 109–44. New York: Oxford University Press, 2020.

Koo, Anita. "Expansion of Vocational Education in Neoliberal China: Hope and Despair among Rural Youth." *Journal of Education Policy* 31, no. 1 (2016): 46–59.

Kostka, Genia. "China's Social Credit Systems and Public Opinion: Explaining High Levels of Approval." *New Media & Society* 21, no. 7 (2019): 1565–93.

Kuhn, Philip A. *Origins of the Modern Chinese State.* Stanford, CA: Stanford University Press, 2002.

Laclau, Ernesto, and Chantal Mouffe. *Hegemony and Socialist Strategy: Towards a Radical Democratic Politics.* 2nd ed. London: Verso, 2001.

Lam, Willy. *Chinese Politics in the Era of Xi Jinping: Renaissance, Reform, or Retrogression?* New York: Routledge, 2016.

———. "The Xi Jinping Faction Dominates Regional Appointments after the 19th Party Congress." *China Brief* 18, no. 2 (2018): 3–7.

———. "Xi Jinping's Ideology and Statecraft." *Chinese Law and Government* 48, no. 6 (November 2016): 409–17.

Lampton, David M. *Following the Leader: Ruling China, from Deng Xiaoping to Xi Jinping.* Berkeley: University of California Press, 2014.

Lampton, David M., Celina Ho, and Cheng-Chwee Kuik. *Rivers of Iron: Railroads and Chinese Power in Southeast Asia.* Berkeley: University of California Press, 2020.

Lan, Pei-chia. "Segmented Incorporation: The Second Generation of Rural Migrants in Shanghai." *China Quarterly*, no. 217 (2014): 243–65.

Larson, Deborah Welch. "Will China Be a New Type of Great Power?" *Chinese Journal of International Politics* 8, no. 4 (Winter 2015): 323–48.

Lee, Sangkuk. "An Institutional Analysis of Xi Jinping's Centralization of Power." *Journal of Contemporary China* 26, no. 105 (2017): 325–36.

Lee, Sarah, and Kevin J. O'Brien. "Adapting in Difficult Circumstances: Protestant Pastors and the Xi Jinping Effect." *Journal of Contemporary China* 30, no. 132 (2021): 902–14.

Leibold, James. "Planting the Seed: Ethnic Policy in Xi Jinping's New Era of Cultural Nationalism." *China Brief* 19, no. 22 (2019): 1–32.

———. "Surveillance in China's Xinjiang Region: Ethnic Sorting, Coercion, and Inducement." *Journal of Contemporary China* 29, no. 121 (2020): 46–60.

———. "Xinjiang Work Forum Marks New Policy of 'Ethnic Mingling.'" *China Brief* 14, no. 12 (2014): 1–12.

Li, Cheng. "A Biographical and Factional Analysis of the Post-2012 Politburo." *China Leadership Monitor*, no. 41 (2013): 1–17. https://www.hoover.org/sites /default/files/uploads/documents/CLM41CL.pdf.

———. "China's Midterm Jockeying: Gearing Up for 2012 (Part 1: Provincial Chiefs)." *China Leadership Monitor*, no. 31 (2010): 1–24. http://media.hoover .org/sites/default/files/documents/CLM31CL.pdf.

———. "China's Top Future Leaders to Watch: Biographical Sketches of Possible Members of the Post-2012 Politburo (Part 1)." *China Leadership Monitor*, no. 37 (2012): 1–10. https://www.hoover.org/sites/default/files/uploads/documents /CLM37CL.pdf.

———. "China's Top Future Leaders to Watch: Biographical Sketches of Possible Members of the Post-2012 Politburo (Part 2)." *China Leadership Monitor*, no. 38 (2012): 1–10. https://www.hoover.org/sites/default/files/uploads /documents/CLM38CL.pdf.

———. "China's Top Future Leaders to Watch: Biographical Sketches of Possible Members of the Post-2012 Politburo (Part 3)." *China Leadership Monitor*, no. 39 (2012): 1–9. https://www.hoover.org/sites/default/files/uploads /documents/CLM39CL.pdf.

———. "China's Top Future Leaders to Watch: Biographical Sketches of Possible

Members of the Post-2012 Politburo (Part 4)." *China Leadership Monitor*, no. 39 (2012): 1–22. https://www.hoover.org/sites/default/files/uploads /documents/CLM39CL2.pdf.

———. *Chinese Politics in the Xi Jinping Era: Reassessing Collective Leadership*. Washington, DC: Brookings Institution Press, 2016.

———. "Was the Shanghai Gang Shanghaied? The Fall of Chen Liangyu and the Survival of Jiang Zemin's Faction." *China Leadership Monitor*, no. 20 (2007): 1–17. https://www.hoover.org/sites/default/files/uploads/documents /clm20cl.pdf.

———. "Xi Jinping's Inner Circle (Part 2: Friends from Xi's Formative Years)." *China Leadership Monitor*, no. 44 (2014): 1–22. https://www.hoover.org /sites/default/files/research/docs/clm44cl.pdf.

Li, Guirong, Jiajia Xu, Liying Li, Zhaolei Shi, Hongmei Yi, James Chu, Elena Kardanova, Yanyan Li, Prashant Loyalka, and Scott Rozelle. "The Impacts of Highly Resourced Vocational Schools on Student Outcomes in China." *China and World Economics* 28, no. 6 (2020): 125–50.

Li, Ling. "Politics of Anticorruption in China: Paradigm Change of the Party's Disciplinary Regime 2012–2017." *Journal of Contemporary China* 28, no. 115 (2019): 47–63.

Li, Shi, Hiroshi Sato, and Terry Sicular, eds. *Rising Inequality in China: Challenges to a Harmonious Society*. New York: Cambridge University Press, 2010.

Li, Shi, Terry Sicular, and Finn Tarp. "Inequality in China: Development, Transition, and Policy." WIDER Working Paper No. 2018/174, United Nations University World Institute for Development Economics Research (UNU-WIDER), Helsinki, December 2018. https://doi.org/10.35188/UNU -WIDER/2018/616-6.

Lim, Darren J., Victor A. Ferguson, and Rosa Bishop. "Chinese Outbound Tourism as an Instrument of Economic Statecraft." *Journal of Contemporary China* 29, no. 126 (2020): 916–33.

Lin, Qianhan, and Wei-Jun Yeung. "Beyond the Middle-School Gates: The Urban-Rural Divergence of School-Work Paths of China's Youth." In *Social Inequality in China*, edited by Yaojun Li and Yanjie Bian, 185–208. London: World Scientific Publishing, 2023.

Ling, Minhua. *The Inconvenient Generation: Migrant Youth Coming of Age on Shanghai's Edge*. Stanford, CA: Stanford University Press, 2019.

Linz, Juan J., and Alfred Stepan. *Problems of Democratic Transition and Consolidation: Southern Europe, South America, and Post-Communist Europe*. Baltimore: Johns Hopkins University Press, 1996.

Lipsky, Michael. *Street-Level Bureaucracy: Dilemmas of the Individual in Public Services*. New York: Russell Sage Foundation, 1980.

Liu, Fu-Kuo. "Ma Ying-jeou's Rapprochement Policy: Cross-strait Progress and Domestic Constraints." In *Political Changes under Ma Ying-jeou: Partisan*

Conflict, Policy Choices, External Constraints and Security Challenges, edited by Jean-Pierre Cabestan and Jacques deLisle, 175–94. New York: Routledge, 2014.

Liu, Qing. "Liberalism in the Chinese Context: Potential and Predicaments." Translated by Matthew Galway and Lu Hua. In *Voices from the Chinese Century: Public Intellectual Debate from Contemporary China*, edited by Timothy Cheek, David Ownby, and Joshua A. Fogel, 45–71. New York: Columbia University Press, 2020.

Liu, Tao, and Qiujie Shi. "Acquiring a Beijing *Hukou*: Who Is Eligible and Who Is Successful?" *China Quarterly*, no. 243 (2020): 855–68.

Liu, Xiaobo. *Zhongguo dangdai zhengzhi yu zhongguo zhishifenzi* (Chinese contemporary politics and Chinese intellectuals). 1990. Reprint, Taipei: Tonsan Publications, 2010.

Looney, Kristen E. "China's Campaign to Build a New Socialist Countryside: Village Modernization, Peasant Councils, and the Ganzhou Model of Rural Development." *China Quarterly*, no. 224 (2015): 909–32.

———. *Mobilizing for Development: The Modernization of Rural East Asia*. Ithaca, NY: Cornell University Press, 2020.

Lorentzen, Peter. "Regularizing Rioting: Permitting Public Protest in an Authoritarian Regime." *Quarterly Journal of Political Science* 8, no. 2 (February 2013): 127–58.

Loyalka, Prashant, Xiaoting Huang, Linxin Zhang, Jianguo Wei, Hongmei Yi, Yingqua Song, Yaojiang Shi, and James Chu. "The Impact of Vocational Schooling on Human Capital in Developing Countries: Evidence from China." *World Bank Economic Review* 30, no. 1 (2015): 143–70.

Luo, Chuliang, Shi Li, and Terry Sicular. "The Long-Term Evolution of Income Inequality and Poverty in China." WIDER Working Paper No. 2018/153, United Nations University World Institute for Development Economics Research (UNU-WIDER), Helsinki, December 2018. https://doi.org/10.35188/UNU-WIDER/2018/595-4.

Luo, Chuliang, Terry Sicular, and Shi Li. "Overview: Incomes and Inequality in China, 2007–2013." In *Changing Trends in China's Inequality: Evidence, Analysis, and Prospects*, edited by Terry Sicular, Shi Li, Ximing Yue, and Hiroshi Sato, 35–74. New York: Oxford University Press, 2020.

Luo, Chuliang, Xu Zhang, and Shouwei Li. "Zhongguo jumin shouru chaju biandong fenxi (2013–2018)" (An analysis of changes in the extent of income disparity in China [2013–2018]). *Social Sciences in China*, no. 1 (2021): 33–54.

Madsen, Richard, ed. *The Sinicization of Religion: From Above and Below*. Leiden: Brill, 2021.

Magnus, George. *Red Flags: Why Xi's China Is in Jeopardy*. New Haven, CT: Yale University Press, 2019.

Mair, Victor. "Language and Ideology in the Written Popularizations of the

Sacred Edicts." In *Popular Culture in Late Imperial China*, edited by David Johnson, Andrew J. Nathan, and Evelyn S. Rawski, 325–59. Berkeley: University of California Press, 1985.

Marshall, Thomas H. "Citizenship and Social Class." In *The Welfare State Reader*, edited by Christopher Pierson and Francis G. Castles, 30–39. Malden, MA: Polity Press, 2006.

Marx, Karl. "The Eighteenth Brumaire of Louis Bonaparte." In *Karl Marx and Friedrich Engels: Selected Works*, 1:394–487. Moscow: Progress Publishers, 1969.

Mastro, Oriana Skylar. "The Taiwan Temptation: Why Beijing Might Resort to Force." *Foreign Affairs* 100, no. 4 (July/August 2021): 58–67.

Mattingly, Daniel C. *The Art of Political Control in China*. New York: Cambridge University Press, 2020.

Meyer, Christian, and Philip Clart, eds. *From Trustworthiness to Secular Beliefs: Changing Concepts of xin* 信 *from Traditional to Modern Chinese*. Leiden: Brill, 2023.

Meyer, David, Victor C. Shih, and Jonghyuk Lee. "Factions of Different Stripes, Gauging the Recruitment Logics of Factions in the Reform Period." *Journal of East Asian Studies* 16, no. 1 (2016): 43–60.

Miller, Alice L. "The Trouble with Factions.' *China Leadership Monitor*, no. 46 (2015): 1–12. https://www.hoover.org/sites/default/files/research/docs/clm46am-2.pdf.

———. "Valedictory: Analyzing the Chinese Leadership in an Era of Sex, Money, and Power." *China Leadership Monitor*, no. 57 (2018): 1–17. https://www.hoover.org/sites/default/files/research/docs/clm57-am-final.pdf.

Minzner, Carl. *End of an Era: How China's Authoritarian Revival Is Undermining Its Rise*. New York: Oxford University Press, 2018.

Miyake, Kunihiko. "Shinzo Abe's No-Nonsense Message to Beijing." Japan Times, December 21, 2021.

Mühlhahn, Klaus. "Reform and Opening: 1977–1989." In *The Making of Modern China: From the Great Qing to Xi Jinping*, 491–526. Cambridge, MA: Belknap Press of Harvard University Press, 2019.

Müller, Gotelind. *Documentary, World History, and National Power in the PRC: Global Rise in Chinese Eyes*. London: Routledge, 2013.

Munro, Donald J. *The Concept of Man in Contemporary China*. Ann Arbor: University of Michigan Press, 1977.

Nathan, Andrew J. "A Factionalism Model for CCP Politics." *China Quarterly*, no. 53 (1973): 34–66.

Naughton, Barry. "The Emergence of Wen Jiabao." *China Leadership Monitor*, no. 6 (2003): 36–47.

Nguyen, Vu Tung. *Flying Blind: Vietnam's Decision to Join ASEAN*. Singapore: ISEAS–Yusof Ishak Institute, 2021.

Nye, Joseph. *Bound to Lead: The Changing Nature of American Power*. New York: Basic Books, 1990.

O'Brien, Kevin J., and Yanhua Deng. "Preventing Protest One Person at a Time: Psychological Coercion and Relational Repression in China." *China Review* 17, no. 2 (June 2017): 179–201.

O'Brien, Kevin J., and Lianjiang Li. *Rightful Resistance in Rural China*. New York: Cambridge University Press, 2006.

———. "Selective Policy Implementation in Rural China." *Comparative Politics* 31, no. 2 (1999): 167–86.

Osterhammel, Jürgen. *Europe, the "West" and the Civilizing Mission*. London: German Historical Institute London, 2006. https://www.ghil.ac.uk/fileadmin /redaktion/dokumente/annual_lectures/AL_2005_Osterhammel.pdf.

Overholt, William H. "Ukraine Offers No Easy Lessons on Taiwan." *Global Asia* 17, no. 2 (2022): 36–39.

Pan, Jennifer. *Welfare for Autocrats: How Social Assistance in China Cares for Its Rulers*. New York: Oxford University Press, 2020.

Pei, Minxin. "China's Coming Upheaval: Competition, the Coronavirus, and the Weakness of Xi Jinping." *Foreign Affairs* 99, no. 3 (May/June 2020): 82–95.

Perry, Elizabeth J. "From Mass Campaigns to Managed Campaigns: 'Constructing a New Socialist Countryside.'" In *Mao's Invisible Hand: The Political Foundations of Adaptive Governance in China*, edited by Sebastian Heilmann and Elizabeth J. Perry, 30–61. Cambridge, MA: Harvard University Press, 2011.

———. "Moving the Masses: Emotion Work in the Chinese Revolution." *Mobilization: An International Journal* 7, no. 2 (2002): 111–28.

Piketty, Thomas, Li Yang, and Gabriel Zucman. "Capital Accumulation, Private Property, and Rising Inequality in China, 1978–2015." *American Economic Review* 109, no. 7 (2019): 2469–96.

Portada, Robert A., Steve B. Lem, and Uttam Paudel. "The Final Frontier: China, Taiwan, and the United States in Strategic Competition for Central America." *Journal of Chinese Political Science* 25, no. 4 (2020): 551–73.

Potter, Pitman. *From Leninist Discipline to Socialist Legalism: Peng Zhen on Law and Political Authority in the PRC*. Stanford, CA: Stanford University Press, 2003.

Pozen, Robert C. "Tackling the Chinese Pension System." Paulson Institute, University of Chicago, July 2013. https://www.brookings.edu/articles/reforming -the-chinese-pension-system.

Pun, Ngai, and Huilin Lu. "Unfinished Proletarianization: Self, Anger, and Class Action among the Second Generation of Peasant-Workers in Present-Day China." *Modern China* 36, no. 5 (2010): 493–519.

Pye, Lucian W. "Factions and the Politics of *Guanxi*: Paradoxes in Chinese Administrative and Political Behaviour." *China Journal*, no. 34 (1995): 35–53.

Qian, Zhenchao, Yuan Cheng, and Yue Qian. "*Hukou*, Marriage, and Access to Wealth in Shanghai." *Journal of Ethnic and Migration Studies* 46, no. 18 (2019): 3920–36.

Ringen, Stein. *The Perfect Dictatorship: China in the 21st Century.* Hong Kong: Hong Kong University Press, 2016.

Roberts, Dexter. *The Myth of Chinese Capitalism: The Worker, the Factory, and the Future of the World.* New York: St. Martin's Press, 2020.

Roberts, Sean R. *The War on Uyghurs: China's Internal Campaign against a Muslim Minority.* Princeton, NJ: Princeton University Press, 2020.

Roche, Gerald, and James Leibold. "China's Second-Generation Ethnic Policies Are Already Here." *Made in China Journal* 5, no. 2 (2020): 31–35. https:// madeinchinajournal.com/2020/09/07/chinas-second-generation-ethnic -policies-are-already-here.

Rogers, Sarah, Jie Li, Hua Guo, and Cong Li. "Moving Millions to Eliminate Poverty: China's Rapidly Evolving Practice of Poverty Resettlement." *Development Policy Review* 38, no. 5 (2019): 541–54.

Romberg, Alan. "From Generation to Generation: Advancing Cross-Strait Relations." *China Leadership Monitor,* no. 43 (2014): 1–23. https://www.hoover .org/sites/default/files/uploads/documents/CLM43AR.pdf.

Ross, Robert S., and Jo Inge Bekkevold, eds. *China in the Era of Xi Jinping: Domestic and Foreign Policy Challenges.* Washington, DC: Georgetown University Press, 2016.

Rozelle, Scott, and Matthew Boswell. "Complicating China's Rise: Rural Underemployment." *Washington Quarterly* 44, no. 2 (2021): 61–74.

Rozelle, Scott, and Natalie Hell. *Invisible China: How the Urban-Rural Divide Threatens China's Rise.* Chicago: University of Chicago Press, 2020.

Rozelle, Scott, Yiran Xia, Dimitris Friesen, Bronson Vanderjack, and Nourya Cohen. "Moving beyond Lewis: Employment and Wage Trends in China's High- and Low-Skilled Industries and the Emergence of an Era of Polarization." *Comparative Economic Studies* 62 (2020): 555–89.

Rudd, Kevin. *The Avoidable War: The Dangers of a Catastrophic Conflict between the US and Xi Jinping's China.* New York: PublicAffairs, 2022.

Salidjanova, Nargiza. "China's New Income Inequality Reform Plan and Implications for Rebalancing." US-China Economic and Security Review Commission, Washington, DC, March 2013.

Schurmann, Franz. *Ideology and Organization in Communist China.* 2nd ed. Berkeley: University of California Press, 1968.

Scott, James C. *Domination and the Arts of Resistance: Hidden Transcripts.* New Haven, CT: Yale University Press, 1990.

Seah, Sharon, Hoang Thi Ha, Melinda Martinus, and Pham Thi Phuong Thao. *The State of Southeast Asia: 2021 Survey Report.* Singapore: ISEAS–Yusof Ishak Institute, 2021. https://www.iseas.edu.sg/wp-content/uploads/2021/01/The -State-of-SEA-2021-v2.pdf.

Seah, Sharon, Joanne Lin, Sithanonxay Suvannaphakdy, Melinda Martinus, Pham Thi Phuong Thao, Farah Nadine Seth, and Hoang Thi Ha. *The State of Southeast Asia: 2022 Survey Report*. Singapore: ISEAS–Yusof Ishak Institute, 2022. https://www.iseas.edu.sg/wp-content/uploads/2022/02/The-State-of -SEA-2022_FA_Digital_FINAL.pdf.

Selden, Mark. *The Yenan Way in Revolutionary China*. Cambridge, MA: Harvard University Press, 1971.

Sewell, William H., Jr. "A Theory of Structure: Duality, Agency, and Transformation." *American Journal of Sociology* 98, no. 1 (July 1992): 1–29.

Shambaugh, David. *China's Future*. Malden, MA: Polity Press, 2016.

——— . *China's Leaders: From Mao to Now*. Medford, MA: Polity Press, 2021.

Shih, Victor C., Wei Shan, and Mingxing Liu. "Gauging the Elite Political Equilibrium in the CCP: A Quantitative Approach Using Biographical Data." *China Quarterly*, no. 201 (2010): 79–103.

Shirk, Susan. *Overreach: How China Derailed Its Peaceful Rise*. New York: Oxford University Press, 2023.

Sicular, Terry. "Will China Eliminate Poverty in 2020?" *China Leadership Monitor*, no. 66 (2020). https://www.prcleader.org/post/will-china-eliminate -poverty-in-2020.

Sicular, Terry, Shi Li, Ximing Yue, and Hiroshi Sato, eds. *Changing Trends in China's Inequality: Evidence, Analysis, and Prospects*. New York: Oxford University Press, 2020.

Smith Finley, Joanne N. *The Art of Symbolic Resistance: Uyghur Identities and Uyghur-Han Relations in Contemporary Xinjiang*. Leiden: Brill, 2013.

Solinger, Dorothy J. *Contesting Citizenship in Urban China: Peasant Migrants, the State, and the Logic of the Market*. Berkeley: University of California Press, 1999.

——— . "Manipulating China's 'Minimum Livelihood Guarantee': Political Shifts in a Program for the Poor in the Period of Xi Jinping." *China Perspectives*, no. 2 (2017): 47–57.

——— , ed. *Polarized Cities: Portraits of Rich and Poor in Urban China*. Lanham, MD: Rowman and Littlefield, 2019.

Sorace, Christian. "Extracting Affect: Televised Cadre Confessions in Contemporary China." *Public Culture* 31, no. 1 (2018): 145–71.

——— . *Shaken Authority: China's Communist Party and the 2008 Sichuan Earthquake*. Ithaca, NY: Cornell University Press, 2017.

Sorace, Christian, Ivan Franceschini, and Nicholas Loubere, eds. *Afterlives of Chinese Communism: Political Concepts from Mao to Xi*. Acton: Australian National University Press, 2019.

Sørensen, Camilla T. N. "The Roots of China's Assertiveness in East Asia: Analysing the Main Driving Forces in Chinese Foreign Policy." *Copenhagen Journal of Asian Studies* 39, no. 2 (December 2021): 10–32.

Starr, Chloe. "From Missionary Doctrine to Chinese Theology: Developing *xin* 信 in the Protestant Church and Creeds of Zhao Zichen." In *From Trustworthiness to Secular Beliefs: Changing Concepts of xin* 信 *from Traditional to Modern Chinese*, edited by Christian Meyer and Philip Clart, 340–59. Leiden: Brill, 2023.

Stenslie, Stig, and Chen Gang. "Xi Jinping's Grand Strategy: From Vision to Implementation." In *China in the Era of Xi Jinping: Domestic and Foreign Policy Challenges*, edited by Robert S. Ross and Jo Inge Bekkevold, 117–36. Washington, DC: Georgetown University Press, 2016.

Stewart, Alexander. "Faith in the Future/Practices of the Past: A Sinicized Islamic Revival among the Hui of Xining." In *The Sinicization of Religion: From Above and Below*, edited by Richard Madsen, 130–47. Leiden: Brill, 2021.

Strafella, Giorgio. "'Marxism' as Tradition in CCP Discourse." *Asiatische Studien / Études Asiatiques* 69, no. 1 (2015): 235–53.

Sun, Yat-sen. "Fundamentals of National Reconstruction (1923)." In *Fundamentals of National Reconstruction*, 76–83. Taipei: Taiwan Chinese Cultural Service, 1953.

Sylvia, Sean, Yaojiang Shi, Hao Xue, Xin Tian, Huan Wang, Qingmei Liu, Alexis Medina, and Scott Rozelle. "Survey Using Incognito Standardized Patients Shows Poor Quality Care in China's Rural Clinics." *Health Policy and Planning* 30, no. 3 (2015): 322–33.

Tam, Tony, and Jin Jiang. "Divergent Urban-Rural Trends in College Attendance: State Policy Bias and Structural Exclusion in China." *Sociology of Education* 88, no. 2 (2015): 160–80.

Tang, Siew Mun, Hoang Thi Ha, Anuthida Saelaow Qian, Glenn Ong, and Pham Thi Phuong Thao. *The State of Southeast Asia: 2020 Survey Report*. Singapore: ISEAS–Yusof Ishak Institute, 2020. https://www.iseas.edu.sg/images/pdf/TheStateofSEASurveyReport_2020.pdf.

Tang, Siew Mun, Moe Thuzar, Hoang Thi Ha, Termsak Chalermpalanupap, Pham Thi Phuong Thao, and Anuthida Saelaow Qian. *The State of Southeast Asia: 2019 Survey Report*. Singapore: ISEAS–Yusof Ishak Institute, 2019. https://www.iseas.edu.sg/images/pdf/TheStateofSEASurveyReport_2019.pdf.

Teiwes, Frederick C. *Politics and Purges in China: Rectification and the Decline of Party Norms, 1950–1965*. 2nd ed. Armonk, NY: M. E. Sharpe, 1993.

———. "The Study of Elite Political Conflict in the PRC: Politics inside the 'Black Box.'" In *Handbook of the Politics of China*, edited by David S. G. Goodman, 21–41. Northampton, MA: Edward Elgar Publishing, 2015.

Tiffert, Glenn. "Peering Down the Memory Hole: Censorship, Digitization, and the Fragility of Our Knowledge Base." *American Historical Review* 124, no. 2 (2019): 550–68.

Tsai, Lily L. "Constructive Noncompliance." *Comparative Politics* 47, no. 3 (April 2015): 253–79.

Tsang, Steve, and Honghua Men. *China in the Xi Jinping Era*. London: Palgrave Macmillan, 2016.

Tubilewicz, Czeslaw. "Friends, Enemies or Frenemies? China-Taiwan Discord in the World Health Organization and Its Significance." *Pacific Affairs* 85, no. 4 (2012): 701–22.

Tynen, Sarah. "State Territorialization through *Shequ* Community Centres: Bureaucratic Confusion in Xinjiang, China." *Territory, Politics, Governance* 8, no. 1 (2020): 7–22.

———. "Uneven State Territorialization: Governance, Inequality, and Survivance in Xinjiang, China." PhD diss., University of Colorado, 2019.

Unger, Jonathan, and Kaxton Siu. "Chinese Migrant Factory Workers across Four Decades: Shifts in Work Conditions, Urbanization, and Family Strategies." *Labor History* 60, no. 6 (2019): 765–78.

Vermander, Benoît. "Sinicizing Religion, Sinicizing Religious Studies." *Religions* 10, no. 2 (2019): 1–23. https://doi.org/10.3390/rel10020137.

Vilela, Andrea. "Pension Coverage in China and the Expansion of the New Rural Social Pension." Pension Watch Briefing No. 11. HelpAge International, London, 2013.

Vogel, Ezra. *Deng Xiaoping and the Transformation of China*. Cambridge, MA: Belnap Press of Harvard University Press, 2011.

———. "The Leadership of Xi Jinping: A Dengist Perspective." *Journal of Contemporary China* 30, no. 131 (2021): 693–96.

Walder, Andrew. "China's Extreme Inequality: The Structural Legacies of State Socialism." *China Journal*, no. 90 (2023): 1–26.

———. "The Remaking of the Chinese Working Class, 1949–1981." *Modern China* 10, no. 1 (1984): 3–48.

Wallace, Jeremy. *Cities and Stability: Urbanization, Redistribution, and Regime Survival*. New York: Oxford University Press, 2014.

Wan, Yi, and Edward Vickers. "Toward Meritocratic Apartheid? Points Systems and Migrant Access to China's Urban Public Schools." *China Quarterly*, no. 249 (2022): 210–38.

Wang, Fei-Ling. *Organizing through Division and Exclusion: China's Hukou System*. Stanford, CA: Stanford University Press, 2005.

———. "Renovating the Great Floodgate: The Reform of China's *Hukou* System." In *One Country, Two Societies: Rural-Urban Inequality in Contemporary China*, edited by Martin King Whyte, 335–64. Cambridge, MA: Harvard University Press, 2010.

Wang, Feng. *Boundaries and Categories: Rising Inequality in Post-Socialist China*. Stanford, CA: Stanford University Press, 2008.

Wang, Frances Yaping, and Brantly Womack. "Jawing through Crises: Chinese and Vietnamese Media Strategies in the South China Sea." *Journal of Contemporary China* 28, no. 119 (2019): 712–28.

Wang, Huan, Sarah-Eve Dill, Huan Zhou, Yue Ma, Hao Xue, Prashant Loyalka, Sean Sylvia, Matthew Boswell, Jason Lin, and Scott Rozelle. "Off the COVID-19 Epicentre: The Impact of Quarantine Controls on Employment, Education and Health in China's Rural Communities." *China Quarterly*, no. 249 (2022): 183–209.

Wang, Jiayu. "Representing Chinese Nationalism/Patriotism through President Xi Jinping's 'Chinese Dream' Discourse." *Journal of Language and Politics* 16, no. 6 (2017): 830–48.

Wang, Lei, Mengjie Li, Cody Abbey, and Scott Rozelle. "Human Capital and the Middle Income Trap: How Many of China's Youth Are Going to High School?" *Developing Economies* 56, no. 2 (2018): 82–103.

Wedeman, Andrew. "Anticorruption Forever?" In *Fateful Decisions: Choices That Will Shape China's Future*, edited by Thomas Fingar and Jean C. Oi, 82–106. Stanford, CA: Stanford University Press, 2020.

———. "The Dynamics and Trajectory of Corruption in Contemporary China." *China Review* 22, no. 2 (May 2022): 21–48.

———. "Flies into Tigers: The Dynamics of Corruption in China." *China Currents* 20, no. 1 (2021). https://www.chinacenter.net/2021/china-currents/20-1/flies-into-tigers-the-dynamics-of-corruption-in-china.

Weng, Wenjie. "The Disciplinary Reform: Sanming and the Post-Mao Civilizing Project, 1978–1984)." Master's thesis, University of British Columbia, 2021. https://open.library.ubc.ca/soa/cIRcle/collections/ubctheses/24/items/1.0413691?o=0.

Whiting, Susan H. "The Cadre Evaluation System at the Grass Roots: The Paradox of Party Rule." In *Holding China Together: Diversity and National Integration in the Post-Deng Era*, edited by Barry Naughton and Dali Yang, 101–19. New York: Cambridge University Press, 2004.

Whyte, Martin King. "China's Dormant and Active Social Volcanoes." *China Journal*, no. 75 (2016): 9–37.

———. "China's Economic Development History and Xi Jinping's 'China Dream': An Overview with Personal Reflections." *Chinese Sociological Review* 53, no. 2 (2020): 115–34.

———. *Myth of the Social Volcano: Perceptions of Inequality and Distributive Injustice in Contemporary China*. Stanford, CA: Stanford University Press, 2010.

———, ed. *One Country, Two Societies: Rural-Urban Inequality in Contemporary China*. Cambridge, MA: Harvard University Press, 2010.

Whyte, Martin King, and Dong-Kyun Im. "Is the Social Volcano Still Dormant? Trends in Chinese Attitudes toward Inequality." *Social Science Research* 48 (November 2014): 62–76.

Wielander, Gerda. *Christian Values in Communist China*. London: Routledge, 2013.

———. "Translating Protestant Christianity into China—Questions of Indigenization and Sinification in a Globalised World." In *Translating Values: Evaluative Concepts in Translation*, edited by Piotr Blumczynski and John Gillespie, 213–36. London: Palgrave Macmillan, 2016.

———. "What China Is Missing—Faith in Political Discourse." In *From Trustworthiness to Secular Beliefs: Changing Concepts of xin 信 from Traditional to Modern Chinese*, edited by Christian Meyer and Philip Clart, 586–608. Leiden: Brill, 2023.

Womack, Brantly. "Asymmetric Parity: US-China Relations in a Multinodal World." *International Affairs* 92, no. 6 (November 2016): 1463–80.

———. "Beyond Win-Win: Rethinking China's International Relationships in an Era of Economic Uncertainty." *International Affairs* 89, no. 4 (July 2013): 911–28.

———. "China and Southeast Asia: Asymmetry, Leadership and Normalcy." *Pacific Affairs* 76, no. 4 (Winter 2003/4): 529–48.

———. "China and the Future Status Quo." *Chinese Journal of International Politics* 8, no. 2 (Summer 2015): 115–37.

———. *China and Vietnam: The Politics of Asymmetry*. New York: Cambridge University Press, 2006.

———. "International Crises and China's Rise: Comparing the 2008 Global Financial Crisis and the 2017 Global Political Crisis." *Chinese Journal of International Politics* 10, no. 4 (Winter 2017): 383–401.

———. *Recentering Pacific Asia: Regional China and World Order*. Cambridge: Cambridge University Press, 2023.

Wong, Yiu Chung. "Independence or Reunification? The Evolving PRC-Taiwan Relations." *Baltic Journal of European Studies* 9, no. 2 (2019): 98–122.

World Trade Organization (WTO). *Global Value Chain Development Report 2019: Technological Innovation, Supply Chain Trade, and Workers in a Globalized World*. Geneva: WTO, 2019.

Woronov, T. E. *Class Work: Vocational Schools and China's Urban Youth*. Stanford, CA: Stanford University Press, 2015.

Wu, Guoguang. "The King's Men and Others: Emerging Political Elites under Xi Jinping." *China Leadership Monitor*, no. 60 (2019): 1–9. https://www.prcleader.org/_files/ugd/10535f_da7effdfa8ad40979f17d561cb845a98.pdf.

———. "New Faces of Leaders, New Factional Dynamics: CCP Leadership Politics following the 20th Party Congress." *China Leadership Monitor*, no. 74 (2022). https://www.prcleader.org/post/new-faces-new-factional-dynamics-ccp-leadership-politics-following-the-20th-party-congress.

Wu, Jieh-Min. "Rural Migrants Workers and China's Differential Citizenship: A Comparative Institutional Analysis." In *One Country, Two Societies:*

Rural-Urban Inequality in Contemporary China, edited by Martin King
  Whyte, 55–81. Cambridge, MA: Harvard University Press, 2010.

Wuthnow, Joel, and Phillip C. Saunders. *Chinese Military Reforms in the Age of
  Xi Jinping: Drivers, Challenges, and Implications*. Washington, DC: National
  Defense University Press, 2017.

Wylie, Raymond. *The Emergence of Maoism*. Stanford, CA: Stanford University
  Press, 1980.

Xie, Yu, Xiaobo Zhang, Qi Xu, and Chunni Zhang. "Short-Term Trends in China's Income Inequality and Poverty: Evidence from a Longitudinal Household
  Survey." *China Economic Journal* 8, no. 3 (2015): 235–51.

Xie, Yu, and Xiang Zhou. "Income Inequality in Today's China." *Proceedings of
  the National Academy of Sciences* 111, no. 19 (2014): 6928–33.

Xu, Jianhua, and Siying He. "Can Grid Governance Fix the Party-State's Broken
  Windows? A Study of Stability Maintenance in Grassroots China." *China
  Quarterly*, no. 251 (2022): 843–65.

Xu, Vicky Xiuzhong, Danielle Cave, James Leibold, Kelsey Munro, and Nathan
  Ruser. *Uyghurs for Sale: "Re-education," Forced Labour and Surveillance beyond
  Xinjiang*. Barton, ACT: Australian Strategic Policy Institute, 2020.

Xu, Zhiyong. *To Build a Free China: A Citizen's Journey*. Boulder, CO: Lynne
  Rienner, 2017.

Yan, Xuetong. "From Keeping a Low Profile to Striving for Achievement." *Chinese Journal of International Politics* 7, no. 2 (Summer 2014): 153–84.

Yang, Dali L. "China's Looming Labor Shortage." *Far Eastern Economic Review*
  168, no. 2 (2005): 19–24.

Yang, Dali L., and Junyan Jiang. "*Guojin Mintui*: The Global Recession and
  Changing State-Economy Relations in China." In *The Global Recession and
  China's Political Economy*, edited by Dali. L. Yang, 33–69. New York: Palgrave
  Macmillan, 2012.

Yang, Guorong. *Xiankui yu Hele: Dui shengming yiyi de niliu tansuo* (*Xiankui* and
  Hele: A contrarian investigation of the meaning of life). Hong Kong: Sanlian
  Shudian, 2010.

Yang, Lixiong. "The Social Assistance Reform in China: Toward a Fair and Inclusive Social Safety Net." Paper presented at the United Nations conference "Addressing Inequalities and Challenges to Social Inclusion through Fiscal, Wage,
  and Social Protection Policies." New York, NY, June 25–27, 2018.

Yang, Yujeong. "The Politics of Inclusion and Exclusion: Chinese Dual-Pension
  Regimes in the Era of Labor Migration and Labor Informalization." *Politics
  and Society* 49, no. 2 (2021): 147–80.

Yao, Shujie. "Economic Development and Poverty Reduction in China over 20
  Years of Reforms." *Economic Development and Cultural Change* 48, no. 3 (April
  2000): 447–74.

Yin, Liangen, and Terry Flew. "Xi Dada Loves Peng Mama: Digital Culture and the Return of Charismatic Authority in China." *Thesis Eleven* 144, no. 1 (2018): 80–99.

Yuan, Youjun. *Xunzhao shidai de xinyang: Dangdai zhongguo guomin xinyang yanjiu* (Searching for a faith of our times: Research into contemporary Chinese citizens' faith). Guangzhou: Guangdong Renmin Chubanshe, 2014.

Yun, Chen. "How to Be a Good Communist." In *Mao's China: Party Reform Documents, 1942–44*, translated by Boyd Compton, 88–107. Seattle: University of Washington Press, 1952.

Zenz, Adrian. "New Evidence for China's Political Re-education Campaign in Xinjiang." *China Brief* 18, no. 10 (2018): 1–45.

———. "'Thoroughly Reforming Them towards a Healthy Heart Attitude': China's Political Re-education Campaign in Xinjiang." *Central Asian Survey* 38, no. 1 (2019): 102–28.

Zenz, Adrian, and James Leibold. "Chen Quanguo: The Strongman behind Beijing's Securitization Strategy in Tibet and Xinjiang." *China Brief* 17, no. 12 (2017): 1–28.

———. "Xinjiang's Rapidly Evolving Security State." *China Brief* 17, no. 4 (2017): 21–27.

Zhang, Chunni, Qi Xu, Xiang Zhou, Xiaobo Zhang, and Yu Xie. "Are Poverty Rates Underestimated in China? New Evidence from Four Recent Surveys." *China Economic Review* 31 (2014): 410–25.

Zhang, Li, and Li Tao. "Barriers to the Acquisition of Urban Hukou in Chinese Cities." *Environment and Planning A: Economy and Space* 44, no. 12 (2012): 2883–900.

Zhang, Xiaobo, Yang Jin, and Wang Shenglin. "China Has Reached the Lewis Turning Point." *China Economic Review* 22 (2011): 543–54.

Zhao, Suisheng. "Chinese Foreign Policy as a Rising Power to Find Its Rightful Place." *Perceptions* 18, no. 1 (Spring 2013): 101–28.

———. *The Dragon Roars Back: Transformational Leaders and Dynamics of Chinese Foreign Policy*. Stanford, CA: Stanford University Press, 2022.

———. "The Ideological Campaign in Xi's China: Rebuilding Regime Legitimacy." *Asian Survey* 56, no. 6 (2016): 1168–93.

———. "President Xi's Big Power Diplomacy: Advancing an Assertive Foreign Policy Agenda." In *Mapping China's Global Future: Playing Ball or Rocking the Boat?*, edited by Axel Berkofsky and Giulia Sciorati, 24–36. Milan: ISPI and Ledizioni LediPublishing, 2020. https://www.ispionline.it/sites/default/files/pubblicazioni/ispi_mappingchina_web_1.pdf.

Zhao, Xiaohang, Yichun Yang, and Yu Xie. "Income Distribution." In *Zhongguo minsheng fazhan baogao, 2020–2021* (Well-being development report of China, 2020–2021), edited by Yu Xie et al. Beijing: Peking University Press, forthcoming.

Zhao, Yuezhi. "The Struggle for Socialism in China." *Monthly Review: An Independent Socialist Magazine* 64, no. 5 (October 2012): 1–17.

Zhou, Guoping. *Zhongguoren queshao shenme? Xifang zhexue jieshou shishang liangge anlie zhi yanjiu* (What are the Chinese lacking? Research into two historical cases of acceptance of Western philosophy). Shanghai: Shanghai Renmin Chubanshe, 2017.

Zhuo, Xinping. *Zhongguo zongjiao yu wenhua zhanlue* (The religions in China and the strategy of culture). Beijing: Shehui Kexue Wenxian Chubanshe, 2013.

Contributors

ALEXSIA T. CHAN is associate professor of government at Hamilton College. She is the author of *Beyond Coercion: The Politics of Inequality in China* (forthcoming).

TIMOTHY CHEEK is professor and Louis Cha Chair in Chinese Research at the University of British Columbia. He is author of *The Intellectual in Modern Chinese History* (2015) and *Propaganda and Culture in Mao's China: Deng Tuo and the Intelligentsia* (1997) and coeditor of *The Chinese Communist Party: A Century in Ten Lives* (2021) and *Voices from the Chinese Century: Public Intellectual Debate from Contemporary China* (2020).

CHIH-JOU JAY CHEN is director and professor at the Institute of Sociology, Academia Sinica. He is a member of the Executive Committee of the International Sociological Association. He was president of the Taiwanese Sociological Association in 2018–19 and a visiting scholar at the Harvard-Yenching Institute in 2014–15.

DAVID DEMES is a PhD candidate in sociology at National Tsing Hua University and a lecturer at Tamkang University, Taiwan. As a freelance journalist based in Taipei, he covers the Sinosphere for various German media.

DENG KAI is a PhD candidate in sociology at National Tsing Hua University. His research focuses on social movements and state-society relations in contemporary China.

ASHLEY ESAREY is associate professor of political science at the University of Alberta. He is coauthor, with Hsiu-lien Lu, of *My Fight for a New Taiwan:*

One Woman's Journey from Prison to Power (2014) and coeditor of *Taiwan in Dynamic Transition: Nation Building and Democratization* (2020) and *Greening East Asia: The Rise of the Eco-Developmental State* (2020).

RONGBIN HAN is associate professor of international affairs at the University of Georgia. He is author of *Contesting Cyberspace in China: Online Expression and Authoritarian Resilience* (2018) and coauthor of *Directed Digital Dissidence in Autocracies: How China Wins Online* (2023).

TONY TAI-TING LIU is assistant professor of international relations at National Chung Hsing University. He was secretary general of the Taiwanese Political Science Association in 2021–23 and a visiting scholar at the Stimson Center in 2022.

MUSAPIR is a pseudonym for a Uyghur scholar based in North America.

KEVIN J. O'BRIEN is Jack M. Forcey Professor of Political Science at the University of California, Berkeley. He is author of *Reform without Liberalization: China's National People's Congress and the Politics of Institutional Change* (1990) and coauthor of *Rightful Resistance in Rural China* (2006).

ANDREW WEDEMAN is professor of political science at Georgia State University. He is author of *From Mao to Market: Rent Seeking, Local Protectionism, and Marketization in China* (2003) and *Double Paradox: Rapid Growth and Rising Corruption in China* (2012).

MARTIN KING WHYTE is John Zwaanstra Professor of International Studies and Sociology, emeritus, at Harvard University. He recently published *Remembering Ezra Vogel* (coeditor, with Mary C. Brinton, 2022).

GERDA WIELANDER is professor of Chinese studies at the University of Westminster. She is author of *Christian Values in Communist China* (2013) and coeditor of *Chinese Discourses on Happiness* (2018).

BRANTLY WOMACK is senior faculty fellow at the Miller Center and emeritus professor of foreign affairs at the University of Virginia. His publications include *Recentering Pacific Asia: Regional China and World Order* (2023), *Asymmetry and International Relationships* (2016), *China among Unequals: Asymmetric Foreign Relationships in Asia* (2010), and *China and Vietnam: The Politics of Asymmetry* (2006).

Index

Figures and tables indicated by page numbers in *italics*

citizenship, pliable, 11, 130, 135, 139–41, 142–45, 145–46

Classic of Rites (Liji), 55, 65n14

Cleannet Bodyguard (Jingwang Weishi) app, 186

climate change, 14, 240

Clinton, Hilary, 237

Cloud Big Data Industrial Development Company, 160

"Common Prosperity" campaign, 98, 110–11, 116, 137

common sense, 70, 76, 77

Comprehensively Deepening Reforms Leadership Group, 51

continuity, vs. change, 138, 250–52

counter-reformation. *See* ideological governance

COVID-19 pandemic: economic effects, 120n19; health code system, 168–70; income inequality and, 95, 110, 116; mass surveillance during, 153, 167–70; Pinghu case study, 167–68, 178n66; Taiwan-China relations and, 214, 215, 217, 221; white paper protests, 156, 170–71, 218; zero COVID policy, 2, 16, 95

cross-strait relations. *See* Taiwan-China relations

Cultural Revolution, 5, 49, 53, 56, 58, 82, 99, 103, 185

Cybersecurity Law (2017), 154, 159, 160–61, 170

Cyberspace Administration of China (CAC), 4, 9, 157, 158–60, 170

danwei (work units), 155

"de-Americanization" (*qu Meiguo hua*), 14

Demes, David, 11–12, 184, 250, 252

democratization, 59, 234

Deng Huilin, 35

Deng Kai, 11–12, 178n66, 184, 250, 252

Deng Xiaoping: achievements and legacy, 17n13, 210; foreign policy, 226, 235; and inequality and poverty, 10, 97; "one country, two systems" plan and, 209; reform Leninism and, 49, 58; "two-term rule" and, 41; Xi's departure from, 3, 4–5, 7, 8, 41, 235

development, 97, 135–37, 230, 232

dibao system (minimum livelihood payments), 100, 120n24, 120n26, 121n27, 251

digital surveillance. *See* surveillance state

Ding Xuexiang, *42*

discourse formation, 70, 73

Dongguan, 133, 134

Duterte, Rodrigo, 234, 242

East Asia Community, 243

East Asia Summit, 243

Economic Cooperation Framework Agreement (ECFA), 208

Economy, Elizabeth, 5–6

education: access to, 103–5, 122n37, 123nn44–45, 129, 142–43, 144, 251; public opinion on, *113*, *114*; Southeast Asia-China exchanges, 233, 246n24

eldercare, *113*, *114*, 115

elite politics. *See* leadership politics

Esarey, Ashley, 41, 250

ethnic policies, 80, 81, 84, 182–83, 188–89, 195

Europe, 15, 218, 227, 240

factions (factional studies): about, 30–31, 36; anti-corruption campaign and, 31–35, *33*, 44, 48n22; future of Xi's faction, 43–44; shifting Politburo balance, 36–37, *38*, 39–40, 41, 44–45

Hu Yaobang, 49, 53, 58, 59, 67n29
Hua Guofeng, 41
Huang Kunming, *42*
Huawei, 9
Hui Muslims, 88n47
hukou system: discrimination based on, 125n54, 131–32; education discrimination and, 104–5, 123n44; efforts to end discrimination, 106–7, 124nn49–51; labor shortages and, 133–34; localization approach, 132, 139; medical insurance and, 100–101; pension coverage and, 102–3; public opinion on, 111–12, *112*, 127n70
human rights (*weiquan*) lawyers, 86n19
Hun Sen, 236

ideological governance: about, 7–8, 52–53; anti-corruption campaign and, 51; historical overview, 53–54; in Qing and Republican China, 53, 54–56; rectification politics, 53, 56–58, 59–61; reform Leninism, 53–54, 58–59; Xi's counter-reformation, 3–4, 50–51, 54, 59–61, 62–64, 70, 251
Ilham Tohti, 182–83
income inequality: about, 9–10, 93–95, 116–17, 251–52; anti-corruption campaign and, 96; "Common Prosperity" campaign and, 98, 110–11, 116; COVID-19 pandemic and, 95, 110, 116; education access and, 103–5, 122n37, 123nn44–45; Gini estimates, 94, 108, *109*, 110, 117n1, 125n59, 126n61; housing and, 110, 118n10; Hu's "harmonious society" programs, 94, 115, 118n7; as inequality in capabilities, 126n68; inequality vs. inequity, 94, 117n4; medical insurance and, 100–102,

101, 121n30; minimum livelihood payments (*dibao* system) and, 100, 120n24, 120n26, 121n27, 251; pension coverage and, 102–3, 121nn32–33; political instability concerns, 93–94; public opinion on, 112–13, 115–16, 127n72, 128n77; rural poverty campaign and, 97–98; and social safety nets and public goods access, 99, 106; taxation and, 96–97, 110–11, 118n9; trends in, 108–10, *109*, 125nn58–59, 126nn61–62; urbanization campaign and efforts to end *hukou*-based discrimination, 106–7, 124nn49–51
Indonesia, *231*, 239, 245n8
inequality, vs. inequity, 94, 117n4. *See also* income inequality
Integrated Joint Operations Platform (IJOP) app, 186
International Civil Aviation Organization, 215
international relations, 226. *See also* foreign policy; Southeast Asia-China relations; Taiwan-China relations
Internet Information Offices, 158–59. *See also* Cyberspace Administration of China (CAC); surveillance state
Islam, 80, 81, 88n47, 166, 184, 187, 191. *See also* religion; Uyghurs

Japan, 218, 237, 238, 240
Jia Qinglin, 34
Jiang Zemin: comparison to Xi, 1, 3; death, 48n32; education access and, 105, 251; factions and, 32, 34–35, 36–37, 39–40, 41; income inequality and, 94, 110; legacy of, 210; policy approach of, 5; reform Leninism and, 53, 54, 58; Taiwan-China relations and, 210

soft vs. hard power, 211–12, 241
Solinger, Dorothy J., 10
Song Tao, 211
South China Sea, 4, 8, 229, 234–35, 238, 239–40, 243, 244
Southeast Asia-China relations: about, 13; background, 228–29; China's economic importance, 230–33, *231*; new normal and opportunities, 229, 240–42, 244; Pacific Asia context, 227; Southeast Asian perceptions of China vs. US, 238–40; and Trump and Biden administrations, 227–28, 229, 237–38; Xi Jinping effect, 234–37, 243–44, 252
State Internet Information Office. *See* Cyberspace Administration of China (CAC)
The State of Southeast Asia survey, 239
Strait Exchange Foundation (SEF), 208, 209
structure, vs. agency, 15, 226, 249, 250–53
Su Chi, 209
Su Rong, *33*, 34, 35
Sun Chunlan, *42*
Sun Lijun, *33*, 35
Sun Tzu: *The Art of War*, 212, 223n17
Sun Yat-sen, 7, 53, 55–56
Sun Zhengcai, 26, *33*, 34–35, 36
Sunflower occupation, 209
surveillance state: about, 9, 11–12, 153, 170–71, 252; COVID-19 pandemic and, 167–70; Cyberspace Administration of China, 4, 9, 157, 158–60, 170; grid management, 154, 155–56, 184, 198n24; health code system, 168–70; institutional evolution of, 154–55; labor-intensive digital surveillance, 161–62; petitioners and, 164–65; real-name registration, 11, 160–61; religious groups and,

166; social credit system, 162–64; synthesized infrastructure, 156–57; white paper protests and, 170–71; in Xinjiang, 184–87, 195, 198n24; Xi's "holistic view of national security," 171n2
synthetic operations centers (*hecheng zuozhan zhongxin*), 156–57

Tahir Hamut Izgil, 191
Taiwan Affairs Office (TAO), 211, 213, 214
Taiwan-China relations: about, 14–15, 207, 220–21, 252; charm offensive, 212–14; COVID-19 pandemic and, 214, 215, 217, 221; deterioration of, 207–10; hard offensive, 214–16; "Message to Compatriots in Taiwan" (1979), 209, 217, 221n3; 1992 Consensus and, 209, 220; Taiwanese developments and, 211, 220–21; war potential, 217–19; Xi's interest in, 210–11, 250; Xi's two-pronged approach, 211–16
Tashpolat Tiyip, 191
taxation, 96–97, 110–11, 118nn9–10
Teiwes, Frederick C., 60
Tencent, 158, 159, 168, 169
Thailand, 230, *231*, 233, 239, 245n8
"Three Middles and One Young" policy, 212
Tibet, 8, 80, 166, 184, 188
Tiger Hunts. *See* anti-corruption campaign
tourism, 96, 212, 232–33
trade, 232
Trans Pacific Partnership (TPP), 228, 234, 238, 244
travel permit, mainland (*taibaozheng*), 212–13
Trump, Donald (Trump administration), 13, 219, 227, 228, 229, 237–40

www.ingramcontent.com/pod-product-compliance
Lightning Source LLC
Chambersburg PA
CBHW031411270326
41929CB00010BA/1407